Provoc*auteurs* and Provocations

Provoc*auteurs* and **Provocations**

Screening Sex in 21st Century Media

INDIANA UNIVERSITY PRESS

This book is a publication of

Indiana University Press
Office of Scholarly Publishing
Herman B Wells Library 350
1320 East 10th Street
Bloomington, Indiana 47405 USA

iupress.org

© 2020 by Maria San Filippo

All rights reserved

No part of this book may be reproduced or utilized in any form or by any means, electronic or mechanical, including photocopying and recording, or by any information storage and retrieval system, without permission in writing from the publisher. The paper used in this publication meets the minimum requirements of the American National Standard for Information Sciences—Permanence of Paper for Printed Library Materials, ANSI Z39.48-1992.

Manufactured in the United States of America

Cataloging information is available from the Library of Congress.

ISBN 978-0-253-05211-7 (hardback)
ISBN 978-0-253-05212-4 (paperback)
ISBN 978-0-253-05213-1 (ebook)

First Printing 2021

CONTENTS

Prologue: Tangled Up in *Blue* 1

PART I. *Provocations*

1. Selling Sex: Scandalous Marketing Campaigns and the Millennial Watercooler Movie 31
2. Full-Frontal Provocation: Male Nudity as Nonphallic Masculinity 69

PART II. *Provocauteurs*

3. Art Porn Provoc*auteurs*: Feminist Critique through Corpo*reality* in the Work of Catherine Breillat and Lena Dunham 165
4. Inbetweener (In)Appropriations: "Bad Queer" Provoc*auteurs* Lisa Cholodenko and Desiree Akhavan 252

Epilogue: Still Taboo? Provocative Acts, Vulnerable Viewing 351

Bibliography 379

Acknowledgments 407

Index 411

Provoc*auteurs* and Provocations

Prologue

Tangled Up in *Blue*

I don't want [my cinema] to resemble life. I want it to be life. I want there to be real moments of life in my films.

Abdellatif Kechiche

[Kechiche] warned us that we had to trust him—blind trust—and give a lot of ourselves. He was making a movie about passion, so he wanted to have sex scenes, but without choreography—more like *special* sex scenes. He told us he didn't want to hide the character's sexuality because it's an important part of every relationship. So he asked me if I was ready to make it, and I said, "Yeah, of course!" because I'm young and pretty new to cinema. But once we were on the shoot, I realized that he *really* wanted us to give him *everything*. Most people don't even dare to ask the things that he did, and they're more respectful—you get reassured during sex scenes, and they're choreographed, which desexualizes the act.

Adèle Exarchopoulos

BY THE TIME *La vie d'Adèle* (*Blue Is the Warmest Color*, Abdellatif Kechiche, 2013) reached US theaters in October 2013, it had already weathered several cycles of controversy. Early on, graphic novelist Julie Maroh protested the adaptation of her 2010 book, which provided the film's source material. Anticipatory rumblings arose about the duration and explicitness of the film's lesbian sex scenes. And its premiere received fevered coverage at the Cannes Film Festival, where, in an unprecedented move, lead actors Adèle Exarchopoulos (whose character is also named Adèle) and Léa Seydoux (who plays Adèle's love interest-turned-girlfriend Emma) were awarded the festival's highest honor, the Palme d'Or. They received the tribute alongside Kechiche in recognition of their creative labors, which, in the view of the festival judges, made them "in a small way also the directors of the film." An exchange of recriminations ensued when Exarchopoulos and Seydoux went public soon thereafter with their objections to the filmmaker's methods. Increasingly testy exchanges developed between them and Kechiche, who eventually called (unsuccessfully) for the film's release to be canceled, claiming, "It has been soiled too much." And, finally, critics launched another round of derision and defense in the lead-up to its theatrical release.[1]

Opening in twenty-five countries, the film went on to make around $15 million worldwide—a substantial return for a foreign-language feature with a 179-minute running time and an NC-17 rating in the United States, where it was ruled ineligible on a technicality for Oscar consideration.[2] As B. Ruby Rich notes in her essay on the film for the Criterion Collection, *Blue Is the Warmest Color* (hereafter, *Blue*) was a "lightning rod" at a moment when France and the United States were on the cusp of legally ensuring marriage equality. Though had it been released a few years later, *Blue* and its accompanying clashes over consent and exploitation would have been caught in the transatlantic crossfire of the #MeToo, Time's Up, and #BalanceTonPorc movements.[3]

Controversy around the film continues to resurface sporadically: when the Criterion Collection released DVD and Blu-ray editions to coincide with Valentine's Day 2014 and again when Kechiche made headlines for auctioning off his Palme d'Or to raise funds for his next project. *Blue* also was a ghostly presence at the 2018 Cannes Film Festival, when jury member Seydoux returned to the red carpet alongside eighty-one other women actors, filmmakers, and activists to protest the festival's long tradition of unbalanced gender representation and then appeared alongside the current Cannes directors to announce a pledge to achieve gender parity within the festival's ranks and to create a more transparent selection process.[4]

Blue is the work brought up most often, by people from all areas of my life, when I mention that I am writing a book on sexual provocation in contemporary screen media. (The other two names that consistently arise are Catherine Breillat and Lena Dunham, to whom this book's third chapter is devoted.) Clearly this says something about the taste profile of my acquaintanceship, but it also reveals much about the film's significance in the current cultural imaginary, being at once singular and paradigmatic of how sexual provocation acts as a driving force for making, selling, consuming, and appraising screen media in the 21st century. The film thus not only provides an apt entry into many of the zones of provocation I explore in this book but also offers an opportunity to reflect at the outset on my own investments in this book's writing. Like nearly every work I have written about in the course of my career studying screen media, this film holds considerable personal significance. More than any other intellectual figure, the much-missed Alexander Doty has been an essential model for my self-imagining as what he called a "scholar-fan," and I follow his lead in acknowledging, grappling with, and embracing the ways in which our personal enthusiasms and histories indelibly inform our critical output.[5]

This book's design has been, however unconsciously, motivated by works and creators I find simultaneously compelling and troubling, with *Blue* serving as an exemplary case for me as well as, evidently, the culture at large. Throughout, I have chosen as case studies texts and figures in which I have a deep-seated personal investment and ones that demonstrate considerable power to provoke—and whose provocations are of a primarily sexual nature. What form that provocation takes, the degree to which it resonates aesthetically and politically, and for which segment(s) of the media audience vary widely. And yet this book attempts to be neither comprehensive nor canonical—thus, many provocations and provoc*auteurs* (as I name media creators for whom sexual provocation is a primary component of their works' themes and brand personae) prominent in the 21st century screen mediascape go unexplored here.[6] Thinking about provocation necessarily entails thinking about the ethical considerations involved both in practicing screen provocation and in writing about it. I heed film philosopher Mette Hjort's call for "a pragmatics of provocation that would allow us to reject certain artistic actions for reasons to do with willful ignorance, lack of understanding, and a failure to think consequentially about cause and effect relations in relation to the inflicting of damage, hurt, or harm." I approach the works here with an eye to determining, as Hjort encourages, whether "goals extending well beyond the individual seem to be at stake" and how coherently, responsibly, and effectively the project of provocation goes about achieving progressive ends for creators and viewers alike.[7]

A layout in the November 2013 issue of *Interview* magazine styled and posed Exarchopoulos and Seydoux to evoke the bohemian dishevelment and erotic languor that costars Marlon Brando and Maria Schneider made famous in *Last Tango in Paris* (Bernardo Bertolucci, 1972), a film that led critic Jonathan Rosenbaum to observe that "sex could be regarded as the ultimate special effect."[8] Positioning *Blue* as the contemporary equivalent of *Last Tango* was a self-aggrandizing gesture that would acquire a darker meaning after Bertolucci, in a 2013 interview at the Cinémathèque Française in Paris, confirmed Schneider's earlier claims (while largely dismissing her concerns) that the film's simulated scene of anal intercourse was unscripted and nonconsensually imposed on her. The interview went viral in 2016 after actor Jessica Chastain and others disparaged the director's methods;

Chastain, in a tweet, labeled the incident "rape."[9] Bertolucci's inflammatory justification for not telling Schneider in advance what the scene would involve, "because I wanted her reaction as a girl, not as an actress," is echoed by Kechiche in the epigraph that begins this prologue.[10] What both directors describe attempting, and reportedly using manipulative means to achieve, was to capture some "real moment" of personal authenticity connected to sexual truth.

While this book elucidates how screen narrative and performance can bring us closer to understanding truths about erotic desire and intimacy, it accepts neither these filmmakers' assertions that such honest revelation can be achieved through duplicitous means, nor their conflation of mediated images with (as Kechiche says) "real moments of life." *Last Tango* offers a sobering example of a film's failure to abide by a "pragmatics of provocation," as Hjort sets out above. The personal harm inflicted outweighs any artistic value added or revelatory insight conveyed. It was (and continues to be) deeply troubling to read and hear Exarchopoulos's and Seydoux's accounts of Kechiche's demands and their having been made to feel (in Seydoux's wording) "like prostitutes." This, more than the form that the film's sexual representations take, is at the heart of my conflicted relation to *Blue*.[11] As the most prominent screen representation of lesbianism since *The L Word* (Ilene Chaiken, Showtime, 2005–9) and a gateway media work for queer youth, *Blue* is a landmark film that deserves to be considered on its merits. Rather than simply allow the film to be "soiled" (as Kechiche claims it has been for him), my analysis will call on our awareness of Kechiche's methods while reading the film as embodying its own self-critical aspects. Without minimizing concerns about the treatment of performers and crew that surrounded *Blue*, I feel grateful that Kechiche failed to prevent the film's release.

Blue presents a complicated entanglement of a kind that cinephiles—especially those with tastes toward the sexually provocative—increasingly find themselves contending with. *New York Times* critic A. O. Scott, in a 2018 piece titled "My Woody Allen Problem," persuasively asserts the impossibility of separating art from artists, especially "when they carry intimate baggage into their work and invite us to sort through the contents." Though Kechiche poses a different set of dilemmas than does Allen, the path forward that Scott proposes fits in the case of *Blue*, as with any work or creator where questions of aesthetics and ethics are so complicatedly intertwined as to render inadequate a simple response of either exculpation or condemnation. Rather than excuse or expunge, we should instead reassess. As Scott remarks, "Reassessment is part of the ordinary work of culture, and in an extraordinary time, the work is especially vital and especially challenging."[12]

With its acquired taint of exploitation having overshadowed the film to the point of shaming the act of its screening (a prominent queer studies scholar all but apologized to me for having programmed it in an academic symposium on sexuality), the risk becomes that *Blue* will be shunned rather than reassessed. In initiating such a personal reassessment here, I argue that, for all its upsetting aspects, *Blue* remains an astounding work for its heartrending exploration of sexual awakening and first love as well as for its political call to action around LGBTQ+ rights (overlooked by those eager to condemn the film for what they saw as its universalist messaging). Additionally, the film offers a subtle (and thus also overlooked) probing of class difference, which acts as a structuring silence in both the tempestuous relationship at the film's heart and in the critical discourse around the film. And, finally, the film maintains a diegetic ambivalence about its own representational strategies. Because this last aspect of *Blue* suggests strategies for contending with its troubling elements, it is my focus here.

First, however, as a prelude to the detailed overview of this book's organization and methodology to follow in chapter 1, it is important to point out that *Blue* shares a great deal with other instances of sexual provocation discussed in this book. Although Kechiche's reputation was already well established in France, *Blue* was his international breakout film, and its sexual explicitness and ability to generate controversy make it a prime example of the "millennial watercooler movie" explored in chapter 1. *Blue* links up with chapter 2's discussion of France's other *succès de scandale* from 2013, Alain Guiraudie's *Stranger by the Lake*—a film whose production history yields a more ethically sound model for shooting explicit sex (and that did not elicit comparable public clamor over its content, as is discussed below). *Blue* serves as an illuminating counterpoint to two further forms of provocations taken up in chapter 2: that of male full-frontal nudity in mainstream media and that of gay male representation that withholds rather than reveals sexual imagery. For lesbian sex, the question seems to be how to screen it (with *Blue* perceived as transgressing lines of moderation and taste); for gay male sex, the question is whether to screen it at all.

Kechiche's crafting of sex scenes that simultaneously project documentary-style realism and alienating stylization will be reassessed in chapter 3's exploration of filmmaker Catherine Breillat. Though the nude female bodies graphically on display in *Blue* conform to the conventional beauty standards from which prov*ocauteur* Lena Dunham's body type diverges, Kechiche films Exarchopoulos with an unflinching focus on her bodily fluids and appetites that parallels both Breillat's and Dunham's wallowing in what I term the corp*orealities* of women's bodies and desires. As a contested entry in the queer canon, owing to its cishet creator and its being disowned by Maroh amid charges of lesbian exploitation and inauthenticity, *Blue* raises issues further explored in chapter 4's assessment of what I name "bad queer" sexual and representational politics. Finally, *Blue*'s route from the Cannes Film Festival to the art house and multiplex, then to Criterion Collection DVD, Netflix streaming, lesbian film-streaming sites such as Buskfilms and One More Lesbian, and even to porn sites such as Pornhub and YouPorn, exemplifies this book's thesis about the convergence of old and new media channels around the point of sexual provocation.

Before stories about the film's troubled production emerged, *Blue*'s sex scenes were under fire for reasons that are themselves worth reassessing. That critics and audiences seemed far more incensed over *Blue*'s Sapphic sex than over the comparably explicit depictions of gay male sex in *Stranger by the Lake* released that same year—albeit unrated in the United States and so with more limited distribution than *Blue*, which received an NC-17—leads Linda Williams to note the overwhelming and disproportionate degree to which lesbian sex scenes are judged by "whether one believes heterosexual men are getting off on it."[13] Indeed, concerns about "lesploitation" (lesbian sexuality presented primarily by and for the male gaze) generated as much controversy as those around cultural appropriation (a straight director adapting a queer graphic novel). *Blue*'s sex scenes superficially share elements with heterocentrist porn's "girl-on-girl" displays, and the prevalence of scissoring/frottage and the recurring use of "reverse cowgirl" positioning drew ire from viewers for their straight porn associations. Yet, as Williams also notes, those positions have ample precedent in lesbian-made porn. And their featured acts might have stemmed from these scenes' reported filming sans choreography and performed by women "not very familiar with lesbian sex" (as Exarchopoulos admits) and unwilling to more suggestively simulate cunnilingus (where Seydoux says she drew the line).[14] More significantly, however, these scenes are composed for suggestiveness rather than for the extreme visibility sought by heterocentric porn and so more closely resemble the art cinema mode Williams has named "hardcore eroticism" to suggest the mix of hard-core pornographic conventions and erotic suggestion created by strategies of "concealing erotic silhouettes, inferred fellation, inferred unprotected [vaginal and/or] anal penetration, and peaceful post-coital moments."[15]

These scenes dispense with the romanticizing gestures that have long defused the threat of Sapphic sex in Hollywood-style treatment. Their stark carnality, especially in a film otherwise devoted to intimate gestures and emotional fathoming, appears to have disconcerted viewers unprepared for a depiction of lesbian sex not as caressing but as fucking. *Blue* clearly declines to emulate examples from the lesbian cinema canon widely credited with feeling authentic and intimate without sacrificing their erotic charge, as in the case of two generally agreed to be among the "best": those in *Bound* (Lana Wachowski and Lilly Wachowski, 1996), on which lesbian "sexpert" Susie Bright consulted, and in the more recent *Duck Butter* (Miguel Arteta, 2018), on which Arteta deferred to co-writer/lead Alia Shawkat, co-lead Laia Costa, and cinematographer Hillary Spera's collaborative choices.[16]

Though Kechiche's camera holds intently on Exarchopoulos's face for sizable portions of *Blue*, the sex scenes wander from this privileging of facial intensity that queer women filmmakers including Desiree Akhavan (discussed in chap. 4) and Stacie Passon (*Concussion*, 2013) deploy to elicit intimacy and sidestep the perceptions of having ventured into fetishistic and pornographic terrain that dogged Kechiche. In her takedown of *Blue* in the *New York Times*, critic Manohla Dargis arraigns Kechiche on this discrepancy, noting that elsewhere he fixates in close-up on Adèle's voraciousness but "does not permit her a similarly sloppy appetite in bed, where the movie's carefully constructed realism is jettisoned along with bodily excesses and excretions in favor of tasteful, decorous poses." This claim that Adèle's "sloppiness" is quarantined from the sex scenes in favor of what Dargis describes as "contained, prettified, aestheticized" images deserves some reassessment, as do descriptions of the film as breaking from its realism when turning to the erotic.[17]

Revisiting these sex scenes reveals that they vary in accord with their location in the narrative trajectory. For example, the

Fig. P.1. *Blue Is the Warmest Color*'s infamous tableau of lesbian sex.

sex that Adèle and Emma have in the full flush of love and in Adèle's childhood bedroom after introducing Emma to her parents (under the guise of being a friend) focuses more intimately and innocently on their faces. Not surprisingly, since they resemble scenes from other films, these moments do not stand out as memorably (for Dargis or others) as do those that resist both Hollywood-style modes of representation and art film's customary integration of sex scenes into the diegetic and spatiotemporal fabric. Kechiche opts to cut to and away from sexual interludes abruptly and in medias res, occasionally employing jump cuts for added discontinuity, almost sealing these sequences off from the recognizable mise-en-scène and denying viewers the "post-coital repose" shots to which they are accustomed (see fig. P.1). Still, on closer examination, these tableaux are also narratively suggestive for showing sex at the emotionally waxing and waning stages of their relationship.

Taken together, the sex scenes stand out for their simultaneous strangeness (compared to norms of narrative cinema) and familiarity (in resembling porn); as such, they provoke an effect of the uncanny. The scenes' much-derided perception as "clinical" (or "surgical," according to Maroh) seems attributable to their being relatively brightly lit, statically shot, frontal (even slightly aerial) compositions. The alienating effect is further enhanced by otherwise atypical elements: discomforting duration, the performers' rather grim countenance, and their occasionally tonally incongruous emitting of what *New Yorker* critic Anthony Lane described as "a fusillade of cries and clutches, grabs and slaps."[18] The closest cousins to *Blue*'s sex scenes may well be those that have gone to similar extremes and elicit a comparable distancing effect, but in the pursuit of laughs. Examples can be found in the exhaustive array of positions enacted by gyrating puppets in *Team America: World Police* (Trey Parker, 2004), the equally limber contortions by amorous gymnasts in *The Bronze* (Bryan Buckley, 2014), and the tampon-extracting, toe-penetrating parody of *Blue* in the pilot episode of *Sally4Ever* (Julia Davis, HBO, 2018–).

What all this dissimilarity, incongruity, and disagreement point to, and what strikes me as most intriguing—and provocative—about *Blue*'s sex scenes, is their divergence both from representational codes for screening sex and from the formal strategies Kechiche employs elsewhere in *Blue*. The pertinent question about this alienation effect is less about Kechiche's intentions and more about the extent to which it is productive and powerful. In rendering sex strangely within the context of narrative cinema, these scenes force us into (self-)assessment regarding their purpose and pleasures.

Blue's sex scenes—specifically the six-minute-long "centerpiece"—recall Chantal Akerman's *Je Tu Il Elle* (1974), which Dargis's review also mentions (and compares favorably to *Blue*). That film's final act features Akerman's unnamed character and a woman suggested to be an occasional girlfriend (played by Claire Wauthion) writhing naked in another scene of extreme duration (ten minutes), also frontally composed and statically shot at a remove, and with a similarly stark, discordant effect conveyed through the black-and-white cinematography and disembodied postsync sound (see fig. P.2). What has always seemed so compelling about this scene (and Akerman's work overall) is

Fig. P.2. Making sex strange: lesbian lovemaking subjected to Brechtian distancing in *Je Tu Il Elle*.

precisely its play between inviting and withholding intimacy to gesture at the simultaneously revealing and resistant properties of the representational image. This tension between seeing and knowing—and thus controlling—the figure(s) held by the gaze informs our understanding of the scopophilic impulse to visually objectify women and suggests Akerman's import for feminist film criticism. That Akerman's scene is celebrated for its elusive toying with spectatorial voyeurism while Kechiche's equivalent scenes are criticized as lacking intimacy and authenticity and for being visually exploitative speaks volumes about the shifting criteria for evaluating such images. Alongside Linda Williams's observation about the tendency to give primacy to straight men's presumed pleasure (or lack thereof), Akerman's being a woman as well as a lesbian and her presence as performer in the scene all seem to validate her authorial strategies where Kechiche's are rendered suspect.

The different contexts of these two scenes are also relevant to how they have been received, with one occurring in an experimental work of the feminist avant-garde and the other in a comparatively commercial and mainstream French art film—however arbitrary or blurry that distinction proves. So while these markedly contrasting responses to scenes that share some features of stylization and affect are noteworthy, what is for Akerman a pervasive visual aesthetic (in *Je Tu Il Elle* and beyond) registers as a break with Kechiche's less stylized, more freewheeling approach elsewhere in *Blue*. Yet I would caution against the tendency (including my own) to exaggerate the characterization of *Blue*'s sex scenes as a departure from the film's "realism," with the analogy to Akerman again proving useful for what has been called her style's "hyperrealism"—a mode by which she documents the everyday with such pronounced fixation and duration as to render it strange.[19] It is this "making sex strange" through the amalgamation of representational codes of porn, experimentalism, and realism that impels spectators into a confrontation with their own pursuit of visual pleasure.

For Kechiche, a Tunisian immigrant who grew up in the Nice *banlieue* adjacent to (but a world away from) Cannes, further anxieties informed *Blue*'s turning of the male gaze of a cishet man of color onto two women of European extraction. The heteropatriarchal authority and cultural capital equipping Kechiche—who at the time of the film's release had come to be considered among the foremost contemporary French directors—were challenged by his dubious "right" (as a straight man) to tell this story and by his being of Arab origins working in a racially oppressive nation and industry. Though it was a lower-profile film, Kechiche noticeably did not receive comparable opprobrium for putting Cuban-born first-time actor Yahima Torres through the paces in her demanding role as the real-life enslaved figure Saartjie Baartman (known as the Hottentot Venus) in his previous feature *Vénus Noire* (*Black Venus*, 2010). Instead, critics divided on whether the film was "abusing" its audience (as at least one critic alleged).[20] Those debates, primarily concerning Kechiche's formally inventive use of unrelenting, extreme close-ups, prefigure what the filmmaker provokes with *Blue*. As James S. Williams characterizes it, there is a dialogue "between those who commend Kechiche's attempt to force the viewer into submission so that we acknowledge our own capacity for spectatorial voyeurism, and those who regard such a strategy as complicit in the very objectification and abjection the film seeks to expose and decry."[21]

The salience of racial politics in *Blue*'s reception emerges particularly in comparison to the relatively muted response to the South Korean art film *Ah-ga-ssi* (*The Handmaiden*, Park Chan-wook, 2016), which was open to similar charges of co-optation by a cishet male filmmaker. It was "inspired by" Welsh novelist Sarah Waters's lesbian cult classic *Fingersmith* (2002) and features lesbian sex scenes of comparable duration and explicitness, and with a fondness similar to *Blue*'s for Sapphic sex tableaux filmed from above. Also premiering at Cannes, unrated in its American release, and with a 144-minute running time, *The Handmaiden* did roughly the same box office as *Blue* in the United States and its other foreign territories (and tripled *Blue*'s domestic total in its home market of South Korea, where it grossed $30 million). That it received but a fraction of the fevered outcry that greeted *Blue* could be due to any number of factors, including *Blue* having left audiences jaded to this particular form of provocation. But it bears noting that *The Handmaiden* did not elicit the same outrage or the same impulse to protect its women actors (if only from the leering male gaze), at least within its Euro-American reception and English-language critical response.

Blue's dense references to Western art's treatment of the female nude makes legible Kechiche's purposeful resistance to representational expectations and conventions (see fig. P.3). Writing about

Fig. P.3. Emma (Léa Seydoux) instructing Adèle (Adèle Exarchopoulos) on the historical art of the male gaze.

Kechiche's work pre-*Blue*, James S. Williams notes the filmmaker's aim to revise the *Beur* cinema tradition in which his career was incubated, signaled by the deliberate shift in Kechiche's interests "from a politics of representation to the (inter)textual and performative processes of cinema itself."[22] *Blue* invites our questioning of Kechiche's authorial control—both its obtrusive presence and its limits—as surely within its diegesis as it would ultimately do in the court of public opinion. By inserting elements of metacommentary not present in the graphic novel, Kechiche directs attention to the assertion of his gendered perspective and his shaping of the film's images and narrative.

Blue opens on a classroom discussion of Marivaux's *La vie de Marianne* (*The Life of Marianne*, 1731–41), to which the film's French title, *La vie d'Adèle*, alludes. The opening lines, "I am a woman. I tell my story," are spoken by an uncredited student called Saïda, whose name and appearance signal her to be of Arab descent. She is stopped by the male teacher (Philippe Potier), who instructs her, "'I am a woman' is a truth. Understand, Saïda? Start from there. You tell your story. It's a truth." With Adèle looking on, this exchange immediately signals that a narrative presented as being by a woman was in fact crafted by one man and subject to the interpretation of another, who "directs" the young woman (of color)'s performance and understanding of it. The "truth" to which it refers is thereby put in question at the outset. After other students take turns at reading, the teacher ends by instructing the class to think about the story's theme of predestination in love. This theme reverberates in the scene soon thereafter in which Adèle and Emma lock eyes at a crosswalk, and it also prefigures Adèle's internal conflict between societal determination and the alternative voiced by Emma's later paraphrasing of Jean-Paul Sartre: "He said we can choose our lives."

In a party scene later in the film, after Emma and Adèle have become a couple, yet another domineering middle-aged man, Joachim (Stéphane Mercoyrol), directs a discussion, this time about the elusive nature of female pleasure and the challenge of its artistic representation. "For you, female orgasm is mystical?" Emma prompts him, smirking slightly. "I'm totally sure of it," he responds. "I'll never understand this because I am a man." Though Emma will later refer to him dreamily, telling Adèle, "He's extremely cultivated. A genius. He knows everything," his pompous holding forth invites us to view him more skeptically. The focus on social stratifications of class and race that permeate Kechiche's earlier work unfolds here along gendered and generational lines. The younger women artists who follow his words but stay largely silent are, though perhaps in thrall, also in need of his patronage. He is, we learn, the "biggest gallery owner in Lille," on whom it is important, Emma says, that Adèle "made a good impression." We next hear his reputation invoked once Emma has landed the coveted show he proffers and is voicing frustration about his exerting control over her work. She complains, "He has a problem with lesbians. There are things I don't want to tell him."

As with the teacher at the film's start, we are encouraged to imagine this ambivalently characterized figure as Kechiche's alter ego. Shortly thereafter another potential Kechiche stand-in appears. Samir (Salim Kechiouche) is a young French Arab actor (as Kechiche himself was at career's start) who probes a reticent

Adèle about her sexual experience with women before relating his own experience of being relegated to stereotypical roles of "terrorists and hijackers" in American film productions. By film's end, having tired of being typecast, he has quit acting. These easily recognizable alter egos importantly illuminate Kechiche's and invite our (self-)questioning of how vectors of gender, age, class, and race affect cultural capital and professional influence. That Kechiche's authorial identification is complexly bound up with these supporting characters as well as with Adèle (whose lower-middle-class background locates her as the "outsider" protagonist, a recurring character type in Kechiche's films that seems informed by his own immigrant perspective) further complicates his self-alignment with a less obvious auteur-surrogate: Emma.

Notably, both party discussions occur in front of a screen on which plays *Die Büchse der Pandora* (*Pandora's Box*, G. W. Pabst, 1929)—the Weimar classic about kept woman Lulu (Louise Brooks), whose flouting of sexual decorum comes to a head in the scene on display within *Blue*, one which is credited as the first lesbian dance sequence put on film. Adèle's dancing with Samir under Emma's watchful eye soon thereafter, and her later dance with a coworker with whom she will have the fling that will lead to her and Emma's breakup, suggest her projection alongside the wanton Lulu as a fallen woman in Emma's view. This projection is reinforced by Emma's sketching Adèle in a self-consciously debauched pose that, Linda Williams notes, recalls Édouard Manet's 1865 painting *Olympia* and is the film's only instance of full-frontal nudity (see fig. P.4).[23] That this is the moment, under Emma's gaze and direction, that Adèle is filmed most fetishistically—in a slow pan up her body that lingers over her entirely shaved pubis—presents Emma as yet another ambivalent stand-in for Kechiche. Curiously, the mise en abyme framing in the scene's next shot permits us to see that Emma has drawn Adèle wearing underpants where she has none, as if to offer her the modesty that the film denies her. The scene adds another

Fig. P.4. Adèle under Emma's gaze and direction, in a pose evoking Manet's *Olympia*.

troubling layer in preemptively displacing a straight male director's conflicted drives (and perhaps guilty conscience) onto his lesbian character, whose otherwise decent (if fickle) comportment turns ugly when Emma, impetuously exiling Adèle after she has admitted to acts of infidelity, administers slaps—ones Seydoux later reported that Kechiche demanded she not simulate.[24]

In both instances, Kechiche could be said to avail himself of a safe stand-in for his own impulses—whether unseemly leering or unconscionable abuse—in a manner that displaces and even romanticizes the bad behavior of his on-screen surrogate. In inviting his identification with the otherwise appealing Emma (whom the film has, up until this point, invited us to revere much as Adèle does), Kechiche avoids the troubling associations that Bertolucci invites with his own Brando-incarnating alter ego, the brutish Paul in *Last Tango in Paris*. At the same time, the French Arab Kechiche might be seen as shielding himself (and his film) from the hostile response that might well greet a male director from a racially minoritized group casting such an overtly desiring eye on white women. Bertolucci's whiteness allowed him to escape—for a time, anyway—the policing of the gaze in a way that a man of color could not. Nonetheless, though these scenes of leering and lashing diegetically implicate Emma, in light of what has been revealed of his working methods, these scenes also stamp Kechiche as (perhaps uncharacteristically) self-knowing for suggesting that *Blue* is crucially a film about a young and naive woman's use by an older, more knowing and privileged artist who harshly casts her out when she no longer fits the idealized image that has endowed her with artistic value.

Much remains to unpack in the film's metacommentary on selling out and "whoring" (the epithet with which Emma violently expels Adèle, whom she suspects of sleeping around). Suffice it to say that, however (un)intentionally, *Blue* enfolds these questions of (lesbian) women's representation within the film's narrative as well as through its pictorial references to visual art with reflexive gestures that, as in James S. Williams's observation, tease out those "performative processes of cinema itself." Recalling Akerman's resistance to being fully seen or known, that Emma's portraiture of Adèle seems at best a superficial semblance and at worst a garish exoticization serves as a reminder that representation is inherently elusive or even intentionally distorting. "It's strange because it is me and it isn't," Adèle says upon seeing Emma's first sketch of her. Her remark prefigures one with which Emma will attempt to overcome Adèle's resistance to becoming a writer. Adèle says, "I can't expose my life to the world." "You can invent rather than expose," replies Emma, in another line that resounds with meaning around "the real moments of life" Kechiche demanded from his actors and the degree to which they submitted to his demand. Recall this chapter's epigraph, in which Exarchopoulos describes her realization that Kechiche wanted her to "give him *everything*."[25] Even as we are invited to register, most prominently in the final scene of Emma's gallery opening, how film affords a fleshing out of that which canvas cannot, Adèle's evident distance from (and discomfort against) the backdrop of her fantasied image spurs us to scrutinize Kechiche's own inventions alongside his methods.

Skadi Loist notes how *Blue* was promoted more as an art film than as (identity-driven) queer cinema to maximize its universalist message for broad audience appeal.²⁶ Yet the film itself goes to pains (albeit subtly) to indicate how Adèle's experience of first love is distinctly colored by its being a lesbian relationship—from its blossoming in the marginalized and politicized queer spaces of gay bars and Pride parades to the bullying and ostracizing by her classmates and from her evasions to her family and their disappearance from the film after she moves in with Emma to her subsequent silence about Emma around her coworkers even as she is made to endure Emma's male pals' inquisitions into their love life.

Half a decade later, thanks significantly to its afterlife streaming on Netflix, *Blue* continues to resonate as a "first contact" film for queer and curious youth introduced to it algorithmically as an LGBTQ+ drama and perhaps without awareness of its "bad object" status (though because of Netflix's obfuscations around viewing numbers, this can only be anecdotally inferred). To judge from the reactions of my students, for whom the concept of the male gaze seems thoroughly inculcated, the film remains both deeply relatable and decidedly problematic for younger generations. Kechiche has fared less well in the public eye; after announcing he would be splitting his new project into two films of three hours apiece, planned distributor Pathé backed out, leading Kechiche to auction his Palme d'Or to help finance their completion. The first installment, the 185-minute *Mektoub, My Love: Canto Uno* (2017), was greeted with derision upon its premiere at the Venice Film Festival for what was described as its directorial self-indulgence and "masturbatory male gaze." Unrepentantly, Kechiche doubled down with the follow-up, 212-minute *Mektoub, My Love: Intermezzo*, which spurred walkouts at the 2019 Cannes Film Festival over its reported excesses, including a seemingly unsimulated cunnilingus scene nearly fifteen minutes long and so much unapologetic leering at the female form that one critic deemed it a "human rights violation."²⁷

Ultimately, it seems, it is not *Blue* itself but its director who will suffer the fallout from the film's multiple controversies, which will indelibly inform his authorial legacy as it has Bertolucci's. As Loist notes, "Without these sustained discussions, which have been perpetually rehashed during various release levels (staggered national releases as well as theatrical and DVD release), the film most likely would not have reached such wide distribution and total grossing revenue."[28] More than merely propelling its long-tail profitability, the scandals around *Blue* forced a reckoning with structural abuses on-set that has ushered in union-mandated standards overseen by "intimacy coordinators" charged with ensuring the safety and comfort of performers filming sex scenes.[29]

Perhaps more than any film since *Last Tango*—along with such contemporaries as *Deep Throat* (Gerard Damiano, 1972) and *Ai no korîda* (*In the Realm of the Senses*, Nagisa Ôshima, 1976)—*Blue* compelled media scholars and casual viewers alike to test their own expressed precepts around screening sex. Furthermore, it did those 1970s films one better by bringing sex between individuals of the same gender fully into that discussion. What makes one sex scene art and another pornography? Why are a sex scene's pleasures for some viewers governed by the responses of others? Why do we place such value on "realism" and "authenticity" in the representation of (especially queer) sex, particularly as we simultaneously insist on its being performative—whether out of protection of its performers or our own security in its classification as not-porn? These are hardly new questions, but they are ones that *Blue* reanimated and reframed from an innovative angle.

Linda Williams singles out for agreement a remark from critic Richard Corliss's review of *Blue* in which he suggests that the issue is not that the film presents an excessive amount of sex, but rather that "one might ask why there is so little in most other movies. Considering that sex is an activity almost everyone participates in and thinks about even more, it's startling and depressing to think about how few movies connect their characters' lives with their erotic drives."[30] Corliss's assessment helps explain the aghast reactions to *Blue*'s sex scenes. Were it not so unusual in nonpornographic movies to see sex scenes of substantial length and verging on the (hyper)real, *Blue*'s would not stand out so markedly in a film that, after all, devotes comparable stretches of screen time to showing characters discussing literature, attending demonstrations, and devouring spaghetti.

Corliss's call also encompasses sex scenes that "connect" with characters' subjectivities and carry significant narrative meaning. Corliss thus echoes Williams's characterization of Hollywood-style sex scenes as "sanitized poses of decorous passion that last no longer than the length of a song—[and thus] effectively quarantine sex from the rest of the film. Sex, in such films, can never be a real part of what the films are about."[31] (But for their alienating qualities, in treating *Blue*'s sex scenes as at least somewhat formally distinct from the rest of the film, Kechiche might seem to effect the same.) Though to avoid screening sex for fear of its seeming excessive or lacking verisimilitude sells both reality and cinematic representation short. As Williams asserts in her seminal 2008 book *Screening Sex* (the scholarly work that most inspires my own), "Not to speak sex in the realistic way of which cinema alone is capable is to leave out an enormous chunk of human life."[32]

Together Corliss and Williams share the viewpoint that piques this book's explorations: that sexual provocation holds the potential to stimulate both screen representation and reception, and that its elision or eradication from the screen restrains this uncannily representative medium's power to (re)shape our sexual imaginaries in productive (as well as pleasurable) ways. As the film critic Ann Hornaday recently inquired, lamenting the paucity of sex scenes in the wake of #MeToo, "Is abstinence really our only option?"[33] Though his unsavory methods are not to be condoned, Kechiche succeeded alongside Exarchopoulos and Seydoux, "also the directors of the film," in creating within *Blue* images of eroticism that would touch off a cultural conversation as riveting, vexing, and affectively charged as the film itself. As chapter 1 will take up, the questions of sex and its representation brought to prominence by mediatized scandals such as the one that surrounded *Blue* have the potential to be put to creatively and politically generative ends, as our post-#MeToo era illustrates.

NOTES

1. The Steven Spielberg–led jury's decision was announced by the festival's then director Gilles Jacob. Maroh characterized the film's sex scenes as "a brutal and surgical display, exuberant and cold, of so-called lesbian sex, which turned into porn." Quoted in Linda Williams, "Cinema's Sex Acts," *Film Quarterly* 67, no. 4 (2014): 9. Kechiche quoted in Kevin Jagernauth, "'Blue Is the Warmest Color' Director Says the Film Shouldn't Be Released and He Thought of Replacing Léa Seydoux," *Indiewire*, September 24, 2013, http://www.indiewire.com/2013/09/blue-is-the-warmest-color-director-says-the-film-shouldnt-be-released-he-thought-of-replacing-lea-seydoux-93327/. Among the concerns voiced about Kechiche's production methods were reports by the French crew's union representation of deplorable working conditions and of the filmmaker's penchant for verbal abuse and endless takes. Exarchopoulos and Seydoux reported its taking ten days to shoot the sex scenes (which comprise roughly ten minutes of screen time). Adèle Exarchopoulos and Léa Seydoux, "The Stars of 'Blue Is the Warmest Color' on the Riveting Lesbian Love Story," interview by Marlow Stern, *Daily Beast*, September 1, 2013, http://www.thedailybeast.com/the-stars-of-blue-is-the-warmest-color-on-the-riveting-lesbian-love-story. While it has been alleged that Exarchopoulos was underage during filming, I can find no substantiated report of this. According to the Internet Movie Database, during the film's production in the spring and summer of 2012, Exarchopoulos was eighteen, the legal age of majority in the European Union.

2. Box office reporting here and throughout this book are taken from Box Office Mojo. Though an NC-17 rating is typically a deterrent for theater chains, Cinemark broke with its historical policy against screening NC-17 titles to book the film (perhaps as a mea culpa for the company's support of California's anti–marriage equality legislation Proposition 8, which resulted in a boycott of the company in 2008), and New York's IFC Center announced it would grant admission to high school–aged patrons.

Blue Is the Warmest Color was determined to be ineligible for an Academy Award nomination for Best Foreign Language Film because it opened in its home country after the stipulated September deadline.

    3. B. Ruby Rich, "*Blue Is the Warmest Color*: Feeling *Blue*," Criterion Collection, February 24, 2014, https://www.criterion.com/current/posts/3072-blue-is-the-warmest-color-feeling-blue. #BalanceTonPorc ("squeal on your pig") is France's equivalent of the US-based #MeToo solidarity movement, both of which work to denounce sexual harassment and assault. Time's Up is a coalition formed by Hollywood actors to support those seeking justice against sexual harassment and assault in the workplace and to promote gender parity in the entertainment industry.

    4. The red carpet protest was organized by groups campaigning under the banner #5050x2020, which calls for gender parity in the French film industry by 2020. The 82 participants signified the number of films by women filmmakers that have screened in the festival's 71-year history (in contrast with 1,645 films by male filmmakers).

    5. See Alexander Doty, *Flaming Classics: Queering the Film Canon* (New York: Routledge, 2000), 1–21.

    6. In formulating the gender-neutral term prov*auteur* by combining *auteur* and *provocateur*, I elect to use the grammatically masculine form for familiarity (the feminine forms are rarely used) and gender parity (as with *actor*, thought to be preferable to *actress*).

    7. Mette Hjort, "The Problem with Provocation: On Lars von Trier, Enfant Terrible of Danish Art Film," *Kinema: A Journal of Film and Audiovisual Media*, 2011, https://doi.org/10.15353/kinema.vi.1236.

    8. Jonathan Rosenbaum, "Real Sex in Movies," October 5, 2018, https://www.jonathanrosenbaum.net/2018/10/real-sex-in-movies/. The *Interview* spread was designed by Karl Templer and photographed by Mikael Jansson. See Zoã Wolff, "Léa and Adèle," *Interview*, November 2013, https://www.interviewmagazine.com/film/lea-seydoux-adele-exarchopoulos.

    9. Chastain tweeted the following response to Bertolucci's interview: "To all the people that love this film- you're watching a 19yr old get raped by a 48yr old man. The director planned her attack. I feel sick." @jes_chastain, Twitter post, December 3, 2016, 3:32 a.m., https://twitter.com/jes_chastain/status/804966641998168064. Chastain was likely responding to Schneider's remark in a 2007 interview that, while the film's sex was simulated, "I felt humiliated and to be honest, I felt a little raped, both by Marlon and by Bertolucci." Schneider quoted in Lina Das, "I Felt Raped

by Brando," *Daily Mail* (UK), July 19, 2007, https://www.dailymail.co.uk/tvshowbiz/article-469646/I-felt-raped-Brando.html.

10. Bernardo Bertolucci, "Bertolucci par Bertolucci," conversation moderated by Serge Toubiana and Jean-François Rauger, *Leçon de cinéma*, Cinémathèque Française, Paris, September 14, 2013, video, 1:57:53. https://www.canal-u.tv/video/cinematheque_francaise/lecon_de_cinema_bertolucci_par_bertolucci.13144. Kechiche quoted in Jonathan Romney, "Women in Love," *Sight and Sound* (December 2013): 41.

11. Seydoux quoted in Kaleem Aftab, "*Blue Is the Warmest Colour* Actresses on Their Lesbian Sex Scenes: 'We Felt Like Prostitutes,'" *Independent* (London), October 4, 2013, https://www.independent.co.uk/arts-entertainment/films/features/blue-is-the-warmest-colour-actresses-on-their-lesbian-sex-scenes-we-felt-like-prostitutes-8856909.html.

12. A. O. Scott, "My Woody Allen Problem," *New York Times*, January 31, 2018, https://www.nytimes.com/2018/01/31/movies/woody-allen.html.

13. L. Williams, "Cinema's Sex Acts," 23.

14. Ibid., 10. Exarchopoulos quoted in Exarchopoulos and Seydoux, "The Stars of 'Blue Is the Warmest Color.'" For the sex scenes, the actors wore prosthetic vaginas (what Seydoux termed "fake pussies"), molded in silicone cast from their bodies. Aftab, "*Blue Is the Warmest Colour* Actresses."

15. L. Williams, "Cinema's Sex Acts," 10, 15, 18.

16. Jude Dry, "Alia Shawkat Made 'Duck Butter' Queer after Male Actors 'Seemed Uncomfortable' with Intimate Sex Scenes," *Indiewire*, April 27, 2018, https://www.indiewire.com/2018/04/duck-butter-alia-shawkat-lesbian-sex-scenes-1201957653/.

17. Manohla Dargis, "Seeing You Seeing Me: The Trouble with 'Blue Is the Warmest Color,'" *New York Times*, October 25, 2013, https://www.nytimes.com/2013/10/27/movies/the-trouble-with-blue-is-the-warmest-color.html.

18. Anthony Lane, "New Love," *New Yorker*, October 28, 2013, https://www.newyorker.com/magazine/2013/10/28/new-love.

19. See Ivone Margulies, *Nothing Happens: Chantal Akerman's Hyperrealist Everyday* (Durham, NC: Duke University Press, 1996).

20. Quoted in James S. Williams, "Re-siting the Republic: Abdellatif Kechiche and the Politics of Reappropriation and Renewal," in *Space and Being in Contemporary French Cinema* (Manchester: Manchester University Press, 2013), 225. Torres reports that while it was a grueling shoot, she felt protected and made comfortable by Kechiche. See Pamela Messi,

"Yahima Torres Talks about Her Role as Sarah Baartman in the Film by Abdellatif Kechiche," *African Women in Cinema*, November 7, 2010, https://africanwomenincinema.blogspot.com/2010/11/yahima-torres-talks-about-her-role-as.html.

21. J. S. Williams, "Re-Siting the Republic," 225.

22. Ibid., 188. *Beur* cinema takes its name from French slang for "Arab" and refers to films made by French filmmakers of North African origin.

23. L. Williams, "Cinema's Sex Acts," 14.

24. Exarchopoulos and Seydoux, "The Stars of 'Blue Is the Warmest Color.'"

25. Ibid.; emphasis in original.

26. See Skadi Loist, "Crossover Dreams: Global Circulation of Queer Film on the Film Festival Circuits," *Diogenes*, November 7, 2016, 1–16. https://doi.org/10.1177/0392192115667014.

27. Zack Sharf, "'Mektoub My Love' First Reactions Enraged by 'Blue Is the Warmest Color' Director's 'Masturbatory' Male Gaze," *Indiewire*, September 7, 2017, https://www.indiewire.com/2017/09/mektoub-my-love-reviews-male-gaze-abdellatif-kechiche-1201873810/. Caroline Tsai, "'Mektoub, My Love: Intermezzo': Abdellatif Kechiche's Torturous, Four-Hour Sequel Is the Butt of the Joke [Cannes Review]," *The Playlist*, May 24, 2019, https://theplaylist.net/mektoub-my-love-intermezzo-cannes-review-20190524/.

28. Loist, "Crossover Dreams," 11.

29. Tambay Obenson, "SAG-AFTRA Issues New Rules for Sex Scenes with 'Intimacy Coordinators,'" *Indiewire*, January 29, 2020, https://www.indiewire.com/2020/01/sag-aftra-intimacy-coordinators-1202206891/. See also Clarissa Sebag-Montefiore, "How to Make Sex Scenes Natural and Nonthreatening? Cue the 'Intimacy Coordinator,'" *New York Times*, January 22, 2019, https://www.nytimes.com/2019/01/22/arts/movie-sex-scenes-safety-intimacy-coordinator.html; and Lizzie Feidelson, "The Sex Scene Evolves for the #MeToo Era," *New York Times*, January 14, 2020, https://www.nytimes.com/2020/01/14/magazine/sex-scene-intimacy-coordinator.html?nl=todaysheadlines&emc=edit_th_200119?campaign_id=2&instance_id=15176&segment_id=20459&user_id=659d4416c49fb088c697ae5b351de3af&regi_id=69986400119.

30. Quoted in L. Williams, "Cinema's Sex Acts," 10.

31. Ibid., 23.

32. Linda Williams, *Screening Sex* (Durham, NC: Duke University Press, 2008), 266.

33. Ann Hornaday, "Sex Is Disappearing from the Big Screen, and It's Making Movies Less Pleasurable," *Washington Post*, June 7, 2009, https://www.washingtonpost.com/lifestyle/style/sex-is-disappearing-from-the-big-screen-and-its-making-movies-less-pleasurable/2019/06/06/37848090-82ed-11e9-933d-7501070ee669_story.html?utm_term=.8d9441e694d5.

PART I

Provocations

ONE

Selling Sex

Scandalous Marketing Campaigns and the Millennial Watercooler Movie

> The visual is essentially pornographic, which is to say that it has its end in rapt, mindless fascination.... Pornographic films are thus only the potentiation of films in general, which ask us to stare at the world as though it were a naked body.
>
> Fredric Jameson, Signatures of the Visible

> The time has come to think about sex. To some, sexuality may seem to be an unimportant topic, a frivolous diversion from the more critical problems of poverty, war, disease, racism, famine, or nuclear annihilation. But it is precisely at times such as these, when we live with the possibility of unthinkable destruction, that people are likely to become dangerously crazy about sexuality.
>
> Gayle Rubin, "Thinking Sex: Notes for a Radical Theory of the Politics of Sexuality"

SEX SELLS.

It is a timeless axiom, and one whose validity has repeatedly been proven in the market for screen media for nearly 125 years. Pornography—the genre that takes selling sex on-screen to its furthest extreme—has been a key driver of screen technology's development and dissemination since cinema's prehistory. As soon as he had settled that legendary bet for Leland Stanford,

Eadweard Muybridge turned his attention from horse locomotion to the movements of (mostly) female nudes documented in his studio photography series.[1] Two additional instances from the early days of motion pictures are illustrative: American cinema's first "hit movie," Thomas Edison's church- and law-defying *The Kiss* (William Heise, 1896), and Mae West's jailing on obscenity charges causing a surge in ticket sales for her Broadway show *Sex*, which paved the way for her hugely successful screen debut in *She Done Him Wrong* (Lowell Sherman, 1933). Since cinema's start, then, screening provocative sexual content has reliably delivered publicity and controversy, commodities frequently convertible into box office profits. "I believe in censorship. I made a fortune out of it," West is known to have joked.

In addition to its vital role in the emergence and rapid popularity of the moving image, sex saved screen media once again, in the 1960s, when racy European "sexploitation" imports held at bay competition from television when other gimmicks in film production and exhibition (such as Cinerama, 3D, and Smell-O-Vision) failed. Likewise, of the three success-making strategies—"sex, swearing and respectability"—attributed to HBO's (Home Box Office) domination of the cable television marketplace since its emergence in the 1970s, arguably the first of these was, and continues to be, the sharpest arrow in its quiver.[2] As chapter 2 will take up, now that the cable television revolution it instigated has waned, HBO continues to hone its sexploitation–meets–quality TV trademark to keep viewers watching and talking. Defying the dispersion of the audience wrought by what FX chairman John Langraf proclaimed in 2015 "peak TV," HBO's *Game of Thrones* (David Benioff and D. B. Weiss, 2011–19) became an irrepressible popular culture phenomenon in no small part because of its perfecting of "sexposition"—the term Myles McNutt coined to describe the series' exaggeratedly prurient use of sex and nudity as backdrop during scenes of narrative exposition.[3] As the coinage implies, sexposition is a strategy resurrected from sexploitation's golden age and both Hollywood's and cable TV's appropriation of it for its own purposes of soft-core titillation.

However perennial, the notion that sex sells has gained renewed force in the digital era, which is characterized by an oversaturation of content in relation to available audiences. So addled are we by overuse of our devices and their domination of our attention that in 2018 *New York Times* technology columnist Farhad Manjoo, furthering Landgraf's warning, professed that we have reached (and possibly now exceeded) "peak screen."[4] Desperate to capture eyeballs and profits, 21st century media producers and products more than ever mobilize sexual provocation as an authorial signature and promotional strategy to stand out in the crowded, fragmented mediascape and marketplace.

As Muybridge's studio photography evidenced, and as Jameson's famous formulation quoted at chapter's start reminds us, cinema developed out of the mutually reinforcing desires to see and to know.[5] From the peephole pleasures made available by the kinetoscope at the turn of the 20th century to the home-viewing privacy realized first by the VHS/VCR revolution and subsequently by the internet and streaming, screens have served as delivery devices for, as often as not, erotically charged material that aims to provoke any number of responses: curiosity, desire, amazement, arousal, outrage, shock. *Thinking* about sex, as Gayle Rubin's epigraph urges, may not seem high on the list of such intended effects, yet this exhibitionistic medium's power to elicit a voyeuristic impulse with potent psychosexual underpinnings would inspire feminist film theory's emergence and continue to drive reflections on cinema as a representational lens for imagining others and ourselves.[6] While many recent deployments of sexual provocation may be on par with sexploitation's sensationalism of the 1960s and 1970s in ultimately commodifying and containing whatever transgressive or subversive potential they might possess, the possibility always remains that these provocative artists and works may resist or undermine sexual hegemonies by provoking alternative ways of screening and imagining cultural logics of desire.

Seeking to recover the radical political force of the provocative, I explore here how provocations and provoc*auteurs* challenge representational and ideological norms around sex and sexuality. Enabled by ever-expanding digital channels of production, distribution, and exhibition, and amplified by virtual forums (e.g., video-hosting sites and social media) for streaming and sharing, the media creators and texts I examine traverse media platforms and market niches, and in so doing transform inveterate cultural scripts to reflect the complexity and contingency of sexuality.

Consider how controversial campaigning and viral marketing work to sell not just film but filmgoing in the posttheatrical era, when movies are increasingly imperiled by competing content (from peak TV to video games to YouTube to TikTok). Scandal and sexually risqué lures are marketing strategies employed across the cinematic marketplace—from Hollywood studio fare to art and indie films—with the aim of producing what I term the *millennial watercooler movie*: a film that cuts through the clutter of content by provoking curiosity and controversy, a work that pushes the edge of what can be said or shown, about which it seems important to have an opinion. Jon Lewis notes that the "real sex films" in vogue in the first decade of the 21st century faced financial challenges due to their usually being theatrically releasable only on the film festival circuit and in the receding domain of the art house cinema, while their afterlives in ancillary markets also suffer as a result of restrictive practices by cable channels and distribution outlets. Thus, these films "are little seen but much talked about."[7]

Lewis's assessment has been complicated, however, by a media market that has grown far more complex, in which short-term profits are sometimes sacrificed in the interest of synergistic brand building or long-tail revenues. Even where the profit incentive lags, these works foster a revitalized market for provocative sexual representations that, for better or for worse, contributes to the "pornification" of popular culture and the mainstreaming of risqué sexual content. From cable TV's sexposition to *Fifty Shades of Grey*'s multiplex-friendly BDSM, this type of content continually raises the bar for what is considered sexually shocking or scandalous on-screen.

A filmmaker's resistance to making cuts to satisfy a ratings board can generate valuable publicity, as can "red-band" (R-rated) trailers ostensibly restricted to mature viewers but highly shareable online. Where a film's commercial viability once depended on its receiving no more restrictive a rating than R (or its equivalent outside the United States), the decreased importance of theatrical exhibition for art and independent film means that receiving an NC-17 rating or forgoing a rating altogether no longer dooms a film. Indeed, an NC-17 rating may draw attention, as in the case of *Blue Is the Warmest Color*. While an extended rollout aimed at building anticipation for a strong opening weekend remains a central marketing strategy for almost all theatrically exhibited films, the tactic has in recent years been supplemented by the free publicity generated by provocative content, whether that content is as fleeting and frivolous as Ben Affleck's "did you see it?" penis-sighting stunt for *Gone Girl* (David Fincher, 2014), discussed below, or as narratively justified and representationally noteworthy as the six minutes of screen time that fortysomething Julie Delpy spends topless in *Before Midnight* (Richard Linklater, 2013). The millennial watercooler movie, then, runs counter both to the blockbuster logic of saturation advertising and opening weekend determinism and to Netflix's algorithm-dependent strategy of dumping huge chunks of original programming, and demonstrates that word of mouth, often driven by online buzz, remains an effective publicity strategy.

An outpouring of recent scholarship has explored screenings of sex deemed extreme, perverse, transgressive, and radical.[8] In venturing into the conversation, I arrive indebted to many scholars, but most of all to pornography studies pioneer Linda Williams, particularly for her deeply considered, steadfast assertion of the ideologically resistant potential of naturalistic screen representations of sex. This book aspires to heed Williams's call for "on/scenities"—"gestures[s] by which a culture brings on to the public scene the very organs, acts, 'bodies and pleasures' that have heretofore been designated ob-off-scene, that is, needing to be kept out of view"—and to join in actively refusing "the continued avoidance of the emotional nature and physical specificity of the sex acts that so importantly punctuate our public and private lives."[9]

The chapters in this book make no attempt to comprehensively cover sexually provocative content; rather, they examine exemplary case studies of sexual provocation in four (sometimes overlapping) categories of contemporary screen media. These categories are (1) mainstream Hollywood-produced and/or -distributed feature films with relatively large budgets and stars; (2) global art cinema, which is increasingly funded by transnational coproduction financing and supplementary public support and entrenched in international film festival economies; (3) US indie filmmaking, which is produced through private financing ventures and dependent on festival and (semi-)independent distribution networks; and (4) television and web series, here encompassing a fairly modest range of basic/premium cable and original online content. I exclude pornography, which exists in a parallel orbit of production and reception cultures that calls for its own coordinated approach. Yet the delineation between art and porn needs troubling, especially as traditional signifiers of pornography (such as erect penises, "money shots," and unsimulated sex) also appear in contemporary art cinema. "The art-sex picture has blossomed so fully it is nearly its own genre," as critic Richard Corliss noted in 2001.[10] Not since the 1960s has the association between art cinema and sexuality seemed so close and so productive. Chapters 2 and 3 parse the work of Alain Guiraudie and Catherine Breillat, provoc*auteurs* who straddle the line between art film and pornography.

Tanya Krzywinska observes that art cinema "often uses the provocation of transgression as a means to lure an audience" even when films are "not particularly transgressive."[11] This discrepancy may arise from misleading sexploitation-style marketing that promises explicit content where there is little to none or from the use of sexually explicit content to ultimately conservative ends. Miramax, the corporate creation of the now disgraced Harvey Weinstein and his brother Bob, frequently worked the former strategy, beginning with the title of its first hit, *sex, lies, and videotape* (Steven Soderbergh, 1989), to promote films with titillating imagery often at odds with their tone and content.[12] One of the more sexually provocative films of recent years, *Bang Gang* (Eva Husson, 2015), takes the latter tack, presenting extended scenes of orgiastic hedonism among French teens only to offer up a conclusion that manages to be both moralizing and wish fulfilling, punishing its youthful libertines with an easily treatable sexually transmitted disease but with nary an unplanned pregnancy or otherwise realistic repercussion in sight. Recognizing this sometimes tenuous negotiation to reconcile sexual provocation with its political potential, Jon Lewis, one of the foremost scholars exploring how sex (and its censorship) has shaped screen history, offers this generous assessment: "There is more to art-house porn than just a willingness to show and tell all. There is a seriousness of purpose and a kind of aesthetic purity to which these films aspire, a gesture toward a new cinematic realism made by filmmakers and actors who are willing to show and do anything and everything for their art."[13]

These provocative works at their best offer powerful reworkings of cultural logics of desire, but they also, in the face of the often-decried death of cinema, revitalize the cultural dialogue around film and help restore it to a place of cultural importance. In their efforts to sustain the market for adult-targeted cinema in an era of family films and fantasy franchises, these scandalous films reaffirm the subversive potential of movie making *and* moviegoing, answering Lauren Berlant and Michael Warner's call to resist those ideologies and institutions of intimacy that, "by making sex seem irrelevant or merely personal ... block the building of nonnormative or explicit public sex cultures."[14]

Looking back to Rubin's quote at the beginning of this chapter, thinking about sex has increasingly become a provocation, so any means of amplifying serious cultural conversations around sex becomes a mode of resistance, and any counterpublic sphere (whether brick and mortar or virtual) for doing so becomes a space of resistance. Writing in the portentous year 1984 while entrenched in an oppressively conservative moment in US history (both socially and politically), Rubin's motives for finding "thinking sex" so urgent seem in retrospect dismayingly clear. The widespread refusal in that era, from the highest levels of power on down, to talk about sex contributed to a pandemic of tragic proportions; the effects of that inaction reverberate today and with exponential impact given the worldwide COVID crisis unfolding as I write this. Though many continue to suffer in concrete, often brutal ways from repressive controls on bodies and sex, what seems like permissiveness—and even dismissiveness—around current norms of sexual behavior in the developed world runs the risk of not taking sex seriously. At a time when provocation is far too often mobilized against sexual freedoms, this book aims to bring provocation back to its radical political roots.

SEXUAL PROVOCATION AS SIGNATURE AND STRATEGY

I start this section, in which I survey this book's structure, with a nod to Carol Siegel's reminder of the diverse, inventive, and sometimes counterintuitive means by which screening sex achieves its representationally and ideologically radical potential. Siegel writes, "A sex radical film is one ... that presents sexuality in a manner that disturbs the liberal concept of a norm, that introduces ideas about sexuality and its impact on society that disrupt majoritarian views of how sex fits into human lives."[15] This book adopts a range of approaches to explore these ideas. As noted in the prologue's discussion of *Blue Is the Warmest Color*, assessing these often disturbing but potentially disruptive (or disturbing *because* they are potentially disruptive) texts compels grappling with tangled metrics of sexual and representational politics, authorial motives and agency, textual affects, personal investments, and intersectional considerations. The book's first half ("Provocations") begins with this chapter's exploration of promotional tactics primed for the millennial watercooler and continues in chapter 2's discussion of the recent proliferation on-screen of full-frontal male nudity, which for most of screen history has been almost completely taboo except in pornography.

Appraising the phallic visual economy circa 2020 through examination of three screen genres—the bromance, the erotic thriller, and quality television—I consider whether the penis's newfound visibility might despectacularize that organ and thus dismantle its discursive construction as phallus and enable a reenvisioning and exploration of male intimacies and queer masculinities. Having established my reasons for singling out these three genres—the bromance frequently foregrounds male homosociality and homoeroticism; the erotic thriller typically eroticizes masculinity; and quality television has been at the forefront of the display of male full-frontal nudity— I then assess how each conventionally works to defuse homoerotic tension and police heteromasculinity. I locate in Jane Campion's work (focusing on her 2003 film *In the Cut*) an alternative means to mobilize the penis's potential as a feminist tool to despectacularize and demystify its symbolic power. I then consider the hypervisibility of gay nudity in Alain Guiraudie's work (focusing on his 2013 film *Stranger by the Lake*) in contrast to the strategy of (mostly) masking queer male genitalia that was adopted by the gay male creators of HBO's *Looking* (Michael Lannan and Andrew Haigh, 2014–16). I argue that this not-showing ultimately enables a still more provocative nonvisual enunciation of sexual truth and fluid desire, conveyed through candid conversation and nonnaming (in which the refusal to label enables erotic desire to elude discursive containment). Whether by appropriating pornographic conventions in rendering male bodies and gay sex hypervisible so as to confront a representational legacy of heterophallicism and queer erasure or by emphasizing narrative and aural (over visual) provocation, these transgressive means of rendering full-frontal male nudity endeavor to achieve what we might think of as "defetishization through representation."

The book's second half ("Provoc*auteurs*") contemplates two cross-generational pairings of screen auteurs who employ sexual provocation as a primary component of their authorial signature. Examining key works by the self-proclaimed "pariah of French cinema" Catherine Breillat and *Girls* creator and controversial Millennial Lena Dunham, and by New Queer Cinema pioneer Lisa Cholodenko and Iranian American bisexual media creator Desiree Akhavan, I explore through these pairings creative influence as well as shared strategies for mobilizing sexual provocation toward feminist and queer ends, and across new channels for making and circulating narratives and emergent forums for provoc*auteur* self-inscription.[16]

While sexual provocation is undeniably a branding tactic, as the work of these four media creators indicates, it is a great deal more. It serves to revise and reenvision representations of sexual subjectivity, embodiment, and identity. Furthermore, my feminist-queer reappropriation of auteurism asserts a demand for recognition of frequently marginalized figures and their creative visions and productive labor without losing sight of how the auteur functions commercially—in Timothy Corrigan's estimation, "as publicity and advertisement, that is, as both a provocative and empty display of material surfaces."[17]

Chapter 3 observes Breillat's and Dunham's flaunting of that which is typically deemed (especially for women) abject, shameful, and not-to-be-looked-at (to twist Laura Mulvey's famous formulation that women in classical narrative cinema connote "to-be-looked-at-ness").[18] Through their shared commitment to screening women's "corpo*reality*"—publicly and naturalistically displaying bodies and acts that are conventionally relegated to the realm of the private and idealized—these provoc*auteurs* stretch the definitional and representational boundaries of what is considered artistic and pornographic to generate a hybrid, politicized mode: art porn.

Long notorious for her blurring of the boundaries between art and pornography and for her focus on acts and desires that typically inspire disgust or revulsion, Breillat is a pioneer of screen provocation and a stylistic and ideological influence on a subsequent generation of women provoc*auteurs* that includes Dunham and Akhavan. Focusing on five Breillat films released since 2000, chapter 3 reads the explicit sex and abject anatomies that characterize her cinema of corpo*reality* as a feminist critique of conventionally fetishistic uses of female eroticism and nudity in both mainstream filmmaking and pornography.

Dunham's own flouting of those representational standards is part of a larger strategy of defiant disrobing and persistent oversharing, from her earliest short films to her social media self-documentation. Locating Dunham as a key successor to Breillat's legacy, the discussion reads the *Girls* creator as shaping her career around a similarly provocative screening of unseemly sex acts and unruly bodies, within an Americanized and predominantly televised context. Central to this strategy is Dunham's self-exhibitionism of her body—culturally and pejoratively inscribed as abject, excessive, and privileged.

Appraising Dunham's screen performances alongside those of Breillat's protagonists (and other art-world provoc*auteurs* whose influence Dunham displays), I assess their mutual enactment of nude embodiment and what I term "sexual self-subjugation" as a route to feminist subject formation. By showing sex as an ambivalent or ambiguous exchange subject to women's self-determination, Breillat and Dunham provocatively and non-prescriptively explore the gray areas of consent while pressing viewers to go beyond neoliberal definitions of the self in terms of individualism and utility. I consider the divisive, and at times vituperative, responses to Breillat's and Dunham's provocations and how both women talk back by reflexively addressing within their work the critics and naysayers.

Chapter 4 considers how sexual and industrial "inbetweeners" Lisa Cholodenko (*High Art, The Kids Are All Right*) and Desiree Akhavan (*The Slope, Appropriate Behavior*) challenge straight and gay sexual and representational politics by presenting intersectionalist, inclusive understandings of queer identity. At the same time that they position themselves outside sexual binaries, these provoc*auteurs* resist entertainment industry binaries of gay versus straight cinema, art versus commerce, and even film versus television versus internet. In doing so, they reject the scripts governing LGBTQ+ cultural producers, who are typically expected to align with either a gay politics privileging identity formation, visibility, and affirmation or a more radical queer politics predicated on subversion. Through their resistance to homonormativity and to queer regulatory regimes, Cholodenko and Akhavan provoke a third way of seeing, and screening, queerness. That they do so not from the far reaches of queer identity and praxis but from the politically and aesthetically moderate confines of marriage equality, bisexuality, and (romantic) comedy makes them (what I call) "bad queers," but with the potential to re-queer queer by further radicalizing the term's meanings and potentials. They reflexively think through questions of identity and imagery in their screen productions, foregrounding negotiations of their own roles as queer media producers.

My analysis of Cholodenko's reception positions her as a bad queer on both sides of the critical/political divide even as her work has received curiously little serious consideration. Cholodenko's 1998 debut film *High Art*, arriving on the tail end of the radical New Queer Cinema moment, provocatively likened lesbianism to heroin addiction.[19] Her subsequent work has remained controversial, even as it has turned in some ways toward the cinematic and political mainstream. *The Kids Are All Right*, released in 2010, seemed to embrace the homonormative and drew a good deal of angry critique in the queer blogosphere, while other Cholodenko projects sideline queer characters entirely and seem designed to resist the policing of queer representation from LGBTQ+ perspectives as much as straight expectations of a lesbian film and filmmaker.

Even as she's been nicknamed the "Persian bisexual Lena Dunham" and anointed her own first feature *Appropriate Behavior* (2014) "a gay *Annie Hall*," Akhavan is similarly resistant to sexual and industrial pigeonholing as a gay filmmaker and the expectations that categorization imposes.[20] Much as Cholodenko provokes consternation across the aisle, Akhavan rejects LGBTQ+ cultural politics' imperatives of pride and positivity and queer political correctness in her (and former partner Ingrid Jungermann's) pioneering web series *The Slope* (whose tagline was "Superficial, homophobic lesbians"). Locating Akhavan as a paradigmatic figure in the emergent genre of the LGBTQ+ web series, I posit that Akhavan's carrying on of New Queer Cinema–inspired irreverence is enabled by the newfound feasibility and financial viability of web production and distribution along with the nichification of media audiences.

Finally, the epilogue invites consideration of what remains provocative in a culture that confoundingly manifests both pornification and sexual puritanism, and what these still-taboo corners of the sexual imaginary reveal when projected and voiced on-screen. Considering two final expressive art forms revived by contemporary realms for taboo talk around sex—stand-up comedy and short fiction—I describe the ongoing political urgency for these considerations of sexual provocation and their reliance on the convergence of old and new media for their dissemination and discursive impact. Noting the affective energies and productive exchanges mobilized by and through social media responses to these recent provocations, I offer a final bid for the radical practice of vulnerable viewing as a route to ensuring advocacy for and openness to challenging material and complex ideas concerning sex and sexuality.

Heeding Siegel's warning at the beginning of this section that graphic or perverse packaging is no guarantee of radical import, the rest of this book focuses largely on what happens after the publicity campaign. I examine the productively provocative meanings the works themselves yield, though still with an eye to their promotional discourse and their reception by critics and audiences in watercooler conversations. Before moving into those provocation analyses and provoc*auteur* studies, I turn to a discussion of the paratextual means of constructing controversial campaigns and inciting public dialogue around films that are sold through sexual provocation—an artful deal that often starts on the film festival's red carpet.

RED CARPET PROVOCATIONS: BRANDING SEX AND/AS ART AT FILM FESTIVALS

The 2015–16 season was the annus mirabilis for sexual provocation at film festivals. The season began with a programming lineup in Park City that critics anointed "Sexy Sundance." In spring, the perennially provocative Cannes festival went to eye-popping extremes with its premiere of Gaspar Noé's explicit 3D sex fest *Love* (2015). The usually conservative Toronto festival mounted an atypically lurid lineup, and a Park City encore was characterized by "fetishes and flatulence." Finally, in February, the 2016 Berlinale sensation *Paris 05:59: Théo & Hugo* (Olivier Ducastel and Jacques Martineau, 2016) began with an eighteen-minute gay sex club orgy sequence.²¹ Sexual provocation has evidently become a dominant publicity strategy on the festival circuit, which has overtaken the foundering art house theater as the predominant distribution vehicle and exhibition venue for art cinema and independent film. Nevertheless, as Marijke de Valck points out, the "scandal film" framing ensures neither commercial success nor critical acclaim. Such films have often underperformed or been underserved by the influential journalists and critics whose attentions are required to keep the scandal aloft.²² A standout in this regard, as noted in the prologue, *Blue Is the Warmest Color* sustained its scandal film notoriety over time by periodic reaffirmations, first in its worldwide premiere at Cannes, then at its US premiere at the Telluride Film Festival, and still beyond. As Mattias Frey notes, "The discourses of outrage and provocation that characterize the scandal film recur in subsequent distribution and reception cycles in theatrical and home-video release."²³ So while more or less effective in distinguishing films from their festival and art house competitors in an ever-widening marketplace, sexual provocation as a promotional tool also proves instrumental in confirming art cinema's cachet as highbrow, cutting-edge, and auteur-driven.

As festivals have proliferated, the festivals, no less than films, must sell themselves. This means retooling their collective appeal—of which the promise of scandalous sexual content is critical, alongside such lures as what de Valck calls signifiers of "scarcity" and the air of sophistication—while creating individual brands that distinguish respective festivals from one another.²⁴ Commenting on the screen imagery and red carpet antics, by turns outlandish and infamous, enacted by Danish filmmaker Lars von Trier and discussed below, his collaborator-muse Charlotte Gainsbourg intuits how provoc*auteurs* serve the dual interests of film festivals to draw attention while differentiating their brand: "I don't think [the provocation] is very interesting; I think it's the sincerity underneath that's interesting and real. I think he's very honest with his work, and the whole provocation is just a farce. But that's who he is also. But it's not something that I take very seriously, and I don't think you're supposed to take it seriously."[25]

Gainsbourg alludes here to the performative use of provoc*auteurism* as a, however paradoxical, means to convey the "real": a concept that underwrites art cinema's oppositionality to the Hollywood style.[26] The rhetorical thrust of much festival discourse around provocative programming resides in attendant promises of naturalistic sexual representation and the sacrifices made for art that its achievement may entail—for the festival-as-entity as well as filmmakers. As Frey reminds us, showing controversial works at film festivals reinforces "that they are liberal, cosmopolitan spaces where productions that may otherwise be subject to censorship enjoy a forum."[27] In reporting on the latest provocations, the critical press will often allude to previous landmarks of sexually daring programming that serve to cement a particular festival's legacy even as new boundaries, it is proclaimed, are being transgressed. Though revealing some similarity to Hollywood's promotional processes of commercialization and containment (which are assessed in the next section), an analysis of art/indie film marketing confirms the efficacy of provocative promotion but suggests a range of possibilities with regard to the ultimate degree of transgression these campaigns (and the films they are selling) transmit. A look at the most prominent international and US festivals, Cannes and Sundance, permits a brief consideration (to be expanded on throughout this book) of how the trope of sexual provocation propels certain films and filmmakers to high-profile visibility as it simultaneously shores up these respective festivals' self-branding as "quality" and "quirky," respectively.

With its historical traditions of defending obscenity and embracing the libertine, France is the nation and Cannes the festival most aligned with sexual provocation (because of this, a high proportion of films discussed in this book are partly or wholly French productions). This is not simply a matter of historical precedent or national sensibility but also one of economic viability, because French films are able to play up their sex appeal (to seem more, in a word, French) without endangering their protection under *l'exception culturelle française* that subsidizes films produced domestically. This laissez-faire attitude, coupled with protectionist measures designed to restrict the flow of Hollywood product into French cinemas, allows provoc*auteurs* and their sexually charged films to gain hold (with cycles such as the New French Extremity with which chapter 3's Breillat is often associated) and sometimes to flourish (as with *Blue Is the Warmest Color* riding its controversial reception at Cannes to worldwide release). Auteurism, itself a French concept, has long been associated with erotic transgression, but several of the most prominent auteurs working today—Breillat and von Trier as well as Xavier Dolan, Gaspar Noé, François Ozon, Albert Serra, and Tsai Ming-liang—are best known not (or not only) for their distinct aesthetic or thematic sensibility but for their penchant for sexual provocation. Film festivals' increasing dependence, as de Valck notes, on "ensuring that there are enough established auteurs participating," creates incentives both for filmmakers to adopt authorial brands as sexual provoc*auteurs* and for festivals and critics to nurture those brands by courting and promoting their high-profile involvement and indulging the scandals they generate.[28]

von Trier serves as an exemplary case in this regard, having been received back into the good graces of the Cannes brass even after making disastrously ill-considered remarks (expressing sympathy for Hitler and admiration for the Nazi aesthetic) at the 2011 festival press conference for his film *Melancholia*. As a result, he was issued a one-year ban as persona non grata (a moniker he would flaunt at Berlin's rival festival that year by wearing a shirt emblazoned with that label and the Cannes logo). Inviting him back in 2014 to screen his real sex film *Nymph()maniac* out of competition (von Trier having already flirted with sacrilege by opening it in Danish theaters on Christmas Day), Cannes would serve as the climax to a multipronged rollout of provocation mobilized from the release of the film's first still—an indistinct image of a beaten-looking Gainsbourg (who plays the film's eponymous lead) lying in an alleyway, which critics and fans found at once anticlimactic, confusing, and troubling.[29]

This use of the teaser "first look" image, an emerging gambit for drumming up advance press coverage and fan anticipation, was followed by a second, more conspicuously charged, image of Gainsbourg suggestively sandwiched between two Black male actors. An even more blatant enticement was offered when a teaser trailer was removed from YouTube for infringing on the site's decency rules regarding sex and nudity (it was reinstated a day later with a warning for viewers). Reportedly inspired by what he deemed to have been the censorious response at Cannes to his previous remarks, von Trier specified a promotional campaign visually arresting enough to do the talking for him. The result, conceived by a noted digital advertising team known as the Einstein Couple, went viral first with its teaser image of the parentheses in the film's title as a stand-in for female genitalia. The image was accompanied by the tagline "Forget About Love" and continued with a series of close-ups of the orgasm-contorted faces of the film's cast members.

A final image of von Trier with duct tape covering his mouth accompanied a press release formally announcing the publicity campaign and the filmmaker's intention to take "a vow of silence" (a nod to the "Vow of Chastity" taken by practitioners of the Dogme 95 film collective of which von Trier is the foremost proponent). The campaign's unattributed borrowing from Beautiful Agony, the subscription-based erotic website founded in 2003 that documents people's faces in the throes of *la petite mort*, encouraged its associations with porn, as did another pre-Cannes promotional image of the cast posed as if on a porn set. In the background, von Trier appears with a digital camera in hand and duct tape again covering his mouth. At Cannes, cast member Shia LeBeouf, having already added fuel to the campaign by disclosing that he submitted a sex tape as audition material, threatened to upstage von Trier by appearing on the red carpet with a paper bag reading "I Am Not Famous Anymore" on his head.

Though *Nymph()maniac* became easily the most talked about film at Cannes that year, it remains uncertain whether the promotional stamina of von Trier's brand, and the festival's touting of it, will prove resilient. His recent work has failed to gain traction, and the political tide has turned against the festival's reverential treatment of controversial male auteurs. Invited back to Cannes in 2018 to premiere his poorly received serial-killer epic *The House That Jack Built*, von Trier was alleged by *New York Times* critic Manohla Dargis to be "trolling" women, and by the *Guardian*'s Kate Muir (who asked the question that incited his appalling remarks in 2011) to be unforgivably flaunting his male privilege during a sensitive cultural moment.[30] Given the walkouts and lackluster response that greeted the film, even as the festival was pledging to address its gender disparity problems, von Trier's proven brand of self-promotion—as he notes, "My problem is really that I'm a crowd-pleaser"—may well have exceeded the limits of taste that Cannes's own canny self-regard insists on.[31] For film philosopher Mette Hjort, the crucial limits were ethical and were surpassed some time ago, when, shortly after von Trier's 2011 debacle, a Norwegian mass murderer who proclaimed his admiration for the filmmaker committed atrocities that recall events in von Trier's 2003 film *Dogville*. Hjort concluded, "To adopt and cultivate the persona of the provocateur to the extent that von Trier does, is, in my view, ultimately irresponsible."[32]

While von Trier may again find himself persona non grata, ultimately Cannes's self-interest seems threatened less by provoc*auteurs* than by the loss of the festival's cultivated reputation for exclusivity and glamour—a reputation it has reinforced by effectively exiling Netflix through its requirement that competition films be released theatrically in France and by instituting a ban on "vulgar" selfies on the red carpet.[33] (The rumored ban on women wearing flats on the red carpet, flouted by barefoot jury member Kristen Stewart at the 2018 festival, has been denied by Cannes officials.) Cannes has long been associated with a cosmopolitanism that accommodates sexual content marked by signifiers of auteurism and artistry, and at a festival with a tradition of *le booing*, to be provocative is perhaps the most strategic play.

Though not always successfully, the festival and its causes célèbres aim to harmonize a highbrow regard for sexual realism with a lowbrow appreciation for showmanship and sensationalism, often framed as a stance against sexual puritanism and censorship. Provo*cauteur* Vincent Gallo and costar Chloë Sevigny (at the time, a couple in real life) mounted an extensive defense at Cannes of their notorious 2003 collaboration *The Brown Bunny* (which features a three-minute scene of Sevigny fellating Gallo). As Mattias Frey documents, Gallo's and Sevigny's defense turned heavily on artistic commitment and personal sacrifice for the goal of sexual realism, though they failed to save the film from its subsequent critical beating.[34]

What some found to be critic-baiting and paparazzi-pandering in the guise of serious art was revitalized as a strategy by provo*cauteur* Gaspar Noé's return to Cannes thirteen years after his highly controversial rape-revenge film *Irreversible* (2002). While the novelty of seeing a cum shot in 3D was enough of a hook to sell *Love* as the latest boundary pusher, its conceit simply updates what had moviegoers of the 1950s ducking from spears and arrows that seemed to emerge from the screen. And given the still intermittent use of 3D exhibition, the gambit proved technologically compromised when the premiere I was to have attended at the Philadelphia Film Festival was delayed interminably when the 3D projector broke down.

Beginning with Steven Soderbergh's *sex, lies, and videotape* premiere in 1989 (which resulted in its sale for a then groundbreaking $1.1 million to Miramax, with an additional $1 million guaranteed for advertising), it has been typical for a film or two on Sundance's annual roster to make headlines for sexual provocation. *Compliance* (Craig Zobel, 2012), which is based on a real-life sexual coercion scam, and *Plemya* (*The Tribe*, Myroslav Slaboshpytskyi, 2014), with its extended sex sequences between deaf adolescents, are two instances. But apart from Ruby Rich's announcement in 1992, in the middle of the culture wars that imperiled the National Endowment for the Arts, that New Queer Cinema had arrived on the Sundance scene, sexual provocation has not been a key aspect of the festival's marketing—until recently.[35]

Sundance has joined Cannes in renewing its support for what has now been named "New New Queer Cinema"—films that exhibit the formal experimentation and postidentitarian irreverence for which the 1990s moment was known. Chapter 4 describes Sundance's function as an incubator then and now for queer provoc*auteurs* Cholodenko and Akhavan. Rather than corral its most incendiary entries into the midnight programming or its "Next" sidebar for emergent and experimental work, Sundance's lineup since 2015 has seen a stable of sexually provocative features enter the main slate and the festival's brand shift from one long associated with American-tinted individualist quirk to an edgier, rawer sensibility. Some of the provocations in Sundance's 2015–16 programming that combined to rebrand the festival and, by association, contemporary US independent filmmaking include the libidinous potty-mouthed gymnasts in *The Bronze*; *The D Train*'s (Andrew Mogel and Jarrad Paul, 2015) daring consummation of its Jack Black–James Marsden bromance; the statutory rape–turned–feminist coming-of-age story *Diary of a Teenage Girl* (Marielle Heller, 2015); the full-frontal swingers comedy *The Overnight* (Patrick Brice, 2015); the flatulence-fueled, walkout-inducing *Swiss Army Man* (Daniel Kwan and Daniel Scheinert, 2016); the fetish documentary *Tickled* (David Farrier and Dylan Reeve, 2016); the sex, drugs, and privilege of *White Girl* (Elizabeth Wood, 2016); and the bestiality–meets–body horror flick *Wild* (Nicolette Krebitz, 2016).

This suggestion that Sundance is moving away from its quirky irreverence toward a taste profile more like the extreme provocations of Cannes was recently reinforced by the most attention-getting entry in its 2018 lineup. *Holiday*, the debut film by Danish writer-director Isabella Eklöf, was reported to feature "the most unsettling rape scene since *Irreversible*."[36] In speculating on the motives driving Sundance's shift toward intensified sexual provocation, we might point to the way it allows the festival's ancillary arms SundanceTV and SundanceNow to vie with cable programming's daring fare while differentiating the Sundance brand from that of fast-rising rival festival South by Southwest. One additional and unlikely competitor, the multiplex cinema, has emerged to challenge Sundance's claim on the US front of sexual provocation. Though enabled by internet-assisted channels of discourse, watercooler status is increasingly hard-won as a result of the dissolution of the mass audience and broadcasting in favor of niche markets and narrowcasting. This chapter's final section will consider several recent films exhibited in wide (rather than limited) release and pitched at a general audience, for which sexual provocation operated as a promotional campaign to propel them to viral levels of public awareness.

SEX AT THE MULTIPLEX

Not since the 1980s–90s heyday of erotic thrillers such as *Fatal Attraction* (Adrian Lyne, 1987) and *Basic Instinct* (Paul Verhoeven, 1992) have adult-themed dramas featuring significant sexual content regularly appeared among the annual top ten highest grossing films at the US box office. At least, not until recently. Apart from the raunchy sexual humor of R-rated bromances like *The Hangover* (Todd Phillips, 2009) and *Ted* (Seth MacFarlane, 2012), the box office leaders are the action films and animated features that comprise a globalized Hollywood's bread and butter. Yet *Sex and the City* (Michael Patrick King, 2008) and *Bridesmaids* (Paul Feig, 2011) nearly cracked the top ten, and "ladies behaving badly" comedies *Trainwreck* (Judd Apatow, 2015), *Bad Moms* (Jon Lucas and Scott Moore, 2016), and *Girls Trip* (Malcolm D. Lee, 2017) all topped $100 million. And with the reliable Nancy Meyers brand—though longer on romance than sex—remaining on the radar, Hollywood studios have kept an eye on potential payouts for wide-release films aimed at adults that dramatically or (more often) comically treat contemporary sexual mores. That market niche has become increasingly the purview of boutique studio divisions (such as Fox Searchlight) and indie distributors (such as Focus Features). Viable returns can be delivered by films ranking in the top twenty or even in the top thirty. Although their prospects in the worldwide market are dimmer and their merchandising potential low to nonexistent, such films are relatively inexpensive to make, have more potential for free publicity through award nominations, and attract a consumer base still willing to buy movie tickets. Particularly noteworthy about this revitalization of sexual provocation at the multiplex is that it highlights women performers and typically targets a female audience.

So while sexual provocation poses no serious challenge to the box office dominance of presold tentpoles, it serves as counterprogramming to the superhero movies that dominate the multiplex, offering spectacularized sex as an alternative to spectacularized violence. Whether *Star Wars* or Pixar, Hollywood's raison d'être since the late 1970s has been films geared toward children of all ages—a fitting turn of phrase given the arrested development the films enable through their fantasies of heroic individualism and American exceptionalism. What is called the "middle class" of movies—those with production budgets in the $5 million to

$25 million (or even $50 million) range—has shrunk drastically, with studio releases swelling into the six figures as indie features recede into microbudgets. Where Hollywood's blockbusters unabashedly shore up ideological constructions of family and nation as redemptive and uncompromised, midlevel studio-produced and/or -distributed films typically package erotic content and contain transgressive meanings in demographically pliable, commercially palatable ways that are not always consistent with the ideological mechanisms of the films themselves. While I will leave extended analysis of this mainstream form of sexual provocation to others, I briefly consider it here to suggest how the Hollywood studio apparatus and theater chains avail themselves of viral marketing strategies and buzz-generating controversy stemming from scandalous sex. In so doing, they provide an alternative business model to the high-stakes speculation that has made Hollywood risk averse when it comes to anything but proven properties and high concept formulas.

The most stupefying evidence of sexual provocation's recent potential for mainstream success is Hollywood's erotic romance trilogy *Fifty Shades of Grey* (Sam Taylor-Johnson, 2015), *Fifty Shades Darker* (James Foley, 2017), and *Fifty Shades Freed* (James Foley, 2018). Those who have analyzed the cultural pull and earning power of the *Fifty Shades* phenomenon—from its origins as *Twilight* fan fiction to the film adaptations' $1 billion earnings worldwide—illuminate how its leveraging of presold property awareness (E. L. James's best-selling books), titillating subject matter (BDSM erotics), and promotional savvy succeeded in making it what Hilary Radner calls "an event film for mums" and a game changer for the woman's film.[37] Particularly impressive to studio executives and industry watchers was its establishment of a lucrative Valentine's Day opening weekend in the February "dump zone" as well as the foreign playability of a film that lacked any A-list stars, significant computer-generated images, or superheroes.

The first installment of the trilogy was the highest-grossing February debut both in US film history and internationally, with ticket sales that topped the $400 million mark after only two weeks. The film's total worldwide gross to date is estimated at $570 million, though the long-tail profits continue to accrue. In contrast with the promotional promises of transgressive content combined with cinematic realism that I refer to as "art porn," the *Fifty Shades* marketing strategy played coy and used commercial ploys. Promotional images featured the lead actors posed to suggest kinky scenarios and asked, "Curious?" A trailer was enticingly set to a remix of Beyoncé's "Crazy in Love" and included as much fetishizing of leading man Christian Grey's luxury lifestyle as of star Jamie Dornan's chiseled torso.

Receipts for the second and third installments fell to around the $370 million mark apiece, but they kept up their strong showing abroad (where roughly 70% of gross profits were made), and the franchise has ultimately proven to be one of Universal's most successful. Though the Kindle and other electronic reading devices were reportedly crucial to *Fifty Shades*' popularity in book form, in that they allowed for furtive reading even in public spaces, the trilogy's robust box office indicated that there was no shame in being seen buying a ticket. Whereas a *Saturday Night Live* parody Amazon ad for Mother's Day 2012 riffed on women reading *Fifty Shades* in secret, comedian Amy Schumer's skit for the 2015 MTV Movie Awards played on her going undercover to the multiplex only to find the lobby crowded with women fans packing vibrators. While the franchise was derisively termed "mommy porn" and "kink for normies," alluding to its romanticizing of BDSM (alongside its eroticizing of conspicuous consumption), BDSM advocates and practitioners took particular offense at the trilogy's representation of BDSM as originating in trauma and enabling neurosis rather than as a sexual subculture oriented around active, informed consent.[38]

Critical response to the films ranged from good-humored eye-rolling to scathing takedowns, while serious assessments by feminist media scholars charge the books and films with regulating transgressive desire into the confines of the Hollywood marriage plot and reducing BDSM to (at best) materialistic commodification or (at worst) eroticized celebration of an emotionally abusive relationship. Yet in proving that women-oriented films could dominate an opening weekend and play abroad without massive star wattage, *Fifty Shades* demonstrated its blockbuster bona fides by being critic-proof.

And so, much as Universal Pictures looked to independent producers' exploitation marketing model in the 1970s to propel *Jaws* (Steven Spielberg, 1975) to its historical position as the first blockbuster, contemporary Hollywood has appropriated art cinema's "scandal film" and its accompanying promotional tactics of shock and sensationalism. The practice of spending a sizable portion of a film's overall budget on publicity is borrowed from exploitation cinema. Today's Hollywood and Indiewood marketing campaigns often approach or equal (or even surpass) a film's production costs.

The commercial potential of this blend of lowbrow sensationalism with higher-end financing was demonstrated by the part softcore porn, part postmodern performance piece *Spring Breakers* (Harmony Korine, 2012). The film made relatively modest profits ($30 million worldwide) but yielded a sufficiently healthy return on its $5 million production budget and played well enough with critics to put its producer Annapurna Pictures and distributor A24 on the map. It managed to do so largely by way of a lurid advertising campaign that positioned former Disney stars Selena Gomez and Vanessa Hudgens as dirtying up their images, presenting the film itself as a sort of hybrid of the *Girls Gone Wild* soft-core porn franchise and Korine's screenwriting debut *Kids* (Larry Clark, 1995). Refusing to convert from trashy to tasteful even when the time came for its Oscar campaign, the film's "For Your Consideration" appeals to Academy Awards voters featured supporting actor favorite James Franco's calls on social media to (echoing his character's tagline) "Consider this shit."

The promotional team behind *Gone Girl* similarly chose to go low with its Ben Affleck penis-sighting stunt, which used social media as the engine to create a "did you see it?" meme around a momentary flicker of full-frontal nudity by its A-list star. The meme appeared to adhere to a marked gender divide—with men reporting having seen it and women having missed it— that conveniently suited the studio's interest in marketing it as a date movie (which was a challenge more because of its "chick lit" origins than its premise of presumed wife killing).[39] As with *Nymph()maniac*, penis sighting was merely one element of a multipronged promotional campaign that borrowed as much from traditional Hollywood tactics as it did from exploitation marketing and viral strategies.

This marketing move can be seen as having been drawn from the same playbook deployed in Production Code–era censorship controversies, such as that drummed up by producer Howard Hughes to ensure the release and subsequent success of his Jane Russell vehicle *The Outlaw* (1943).[40] It also recalls Miramax's ingenuity with *The Crying Game* (Neil Jordan, 1992)—and before it Alfred Hitchcock's with *Psycho* (1960)—in their manipulation of critics and early viewers (and in *Gone Girl*'s case, the Gillian Flynn novel's scores of readers) into spoiler avoidance.[41] In fact, penis sighting was a final effort to keep people talking about *Gone Girl* after its opening weekend but before its Oscar campaign reheated its buzz. The tactic was part of a long campaign that began with an advance ploy drawn from *The Blair Witch Project*'s (Daniel Myrick and Eduardo Sanchez, 1999) pioneering of the "mockumentary" approach and online interactive campaign, in which a fabricated tip hotline for the missing Amy Dunne (Rosamund Pike's character) appeared as an "Easter egg" in early trailers and print ads and, when dialed, treated callers to a chilling reading of the opening lines of Flynn's novel.

Rewarding ardent fans in a different sense, the exaggerated beefcake billing for *Magic Mike* (Steven Soderbergh, 2012), which nods nostalgically to *The Full Monty* (Peter Cattaneo, 1997) while promising far better abs, helped make that film a sleeper hit that took in $167 million worldwide against a $7 million production budget. Its reported appeal for gay men in the United States, who flocked to the film in numbers not seen since the release of *Brokeback Mountain* (Ang Lee, 2005), seems to have owed much to the redirection of its promotional campaign from its initial framing as a romantic comedy (playing up the heterosexual coupling of stars Channing Tatum and Cody Horn) to one that targeted the gay press and brought supporting cast member and out gay actor Matt Bomer to the forefront along with Tatum's naked posterior, which was put on display in the film's red-band trailer.[42] In a rare instance of the film industry overcompensating in favor of the female audience, the promotional campaign for the sequel *Magic Mike XXL* (Gregory Jacobs, 2015) doubled down on its appeals to women, sacrificing the previous outreach to (especially gay) men and with them a substantial portion of the first film's box office (though the absence of star Matthew McConaughey and director Soderbergh alongside blockbuster competition during the July 4 opening weekend seem also to blame).

Although the first film's promotional imagery was hardly subtle, *Magic Mike XXL* came on to its prospective audience with a teaser poster centered on Tatum's crotch and bearing the cut-to-the-chase tagline "Coming." Two years later, *Girls Trip* would use a similar blend of sexual come-on and double entendre with publicity images featuring the four women leads framed between the legs of a man wearing only boxer briefs, accompanied by a tagline promising "You'll Be Glad You Came." Interestingly, then, the same promotional gambit that drew gay men to *Magic Mike*—downplaying the heterosexual love story in favor of dirty dancing and derrieres—worked on straight women. An astounding 96 percent of the US opening weekend audience for *Magic Mike*

XXL was estimated to be female, up from 73 percent for *Magic Mike*. Even if, like a live performance by "male entertainers," the Magic Mike films are fairly chaste, these promotional appeals to women are not false advertising. As critic Wesley Morris wrote in his review of *Magic Mike XXL*, "I've never watched a movie more aware of the fact that it is not speaking explicitly to men, not even gay ones."[43] Moreover, in having established this gendered branding, the Magic Mike mini-franchise has landed on a longer-tail profit source in the phenomenon of movie nights and viewing parties and a cottage industry of bachelor and bachelorette party–friendly "live all-male revues" and "authorized tribute shows," including the Magic Mike Live show in Las Vegas "presented by Channing Tatum."[44]

Even as it has made a contribution to revitalizing communal moviegoing, the Magic Mike phenomenon's connection to the wedding-industrial complex may undercut these films' potential for radical provocation. As Berlant and Warner posit, public sex cultures resist "the privileged institutions of social reproduction, the accumulation and transfer of capital, and self-development," so we might view Magic Mike's indirect investments in marriage and consumption as problematically heteronormative (or homonormative, given the renewed appeals to its gay male constituency for bachelor party patronage).[45] Yet a significant component of the first film, taken up in the critical discourse around it, was a critique of capitalism that undergirded its narrative focus on recession-era Floridians finding steadier employment in stripping than in the disappearing pool of blue-collar jobs—a narrative element through which *Magic Mike* thematizes its own role in selling sex.

Like *Fifty Shades'* domination of Valentine's Day weekend, these women-targeted films are shoehorning their way into a summer release schedule that has long been the province of the young male and child/family quadrants, and they demonstrate that female-centered desire and sexual fantasy can sell mainstream cinema. In addition to illustrating the pull of sexual provocation in mainstream film production and its potential to create millennial watercooler movies, these films serve as Hollywood case studies with corollaries in chapters to come. *Gone Girl* and the Magic Mike films introduce chapter 2's examination of male full-frontal nudity (or its titillating possibility) as a potential route to de-phallicizing the penis and queering masculinity, while *Fifty Shades*' foregrounding of BDSM eroticism previews the discussion in chapter 3 of women provoc*auteurs* who explore what I call sexual self-subjugation. Additionally, these sexually provocative Hollywood movies featuring women behaving badly, both in and out of the bedroom, align with chapter 4's bad queer provoc*auteurs* in offering an irreverent alternative to mainstream content, whether that mainstream is defined as family-friendly fare or GLAAD-approved homonormativity.[46]

Although my focus here has been on sexual provocation's use as a means to revitalize film festivals and moviegoing in a post-theatrical era, these discussions suggest how millennial watercooler movies need not play—or yet, or still, be playing—in a theater near you to have impact. Online promotional strategies from teaser images to red-band trailers ensure that the attention and discussion they elicit start long before the festival premiere or release date. And despite our diminishing cultural memory, the online infrastructure that increasingly offers such films an afterlife in streaming—particularly on curated sites such as Fandor and Mubi—finds prospects for long-tail profits in those memorably provocative films. With such films' newfound dependence on at-home virtual cinema viewing in the wake of 2020's COVID-related theater closures, appeals such as that made by the first-run trailer for Sadean historical drama *Liberté* (Albert Serra, 2020), "available now to watch from the *dis*comfort of your living room," are bound to prevail.

On this note, though I focus here on the millennial watercooler movie, by no means is the link between sexual provocation and digital-era promotion a film-only phenomenon. Indeed, the watercooler concept was popularized in reference to communal television viewing before the all-at-once release model, on-demand and time-shifting options, and binge-watching practice came to eclipse such real-time spectatorship. Instead, notes *Atlantic* critic Nolan Feeney in reporting on *Breaking Bad*'s (AMC, 2008–13) final and most-watched episode, "The technologies that often get blamed for bringing about the end of water-cooler TV are actually encouraging all kinds of viewers to take part in television as it happens."[47]

This book will traverse television and web series, and the epilogue even revisits old media (in the form of *The New Yorker*) born anew through new media virtual and viral networking. Indeed, these issues of communal reception and cultural conversations become ever more pronounced in thinking about watercooler TV. Much as movies have spread across screens and spaces, television has also become less entrenched in the home and less anchored to the televisual apparatus, having migrated to cordless mobility and personal screens that are often blamed for encouraging audience fragmentation and individual and political solipsism. But what is often characterized as immersive, addictive spectatorship need not keep viewers hermetically isolated and silent as long as social media's potential as a virtual watercooler and counterpublic sphere is embraced. Another contemporary phenomenon, the live tweeting of television, attests to this potential for provoking critical discussion around series finales, awards shows, live musical theater specials, and other event programming.

Yet as digital technologies and forums for conversing around media proliferate—as this chapter emphasizes at its start—so has content. Alongside the concern of silencing is the possibility that cultural dialogue will turn to monologues and that the communities these virtual spaces enable will turn into echo chambers. Evidence of and repercussions from this echo-chamber effect are already abundant in the political sphere, where screen media have played a significant role in the creation of isolated and antagonistic publics. While those matters loom behind, though lie outside, the purview of this book, I remain mindful of the unique power of the moving image and its ability to persuade and to transform our understanding of the world.

Today's political climate makes frighteningly clear how this power can be mobilized toward tyranny and division, and this current reality makes it all the more important to reaffirm the potential of screen narratives to cultivate and deepen our humanity. As the writer and publisher Dave Eggers expressed in a 2018 *New York Times* editorial lamenting the Trump administration's contemptuous dismissal of the arts, "But with art comes empathy. It allows us to look through someone else's eyes and know their strivings and struggles. It expands the moral imagination and makes it impossible to accept the dehumanization of others. When we are without art, we are a diminished people—myopic, unlearned and cruel."[48] It is a sentiment regularly sounded in the academy as the arts and humanities and the institutions that support them falter and even wither.

With the proliferation of screen media—in 2018, 495 scripted television series were aired and around 870 films released in the United States alone—it is increasingly rare that people are watching the same thing, much less watching it at the same time. Hence, the need, recalling Rubin, "to think about sex" on-screen as a means to bring us into cultural conversation—whether at the film festival, the art house, the multiplex, in our individual living rooms, or connected virtually via our electronic devices. In the wake of cross-platform marketing strategies, diversified entertainment options, and dispersed audiences, the "sex sells" strategy is both pervasive and productive. It also, as mentioned at the outset, calls for a recovery of the political potential of provocation. In her book-length meditation on the *Fifty Shades* phenomenon, sociologist Eva Illouz concludes that "its effect is performative, changing sexual and romantic practices while speaking about them."[49] Befitting its topic, this book itself aims to be performative as well as provocative, to serve as a polemical response to the silencing around sex within the academy and in the culture more broadly. After all, to think and speak about sex—especially in these deeply troubled times—is itself a provocation.

NOTES

1. In the 1870s Eadweard Muybridge conducted and published a series of motion studies using time-lapse photography; some of the earliest of these, made at the behest of industrialist and politician Leland Stanford, aimed to determine whether in a horse's gait there is an instant at which all four hooves leave the ground (there is); these experiments are widely considered to have provided the practical and conceptual impetus for motion picture technology.

2. See Janet McCabe and Kim Akass, "Sex, Swearing and Respectability: Courting Controversy, HBO's Original Programming and Producing Quality TV," in *Quality TV: Contemporary American Television and Beyond* (London: I. B. Tauris, 2007), 62–76.

3. Myles McNutt, "Game of Thrones: 'The Night Lands' and Sexposition," *Cultural Learnings*, April 8, 2012, https://cultural-learnings.com/2012/04/08/game-of-thrones-the-night-lands-and-sexposition/.

4. Farhad Manjoo, "We Have Reached Peak Screen: Now Revolution Is in the Air," *New York Times*, June 27, 2018, https://www.nytimes.com/2018/06/27/technology/peak-screen-revolution.html.

5. Fredric Jameson, *Signatures of the Visible* (New York: Routledge, 1990), 1.

6. Gayle Rubin, "Thinking Sex: Notes for a Radical Theory of the Politics of Sexuality," in *Culture, Society and Sexuality: A Reader*, 2nd ed., ed. Richard Parker and Peter Aggleton (New York: Routledge, 2007), 143. For the foundational treatise of feminist film theory, see Laura Mulvey, "Visual Pleasure and Narrative Cinema," *Screen* 16, no. 3 (October 1975): 6–18.

7. Jon Lewis, "Real Sex: Aesthetics and Economics of Art-House Porn," *Jump Cut*, no. 51 (Spring 2009), http://www.ejumpcut.org/archive/jc51.2009/LewisRealsex/index.html.

8. Examples include Lindsay Coleman, ed., *Sex and Storytelling in Modern Cinema: Explicit Sex, Performance and Cinematic Technique* (New York: I. B. Tauris, 2016); Lindsay Coleman and Carol Siegel, eds.,

Intercourse in Television and Film: The Presentation of Explicit Sex Acts (Lanham, MD: Lexington Books, 2018); Mattias Frey, *Extreme Cinema: The Transgressive Rhetoric of Today's Art Film Culture* (New Brunswick, NJ: Rutgers University Press, 2016); Joel Gwynne, ed., *Transgression in Anglo-American Cinema: Gender, Sex and the Deviant Body* (New York: Wallflower, 2016); Tanya Horek and Tina Kendall, eds., *The New Extremism in Cinema: From France to Europe* (Edinburgh: Edinburgh University Press, 2013); Aaron Michael Kerner and Jonathan L. Knapp, eds., *Extreme Cinema: Affective Strategies in Transnational Media* (Edinburgh: Edinburgh University Press, 2016); Darren Kerr and Donna Peberdy, eds., *Tainted Love: Screening Sexual Perversion* (New York: I. B. Tauris, 2017); Carol Siegel, *Sex Radical Cinema* (Bloomington: Indiana University Press, 2015); and John Tulloch and Belinda Middleweek, *Real Sex Films: The New Intimacy and Risk in Cinema* (New York: Oxford University Press, 2017).

9. Linda Williams, *Hard Core: Power, Pleasure, and the "Frenzy of the Visible,"* expanded ed. (Berkeley: University of California Press, 1999), 282; Linda Williams, *Screening Sex* (Durham, NC: Duke University Press, 2008), 298.

10. Richard Corliss, "Films That Are Good in Bed," *Time*, November 18, 2001, http://content.time.com/time/magazine/article/0,9171,184984,00.html.

11. Tanya Krzywinska, *Sex and the Cinema* (New York: Wallflower, 2006), 110.

12. See Alisa Perren, "sex, lies and marketing," *Film Quarterly* 55, no. 2 (2001): 30–39.

13. Lewis, "Real Sex."

14. Lauren Berlant and Michael Warner, "Sex in Public," *Critical Inquiry* 24, no. 2 (Winter 1998): 553.

15. Siegel, *Sex Radical Cinema*, 26.

16. Breillat quoted in Benjamin Secher, "Catherine Breillat: 'All True Artists Are Hated,'" *Telegraph* (London), April 8, 2005, https://www.telegraph.co.uk/culture/film/starsandstories/3672302/Catherine-BreillatAll-true-artists-are-hated.html.

17. Timothy Corrigan, "The Commerce of Auteurism," in *A Cinema without Walls: Movies and Culture after Vietnam* (New Brunswick, NJ: Rutgers University Press, 1991), 106.

18. See Mulvey, "Visual Pleasure and Narrative Cinema": 6–18.

19. Critic B. Ruby Rich coined the term "New Queer Cinema" in response to queer independent film and video work on view at Sundance

and other festivals and made the case for its being, more than a film movement, a "moment." See Rich, "A Queer Sensation," *Village Voice*, March 24, 1992, 41–44.

20. Akhavan quoted in Nick Dawson, "Desiree Akhavan and Ingrid Jungermann," *Filmmaker*, 25 New Faces of 2012, 2012, https://filmmakermagazine.com/people/desiree-akhavan-and-ingrid-jungermann/#.WXilPIqQxsM.

21. See Ramin Setoodeh and Brent Lang, "Sundance 2015: The Festival of Sex on the Slopes," *Variety*, January 29, 2015, https://variety.com/2015/film/markets-festivals/sundance-2015-the-festival-of-sex-in-the-slopes-1201418884/; Ryan Lattanzio, "From Gaspar Noé to Jeremy Saulnier, Cinema Provocateurs Head to Toronto," *Indiewire*, August 11, 2015, https://www.indiewire.com/2015/08/from-gaspar-noe-to-jeremy-saulnier-cinema-provocateurs-head-to-toronto-185575/; Brooks Barnes, "At Sundance, a Focus on Fetishes and Flatulence," *New York Times*, January 24, 2016, https://www.nytimes.com/2016/01/25/movies/at-sundance-a-focus-on-fetishes-and-flatulence.html?emc=edit_th_20160125&nl=todaysheadlines&nlid=6998640&_r=0.

22. Marijke de Valck, *Film Festivals: From European Geopolitics to Global Cinephilia* (Amsterdam: Amsterdam University Press, 2011), 155–56.

23. Frey, *Extreme Cinema*, 66.

24. See Marijke de Valck, "Conversion, Digitization, and the Future of Film Festivals," in *Digital Disruption: Cinema Moves On-Line*, ed. Dina Iordanova and Stuart Cunningham (St. Andrews, Scotland: St. Andrews Film Studies, 2012), 117–29.

25. Quoted in Jane Birkin and Charlotte Gainsbourg, conversation moderated by Dennis Lim, Film at Lincoln Center, New York, January 29, 2016, accessed on *The Close-Up*, no. 69, February 3, 2016, audio, 45:05, https://www.filmlinc.org/daily/the-close-up-jane-birkin-and-charlotte-gainsbourg/.

26. For a discussion of art cinema's ontological categorization in relation to Hollywood-style cinema, see David Bordwell, "Art Cinema as a Mode of Film Practice," in *Film Theory and Criticism*, 7th ed., ed. Leo Braudy and Marshall Cohen (New York: Oxford University Press, 2009), 649–57.

27. Frey, *Extreme Cinema*, 57.

28. de Valck, *Film Festivals*, 157.

29. *Nymph()maniac*'s sex scenes are comprised of footage of hardcore actors performing sex digitally composited with scenes of the top-billed actors simulating sex. For response to the film's first still, see for

example Alex Billington, "First Look: Charlotte Gainsbourg in Lars von Trier's 'Nymphomaniac,'" *First Showing*, February 6, 2013, https://www.firstshowing.net/2013/first-look-charlotte-gainsbourg-in-lars-von-triers-nymphomaniac/.

30. Manohla Dargis, "Is Lars von Trier Trolling Us?" *New York Times*, May 16, 2018, https://www.nytimes.com/2018/05/16/movies/lars-von-trier-the-house-that-jack-built-cannes-film-festival.html; Kate Muir, "Lars von Trier's Cannes Return Proves Festival Is Still in Thrall to Male Privilege," *Guardian*, April 20, 2018, https://www.theguardian.com/film/2018/apr/20/lars-von-trier-persona-non-grata-cannes-film-festival-times-up.

31. Quoted in Dargis, "Is Lars von Trier Trolling Us?"

32. Mette Hjort, "The Problem with Provocation: On Lars von Trier, Enfant Terrible of Danish Art Film," *Kinema: A Journal of Film and Audiovisual Media*, 2011, https://doi.org/10.15353/kinema.vi.1236.

33. As of this writing, in the wake of the cancellation of Cannes 2020 due to the coronavirus pandemic, Cannes and Netflix remain unreconciled despite its artistic director Thierry Frémaux having made public the festival's intention to screen Netflix film *Da 5 Bloods* (Spike Lee, 2020) out of competition; Lee's latest feature was not among the fifty-six films subsequently announced to have received a 2020 Official Selection label.

34. See Frey, *Extreme Cinema*, 174.

35. See Rich, "A Queer Sensation." Some of the films categorized as New Queer Cinema were funded by National Endowment for the Humanities grants and so were included among those subject to conservatives' outcry against public funding of allegedly obscene artwork.

36. Eric Kohn, "'Holiday' Review: Devastating Danish Drama Has the Most Unsettling Rape Scene Since 'Irreversible'—Sundance 2018," *Indiewire*, January 26, 2018, https://www.indiewire.com/2018/01/holiday-review-isabella-eklof-rape-sundance-2018-1201921797/.

37. See Hilary Radner, *The New Woman's Film: Femme-centric Movies for Smart Chicks* (New York: Routledge, 2017), 173–89.

38. See Francesca Tripodi, "Fifty Shades of Consent?" *Feminist Media Studies* 17, no. 1 (2017): 93–107.

39. For reporting on the he saw it/she didn't divide, see Kyle Buchanan, "How to See Ben Affleck's Penis in *Gone Girl*," *Vulture*, October 1, 2014, https://www.vulture.com/2014/10/how-to-see-ben-affleck-nude-penis-gone-girl.html.

40. The Production Code Administration (PCA) was the chief regulating body for the censorial code put into strict effect in 1934 by the Motion

Picture Producers and Distributors of America (MPPDA) in an attempt to ward off regulation of motion picture content by federal and state governments, which were under persistent pressure from religious and moral groups to "clean up" the movies. Believing that self-regulation would be the more satisfactory option, the PCA took as its guiding principle, "No picture shall be produced which will lower the standards of those who see it." The PCA regularly demanded of filmmakers that modifications be made or denied them outright its seal of approval, considered a necessity for a film's chance at financial success. With the influx of foreign films (not as strictly subject to Code regulation) into US theaters starting in the 1950s, and after defiance expressed by a few US directors who chose to release their films sans seal, the PCA's authority was gradually dispelled. In 1968, the Code was replaced with the ratings system that remains in place today, overseen by a contemporary version of the MPPDA now known as the Motion Picture Association of America (MPAA).

41. Miramax pressured critics to keep secret (while coyly alluding in its promotional campaign to) *The Crying Game*'s second act reveal that the male lead's hitherto love interest—presumed by him and viewers to be a cis woman—is anatomically male. Publicity for *Psycho* played up Hitchcock's insistence to theater owners that no one be admitted after film's start and offered titillating details on the filming of the famous shower scene, ingeniously obscuring the shock of star Janet Leigh's killing off only 45 minutes into the film.

42. Eric Piepenburg, "'Magic Mike' Is Big Draw for Gay Men," *New York Times*, July 4, 2012, https://www.nytimes.com/2012/07/05/movies/magic-mike-with-channing-tatum-draws-gay-men.html.

43. Wesley Morris, "Hump Day: The Utterly OMG 'Magic Mike XXL,'" *Grantland*, July 2, 2015, http://grantland.com/hollywood-prospectus/hump-day-the-utterly-omg-magic-mike-xxl/.

44. Tatum is credited on the Magic Mike Live website as having conceived and directed the show; see https://magicmikelivelasvegas.com/.

45. Berlant and Warner, "Sex in Public," 553.

46. GLAAD is a US nongovernmental media monitoring organization. In characterizing neoliberalism's redefining of LGBTQ+ identity, Lisa Duggan coined the phrase "the new homonormativity," defined as "a politics that does not contest dominant heteronormative assumptions and institutions, but upholds and sustains them, while promising the possibility of a demobilized gay constituency and a privatized, depoliticized gay culture anchored in domesticity and consumption." Duggan, "The New

Homonormativity: The Sexual Politics of Neoliberalism," in *Materializing Democracy: Toward a Revitalized Cultural Politics*, ed. Ross Castronovo and Dana D. Nelson (Durham, NC: Duke University Press, 2002), 179.

47. Nolan Feeney, "Netflix and On-Demand Aren't Killing 'Water-Cooler TV'—They're Saving It," *Atlantic*, September 30, 2013, https://www.theatlantic.com/entertainment/archive/2013/09/netflix-and-on-demand-arent-killing-water-cooler-tv-theyre-saving-it/280113/.

48. Dave Eggers, "A Cultural Vacuum in Trump's White House," *New York Times*, June 29, 2018, https://www.nytimes.com/2018/06/29/opinion/dave-eggers-culture-arts-trump.html.

49. Eva Illouz, *Hard-Core Romance*: Fifty Shades of Grey, *Best-Sellers, and Society* (Chicago: University of Chicago Press, 2014), 77.

TWO

Full-Frontal Provocation

Male Nudity as Nonphallic Masculinity

Precisely because the penis has remained hidden for so long, in some ways it has become the last great taboo in our culture.

Peter Lehman, *Running Scared: Masculinity and the Representation of the Male Body*

America fears the penis and that's something I'm going to help them get over.

Judd Apatow

21ST CENTURY "DICK FLICKS": REVISING THE MELODRAMATIC/COMIC PENIS DICHOTOMY

The year 2014 proved a tipping point for imagery of and discourse around the visibility of the penis. VH1 premiered its reality series *Dating Naked*; pop star Justin Bieber was alleged to have inflated his manliness in a series of Calvin Klein underwear ads; actor Jon Hamm addressed the internet meme devoted to documenting his endowment with a plea to "lay off"; and, as explored in chapter 1, Twentieth Century Fox's publicity campaign for *Gone Girl* incited a "did you see it?" debate over whether Ben Affleck's penis could be glimpsed in a shower sequence.[1] Male nudity continues to proliferate in reality television, with a recent (and earliest out of the gate) instance being the opening-scene genital flashing in the pilot of the short-lived UK series *Bromans* (Karl Warner and Peter Tierney, ITV2, 2017), which featured male contestants competing gladiator-style. Fan sites and Tumblrs devoted to "penis peeping" have also proliferated despite Hamm's entreaties. These sites trade on celebrity exposures such as the shot of Tom Hardy that was leaked in 2016 from the set of the television series *Taboo* (Chips Hardy, Tom Hardy, and Steven Knight, BBC One/FX, 2017–), which provoked a paparazzi flap around which the show's publicity campaign was then launched.[2] A more premeditated promotional gambit involved some suggestive sweatpants worn by Justin Theroux, lead of HBO's *The Leftovers* (Damon Lindelof, 2014–17), that were used as a "running joke" between the show's creator and audience.[3]

These appearances of the penis in popular culture were predictably matched by male nudity making waves in artistic circles—from a full-frontal Shia LeBeouf going viral in a 2012 music video for Icelandic art-rock band Sigur Rós to art film director Gaspar Noé bestowing on cinema its first 3D penis with 2015's *Love*. Already an increasingly infamous meme in an age of sexting "dick pics," with the Anthony Weiner scandal in 2011 providing the most high-profile yet debased episode to date, male genitalia so thoroughly pervaded the small screen that *Vulture* scribed a year-end trend piece titled "Why Full-Frontal Male Nudity Was All Over TV in 2015."[4] Though it goes unmentioned by *Vulture*, the US presidential campaign under way in 2015 also gave penis talk prominent play on the political stage, as then candidate Donald Trump's assured voters, "I guarantee you, there's no problem" with the size of his manhood. His statement was subsequently discredited when sex performer Stormy Daniels cast aspersions on the presidential genitalia on the talk show circuit and in her tell-all memoir. The penis's crossover cachet extended even to that most mainstream and commercial of realms, the Hollywood superhero franchise, when Marvel's *Deadpool* (Tim Miller, 2016) borrowed *Gone Girl*'s peek-a-boo ploy as one of a range of tactics to endow the film with edgy antiheroic cred. The strategy succeeded to the tune of $760 million box office.[5]

Penises, particularly erect ones, rarely make the cut for the R rating in the United States or its equivalents abroad. Yet, as was established in chapter 1, to exceed the boundaries of the R rating these days generally proves a bonus in terms of publicity, if not profitability—one reason for the abundance of penis sightings of late after being a representational rarity long after the loosening of censorship restrictions in the 1960s.[6] The film scholar who has written most extensively and thoughtfully on this topic, Peter Lehman, indicates that, in realms of screen imagery where pornographic projections of phallic excess—that is, visualizing the penis as erect and all-powerful—is not permitted, the traditional strategy has been to keep the penis veiled. The reason for this, according to Lehman, is that "the sight of the actual organ threatens to deflate and make ludicrous the symbolic phallus."[7]

One particularly pronounced representational strategy in this regard has the penis exaggeratedly and teasingly referenced but never revealed in a way that, Lehman describes, "simultaneously foregrounds the display of the male body and protect[s] it from the spectacle it circles around. These awkward visual structures that deny the view of the genitals are compounded when we hear characters talk about the penis, but we are denied the view of it."[8] Actor Viggo Mortensen's naked fight scene in *Eastern Promises* (David Cronenberg, 2007) is a vivid example of such foregrounding that (though it is not diegetically discussed) provokes spectatorial parsing and freeze-frame scrutiny, while the steel workers–turned–strippers of *The Full Monty* never deliver a visual payoff on the title's verbal titillation. Lehman further notes that, in addition to its risk of undermining phallic authority, full-frontal nudity renders the male body vulnerable to women's evaluation and incites homophobic anxiety around the desire to look. As Lehman observes, "What is lost amid all this careful regulation is the variety of actual penises that are not asked to bear the burden of representing anything other than what they are—penises, in other words, that are neither more nor less than penises."[9]

Recouping this loss, some recent instances of unveiling the penis on-screen paradoxically de-spectacularize male embodiment by rendering it naturalistically and nonphallically, working to overturn a representational norm not confined to contemporary visual media alone. As Elizabeth Stephens notes, even in earlier historical eras when the penis enjoyed visibility across artistic forms high and low, phallic representation has largely been nonnaturalistic, "eliding its relationship to the physical penis in ways consistent with contemporaneous concepts of phallic masculinity." As Stephens observes, artistic traditions from the ancient world forward have represented the penis in a range of ways, always with the aim of phallic signification as determined by that culture (i.e., rational self-control for the Greeks versus enviable, fearsome potency for the Romans).[10] To revise this representational regime so thoroughly as to relieve the penis of its phallic signification, to render it merely a penis, constitutes a formidable shift.

While acknowledging that naturalism is not a surefire aesthetic or ideological means to de-phallicize male corporeality, I remain skeptical of the view that derisively regards nude scenes as without progressive potential, as in film critic Roger Ebert's pronouncement, "Genitals, of either sex, reduce any scene to a documentary. Nudity below the waist is fatal to the dramatic impact of any scene, drawing attention away from the characters, dialogue, and situation."[11] Ebert here expresses disdain for documentary, an ostensibly "reduced" mode of representation inferior to that of dramatic fiction, as well as a disbelief that full-frontal nudity might enable or enhance narrative insights or effects. Full-frontal nudity need not inevitably be spectacular, as Ebert suggests, but may indeed lend itself to narrative development while also displaying the truth-revealing dimension of documentary in its privileging of the real. It bears noting, however, that among this recent upsurge of naturalistic male nudity, a number of the penises on display are prosthetic—a factor that complicates my notion of naturalistic nudity and its potential for conveying corpo*realities*: screen representations of unidealized embodiment that chapter 3 explores in relation to female anatomies and feminist ideologies.

In large part, male celebrity nudity in narrative cinema has been the province of a handful of dramatic actors whose star personae skew toward the perverse (Harvey Keitel) or libertine (Ewan McGregor). Occasional one-offs include actors such as Tom Berenger "going native" in *At Play in the Fields of the Lord* (Hector Babenco, 1991) and Bruce Willis delving into erotic thriller territory in *Color of Night* (Richard Rush, 1994). The interest in celebrity nudity that fuels such gawker sites as *Mr. Skin* (and its male nudity offshoot *Mr. Man*) points to a particular modality of visual pleasure that encompasses more than erotic impulse. The desire to visually verify in such instances appears equally fueled by curiosity (and ensuing judgment) and by the context in which a star appeared naked (how early in one's career or for how artful a project), and, of course, with an eye to evaluating appearance (size, shape, and, where female breast exposure or male prosthesis is concerned, authenticity). Following actor Halle Berry's reputed half-million-dollar salary bump for appearing topless in *Swordfish* (Dominic Sena, 2001), increasingly the interest also lies in the contractual negotiations and compensation surrounding nudity clauses.

Of course, merely unveiling an average-size, flaccid penis in a nonspectacular mise-en-scène is not necessarily sufficient to detach it from its phallic signification. As Lehman notes, a scene of male full-frontal nudity in Pedro Almodóvar's *What Have I Done to Deserve This?* (1985) signifies differently when accounting for the inflection of a gay-identified filmmaker, for whom any reference to the phallic visual economy will necessarily be "caught in the contradiction of both challenging and reinforcing dominant sexual codes."[12] In that case, Almodóvar's display of an undersized, flaccid penis works to resignify its association with weakness and failure, even as it also performs a parodic critique of inflated heteropatriarchal notions of the phallus. Lehman's broader point is that any specific instance of penis display is subject to a complex constellation of narrative context and author-reader-text relations and must be understood in that context.

Conversely, the penis may be displayed to spectacular effect that ultimately renders it defetishized, as in the performance art contortions of *Puppetry of the Penis* creator Simon Morley or "supermasochist" Bob Flanagan. In such displays, the male body's hypervisibility and (often jaw-dropping) pliability paradoxically renders the penis ordinary, de-eroticized, abstract, or all-too-human. Singling out instances of nonphallic full-frontal male nudity on-screen, both in and out of erotic contexts, counters a history of corporeal representation that has fetishized the penis-as-phallus and thereby dismembers (so to speak) its symbolic power. In focusing on the penis, then, my goal is not to reinforce its phallic mythology but rather to demystify it, to scrutinize its corpo*reality*, so as to dismantle its discursive construction as phallus. As Lehman notes, "Silence about and invisibility of the penis contribute to phallic mystique. The penis is and will remain centered until such time as we turn the critical spotlight on it."[13] Richard Dyer, Richard Fung, and Alexandra Juhasz have each contributed cogent considerations of how the penis has been represented in queer contexts. While this chapter builds on their explorations, as well as on equally estimable work by Hannah Mueller on the treatment of male nudity in contemporary television drama, that Lehman's remains the singular, if invaluable, perspective on the penis's heterophallic significations in mainstream cinema points to a theoretical lacuna in this realm—one that this chapter aims to address.

Amid these questions of (in)visibility, representability, and provocation, I see female full-frontal nudity as subject to significations distinct from those of male full-frontal nudity, owing to its manifestation in a cultural context in which women's bodies are subject to intense surveillance and scrutiny while men's bodies are policed in accord with (hetero)masculinist overvaluation. In distinguishing between gendered approaches to screening nudity, I do not mean to ratify binarisms of sex and gender. Much as this book's prologue pointed to the distinction governing scenes of same-sex eroticism in heterosexist contexts—whereby lesbian sex is highly variable in its degree of provocation given its mainstream fetishization while male same-sex eroticism remains in itself provocative—on-screen nudity should be assessed in terms of equity, not equality. Chapter 3 gives sustained consideration to ways in which female nudity can be performed on-screen for purposes of defetishization, and the strategies discussed therein align with this chapter's appreciation for naturalistic representations of nudity. So while there are commonalities in how media creators might go about mobilizing full-frontal nudity more effectively overall, appraising on-screen nudity requires taking into account gendered disparities both societal and anatomical. Until recently, female full-frontal nudity has been vastly more visible outside of pornographic representation, though one might claim male sexual embodiment to be more representable given that male genitalia are more prominently visible and the state of male arousal more easily legible. As discussed in chapter 3, both the provocation and defetishizing potential in screening female full-frontal nudity derives precisely from the drive to capture those less easily represented aspects of female embodiment.

In considering a range of recent screen representations that work to demystify male embodiment, I first assess the representational schema that Lehman constructs for its continuing relevance for and difference from contemporary screen treatments of the now more visible penis. I then appraise the penis's potential as a feminist tool as well as its capacity to acknowledge and affirm, rather than disavow and displace, gay *and* homosocial male intimacies and queer masculinities. In particular, I explore three screen genres—the bromance, the erotic thriller, and "quality television" (as artistically ambitious shows aimed at a niche audience have come to be known)—already noted for their inclinations toward foregrounding male homosociality and homoeroticism, eroticizing masculinity, and displaying full-frontal nudity, respectively. Of course, the nudity encountered in these genres remains predominantly that of cis women, whose fetishized form serves as a structuring presence. The bromance (and its progenitor, the male buddy film) must defuse its homoeroticism with reassuring displays of women as sex objects. The erotic thriller is easily conflated with straight soft-core pornography. And quality television is premium cable's mode of distinguishing itself from (in the United States) network TV regulated by the Federal Communications Commission (FCC).[14] Noting how these genres have historically adhered to heterophallic mythologizing, I focus on key texts that, in foregrounding male nudity, critique and revise those genres' representational and ideological codes in ways that ultimately render the unidealized and hence de-phallicized corpo*realities* of these screened bodies.

In observing that "both avoiding the sexual representation of the male body and carefully controlling its limited explicit representations work to support patriarchy," Lehman reveals a representational and ideological regime in narrative cinema where 21st century incentives for screening sexual provocation vie with the need to maintain the double standard around women's sexual objectification.[15] In pornography, the penis occupies the center of the spectacle, while in other forms of screen media, the mandate that the penis remain veiled (or at least strictly confined to two forms of established visual coding, discussed below) conflicts with contemporary incentives to transgress the already fraying boundaries of sexual provocation through ever more outrageous novelty and boundary pushing. The result has been to keep male full-frontal imagery consigned to opposite ends of a representational spectrum that uses extreme, overdetermined, and therefore nonnaturalistic means of imagining the penis. As Lehman formulates, the penis's rare appearances outside pornography have been and continue to be largely confined to a polarized dichotomy of melodramatic and comic: "At one pole, we have the powerful, awesome spectacle of phallic masculinity, and at the other its vulnerable, pitiable, and frequently comic collapse."[16]

While Lehman's work valuably maps the lay of the land at millennium's end, the ground shifts as male full-frontal nudity becomes a more commonly employed strategy of provocation and thus a more frequently encountered feature on-screen. Through analysis of two films that take male sexual embodiment as their central preoccupation, the following two sections demonstrate how 21st century appearances of the penis still tend to fall within the melodramatic/comic dichotomy that Lehman formulates, even as that dichotomy has been revised for a contemporary audience acclimated to male full-frontal nudity's more frequent appearances and knowledgeable about its representational and ideological coding.

BROMANCING THE COMIC PENIS IN *THE OVERNIGHT* (PATRICK BRICE, 2015)

My earlier work *The B Word* discusses the importance of the bromance cycle—that early-aughts Hollywood studio hybrid of buddy film and romantic comedy—for (however comically) challenging heteronormativity. My analysis demonstrates how the bromance foregrounds and negotiates homosocial relations though the transformation of a male same-sex bond that initially resists, but eventually accepts, compulsory heterosexuality's privileging of the opposite-sex couple.[17] I find the bromance cycle also at the center of the new millennium's transformation in the "comic penis," and with those ideological underpinnings largely maintained. Deployed to relieve what contemporary comedy maestro Judd Apatow diagnoses in the epigraph at the beginning of this chapter as a national penis anxiety, the bromance plays for laughs what its dramatic progenitor, the male buddy film, worked violently to contain: the threat of emasculation.[18] The bromance recasts the contemporary man as more heteroflexible than his homophobic forbears, yet defuses any real threat to heteromasculinity by means of the cycle's comic disavowal of "man love." Through its reliance on ironic humor aimed at a knowing liberal audience for whom the traditional buddy film's overt misogyny and homophobia have become unacceptably retrograde, the bromance appears representationally disengaged and thus ideologically lighthearted and guilt-free.

The heyday of the bromance could be mapped from the shocking sight gag of Ben Stiller's (prosthetic) testicles stuck in a zipper in *There's Something About Mary* (Bobby Farrelly and Peter Farrelly, 1998) to the cringe-inducing interval that elapses after Jason Segel drops his towel in dismay at being dumped by girlfriend Kristen Bell in the opening scene of *Forgetting Sarah Marshall* (Nicholas Stoller, 2008) (see fig. 2.1). Along the way, each new bromance seemed obligated to up the ante of raunchy transgressions and homoerotic innuendo that served as a release valve for these movies' anxieties around millennial masculinity and male homosociality.[19] A comparison of these two films, from opposite ends of the bromance timeline, illuminates this transformation.

While Lehman's finding that "penis jokes are usually throwaways with unattractive male characters as their object" still frequently holds true, *There's Something About Mary* lands its genital humiliation roundly on its comic hero (rather than tossing it to a supporting player) and endows it with narrative weight beyond a one-liner.[20] Moreover, with Stiller himself having ushered in

Fig. 2.1. Leading man Jason Segel's full-frontal appearance in *Forgetting Sarah Marshall*.

the "Frat Pack" of angsty neurotics and overgrown adolescents who populate the bromance, the unappealing male character had become the bromance's leading man. Nevertheless, *There's Something About Mary* epitomizes the male genitalia–as–joke representation as Lehman characterizes it, with its startling yet fleeting appearance pitched for maximum shock value, its nonnaturalistic display in extreme close-up detached from any personhood and patently artificial, and its presenting a male character's humiliation in specifically emasculating terms signaled by the paramedic's announcement: "We've got a bleeder."

A decade later, the Apatow-produced *Forgetting Sarah Marshall* gave the penis more naturalistic treatment in its uncomfortable duration on-screen and manifestly unfaked display. In making a flaccid, average-size penis hypervisible, *Forgetting Sarah Marshall* overturned the representational rules of the comic penis. But *Forgetting Sarah Marshall* also demonstrates a 21st century sensibility with regard to sexual provocation in attaining the desired comic and ideological relief of the penis as sight gag without appearing to reinforce its phallic signification. As opposed to the conventional comic treatment, in which the actual penis is compared unfavorably with its unseen, phallic Other, accomplished by means of aligning it with abject supporting characters and the incorporation of what Lehman terms "penis-size jokes," here we laugh at *seeing* Segel's penis without feeling we are laughing *at* his penis.[21] Though the scene provokes an equally wincing response to its owner's figurative emasculation as did *There's Something About Mary*, the response is one of pity rather than horror. Peter Lehman and Susan Hunt posit that the scene ultimately functions to affirm the soft-bodied Segel character's average physique but "mind guy" intellect as preferable to that of the virile but imbecilic "body guy" played by Russell Brand.[22] Though Segel's character is pitiable for being caught with his proverbial pants down, that exposure ultimately forges identification with his more "evolved" character, much as Segel the star ups his cred for being "man enough"—that is, not overly concerned with his manliness—to drop trou (or in this case, towel).

Like *Forgetting Sarah Marshall*, several US independent films take the bromance as their point of departure, implicitly referencing this genre to revise its still largely latent anxieties of emasculation and enunciations of homoerotic desire. Noteworthy examples include Lynn Shelton's feminist mumblecore feature *Humpday* (2009), whose frank investigation of the thin line between homosocial and homoerotic I discussed in *The B Word*, and *The D Train*, whose publicity campaign's withholding of its bromance boundary crossing led to a scandal at Sundance.[23] While *Humpday* is far and away the more thoughtful of the two, both films rely on comic framing akin to that of *Forgetting Sarah Marshall* but stop short of going full-frontal to guard against what might seem an overly bracing confrontation with male same-sex eroticism and perhaps to preserve their leading men's straight star personae.

Where these and other indie bromances hesitate to couple too closely their displays of homoerotic desire and male nudity, *The Overnight* ventures there, albeit with recourse to prosthetics.

Written and directed by "mumblegore" filmmaker Patrick Brice (*Creep, Creep 2*) and produced in the Duplass Brothers' indie incubator, *The Overnight* employs the provocative premise of an adult playdate that veers into uninhibited extremes as a venue for screening male corpo*realities* and queer masculinities. Penis fixation, if no actual penis, announces itself in the film's opening scene, which shows married couple Alex (Adam Scott) and Emily (Taylor Schilling) mid-coitus. An almost comically thrusting and moaning Alex implores Emily to tell him he "has a giant dick." She complies but asks him in turn to "do circles," evidently a request she has made before. As both partners near climax, Alex pulls out and each begins (off-screen) to masturbate hurriedly in an unsuccessful attempt to orgasm before their napping son intrudes. It is a now-clichéd scene of child-induced coitus interruptus, but one that, in its mutual onanism, establishes without clarifying the couple's somewhat curious sexual dynamic.

Subsequent scenes indicate that Alex's need for reassurance may extend beyond the bedroom. Having recently relocated to Los Angeles for Emily's job, Alex's newfound status as primary caregiver to their child leaves him devoid of adult companionship and dispirited as his suited spouse rushes to the office. Alex rebuffs Emily's motherly encouragement to try meeting people with, "Am I seven years old?" But the snub he goes on to receive from hipster dads at the park confirms his uncool status. Yet his hopes, and ego, are boosted a moment later with his introduction to stylish smooth-talker Kurt (Jason Schwartzman), who invites Alex's family to join his for dinner. What ensues, once the kids are asleep, is an increasingly unrestrained evening in which Alex and Emily come to suspect that Kurt and his sexy French wife, Charlotte (Judith Godrèche), are swingers. "This is California—maybe this is what dinner parties are like," Alex says blithely, eager to coax along the more cautious Emily.

Yet the scenario that develops is nothing so pedestrian as partner swapping, as Kurt and Charlotte come to reveal their particular interests (his, anal portraiture; hers, administering "happy endings" to strangers at a local massage parlor; theirs, producing and performing in, respectively, lactation pornography). Nor does the predictable pairing off occur as expected. While the women bond in the bedroom that Charlotte reveals is hers alone ("There are things I do here that nobody knows about"), Kurt lures Alex into his studio to show off his recent work ("This series is called *Portals*") and entices him onto all fours to pose before Emily interrupts, "just as we were getting to the good part," says Kurt.

What follows constitutes the film's turning point, in a scene featuring not one but two penises, wherein Kurt prods Alex to release his inner cockiness regardless of what might seem lacking in his manhood. When the already pants-less Kurt proposes the foursome go skinny-dipping, Alex pulls Emily aside to confide anxiously his concern at measuring up to the "giant goddamn horse cock" clearly outlined through Kurt's briefs. Kurt intervenes and, with some goading, gets Alex to come clean: "I have an abnormally small dick," he confesses shamefully. "I still have this dick from middle school on my body." When Emily supportively (if not so convincingly) demurs that it makes no difference to her, Alex turns with irritation to say, "If I make circles it's okay; it's like I have a big old ding-dong." Alex is taken to task by the persistent Kurt, who orders him to "Stop moping around like a little bitch. Take that thing and you own it. You're a stud horse." An emboldened Alex joins Kurt in a striptease that ends with their prostheses (underwhelming and overwhelming, respectively) dangling as a cheering Charlotte and incredulous Emily look on (see fig. 2.2).

Scott's revealing performance here one-ups, paradoxically by means of downsizing, other male actors who have subjected their genitals to scrutiny for comic effect—namely, Segel in *Forgetting Sarah Marshall*—while simultaneously assuring us of its inauthenticity as an obvious prosthesis. Clearly this scene's subversive potential is limited by its reliance on prosthetics. Their

Fig. 2.2. Flaunting the comic (prosthetic) penis in *The Overnight*.

exaggeratedly contrasting sizes are not just nonnaturalistic but, displayed in the same frame, provoke astonishment both comic (in rendering visual the penis-size joke) and melodramatic (in unfurling its spectacular inverse).

This purposefully unconvincing display brings to mind Adam Scott's other prosthetic-enabled full-frontal performance, in the pilot for HBO's short-lived relationship drama *Tell Me You Love Me* (Cynthia Mort, 2007), in which his character is manually stimulated by his wife. That scene, directed by feminist filmmaker Patricia Rozema, is narratively significant as the couple—struggling to conceive a child and attempting to revive their flagging intimacy—employ a natural-looking prosthetic penis that viewers might easily mistake for Scott's own. The prostheses used in *The Overnight*, on the other hand, clearly lack verisimilitude—and any viewer confusion was set straight by the actors' firm disclaimers in their promotion of the film.[24] That the manly penis comes affixed to confident Kurt and the boyish penis to insecure Alex might seem to endow the spectacularly large penis with phallic authority and shade the comically small penis with emasculation. And yet both penises are obviously prostheses; the fantasy "giant dick" is as artificial as the "middle school" dick, signaling the falsehood of both as signifiers of manliness and its lack, respectively.

It bears mentioning that Charlotte, her breasts already displayed in the lactation video screened diegetically, doffs her underwear in this scene—and not only is no prosthesis involved, but no merkin appears in use either. That this elicits no diegetic commentary and presumably less audience attention than the penis pas de deux is suggestive of just how nondramatic female nudity remains by comparison. That French actress Godrèche performs full-frontal nudity but US actress Schilling remains clothed is further indication of how female nudity remains more typical in the European art film milieu that Godrèche comes from—although Schilling appeared topless at the outset of her starring role in the Netflix series *Orange Is the New Black* (Jenji Kohan, 2013–19).

It would be easy to spurn these male performers' risk-free self-exposure and the scene itself as emptily provocative, and perhaps even as reinforcing phallic authority in the way that penis-size jokes typically do. Yet *The Overnight* proves both too sympathetic to Alex's body shame and too canny about its indie audience's distaste for dick jokes to be so handily dismissed. Similar to *Forgetting Sarah Marshall*'s sleight of hand, *The Overnight* performs an ironic maneuver wherein it delivers the penis-size joke while disavowing the phallic endorsement it usually constitutes. Like the film itself, Kurt remains poker-faced in assuring Alex, "I wasn't putting my dick next to yours to do anything, man," leaving viewers as uncertain as Alex about the veracity of both potential meanings contained in Kurt's words. As much as the affable Scott's casting encourages our identification with his character (as with Segel's in *Forgetting Sarah Marshall*), the film's repeated infantilizing of Alex—aligning him with his young son in wearing shorts and overindulging on pizza, and noting his professional usurpation by Emily—threatens to conflate his childish character with his undersized stature, and to belittle his ensuing transformation into greater self-acceptance. Though deadpan in doing so, the film invites us to regard Alex's newfound confidence as both delusional and drunken. Gushing to Emily, "I feel like I just gave birth to myself. I love my dick. Kurt brought me to a place where I can say that. This is so good for our sex life, for our everything," an intoxicated Alex promptly retches poolside.

Meanwhile, the manly status afforded Kurt by Alex's obvious envy is boosted further by affirmations from both women. Charlotte tells Emily meaningfully, "Kurt has a lot to offer, as I'm sure you saw," after which Emily has trouble denying Alex's allegation, "The moment [Kurt] whipped that thing out you've been thinking about it." Though it is couched in terms of a long-time monogamist's curiosity about other men, Emily essentially confirms her dissatisfaction with Alex's penis size: "I think it's weird that we have to jerk off next to each other to come. And I really think that it sucks that you lust after another woman's breasts." Again, what we might read as sensitivity or doublespeak on Emily's part spares Alex the humiliation that a scornful penis-size joke would provoke yet still allows for a brutally honest acknowledgment that size matters. It turns out, though, that size does not matter enough to be a determining factor in coupling, as Alex and Emily reconcile by film's end. However, no discussion occurs about how they might accommodate what Emily declares is "a real thing, and I don't think we can deny it. I think that you think about other women, and I think about other men." Like Alex and Emily, *The Overnight* itself enfolds the issue of penis size into one of long-term monogamy and ultimately backs away from addressing either. The film thus skirts the opportunity that Lehman and Hunt imagine: "If, however, the variety of penises repressed from representation is made visible, this may lead to an awareness of a similar variety of masculinities and sexualities: some may be penetration-centered; some may not."[25]

The Overnight's turn away from questions of penis size to those of (non)monogamy and sexual preference broaches seriously another topic that has typically received comic treatment, yet here, too, there is an unfortunate lack of follow-through. In pitting new-to-town naïfs against affluent urbanites, *The Overnight*'s setup recalls such cult sex comedies as *Bob & Carol & Ted & Alice* (Paul Mazursky, 1969) and *Score* (Radley Metzger, 1974). Certainly class envy informs Alex's awe of prosperous entrepreneur Kurt, whose grand house and trophy wife metaphorically reinforce his other endowment. Yet the expected orgy scene departs from the sex comedy formula with a culminating twist that offers a further challenge to the large penis's correlation with heterophallicism. Having fallen into bed, the expected opposite-sex pairing off is interrupted by Kurt's revealing that he has come to feel sexually attracted to men and to Alex in particular. With both women nodding their approval and looking on supportively, Kurt and Alex kiss—and just as the foursome begins to proceed, another child-instigated case of coitus interruptus puts an end to the evening. Though the kiss lasts no longer than similar moments in other bromances (Hollywood and indie) that have dared to enter this territory, it is neither played for laughs, as in the climactic kiss between Will Ferrell and Sacha Baron Cohen in *Talladega Nights: The Legend of Ricky Bobby* (Adam McKay, 2006), nor is it immediately punctuated by a negative declaration of how "terrible" it was, as with the kiss between *Humpday*'s male pals. So while the scene's overall sober tone offsets the film's ironic treatment of its sexual and representational transgressions, its disruption allows the film to end nursing the same ambiguity it has employed throughout. On one hand, Kurt's queer identity confounds the dictates of the melodramatic/comic binary, dislodging the phallus's reassuring imprimatur of heteromasculinity. Though its melodramatic unveiling during the pool scene might have seemed justified by Kurt's characterization as sexually perverse, by film's end, Kurt's now affirmed queer masculinity undoes the melodramatic penis's "shocking" connotations while also challenging mainstream cinema's representational mandate to keep queer male corporeality and desire concealed and desexualized.

Subsequently learning in the film's final scene that Kurt and Charlotte are also staying together is troubling for the way that it, too, glosses over their established erotic incompatibility and for how it remains silent on the subject of the woman's sexual fulfillment. Again the film's equivocation permits us to interpret ironically Kurt's announcement that they have begun therapy and his gratitude to Alex and Emily ("You walked us down the aisle"). Though it goes unconfirmed, we might read this as a nonpathologizing effort at constructing a nonconventional partnership, but more literally it suggests the couple's "going straight" and the film's own recapitulation to bromantic family values, with male friendship affirmed but reassuringly de-eroticized and subordinated to heterosexual coupling.

RECASTING THE MELODRAMATIC PENIS IN *SHAME* (STEVE MCQUEEN, 2011)

In Lehman's formulation, the "melodramatic penis" acts as narrative cinema's compensatory substitute for pornography's fetishistic displays of erection and ejaculation. It, too, is (as Lehman writes) "provoked by an extraordinary event that guarantees the sight will have a major impact," yet the melodramatic penis disavows its spectacular nature by "itself never appear[ing] to be the cause of the shocks but, rather, accompany[ing] the revelation of something shocking: transvestism, adultery, incest." However unassuming its disavowal through displacement, the melodramatic penis nonetheless, Lehman concludes, "still seeks to block a penis from merely being a penis."[26] In the films that Lehman discusses, the melodramatic penis belongs to either a supporting character or a lesser-known actor, or often both. But the increasing willingness of A-list male stars to go full-frontal demands a reassessment of the visual and narrative import of screening the penis. Where a well-known actor might reasonably consent, as in *Forgetting Sarah Marshall*, to being the gentle butt of the joke, taking on a role that invokes the melodramatic association of the penis with perversity that Lehman observes is a bigger risk. Yet the melodramatic penis has no more disappeared from view than has the comic penis, and it, too, has been inflected so as to accommodate the new normal of high-profile visibility.

A prominent example of this new approach to screening melodramatic male nudity is the NC-17-rated *Shame*, a critically lauded portrait of an emotionally stifled sex addict, Brandon (Michael Fassbender), whose compulsion becomes uncontrollable following the intrusion of his self-destructive sister Sissy (Carey Mulligan) back into his life. Cowritten and directed by British artist-filmmaker Steve McQueen, *Shame* is, in effect, a bromance gone bad—a nightmarish fulfillment of the bromantic drive to avoid adult heterosexual intimacy in favor of self-gratification. Fassbender's appearance fully nude, sans prosthesis, occurred in the same year as his first leading role in a superhero franchise film with *X-Men: First Class* (Matthew Vaughn, 2011). The crossover achievement was much noted in *Shame*'s reviews and with *Time*'s Richard Corliss announcing, "Magneto lets it all hang out."[27] But where *Shame*'s critical reception and awards season publicity campaign fixated on the Oscar-nominated Fassbender's nudity, the film itself presents that nudity as definitively nonmelodramatic. Only two scenes into the film, Brandon twice passes naked across the screen en route to and from the bathroom, where he is seen (from the back) and heard urinating (see fig. 2.3). Although his penis is unmistakably visible on each pass, it is partially obscured in shadow and then disappears for the rest of the film. Brandon's head is mostly out of frame, introducing a visual motif in which he appears in frontally composed static shots with his head partly or wholly elided, signaling his emotional detachment and deference to his bodily drives. The artful shadowing and semiconcealment of Fassbender's face might lead

Fig. 2.3. Leading with full-frontal nudity: Michael Fassbender in *Shame*.

viewers to conclude that a prosthesis or body double was used, were it not for the actor's proud claim to have performed the scene himself. By appearing early in the film, narratively unannounced, and in a sequence representing daily routine, this penis's manifestation opposes the melodramatic mode that Lehman describes in every respect but one: its considerable size. This factor, along with the nudity's nonmelodramatic narrative placement, protects Fassbender's star persona.

In contrast, when Brandon experiences impotence while attempting emotionless sex with a coworker, his penis remains hidden, necessarily veiled at this moment of failure, when to see it would disrupt its signifying power. Tellingly, this is also the case in a later scene in which Brandon has an anonymous sexual encounter in a gay club. As Brandon's sexual excesses build to a frenzied denouement, the camera's gaze repositions itself on Brandon's face, which becomes a rictus of desperate, torturous effort, in keeping with the film's depiction of Brandon's sex addiction as originating in his psyche rather than the body. Thus, in *Shame*, what would conventionally have been a melodramatic unveiling of the perverse penis is adapted to accommodate a male star's self-display, permitted while his character still retains his reassuring heteromasculine vigor.

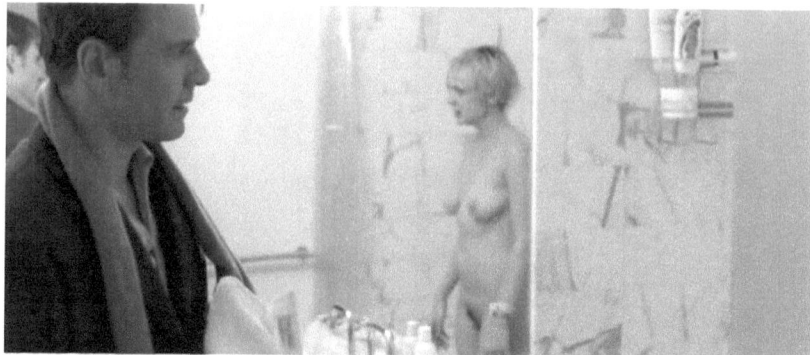

Fig. 2.4. A loaded moment between siblings in Carey Mulligan's first appearance on-screen in *Shame*.

Yet, perhaps owing to the residual anxiety prompted by the penis's appearance, a further displacement is needed to keep signifiers of perversity or emasculation from accruing to this penis-as-phallus. Unsurprisingly, it is the woman's body that assumes those melodramatic attributes of sexual pathology and lack that Fassbender's full-frontal exhibition cannot integrate. *Shame* effectively displaces onto female nudity the penis's melodramatic signification by means of a full-frontal shot of Sissy, harshly lit and held for a disconcertingly extended, minute-long take. This melodramatic reveal evokes a horror movie, as Brandon arrives home to hear his bathroom shower unexpectedly running and the swooning chorus of Chic's disco classic "I Want Your Love" playing at full volume on his stereo. Armed with a baseball bat, he bursts in on a terrified Sissy—our first glimpse of her, though we had heard her voice previously on Brandon's voicemail recording, pleading with him to pick up, in the same scene in which Brandon is seen nude (see fig. 2.4).

Further linking these two instances of full-frontal nudity, Chic's still-blaring lyrics suggestively echo Sissy's pleas in that earlier scene, hinting at what Alistair Fox finds to be her "suffer[ing] from a love addiction that is a corollary to her brother's sex addiction."[28] Brandon disquietingly continues to look at her. She meets his gaze and launches into a defense of having arrived unannounced, making little effort to cover herself as we look on from a conspicuously voyeuristic vantage point that reveals her mirrored reflection. Fear is quickly replaced by the disturbing revelation of these siblings' (quasi-)incestuous bond. Sissy's body thus takes on the perverse signification that Brandon's is spared, a smooth displacement of melodrama onto a female body that already disproportionately bears the cultural inscription of shame.

Though its approach to screening female nudity is so unorthodox as to be unnerving, *Shame* received much more voluble response to its male nudity. What discussion there was of Mulligan's full-frontal appearance noted not just the scene's disturbing aspects but also her body's "realness." In contrast were exclamations over the supposed exceptionality of Fassbender's nudity. "Just having Michael walk naked round a corner onscreen caused a stir," commented director McQueen.[29] Such statements seem driven by a lingering need to compensate for the still discernable stigma that clings to Fassbender's penis shot despite the film's displacement of its perverse connotations to Sissy. The paratextual overcompensation that followed reassured viewers of Fassbender's healthy manhood. For example, actor George Clooney addressed his fellow Best Actor nominee during his acceptance speech at the 2012 Academy Awards, saying, "I would like to thank Michael Fassbender for taking over the frontal nude responsibility that I had. Really Michael, honestly, you can play golf like this [*motioning*] with your hands behind your back." Fassbender himself joined in on the self-aggrandizing, joking that his father was "very proud" upon seeing the full-frontal scene.[30]

Ultimately Fassbender's nudity conferred the opposite of shame on his star persona. He received his peers' and fans' respect for his artistic courage, even as some speculated that all this penis chatter cheapened the role and cost him the Oscar. Considering the far less voluble response to another full-frontal appearance for an acclaimed role in a comparable sex-themed art film—that of Peter Sarsgaard in *Kinsey* (Bill Condon, 2004)—Lehman and Hunt note that the character's average-to-undersized penis is shown as neither a personal source of discomfort nor a hindrance to his satisfying his (male and female) partners.[31] Where Sarsgaard's full-frontal performance was downplayed in the film's promotion, given its nonmelodramatic stature and nonphallic signification, Fassbender's was melodramatically played up to promote its association with his character at his most heterophallically empowered. So while Lehman's formulation that an unveiled penis must be accompanied by melodramatic or comic affect holds true here, that affect has shifted from being realized on-screen to being played out paratextually—where this newfound representational willingness to depict "casual" full-frontal male nudity is not so casually subsumed within popular discourse. In effect, then, the penis remains melodramatic despite its diegetic underplaying, and the response it provokes is displaced from characters in the film to spectators themselves.

Thinking back to the prologue's focus on the controversy surrounding Abdellatif Kechiche's authorship in *Blue Is the Warmest Color* encourages a consideration of the complex cultural metrics that permitted McQueen, who is Black and at the time of *Shame*'s release was married to a woman, to sidestep any homophobic insinuations that his attention to Fassbender's body might otherwise have encouraged. Yet they also enabled McQueen, unlike Kechiche, to avoid the racial controversy that sought to discipline a man of color's gaze at, and representational control over, white bodies.

Shame's full-frontal reveal might also be compared with that of Anglo-American cinema's only rival to aforementioned Miramax spoiler-proofed *The Crying Game* for the most-discussed melodramatic display of the penis: *Boogie Nights* (Paul Thomas Anderson, 1997). In the film, porn performer Dirk Diggler's (Mark Wahlberg) star attribute, the object of so many admiring remarks and awe-filled stares throughout the film, receives its much-anticipated unveiling at film's end. Appearing in the film's opening sequence rather than its final shot, *Shame* declines to create such suspense narratively; instead, it stokes the awe of its nondiegetic audience and thus aligns more closely with porn's phallically charged but still authentic marvel (in that no prosthesis is present). Precisely because of the mystique built up around it, Diggler's penis carries the expectation that it, as Lehman notes, "better look as much like the supposed awesome spectacle of an erection as possible."[32] Thus, its eventual materialization must be a fabrication—no mere mortal penis would do. Of course, some of porn's male performers offer a spectacular excess that strains plausibility, but writer-director P. T. Anderson's choice to use a prosthesis renders the melodramatic penis's intended effect of disbelief literally—it is not believable. This image of penis-as-phallus as blatantly artificial serves the narrative at this culminating moment in which a humbled Diggler has come to recognize himself as a mere human. The mantra he recites in the lead-up to exposing himself ("I'm a star ... a big bright shining star") serves as performative pep talk—surely intended as an homage to the final scene in *Raging Bull* (Martin Scorsese, 1980), where washed-up Jake LaMotta (Robert De Niro) prepares to go onstage—by which Diggler (re)constructs his hypermasculinity even while disclosing that it is a mere role.

Comparatively, *Shame* may appear to shore up phallic mystique by equipping Brandon with a real penis sized to suit his excessive drives, yet one might more generously allow for a metaphorical interpretation that sees Brandon's as a burdensome penis with a propensity for dysfunction—as happens when Brandon attempts to merge sex and intimacy in an encounter with a disarming woman coworker and finds himself unable to perform. Viewed this way, Fassbender's penis is narratively naturalistic (its purpose is humanizing rather than fetishizing) but discursively melodramatic (provoking awe and respect)—a paradoxical result of the penis's longtime veiling and of contemporary Western culture's size worship. The public response to *Shame* reveals that the relative ubiquity of female nudity in contrast with the paucity of male nudity challenges the latter's potential not so much to be, but to be read as, naturalistic. The discussion later in this chapter of filmmaker Alain Guiraudie's work suggests that one solution to this representational challenge, whereby the penis's appearance seems inevitably to provoke melodramatic response, might be to make the penis ubiquitous.

FEMINIST AND QUEER REPRESENTATIONS OF FULL-FRONTAL NUDITY IN THE EROTIC THRILLER

Conceiving representational strategies for de-phallicizing the penis calls for imagining approaches that, as Alexandra Juhasz describes, "unlink genitals from their gendered homes, that sever biology from destiny ... [to] instruct us that a proactive political practice can occur whenever bodies (or body parts) are separated from their culturally determined duties." As Juhasz suggests, such an approach would dislodge the penis as the privileged signifier of heteromasculinist privilege and dismantle the gender binary determined by an either/or relegation of anatomical sex. Juhasz focuses on cases in which nonphallic masculinity is conceived by "imagin[ing] a penis that does not refer back to a man," and thus disrupts the penis-as-phallus's signification of biologically determined masculinity and its ostensibly intrinsic power.[33] Juhasz cites the cinematic use of the dildo in lesbian contexts. Another strategy entails screening the penis in trans or non-binary contexts that are respectful and affirmative (as opposed to the many insensitive or offensive representations that continue to appear). Such instances of full-frontal nudity by trans or non-binary performers in mainstream media are rare, though a noteworthy exception, featuring recurring cast member Davina (Alexandra Billings), occurred in the fourth season of *Transparent* (Joey

Soloway, Amazon, 2014–19; 4.2, "Groin Anomaly").[34] So Mayer explores yet another representational strategy wherein screening "soft cock" (whether skin or silicone) "detaches [the penis] from binary conceptions of masculinity, making it mobile and gender-fluid."[35] Building on these approaches, I consider two additional cases with equal potential for dismantling phallic authority, in which the nondetachable (as opposed to strap-on) cisgender penis signifies not merely nonphallic but feminist and queer masculinity.

Consonant with the "dick flick's" revision of the penis's melodramatic/comic dichotomy discussed in the previous section, recent takes on the erotic thriller have expanded the role and meaning of full-frontal representation for the 21st century. This move coincides with what Linda Ruth Williams notes is the genre's having been "annexed by the highbrow auteur, with a select series of prestigious or notorious titles emerging around the new century."[36] Two such provoc*auteurs*, New Zealand–born, Australia-based screenwriter-director-producer Jane Campion and French filmmaker Alain Guiraudie, stage investigations of (and interventions on) the erotic thriller that herald a critical departure from Douglas Keesey's characterization of the genre circa 2001: "The erotic thriller's transgression of limits involves only the female body, not the male. The penis is not exposed but remains veiled, the better to preserve its myth of phallic power."[37] In following this cultural dictate to keep the penis veiled, the conventional erotic thriller sustains the genre's "safe" soft-core eroticism and thus serves the presumed desires of its primary constituency, the female audience. Yet, in their book-length studies of the erotic thriller, Nina K. Martin and L. R. Williams both suggest that the genre resists gendered structures of representation as well as heterophallic codes of signification in ways that women viewers may also find appealing yet are only arguably revisionist—or feminist.

As Martin notes, in the erotic thriller, "Male bodies are also objectified . . . [with] women positioned as looking, watching, gazing, and acting on their desires."[38] And as L. R. Williams finds, the erotic thriller regularly undermines phallic authority through its characterization of the desiring man in sexual thrall, for whom "the erect penis signals not sovereign authority but men's lack of control."[39] This trope of the lustful "fall guy"—the sexual plaything of a criminal woman who goes on to frame him—transforms the penis from phallic signifier into, as L. R. Williams terms it, a manipulable "tool[ ] of female greed."[40]

This narrative structure, seen in such films as *Body Heat* (Lawrence Kasdan, 1981) and *The Last Seduction* (John Dahl, 1994), clearly borrows heavily from film noir and as such plays more to male anxieties and pleasures than does the more female-oriented erotic thriller. Yet the erotic thriller's resistance to patriarchal cinematic conventions in the ways Martin and L. R. Williams identify nevertheless reinscribes gendered structures of representation and phallic signification—by merely substituting the man as submissive object and the woman as domineering voyeur and by handing off the penis from man to woman without divesting it of phallic authority. The provoc*auteurs* discussed below attempt a more substantively revisionist treatment of the erotic thriller's sexual mythologies that challenges the objectifying gaze (on men and women alike) and represents male nudity and sex nonphallically.

THE PENIS AS FEMINIST TOOL IN JANE CAMPION'S *IN THE CUT* (2003)

No woman filmmaker (except perhaps Catherine Breillat, discussed in chap. 3) is better known for her penchant for screening penises than Jane Campion—most famously Harvey Keitel's in *The Piano* (1993). Across her three decades to date of feature filmmaking, Campion has employed female and male full-frontal nudity in ways that reveal and reverse gendered dynamics of power and pleasure. Campion's 2003 erotic thriller *In the Cut* is an exemplary case. Adapted from Susanna Moore's controversial 1995 novel about a literature professor who becomes involved with a murder investigation and the police detective working the case, *In the Cut* casts American rom-com sweetheart Meg Ryan radically against type as Frannie Avery, a brittle, sexually adventurous single woman. Having importantly shifted the novel's setting to a wary post-9/11 downtown Manhattan (Campion filmed on location during the summer of 2002), *In the Cut*'s deliberately voyeuristic cinematography portrays Frannie and the film's other women characters as constantly surveilled by patriarchal authority figures both official and unofficial, whose observation is said to be for the women's safety but who are shown to be ineffectual, if not directly endangering those women.

While the camera's roving gaze mimics that of the watchful men probing women's bodies and spaces, Campion renders these visions opaque by troubling the visual pleasure and meaning of what is seen. The female flesh on display at an exotic dancing venue aptly named the Baby Doll Lounge calls attention to US culture's commodification of female sexuality, even as Campion refrains from condemning such actions or images, and even arguably revels in their exhibition. Yet Campion troubles such scenes' conventional visual exploitation by including within the frame images that are typically left off-screen in depictions of what is, after all, a female workplace: the children supported and cared for by an alternative family of women looking out for one another. Similarly, scenes depicting half sisters Frannie and Pauline (played by Jennifer Jason Leigh) convey their emotional intimacy through their bodily comfort in various states of undress, dancing together, walking arms entwined, and sharing each other's beds. If Campion uses a provocative amount of nudity, then she also uses nudity provocatively. Its treatment does not permit the reassuring disengagement from women's humanity on which fetishism relies.

Campion confines full-frontal nudity (male and female) to two key scenes in which the female body is atypically downplayed and the female gaze just as atypically foregrounded. In the first instance of full-frontal male nudity, Frannie happens on a shadowy encounter in a bar's basement, where a man whose face is obscured in darkness receives fellatio from a woman we later learn becomes a murder victim shortly after. Threatened with an NC-17 rating from the Motion Picture Association of America, Campion cut from this scene for the film's US theatrical release two shots of the man's erect penis; those shots are restored on the unrated DVD version. In becoming an unknowing eyewitness to the sexual lead-up to a grisly murder, Frannie remains still and partly hidden in the shadows, but her voyeurism is compromised by the man's awareness of her looking. Though neither she nor we can see his face to verify his returned gaze, he registers his knowledge of being observed by reaching down to gather up the woman's hair, providing Frannie a clearer view. In subsequent cuts to close-up framing, Campion accords the audience the same view. In one of many such moments in the film, here a woman's presumption in assuming the actively desiring gaze serves as enticement for a challenging, even violent male reciprocation. Noticeably, Frannie's viewing in the basement is done while wearing glasses, that visual signal of a woman's intellect and associated undesirability, and certainly these reprisals for women's looking conform to cinefeminism's findings regarding the thriller and horror genre's punishment of inquisitive, (sexually) active women.[41] Frannie's gaze usually is one that seeks information and inspiration—in poetry posted in the subway, in the slogans emblazoned on the clothing of passersby, in the street slang that she meticulously records. But as indicated by Frannie's taking in more than just the sex act on display to note as well an incriminating tattoo, her inquisitive gaze shares with her desiring gaze the capacity to put her in harm's way.

The first glimpse of the man's penis, erect, in extreme close-up, is the sort of fragmented, disembodied phallic imagery associated with porn. Yet ultimately it is not porn-like, in that it is not a real penis but a prosthesis, something viewers would likely not notice (unlike *The Overnight*'s prosthetic penises, this one is not so artificial or excessive-seeming as to provoke laughter or disrupt the scene's verisimilitude) but which was reported by Campion in the unrated film's DVD commentary.[42] Because the man's face is obscured, a body double would have been feasible, so this choice to use a prosthetic, alongside our knowledge of it (even if communicated paratextually), bears importantly on the film's meaning.

Ultimately this inauthentic penis is as misleading a signifier as that of the scene's other narratively critical detail revealed in close-up: the three of spades tattooed on the man's inner wrist. This misdirection will lead Frannie to misjudge the murderer's identity after she glimpses the identical tattoo on the wrist of love interest Detective Malloy, played by Mark Ruffalo. Misunderstanding the object of her glance to be his fountain pen, he says, "It's fake. It's a cop thing." The film's conclusion reveals that the killer is Malloy's partner, Detective Ritchie Rodriguez (Nick Damici). The visual resonance of his penis with porn equates phallic excess with sadistic masculinity. Yet that this phallic signifier is also fake, merely a prop, signals the fabricated link between the penis and masculinist authority that must be continually reinforced through displays of power. Fittingly, this patriarchal agent is a male cop rendered figuratively emasculated. On modified duty, his service weapon and badge confiscated as punishment for violent behavior (against his wife, tellingly), Rodriguez is reduced to carrying another prosthetic toy, a water gun. Instead of serving as an anatomical authenticator of man's innate claim to patriarchal authority, then, this prosthetic penis in the act of being fellated reveals patriarchy's need to shore up masculinity through constant, if fraudulent, displays of phallic fetishism. Yet because it is left ambiguous whether it was Malloy or Rodriguez being serviced in the bar basement, the film does not necessarily condemn the act of being fellated.

The next penis to appear in *In the Cut* is not prosthetic and belongs to lead actor Mark Ruffalo. After Frannie is knocked down in the street by an unknown assailant, Malloy insists on reenacting the attack to aid in her recollection of details and so assumes the attacker's position. What follows, in an evident blurring of pleasure and danger, is Frannie's attack erotically reimagined as foreplay. Alongside its cinematographic rendering of women under pervasive surveillance, *In the Cut* stages several acts of men forcing themselves on women and invading their space, indicating the normalized presence of such forms of physical and spatial violation in women's lives. In contrast, at this moment of seduction with Malloy, Frannie is heard to give clear consent, saying, "Yes," and—in a nod to the film's commitment to depicting sex naturalistically—she is shown retrieving a condom before joining him in bed. The sex that follows constitutes another reenactment, this time of the basement scene, though with differences as crucial as that of their foreplay's distinction from Frannie's actual attack. While this slippage between killer and lover clearly fits the erotic thriller's penchant for associating desire with danger, the more provocative move on Campion's part is to suggest that women's sexual fantasies are distinct from any actual wish to be, or experience of being, harmed or violated.

Much as Frannie had, in an earlier scene, brought herself to climax by reimagining the basement scene with Malloy as the mystery man, Campion stages their first sexual encounter as an eroticized but nonphallic reenvisioning of the ominous, all-too-phallic scene Frannie witnessed. In contrast to her sister Pauline's remark that "I remember every guy I ever fucked by how he liked to do it, not how I wanted to do it," here Frannie orchestrates the situation to conform to her fantasized reenvisioning. This sex scene is bookended with elements that recall the basement scene and Frannie's subsequent, onanistic reimagining of it. Malloy starts out sitting with his hands crossed behind his head, as had the mystery man in the basement, while Frannie lies facedown, as she had while masturbating. The scene ends with the click of Malloy's lighter echoing that of the sound that first drew Frannie to

Fig. 2.5. In service to women's pleasure: Mark Ruffalo's casual full-frontal nudity in *In the Cut*.

the basement scene. Yet the sex here is decisively less phallic than that in the earlier scene; instead, we see Malloy orally pleasuring Frannie so that she achieves orgasm. An ellipsis follows, and a satisfied Frannie resettles beside him to ask, "I want to know how you did that to me. Someone taught you. Who was that?" Before he can provide an answer, she ventures her own assessment: "An older woman." As Malloy then recounts his boyhood education by an (indeed) older woman who acted as his sex teacher, his penis is briefly visible in frame (see fig. 2.5). That it is flaccid and neither illuminated nor in close-up visually contrasts with the killer's prosthetic penis. Rather than visually thrusting into the frame, detached and abstracted, Malloy's penis is average-sized and comes into view naturally, as if by accident, as he adjusts the bedsheet. Where the prosthetic penis adhered to pornographic coding as phallic spectacle connected to male domination and pleasure, Malloy's penis is neither the melodramatic center of the scene, nor is his pleasure its priority. Indeed, the penis is not even the source for that which is central to the scene: female pleasure.

In analyzing *American Gigolo* (Paul Schrader, 1980) and its display of star Richard Gere's body, Lehman locates the film's penis anxiety in "its contradictory impulses of wanting simultaneously to show Gere's body and to cover it up." Noting the postcoital scene's use of an unmotivated long shot to distance us from Gere's unveiled penis, Lehman concludes, "The [scene's] speech foregrounds the male character's subjectivity even as the logic of the scene seems to objectify him and foreground the woman's subjectivity and her look."[43] Lehman's analysis is useful in illuminating how Frannie and Malloy's postcoital scene, which is similar in content, is shot with a formal logic that *American Gigolo* disrupts. We see each partner from the visual perspective of the other, and there is a balance of gendered gazes, subjectivities, and pleasures. As Malloy recounts his sexual initiation, their sex starts up again—cleaving the sequence into mirrored halves each portraying sex acts (first anilingus then cunnilingus followed by vaginal intercourse) aimed at female and male orgasm, respectively—though the scene's second half fades out midway without verifying Malloy's completion. Although it still attends to both partners' pleasures, this two-part sequence ruptures the "shared orgasm" myth of the Hollywood-style sex scene as well as heterosexist pornography's fixation on the so-called money shot visualizing male pleasure.

Identifying a narrative trend among films from the 1990s onward (but dating back at least as far as *Lady Chatterley's Lover*) involving an upper-class woman's sexual awakening under the influence of a working-class man, Lehman and Hunt pronounce this "body guy" genre as "tied to an overvaluation of a certain kind of masculinity, male body, and male sexual performance and a simultaneous anti-intellectual devaluation of the world of the mind and the intellect."[44] In her presentation of the sexual dynamic between a blue-collar man and an intellectual, sophisticated woman, Campion diverges from the erotic thriller's objectification of the working-class male in reproving Frannie for fetishizing Malloy and challenges the genre's anti-intellectualism through Frannie's reckoning with her flawed mode of reading people. From their first meeting, when she insists on verifying his identity before allowing him to enter her apartment, Frannie, as a woman living alone, views Malloy with understandable wariness, even if she will continue to overlook the significance of his being the sole male character not to intrude at will into her space. When Frannie describes Malloy as having a mustache, Pauline responds, "They all have that," conflating cops as one uniform gendered and classed category. But as the tattoo will reveal, such skin-deep indicators are misleading. In accordance with the body guy narrative, Frannie views Malloy with an overvaluation of his sexual worth that causes him to withdraw from her expectation of sex, reproaching her, "You wouldn't go nowhere with me if I didn't fuck you." In taking Frannie to task here, Campion confronts and challenges the erotic thriller's indulgence of a female gaze that merely reverses gendered patterns of visual objectification. Campion by no means aims to prevent Frannie's (or the film viewer's) visual pleasure in Ruffalo's handsome form—indeed, the film very much indulges that pleasure—but rather to challenge Frannie's consignment of Malloy to merely sexually exploitable status. So, too, does Malloy depart from the body guy trope in his unremarkable penis and attentive style of lovemaking, much unlike the body guy genre clichés of "large penis for sustained deep penetration" and "forceful penile thrusting" that Lehman and Hunt identify as pernicious influences on popular conceptions of what constitutes good sex.[45]

A further aspect of *In the Cut*'s revision of the body guy trope and the erotic thriller emerges in comparison to *American Gigolo*, where, as Lehman observes, Gere's character, Julian, in his "to-be-looked-at-ness" and in the passive role he inhabits, is feminized throughout the film. Lehman and Hunt observe this characteristic feminization of the working-class male—paradoxical given the masculine sexuality he embodies—throughout the body guy genre and argue that this alliance with femininity denies Julian possession of "proper" masculinity.[46]

In her astute reading of *In the Cut*, Sue Thornham notes the importance of Malloy's utterance, late in the film, "I'm starting to fucking feel like a chick here."[47] He is, at this moment, latched to a radiator with his own handcuffs, having just submitted to Frannie's straddling him and following his urging to "fuck yourself." Powerless to defend himself physically, Malloy expresses his figurative emasculation derisively with the verbal substitute ("chick") of male street slang, which linguistic scholar Frannie notes is "always sexual or violent or both." But Malloy's pronouncement, though voiced in protest, might alternatively be read as an imagining of nonphallic masculinity, by which feeling "like a chick" could signify his openness to being sexually dominated toward the aim of female pleasure as well as his extension of trust in making himself emotionally as well as physically vulnerable. Just as the earlier scene's unveiling of the flaccid penis departed from its melodramatic or comic treatment elsewhere, in which its physical vulnerability renders it subject to ridicule or connects it to perversion, Malloy's self-exposure here verifies his nonphallic masculinity and hence his deserving Frannie's love. *In the Cut* ultimately revises the mind/body opposition insisted on by the body guy genre to suggest that mutual respect and emotional openness are imperative.

The misleading tattoo serves as a somber warning for Frannie of the importance of careful close reading—of not relying on superficial analysis and skin-deep indicators. *In the Cut*'s tentatively happy conclusion keeps its characters' evolution ambiguous, but it would seem that Frannie has crossed the line that had kept her at a remove from those whose street slang she consumed for her own intellectual and cultural benefit, much like a tourist. This is not to say that Frannie abandons intellectualism or willfully misreads, as Thornham notes the erotic thriller heroine has traditionally done in an eroticization of the disarticulation that befalls women who subordinate their voices in coupling under patriarchy.[48]

In the Cut departs from both the body guy genre and the romance narrative (of which, as Thornham demonstrates, the erotic thriller is very much an example) to posit Frannie's intellectual practice of close reading as lifesaving. Only in misreading (via superficial cues gleaned from an objectifying gaze) does she endanger herself. Owing to Campion's powerful "sense of cock," to adopt Malloy's phrase for what distinguishes a good blow job from a bad one, here the penis acts as a feminist tool to undo the inherent penis-as-phallus signification and to integrate femininity and masculinity within the same subjectivity rather than keeping them bifurcated through gender. In the next section, I evaluate this revisionary potential for screening nonphallic male nudity—that is, penises that resist the mandate Lehman identifies to reinforce heteromasculinity—against the politics of representing gay male corporeality and desire.

QUEERING PENISES AND FLAUNTING GAY SEX IN *L'INCONNU DU LAC* (*STRANGER BY THE LAKE*, ALAIN GUIRAUDIE, 2013)

More than twenty years into his filmmaking career, *Stranger by the Lake* became Alain Guiraudie's breakout film when it caused a sensation at the 2013 Cannes Film Festival. It premiered in the "Un Certain Regard" section dedicated to promoting nontraditional visions, went on to win the Queer Palme award (beating out *Blue Is the Warmest Color*, which won the top Palme d'Or), and was picked up for North American and UK distribution by queer-friendly Strand Releasing and Peccadillo Pictures, respectively. Though a marginally known figure even in France, Guiraudie's provoc*auteur* signature had been long in evidence. His early feature *Ce vieux rêve qui bouge* (*That Old Dream That Moves*, 2001) introduces the full-frontal nudity and queer erotics that would become staples of Guiraudie's work. So, too, has Guiraudie long prodded at the representational norms of gay identity politics, from centering his films in untrendy rural milieus and among working-class laborers and otherwise peripheral, nonaspirational characters who exhibit fluid sexual behaviors but staunchly refuse identitarian scripts. An example of his characters defiantly perverting the coming-out paradigm can be found in the middle-aged gay man who falls in love and runs off with a sixteen-year-old girl in *Le roi de l'évasion* (*The King of Escape*, 2009).

Not until *Stranger by the Lake*, however, did the openly gay Guiraudie join the pantheon of French queer filmmakers recognized in international cinephile circles that includes Christophe Honoré, François Ozon, and André Téchiné. Of this triad of contemporary French queer cinema, Ozon seems to exhibit the most commonality with his contemporary Guiraudie (born three years apart) in their antibourgeois irreverence, character and thematic inscrutability, and unabashed reveling in visual pleasure. In spurning calls for positivity and palatability, Guiraudie's incendiary politics of queer representation aligns him with a transnational cinematic legacy of queer provoc*auteurs* stretching from Rainer Werner Fassbinder to Bruce LaBruce to Tsai Ming-liang. Yet with *Stranger by the Lake*, Guiraudie issued a singular provocation in blatantly appropriating gay stereotypes and using ironic distancing to render their meaning ambiguous. In so doing, Guiraudie insists on the queer-identified artist's right to reclaim and resignify "bad objects."

Stranger by the Lake is set entirely around an idyllic lakefront gay cruising spot in southern France. The plot concerns the drowning of a man by his fickle lover Michel (Christophe Paou), a crime witnessed by Franck (Pierre Deladonchamps), who nonetheless becomes sexually involved with Michel soon thereafter. As provocative as any film by Catherine Breillat or the other enfants terribles of the New French Extremity (to be discussed in chap. 3), *Stranger by the Lake*'s chief provocation for mainstream audiences—its appropriation of pornographic conventions in rendering male nudity and gay sex hypervisible—presumably would bother LGBTQ+ viewers less than its restaging of the representational and cultural legacy conflating queer men with promiscuity and pathology. Yet its reported success in both targeting and finding favor with LGBTQ+ viewers suggests this audience found its evocative nostalgia for pre-AIDS sexual freedoms and apparent reverence for the queer transgressive works of Bataille and Genet refreshingly unsanitized.[49]

Having also garnered broader critical acclaim (most notably at Cannes), the film performed respectably if not nearly as robustly as *Blue Is the Warmest Color* in its theatrical release and streaming afterlife. However nonplussed audiences may have been by the film's play with homophobic clichés, any outrage from watchdog groups such as GLAAD seems to have been abated by its critical seal of approval (and perhaps drowned out by the controversy around *Blue Is the Warmest Color*, which was released around the same time). And *Stranger by the Lake*'s relatively limited release allowed it to fly mostly under the radar of moralizing conservatives and risk-averse theater owners.[50] More intriguing still, and indicative of producer mindsets and consumer tactics around 21st century media, was the way in which the film's porn styling "astutely sets itself up for eroticized online analysis," as Noah A. Tsika notes. Tsika observes that Guiraudie "galvanized the gay-identified erotic blogosphere not by omitting sex but by prominently featuring it, in all its hardcore glory," and notes that the film's producers actively encouraged the user-produced content and interactive online reception that ensued.[51]

As Susan Bordo observes, gay male aesthetics have been instrumental in bringing sexualized male imagery to the mass market since the 1970s by encouraging "a new willingness to visually foreground the sexuality of male hips and buttocks, and, ultimately, male genitals."[52] For all the influence Bordo notes, little attention has been paid to nonpornographic screen representations of the penis in gay/queer content and spectatorial contexts. As the panicked cultural response to *The Crying Game* in the wake of distributor Miramax's controversy-stoking publicity campaign made evident, the penis's appearance acquires compounded signification when associated with queerness. Hence, the many infamous cases of desexualized mainstream screen representations of romantic/erotic relationships between men, including the public service announcement–style warning at the start of the pioneering studio-produced gay drama *Making Love* (Arthur Hiller, 1982); the chasteness imposed on the gay couple, never shown kissing, in *Philadelphia* (Jonathan Demme, 1993); the shrouded goings-on atop *Brokeback Mountain* (Ang Lee, 2005); the belated first kiss between a same-sex married couple in season two of *Modern Family* (Steven Levitan and Christopher Lloyd, ABC, 2009–20); and the panning away from the lovers' commingled bodies in *Call Me by Your Name* (Luca Guadagnino, 2017). Queer narratives made at the far reaches of independent and art cinema realms, with less need to maintain mainstream palatability than those crossover hits, still circulate in a media ecosystem that insists on the veiling of male genitalia and gay sexual intimacy for commercial gain, as the 2020 censoring of the streaming version of *God's Own Country* (Francis Lee, 2017) indicates.[53] Nevertheless, in the framework of a queer scenario featuring queer characters, the penis's appearance does not speak phallic authority or provoke homophobic retaliation in the same way, and so the metric for sizing up penis representation must be reconfigured in these queer contexts.

My supposition in this chapter—that screening male nudity explicitly yet naturalistically holds the greatest potential for defetishizing the penis—requires qualification when extended to a queer context. The penis fetishism on display in gay pornography or other queer cultural production (Tom of Finland erotica, for example) operates in a performative mode and within a sociopolitically marginalized context that, as in the case of the lesbian dildo, should not be equated with heteropatriarchal fetishizing of the penis-as-phallus. Apart from this representationally similar but ideologically distinct penis fetishism, queer approaches to unveiling the penis significantly diverge from the heterophallic reliance on the comic/melodramatic dichotomy. They need not necessarily adopt the naturalistic mode that I have advocated as the most effective strategy for de-phallicizing the penis's signification in nonqueer contexts.

As Gary Needham observes, a new visibility of the penis in recent French queer and feminist filmmaking involves "the foregrounding of the body's penis itself both in its magnified presence through the close-up and its ideological insecurity transformed by the conspicuous presence of the prosthetic strap-on."[54] The prosthetic's defetishizing, resignifying potential has already been glimpsed in *The Overnight* and *In the Cut* (considered above) and will return in chapter 3's discussion of Breillat's *Sex Is Comedy*. But while *Stranger by the Lake* features close-ups of penises, they occur solely in moments when the presence of body doubles required tight shots, and no prosthetics were used. (Reportedly, Guiraudie initially planned to use prosthetic penises and fabricated cum shots, but when the choreography proved unconvincing and uncomfortable for the actors, porn performers were substituted as stand-ins.)[55] Owing perhaps to its nostalgic tone and arcadian affect, *Stranger by the Lake* opts out of the contemporary trend for performative abstraction of the penis identified by Needham in favor of reinstating the "casual nudity" that Needham characterizes as French cinema's more conventional approach and that Lehman and Hunt associate with 1970s narrative cinema.[56] This naturalistic framing, which regards full-frontal male nudity, in Lehman's aforementioned formulation, as "neither more nor less than penises," acquires a dual purpose when depicting male same-sex eroticism: to de-phallicize the penis and to naturalize (that is, to render familiar and unstigmatized) gay sex and queer masculinities.

Guiraudie reflexively engages the erotic thriller to offer a queer reassessment of the *homme fatal*, a term coined by Andrew Spicer to identify film noir's male villain, described as possessing "an exciting mixture of cunning, cool calculation, manipulative charm and deep rooted sexual sadism."[57] Though less iconic than noir's femme fatale, the *homme fatal* is vital to the erotic thriller, because, as L. R. Williams notes, he "shift[s] generic emphasis and influence, from the characteristic male-focused point of view of noir to a female sympathy which looks more like 1940s female Gothic."[58]

Still another shift occurs when the erotic thriller queers its central couple—the protagonist and his or her object of investigation and, inevitably, desire. The erotic thriller has treated lesbian couplings in films such as *Bound* and *Mulholland Drive* (David Lynch, 2001), alongside connotatively queer male couplings such as those in *Internal Affairs* (Mike Figgis, 1990) and *The Talented Mr. Ripley* (Anthony Minghella, 1999). Yet few explicitly gay male couplings have surfaced in the genre. In *Stranger by the Lake*, queer desire and gay identity transform the dynamic between protagonist and *homme fatal* and push the erotic thriller beyond its entrenched heteronormativity and what Nina Martin observes is its "pervasive anxiety surrounding the construction of gender."[59] *Stranger by the Lake* exhibits what L. R. Williams references as the Gothic-influenced shift in perspective away from noir's heteropatriarchal male protagonist, yet here the move is more unambiguously queer in aligning the audience's point of view and sympathy with a gay man, Franck (rather than with the erotic thriller's customary female protagonist). Moreover, the *homme fatal* is reincarnated as an explicitly queer figure— another gay man, Michel—and more radically still, his traditional villainy and duplicity is depathologized (if still regarded with ambivalence, as discussed later).

Noting Spicer's association of the *homme fatal* with "connotations of sexual perversity as well as sadism," the erotic thriller's juxtaposition of sex and danger and its staging of voyeurism and sexual exhibition have provocative implications when screening queer male corporeality and eroticism.[60] Significantly, Guiraudie's foregrounding of queer desire's relation to death engages the erotic thriller within a queer praxis that, Max Cavitch notes in writing about Ozon, another French provoc*auteur* engaged in queering the erotic thriller, "has been both a sustained response to a particular history of loss and an important contribution to the ongoing psychosocial project of theorizing mourning."[61]

As indicated by the archetypal signposts emblazoned throughout *Stranger by the Lake*'s trailer ("A Lake," "A Stranger," "A Witness to a Murder") and the repeat references to Hitchcock (both in critics' blurbs and intertexual allusion), interspersed with carnally charged dialogue and images, *Stranger by the Lake* was packaged as a consummate erotic thriller but one enlivened by its equally unmistakable gay male twist. This "same, but with a difference" branding is central to the film's critique of conventional erotic thrillers, as L. R. Williams defines them: "noirish stories of sexual intrigue incorporating some form of criminality or duplicity, often as the flimsy framework for on-screen softcore sex."[62] By eliminating the whodunit element from an already loosely plotted story, Guiraudie dispenses with much of the genre's expository pretense to distill sequences down to their sexual mechanics, set to the beats of gay cruising, as Richard Dyer narrates them: "Even if all that is involved is a fuck between two men, there are the following narrative elements: the arrival on the scene of the fuck, establishing contact (through greeting and recognition, or through a quickly established eye-contact agreement to fuck), undressing, exploring various parts of the body, coming, parting."[63]

Though it emerged out of the 1980s home-video revolution that transformed porn consumption, the erotic thriller, with its spectacularized if simulated sex, both flaunts and disavows its adjacency to porn. In contrast, Guiraudie blatantly acknowledges this proximity by incorporating porn's aesthetic of realness and distinctive elements—namely, male genitalia and the money shot

Fig. 2.6. Quotidian full-frontal male nudity in *Stranger by the Lake*.

of male ejaculation, both of which are banished from the conventional erotic thriller. In its ubiquitous male full-frontal nudity and unsimulated sex scenes (performed by stand-ins), *Stranger by the Lake* foregrounds what the conventional erotic thriller conceals: the realness of bodies and sex (see fig. 2.6).

As Linda Williams notes of the film's corpo*realities*, "Here is a film that allows its audience to watch penises as appendages that are just there as well as in those moments when they are more than just there."[64] This combination of quotidian nudity and explicit yet naturalistic sex counters not just erotic thriller conventions but Hollywood's desexualization of queer masculinity as well. At the same time, *Stranger by the Lake*'s disassociation from porn is pronounced, its art cinema ambiguity and meta referentiality preventing wholly pleasurable, immersive scopophilia. Rather than being received as half measures on both counts, this literal and figurative conflation of pornographic and art film elements strikes a sweet spot, as Noah Tsika notes, that "make[s] clear that, for a certain, sexually explicit subset of queer cinema, such adjacency [between gay-identified pornographic and nonpornographic audiovisual productions] means everything, forming the basis not simply of a broad iconographic style—a consistently 'porny' aesthetic—but also of narrative itself, of the 'hot' reflexivity with which a story might unfold."[65] In so doing, *Stranger by the*

Lake's hybrid approach to screening sex works to blur and question, rather than divide and define, categories of erotic thriller, art cinema, and porn.

The unveiled, unrepressed naturalism with which *Stranger by the Lake* represents bodies and sex signals Guiraudie's deconstruction of the erotic thriller's reliance on romanticized sexual fantasy to examine the genre's driving motives in a specifically and explicitly queer context that the genre has largely evaded. Far surpassing the dangerous desire that arouses *In the Cut*'s Frannie and many other erotic thriller heroines, the disavowal required of protagonist (and possible next victim) Franck exceeds narrative conventions because viewers are uncharacteristically *not* held in suspense about the *homme fatal*'s culpability. We observe Michel clearly enough, as Franck does, drowning his clingy lover—and so the investigative will to knowledge typical of the thriller is refocused instead on the questions of why Franck allows himself to be seduced by a murderer and whether he will fall prey to the figurative and literal man-killer. In leaving motive inconclusive and the case unresolved, *Stranger by the Lake* resists the teleological structure of the investigation narrative in a way befitting the similarly confounding desires and shifting sexual subjectivities that the film thematizes. And so *Stranger by the Lake* epitomizes the erotic thriller's juxtaposition of pleasure and danger and hyperbolizes its sexual ethos as defined by L. R. Williams: "the moment of highest erotic charge being also the moment of most extreme moral culpability."[66]

Moreover, through Guiraudie's reflexive signaling of the gaze through his frequent use of point-of-view shots, *Stranger by the Lake* probes the audience's own desiring drives. Fittingly, this perspective appears most intensively in the vantage point from which we see Michel's first murder, with onlooker Franck's voyeuristic positioning as redolent of cinematic spectatorship as that of James Stewart's chairbound L. B. Jefferies in *Rear Window* (Alfred Hitchcock, 1954). We viewers are complicit in desiring

Franck's sexual communion with murderous stud Michel and, as such, long to be taken over by the cinematic image and vicariously endangered. Yet also feeling it safer just to watch, we are given as a less flattering on-screen surrogate the pitiable voyeur Eric (Mathieu Vervisch), forever lurking on the margins, a pasty-skinned mortal among golden gods. Rather than perceiving *Stranger by the Lake* as critic Wesley Morris does—as "organiz[ing] a moral universe around the absurd lawlessness of sexual attraction"—I find the film to acknowledge the very impossibility of doing so, at least within the realm of sexual fantasy such as that which cinema projects.[67]

Nearly Bressonian in its minimalist mapping of the rhythm of genre, *Stranger by the Lake*'s pared-down narrative structure comprises sequential days each beginning and ending in the parking lot adjacent to the lake. This repetition-with-a-difference sequencing suggests an attempt to master some anxiety through reenactment. Accordingly, Franck's and our shuttling between the scopophilic wish fulfillment provided by porn and the imagined mastery over nightmarish anxiety commingles Eros and Thanatos—pleasure principle and death drive—to mobilize the erotic thriller as a means to relieve libidinal energies and primal fears for character and viewers alike. *Stranger by the Lake*'s back-to-back pairing of the money shot—as sexual anthropologist Tim Dean notes, "the visual evidence of momentarily losing control"—with the murder-by-drowning scene suggests how the two scenes and their pleasure/danger significations mirror each other.[68] Certainly *Stranger by the Lake* demonstrates the ongoing viability of what Timothy Corrigan describes as the incoherent text, one bearing the postmodern symptom of resistance to legibility and interpretation and so "forc[ing] audiences to turn to the contours and choices of their own responses."[69] Through fleeting dialogue about safer sex, but more so in Michel's metaphorical embodiment of the sexual killer, *Stranger by the Lake* obliquely references the specifically queer source of this anxiety needing mastering, that which Foster Hirsch notes is a structuring absence in the erotic thriller: HIV/AIDS.[70] It is possible—even tempting, given its overdetermined conflation of casual sex with death—to read *Stranger by the Lake* as a conservative text cautioning against gay promiscuity. Were it not so unwieldy a moral tale, it could well be read as indicting "barebacking"—the practice of having condomless anal sex—as "tantamount to murder," as controversial gay health advocate Larry Kramer did in a 2004 speech.[71]

The art film ambiguity and affective pleasures suffusing *Stranger by the Lake*, however, cloud any meanings that appear to condemn its erotic or moral transgressions, just as the film resists the teleological conclusiveness that serves as the erotic thriller's means of reinforcing status quo ideology. In so doing, Guiraudie alludes to similarly opaque erotic thrillers in which queer readings and pleasures resist containment through interpretative means—among them William Friedkin's 1980 film *Cruising*, which, with its closeted gay killer who murders would-be lovers in infernal nocturnal settings, is a veritable inversion of *Stranger by the Lake*.[72] Another film to which *Stranger by the Lake* clearly pays homage, gay porn classic *Boys in the Sand* (Wakefield Poole, 1971), itself played irreverently on the earnest gay self-flagellation of the crossover stage production *The Boys in the Band* (the film version of which, released in 1970, was also directed by Friedkin). Poole's film was, as José B. Capino has discussed, as much a porn/art hybrid as Guiraudie's (it features a classical instrumental score and self-reflexive stylized fantasy sequences).[73] The choice by (most) viewers to embrace rather than protest *Stranger by the Lake*, then, seems itself an irreverent yet distinctly queer mode of spectatorship, as potentially self-incriminating as Franck's alliance with Michel, yet one that we could attribute to a distaste for the sanitizing of so much contemporary gay cultural product and homonormative politics.

In her discussion of *In the Cut*, Sue Thornham argues that the myth of romance proposed by the *homme fatal* in the

Gothic-inflected erotic thriller eroticizes women's oppression in heteropatriarchal coupling. As such, it is a masochistic (and, Thornham argues, distinctly postfeminist) fantasy wherein the actual source of narrative anxiety stems less from dangerous sex than from heterosexual coupling—a self-destructive proposition, she argues, for women under patriarchy.[74] Though Franck could be said to resemble a Gothic protagonist in eroticizing and romanticizing his submission to Michel's Bluebeard-like seductive murderer, when viewing the two as a queer outlaw couple, the threat becomes less heteropatriarchal than homonormative. Here again Guiraudie's hybridized approach to the erotic thriller troubles—through its art cinema attributes of ambiguity and irony—the genre's customary containment and condemnation of the monstrous *homme fatal*. Alongside that anarchic resistance to the genre's reinstatement of the ideological status quo, through its alignment with porn *Stranger by the Lake* also asks to be linked to the fantasy of untrammeled sexuality, "a predominant one in gay cultural production," Dyer observes, that proffers "a utopian reconciliation of the desire for romance and promiscuity, security and freedom, making love and having sex."[75] Much as the femme fatale's criminal sexuality disrupts heteronormativity, *homme fatal* Michel's enticement to casual sex flouts homonormativity's privileging of monogamy and domesticity. Moreover, Michel and Franck defy safer sex edicts to indulge in an act in which, as Tim Dean documents in *Unlimited Intimacy*, his 2009 study of the barebacking subculture, "the abandonment of condoms is motivated not only by a lust for enhanced physical sensation but also by a desire for certain emotional sensations, particularly the symbolic significance attached to experiences of vulnerability and risk."[76]

With mustachioed Michel's rough trade allure and the Edenic sexual playground devoid of contemporary temporal markers alluding nostalgically to the pre-AIDS hedonism of gay culture and gay porn, *Stranger by the Lake* reflexively stages a utopian fantasy that is also anarchic, unencumbered by the erotic thriller's sexual and moral precautions. Remembering L. R. Williams's characterization of the erotic thriller as the "rich person's pornography," a further anarchic element infuses the taste transgression that transformed a Cannes-certified cinematic artwork into, as Tsika describes its second life online, "an explosion of digital productions that showcase the film's money shots ... with their gorgeous, enormous cocks and torrents of cum."[77] In this way, *Stranger by the Lake* and its reception recall Lee Edelman's envisioning of sexual jouissance as freeing the queer subject from a heteronormative ethos of reproductive futurism that maligns queerness by associating it with negativity.

Fittingly, Edelman's urging in *No Future: Queer Theory and the Death Drive* (2004) for a queer antisociality and oppositionality that is future negating, in which "sex can be envisioned as a subjective escape from a future pull that seems inevitable," caused consternation for queer activists and theorists comparable to that provoked by Guiraudie's vision.[78] Though Franck may plead with Michel to make their relationship less unconstrained, his ultimate surrender to Michel's fatal embrace prompted critic Wesley Morris to conclude that Guiraudie was issuing "a damning indictment of a strain of gay life. It's not marriage that frays the fabric of community. It's sex."[79] Consonant with Dean's assessment of barebackers' motives, I read the film's ending in more romantic if still fatalistic terms as suggesting that to fully open oneself to sexual and emotional concupiscence is to risk death, along the lines of Bataille's axiom that eroticism is "a psychological quest not alien to death."[80]

In Guiraudie's narrative, the true strangers by the lake are Henri (Patrick d'Assumçao), a vacationing widower and closeted bisexual whom Franck befriends, and Inspector Damroder (Jérôme Chappatte), dispatched to investigate the murder. Both prove determined to police queer male desire, imposing logic and surveillance that shames gay men as superficial, promiscuous, and amoral. As Inspector Damroder questions Franck, "One of your own was murdered, and you don't care? You guys have a strange way of loving one another sometimes. Show some concern, if only for yourself." Franck's protest, "We can't stop living," is voiced feebly but speaks volumes in its resistance to externally imposed determinations of ethical, productive forms of community mourning and sexual citizenship.

Reading *Stranger by the Lake* as a rejoinder to dominant heterosexual bourgeois culture's actual and affective denial of queer belonging, Karl Schoonover and Rosalind Galt posit that the transgressive relationship between Franck and Michel "makes felt their impossible relationship to the moral and their exclusion from the social world."[81] The crackdown on nudity and sex initiated by Inspector Damroder's intrusion into and panoptical gaze upon this formerly safe space recalls conservative uses of HIV/AIDS as justification for denigrating and destroying queer practices and cultures such as those deemed "bad sex" and condemned for their antiromantic "negativity." In "Thinking Sex," Gayle Rubin itemizes the former: "Bad sex may be homosexual, unmarried, promiscuous, non-procreative, or commercial. It may be masturbatory or take place at orgies, may be casual, may cross generational lines, and may take place in 'public,' or at least in the bushes or the baths." In "Is the Rectum a Grave?" Leo Bersani echoes Rubin in elucidating how the latter can similarly subvert the cultural sex hierarchy: "Negativity in art attacks the myths of the dominant culture—the pastoral myth, for example, of sexuality as inherently loving and nurturing, of sexuality as continuous with harmonious community. Only by insisting on the bleakness, the love of power, even the violence perhaps inherent in human relations can we perhaps begin to redesign those relations in ways that will not require the use of culture to ennoble them."[82] Not only queer sex but its screened representation and spectatorship are subject to this regulatory regime, and here again Guiraudie's reflexivity gives the film resonance. Even as *Stranger by the Lake*'s nostalgic recall of gay porn texts has rejuvenated their afterlife in the erotic blogosphere, we are compelled to reflect on the obliteration of cruising sites and gay porn theaters, alongside other queer "sexual publics," by sweeping governmental and moral prohibitions.[83]

As Dean notes about cultural resistance to Otherness as barrier to the unlimited intimacy he promotes, "The figure of *the stranger* evokes concerns about safety and risk that remain irreducible to the question of 'safe sex.'"[84] Thinking back to the anxieties policing the penis's heterophallic representation, this fear of Otherness constitutes another rationale for its visual fetishization. As Elizabeth Stephens suggests, the money shot's overvaluation of ejaculation compensates for the subsequent deflation of the phallus into the flaccid penis. At the same time, the fetishizing shot disavows what is perhaps more troubling still: the "disrupting subjective coherence and dissolving [of] the body's boundaries" that sex entails.[85] Where *homme fatal* Michel embodies Edelman's call for a defiant antifuturity and antisociality to embrace what Bersani calls "the unintelligibility, even the inhumanity inherent in sexuality," Franck signifies how erotic intimacy, as an escape from subjectivity through a significant encounter with another/an Other, in being deindividuating, forges human connectedness.[86]

More than being merely a cautionary tale or a nostalgic looking back, *Stranger by the Lake* offers a return to the past in the present, to embrace what Dean calls a "positive ethics of cruising [that] involves not just hunting for sex but opening oneself to the world" through desubjectifying engagements with strangers that forge empathy. Through its incorporation of gay subcultural practices and gay porn tropes—specifically barebacking's consanguinity, which Dean argues "gives physical form to what should be understood as an ethical disposition of vulnerability to the other"—*Stranger by the Lake* challenges the erotic thriller's sexual paranoia and the *homme fatal*'s perversity by depathologizing, without defusing altogether, the threat of sex and of love.[87] Both require one to risk a literal or figurative killing off of oneself, and Franck's submission to *la petite mort* constitutes acceptance of the dangers of sexual and emotional intimacy that are not reassuringly assuaged, but rather tentatively faced, by film's end. *Homme fatal* Michel is still at large, and by killing Inspector Damroder has reclaimed the lake as a queer sexual public space, just as Guiraudie reclaims gay sex for art film production and exhibition and integrates its explicit, politicized representation in the erotic thriller to suggest how the genre might confront its own sexual repression.

Guiraudie's more recent feature, *Rester vertical* (*Staying Vertical*, 2016), makes good on his vow to "go further in my representation of sex," by including a Courbet-inspired close-up of a woman's genitalia in the course of a graphic childbirth scene, alongside an extended long take sequence, set to Pink Floyd, of intergenerational anal sex between two men in the course of the younger assisting the older's suicide. This insistence on pushing past the typically prettified, sanitized images of female nudity and gay male intimacy to expose bodily recesses and processes as well as the mechanics of sex puts Guiraudie in stride with compatriot Catherine Breillat's approach to screening female embodiment (taken up in the next chapter) as well as with the procedural approach toward gay sex employed by HBO's *Looking*, discussed below. As Guiraudie continued, "Because that's yet another thing, in terms of controversy, for a homosexual to show female sex. Straight sex. Sexual organs, of men, older men, younger men, older women, younger women, giving birth, with a vagina. The problem is, doing it in a non-provocative way, not pornographically."[88]

Guiraudie's equation of provocation and pornography, and his distancing his work from both, seems not so much disingenuous as self-effacing about his achievement in undoing these discursive and representational constructs. In dissolving such hierarchical divisions governing good and bad objects and erotics, Guiraudie's leveraging of full-frontal provocations to envision male corp*orealities* and queer masculinities proves especially stimulating. Yet that he does so in 21st century art cinema, as rarefied a realm as *Stranger by the Lake*'s sylvan setting, necessarily limits their representational and ideological impact. The next section explores another queer challenge to representational politics for screening the penis that is played out on the adjacent minefield in which pornographic codes encroach on "quality" cultural zones. In considering how a premium cable television series about gay men proved provocative by averting rather than courting the pornographic, we are compelled to ask what is revealed by keeping the penis from view.

IT'S NOT PORN, IT'S HBO: FULL-FRONTAL QUALITY TV

From HBO's "sex, swearing and respectability" and Showtime's "No Limits" to the T&A (and increasing P) abounding on basic cable channels such as AMC, Starz, and FX, quality television has become a potent showplace for full-frontal nudity in the contemporary mediascape.[89] A much-contested term since its coining, *quality television* is generally understood to refer to programming that is relatively complex and sophisticated both aesthetically and narratively, that caters to a specialized audience characterized as having highbrow tastes, and that uses controversial content as a crucial mode of product differentiation. HBO has been at the forefront of quality television's strategic use of transgressive audiovisual elements (including explicit language, violence, and especially sex).[90] The network has acquired a reputation sufficient to elicit in 2014, from comedy website College Humor, a parody ad titled "It's Not Porn, It's HBO." In the ad, an ensemble of actors "somewhere in L.A." gleefully report being cast in roles in which they perform outrageous sexual acts redolent of porn but unmistakably referencing those featured in series on the channel with, the ad's self-congratulatory voice-over reminds us, "108 Emmy nominations."

Though HBO continues its reign as the porn-adjacent exemplar, it has been challenged in recent years not only by its perennial competitor Showtime but by the proliferation of basic cable and streaming sites, including Amazon Prime Video, Facebook Watch, Hulu, Netflix, and YouTube—all of which are also partly or wholly outside the FCC's jurisdiction and with equal interest in eliciting attention and growing their subscriber and user bases. Given the glut of (old and new) television channels and the sexual cornucopia exhibited therein, branding one's content singularly around sexual provocation—even in the guise of delivering quality—seems to have reached a saturation point that calls for more distinctive messaging and audience targeting. Most poised to be HBO's heir apparent, the basic cable channel Starz elevated its brand visibility and reputation with its canny merging of nudity with lowbrow cult genres and quality aesthetics.[91] Developing their brand strategy to envelop distinctly trans, queer, and feminist perspectives alongside sexual provocation, in 2019 HBO revitalized its image by debuting *Euphoria* (Sam Levinson, 2019–), featuring a trans teen lead and discussed below; *Work in Progress* (Tim Mason and Abby McEnany, 2019–), starring self-described "fat, queer dyke" comedian McEnany as herself; and *Mrs. Fletcher* (Tom Perrotta, 2019–), a sex-positive and consent-minded adaptation of Perrotta's 2017 novel, about a middle-aged single mom (Kathryn Hahn) whose discovery of MILF porn launches her midlife reinvention.

Amid this glut of sexually explicit imagery, the question persists of why male full-frontal nudity remains disproportionately underrepresented, and why, when it does appear, it is often not in a sexual context. As Hannah Mueller notes, "Instead, male nudity is predominantly used as a means of negotiating power relations ... [and] is associated with surrender and humiliation." Surveying the expanse of still mostly female full-frontal nudity across contemporary quality television drama, Mueller observes:

> The concept of quality has become increasingly entangled with strategies of transgression and masculinization in the production and the marketing of quality TV drama. The conflation has resulted in the visualization of blatantly conservative gender norms,

a strict gender binary, the revival of the cinematic male gaze on the small screen, the voyeuristic exploitation of female homosexuality, and the oscillation of male homosexuality between invisibility and violence. These visual strategies unabashedly prioritize straight, male audiences over female or queer viewers, but they are legitimized in the name of creative vision and authenticity, thus associating quality with the heterosexual male spectator.[92]

Unsurprisingly, the heterophallicism Mueller maps was slow to give the unveiled penis visibility remotely equal to that of female nudity—a disparity that was itself mocked with additional parodies. Actor Kevin Bacon, who has appeared naked on-screen in multiple roles, appeared in the role of celebrity spokesperson for a (fake) media activist movement named #Freethebacon, disseminated through a 2015 Mashable parody video taking Hollywood to task for not giving equal visibility to the male member. Additionally, HBO was singled out for the one significant way in which it did not resemble porn. A 2013 mock public service announcement also created by College Humor and titled "HBO Should Show Dongs," featured a quartet of women actor-comedians playing HBO female viewers pleading for "genital equality" in the form of more "premium penis."

Alongside such parodies, an increasingly voluble monitoring of the penis's striking absence was undertaken by TV critics and bloggers, who singled out shows in which expected reveals were not forthcoming. Showtime's *Masters of Sex* (Michelle Ashford, 2013–16), a fictionalized portrayal of famed sex researchers Masters and Johnson, featured considerable and consistent female nudity, including that of lead actor Lizzy Caplan, but avoided showing a single penis. By the series' final season, rather than caving in to the call to "show dongs," *Masters of Sex* seemed to respond by scaling back the female nudity in an attempt to forestall further questioning. Critiques of the show argued that these omissions of penile representation undermined what was perceived as dephallicizing discourse in the series' story lines, which, in keeping with its real-life inspirations, worked to clarify cultural (mis)conceptions regarding, for example, the relation between penis size and sexual performance (1.11, "Phallic Victories").[93]

More recently, HBO appeared to be attempting to head off similar critiques brewing in the wake of the #MeToo and Time's Up movements by starting the second season of the prestige sci-fi drama *Westworld* (Jonathan Nolan and Lisa Joy, 2016–) with a full-frontal nude appearance by male cast member Simon Quarterman, whose press around the episode eagerly framed his choice as predicated on balancing the extensive female nudity (by series lead Thandie Newton particularly) throughout season one. Fittingly, it is Newton's character Maeve who orders Quarterman's Lee Sizemore to strip during the robot rebellion that commences season two (2.1, "Journey into Night").[94] So, too, is the first season of HBO's self-consciously "transgressive teen soap" *Euphoria* "doing [its] part to redress the premium-cable gender imbalance when it comes to nudity," in the estimation of a *New York Times* critic who, while acknowledging the show's boundary-pushing representation of its young characters doing drugs, feeling suicidal, and having copious amounts of sex, nevertheless concluded, "But what sets it apart is penises. Miles and miles of penises, in locker rooms, video chats, selfies and grainy home videos. They populate dating apps, uncomplainingly accept condoms and in one case get masturbated in plain view of a webcam. Even for HBO, it's more penises than we've seen since 'Oz,' and that was set in a men's prison."[95]

In the sixteen-year span between *Oz* and *Euphoria*, however, HBO maintained its heavily weighted double standard even in the case of *Hung* (Colette Burson and Dmitry Lipkin, 2009–11), in which the much-anticipated reveal of its gigolo protagonist Ray Drecker's (Thomas Jane) titularly referenced member was delayed until halfway through the show's final season, and then offered up only its top half in obviously prosthetic form (3.4, "Fuck Me, Mr. Drecker or Let's Not Go to Jail"). In the context of the show, which focuses on a divorced middle-aged father turning to sex work to stay financially afloat in recession-era Detroit, Ralph J. Poole argues that this melodramatic display serves as a necessary culmination to the show's use of penis-as-phallus symbolism as a means of preserving the down-and-out Ray's manhood.[96] The cultural significations of phallic plentitude override whatever sexual realism the narrative achieves, as Ray is forced to confront early on that his exceptional physical endowment alone does not ensure the satisfaction of his female clientele. Yet while *Hung* ends up reinforcing the large penis's status-conferring value as the last redoubt for the otherwise disempowered white male, we are again compelled to consider how the obvious use of an oversized prosthetic frames the penis-as-phallus as transparently inauthentic. Furthermore, that the reveal occurs during a fantasy role-play that has Ray (partly) attired to recapture his youthful ballplayer glory for a former student paying for his services underscores how this penis is effectively reduced to a prop in this patently pretend costuming. À la *Boogie Nights*' Dirk Diggler (to whom *Hung* clearly owes a debt), by virtue of its performative presentation and its eliciting pathos rather than awe or abjection on behalf of the protagonist (rather than a supporting character), this penis resists consignment to either pole—the powerfully melodramatic or humiliatingly comic—and thus constitutes a subversion of the previously discussed representational dyad.

Although most instances of the unveiled penis across the contemporary television landscape may conform to the heterophallic dictates observed by Lehman and Mueller, given their sheer number in recent years relative to what was on view before, one might expect that more varied modes of representation would have emerged. In the preface to his updated 2007 edition of *Running Scared*, Peter Lehman posits, "HBO is mature about male nudity and the penis in a manner that leaves Hollywood in the dust"—an appraisal that the recent parodies would seem to contest or at least qualify.[97]

To consider a few additional instances of HBO's penis programming over the years, I look beyond the stylized and often fantasy-based realm of dramatic series on which Mueller focuses as well as programming that manifests what Janet McCabe and Kim Akass describe as quality television's penchant for "enclosing the profane in a discourse of historical verisimilitude."[98] Looking to assess representations rooted in more contemporary realist contexts and treated more naturalistically, I find that both textual meaning and affective response work to resist the shoring up of heterophallicism that Mueller finds symptomatic of so much of television nudity and to disrupt the dichotomy between phallic spectacle or comic collapse that Lehman detects in the screen penis schema.

Unsurprisingly, the penis has received innovative treatment of this sort from the HBO provoc*auteur* Lena Dunham (featured in chap. 3). Her six-season run of *Girls* was bookended by two noteworthy instances of male full-frontal nudity. While neither instance fully succeeds in undoing the comic/melodramatic dichotomy or the show's history of disproportionately revealing female nudity, each frames the penis in a way that undermines its phallic signification by rendering it absurd yet all too human. In *Girls'* first season, Dunham's Hannah (and viewers) are exposed to her hapless father Tad (Peter Scolari) slumped on the bathroom tile, flaccid penis in full view, after he slips in the shower mid-tryst with his wife, Loreen (Becky Ann Baker) (1.6, "The Return"). Given its humiliating context and the physically unprepossessing, anything but alpha male Tad, the scene skews closer to the Lehman-identified comic penis. Yet it neither invites a mockery of penis size nor of Tad's manhood (indeed, he had been demonstrating his virility at the time of his fall). Rather, because the scene is about the shortcomings that arrive with age ("I'm just realizing that I'm growing old," Tad laments afterward), this penis scene resists relegation to the comic register. The laughter it provokes originates in and invites commiseration with the awkwardness of the father-daughter discomfort, in which the real but underwhelming penis amounts to a mortifying yet humanizing twist on the primal scene. Much as Dunham's own nudity in *Girls* works to defetishize and humanize female embodiment as corp*oreality*, as chapter 3 will argue, this treatment of the penis as naturalistic rather than melodramatic/comic contrasts with the spectacular phalluses of most quality television programming, even as this scene's singularity across the first five seasons of *Girls* necessarily limits its impact.

Not until its sixth and final season did *Girls* venture another significant, if also discomforting, penis reveal: that of the erect (prosthetic) penis that otherwise fully-dressed Chuck Palmer (Matthew Rhys) foists on Hannah as his final challenge to her in their episode-long debate over sexual power dynamics (6.3, "American Bitch").[99] Not visibly fake in the way of Ray Drecker's in *Hung*, but also not immediately (and wincingly) convincing as was father Tad's in season one, this penis's incongruous presence and uncanny appearance is meaningful given the context in which it is introduced and just as swiftly (and without forthcoming explanation from Chuck) withdrawn. Definitively not a naturalistic element of the scene in the way that Tad's is, the appearance of Chuck's penis is so disorienting that it throws Hannah and leaves her unsure how to respond.

Though the scene remains tonally light, it bears more than a shadow of resemblance to another much-discussed scene from the 2017 television season that made topical reference to real-life power plays. That scene, on comedian Tig Notaro's autobiographically inspired series *One Mississippi* (Diablo Cody and Tig Notaro, Amazon, 2015–17), indirectly addressed the rumors already swirling about that show's executive producer Louis C.K. It positioned Notaro's character's female producer Kate (Stephanie Allyne) on the receiving end of a male coworker's licentious behavior during an office meeting (2.5, "Can't Fight This Feeling"). In this instance, the penis remains unseen (though its looming presence is felt), but both scenes convey the discombobulating and dismaying effects of such experiences as their rampant occurrence in the entertainment industry (and beyond) was increasingly coming to light. In so doing, the scenes employ penis representation (or its lack) to critique phallicism on- and off-screen.

In a departure from the melodramatic treatments of male full-frontal nudity that Hannah Mueller finds in much quality TV drama, several other HBO half-hour dramedy series reconfigure the comic penis in a ratio of minimal visibility for maximum impact. Five years prior to the run of his follow-up hit series on FX, and before he became Hollywood persona non grata in the wake of sexual misconduct allegations to which he eventually confessed, the short-lived *Lucky Louie* (Louis C.K., HBO, 2006–7) featured the first iteration of comedian Louis C.K.'s portly, pale, and put-upon alter ego. The series attempted to hybridize HBO's raw sensibility with the formal attributes of the traditional network sitcom (it was filmed using a multiple camera setup in front of a live studio audience and employed a laugh track). In a 2011 interview, C.K. relates how there came to be male full-frontal nudity on *Lucky Louie*: "HBO was asking us why there was no nudity on the show, and what they really meant was, 'Why wasn't Pamela Adlon, who played my wife, nude?' When I hired Pam, I didn't tell her she was going to be doing anything like that. It wasn't supposed to be that kind of show. So I said, 'You know what, I'll do it.' And I did that episode, and they were like, 'O.K., we have plenty of nudity, thank you.'"[100]

The episode to which he refers, the season's second, has thirty-seven-year-old Kim (Adlon) experiencing the first orgasm of her seven-year marriage and, it is implied, her life (1.2, "Kim's O"). After the initially flummoxed Kim figures out why their sex had felt different this time, she praises Louie for having "done good, honey." She pats him encouragingly and tells him, "Go get yourself a snack." Like a puppy, he eagerly and obediently jumps out of bed, providing a glimpse of his genitals that, framed in the same medium long shot standard to sitcom setups, makes for a nearly undiscernible blur as he streaks past. Compared to the comic penis that Lehman describes, this instance of full-frontal nudity does not linger long enough for a penis-size joke to be viable, and while it comically belittles by infantilizing the character, there is compensation in his having just proven (albeit belatedly) his sexual prowess.

For HBO this was a notably early instance of penis unveiling, particularly by a show's lead. Louis C.K.'s subsequent series *Louie* (FX, 2010–15) did not replicate this type of unveiling despite the basic cable channel's openness to showing full-frontal nudity and his character's corporeal candor. Though relatively fleeting and still categorically comic, *Lucky Louie*'s full-frontal scenes—which included another instance of male nudity (by another recurring male character) but remained an outlier among HBO shows for not showing female nudity—sparked a "did you see it?" debate (of the sort described in chapter 1's discussion of Ben Affleck's fleeting full-frontal in *Gone Girl*) and bolstered both the show's reputation for sexual (and relational) realness and, ironically enough, the performer's for gender parity and sensitivity.

More recently, the HBO series *Togetherness* (Jay Duplass, Mark Duplass, and Steve Zissis, 2015–16) attempted to revive married couple realism for the 21st century (albeit without the throwback sitcom aesthetic). Co-creator and co-lead Mark Duplass points to the pivotal role to be played by male nudity: "It's less about making something sexy and brilliant that you can masturbate to and more about showing in an honest way what the bedroom looks like and what relationships look like."[101] In practice, however, season one of *Togetherness* borrowed the "did you see it?" move from the *Lucky Louie* playbook, with Duplass claiming bragging rights for a full-frontal shot so fleeting that it barely registered visually on screen.

Its occurrence takes place in a scene between longtime marrieds that has Michelle (Melanie Lynskey) attempting to spice up their sex life by playing dominatrix with her husband Brett, played by Duplass (1.2, "Handcuffs"). Ordered to take off his underwear, Brett pulls down his boxer briefs to momentarily reveal his genitalia, before submitting naked and on all fours to a short spanking session that ends abruptly when Michelle accidently slaps Brett's balls. (As with Fassbender's full-frontal shots in *Shame*, that Duplass's face does not appear in the same frame as the penis may be intended to discourage the image's dissemination online.)

Not nearly so flattering as C.K.'s feat of wife-pleasuring, Brett's penis emerges (though barely) within a comic scene that all but emasculates him first as a sexual submissive, then, by scene's end, cowering in a fetal position with his young daughter's Strawberry Shortcake ice pack pressed to his testicles. Although Brett appears naked and on all fours for a substantial portion of the scene, the "did you see it?" element is even more pronounced here than in *Lucky Louie* and seems hardly equivalent to what Duplass credits himself with in saying, "If I'm asking [costars] Amanda Peet and Melanie Lynskey to be naked, I better be damn willing to do it myself."[102] Over its two-season run, *Togetherness* did in many ways fulfill Duplass's aim of representing relationships honestly, but male full-frontal nudity played a minor role—even if Duplass would take another opportunity in season two to demonstrate his commitment to gender parity by performing another, slightly longer, but still fleeting, full-frontal scene (2.6, "Geri-ina"). As discussed in chapter 4, Duplass would go on to another full-frontal reveal that was more visually legible and of substantially longer duration in *Creep 2* (Patrick Brice, 2017).

No doubt in response to this emergent call for equal-opportunity nudity and the publicity such provocations were found to attract, the floodgates for full-frontal male nudity opened. It has become practically de rigueur for series creators to anoint themselves, as *The Leftovers* creator Damon Lindelhof did in 2017 amid a final season featuring multiple male full-frontal shots, as purveyors of penis: "There's an incredible disproportion between naked women and naked men on television. And if you're going to do a show on HBO, which is one of the few places where you can do full-frontal nudity, there's no excuse not to show more dongs. I'm passionate about it. I'm just the beginning of the vanguard, but I want to normalize male nudity on television."[103]

Strategically deployed to establish edgy credibility for quality television and to incite reactions in critical discourse and social media before being quickly and skittishly withdrawn, the penis comprises the 21st-century cable equivalent of other short-lived sensationalist scenarios that characterized what used to be called sweeps week. HBO has proven fairly typical of quality television in representing nudity and sex more provocatively than naturalistically. Given this enduring reliance on the comic/melodramatic dichotomy even when reconfigured for a 21st century sensibility that eschews penis-size jokes while reconstituting the phallus as spectacle, one might well ask whether gay male representation should take another representational route. My final example of 21st century treatments of male nudity is provocative precisely because it elides the full-frontal displays that audiences have come to expect from quality television. That it does so within a gay milieu almost as sexualized as *Stranger by the Lake*'s adds contour to my previous contemplation of the penis's sexual and representational politics outside the heterophallic regime.

"BORING AT LAST" GAY REPRESENTATION IN HBO'S *LOOKING* (MICHAEL LANNAN, 2014–16)

A collaboration between American screenwriter-producer Michael Lannan and British filmmaker Andrew Haigh, *Looking* is set in contemporary San Francisco and centers on three gay friends. White-bred Patrick (Jonathan Groff) is a twenty-nine-year-old game designer who at the start of the series is yet to have a long-term relationship with a man. Agustín (Frankie J.

Alvarez) is a hard-partying Cuban American sometime artist. And Dom (Murray Bartlett) is a mustachioed hunk pushing forty but still waiting tables and chasing sexual conquests. Polarizing upon its debut, *Looking* was alternately "lauded for eschewing easy pay-cable provocation" and derided for that same lack of provocation.[104] "Why Is *Looking* So Boring?" asked the headline for a *Slate* think piece, to which a *Daily Beast* headline affirming the sentiment and the show replied, "Yes, *Looking* Is Boring. It's the Drama Gays Deserve."[105] *Slate*'s Brian Lowder's put-down of *Looking* as "a PSA for how the mainstream increasingly expects gayness to look—butch enough, politically apathetic, generally boring" called out the show's perceived homonormativity.[106] But other critics were less concerned that *Looking*'s characters were too bourgeois and self-absorbed to be at the barricades, and their assessments were more ambivalent. Rich Juzwiak in *Gawker* likened *Looking* to "paging through a magazine in a dentist's office" but, by the end of his review, extolled the show for a distinctive achievement: "Gay men get to be boring at last."[107]

While these responses indicate several representational pressure points, consternation over the show's lack of male nudity and its treatment of gay sex was particularly pronounced, and this will be the focus of this chapter's final consideration of full-frontal provocation. As the series' title announces, *Looking* focuses on (self-)examining contemporary politics of queer representation. Putting *Looking*'s representations of gay male corporeality and intimacy in dialogue with queer critical concepts of visibility and authenticity, we can consider the reasons for and implications of the show's significations for screening nonphallic masculinities.

Perhaps, then, the most surprising aspect of 2014 as "year of the penis" was that *Looking*, despite appearing at a time of considerably greater permissiveness in cable programming, was perceived as substantially less sexually provocative than quality television's first major foray into gay men's lives. Showtime's landmark *Queer as Folk* (Ron Cowen and Daniel Lipman, 2000–5) had been adapted from a UK series and released nearly fifteen years before. Presumably this was good news for those critics who expressed dismay, as did Anthony Tommasini of the *New York Times* in a much-debated piece, at *Queer as Folk*'s "retro depiction of gay cruising and its obsessions with youth, abs and drugs . . . just fantasy, come-ons, blunt advances, quick acceptance or rejection, and even quicker sex."[108] Not unlike *Stranger by the Lake*, *Queer as Folk* reveled in its complicity with homophobic stereotyping, announcing in voice-over in the series' opening line, "The thing you need to know is, it's all about sex." Whether eliciting raves or hand-wringing, the responses to *Queer as Folk* were a far cry from the characterizations of *Looking* as boring. Yet, as Tommasini went on to note, the earlier show lacked visual audacity and hard-core realism in screening bodies and sex: "True, the acts, anal and oral, have never been so casually presented on mainstream television. But, this being mainstream television, any glimpse of genitalia is assiduously [sic] avoided, and the promised shock is further undercut by the soft-porn quality of the directing."[109] That depictions of anal and oral acts between men, which Tommasini concedes were transgressive for their day, remain so in *Looking*'s more contemporary moment indicates the extent to which gay sex remains visually taboo. Importantly, Tommasini does not object to sexual explicitness but rather its titillating treatment, so he would presumably find *Looking*'s naturalistic approach to filming sex, discussed below, more to his liking than the soft-core porn style he attributes to *Queer as Folk*. Yet where "mainstream television," as Tommasini terms it, has clearly come around to revealing genitalia, in *Looking* full-frontal nudity appears only sporadically, not until the second season, and not in sexual contexts. But as Tommasini's remarks remind us, where *Queer as Folk*'s transatlantic reception elicited disapproval for its soft-core sex from a segment of the gay viewing audience, *Looking* was derided for not sharing a similar degree of explicitness and for being comparatively staid in keeping the penis under wraps.

Responding to *Looking*'s alleged sexual normativity, Wesley Morris finds that the series "feels like a breakthrough for TV, not for the sex, exactly, but for the lack of hysteria or gymnastics with which the sex is conducted. Anyone who's watched *Queer as Folk* or *The L Word* might find relief in sex that's after something other than revenge or sport or a disturbance of the pay-cable peace."[110] The hypersexualized legacy left by *Queer as Folk* and *The L Word* was not on the minds of viewers alone, but clearly factored in to the show's conceptualization by its creators and HBO. *Looking* could also be said to have borrowed from those series a strategy that Candace Moore terms *heteroflexibility*, which employs characters and narrative elements designed to solicit straight-identified viewers who are queer curious and empathetic.[111] *Looking*'s sexually naive, frequently judgmental protagonist Patrick functions to acclimate straight viewers into the show's queer realm. By regularly admitting to his own queer shame and self-loathing, Patrick assuages any residual homophobia among viewers, while his partial ignorance of gay idiom and rites affords opportunities for the straight audience's edification, as when his pals inform him that referring to someone as having a "house in Virginia" signifies their HIV-positive status. Less contested than its negotiation of viewer expectations for sexual (in)explicitness, *Looking* navigates its audience's varying degrees of fluency with the queer lexicon by embedding its educational moments in an often-deft display of code-switching, as befits the series' preference for naturalism over didacticism.

From the start, then, *Looking* was both consonant and dissonant with quality television's previous LGBTQ+-targeted programming as well as with HBO's programming lineup. As heir apparent to *Queer as Folk* and *The L Word*, *Looking* constituted HBO's poaching of the queer programming niche that its chief competitor had carved out with those earlier ventures. Seeking to distance *Looking* from its Showtime forebears even as it angled for their fan base, HBO was likely unbothered when *Looking* was dubbed by critics as "*Girls* for gays," seeming similar enough in format (half-hour dramedy) and content (neurotic, relatively privileged young people negotiating sexual hang-ups and relationship drama). However thin the comparison, *Looking* did echo *Girls* in diversifying HBO's audience and brand (from a gender and sexuality standpoint, at least) without losing its sexually edgy image. The channel's reputation as home to bad-boy antiheroes and their cocksure creators had reached a saturation point. Though in its visual chasteness *Looking* did not resemble *Girls* (or virtually any HBO series), in spearheading HBO's expansion into beyond-heteronormative territory, *Looking* delivered a queering of the cable juggernaut's image in ways analogous to *Girls*' feminist provocations, which are discussed in chapter 3.

Looking's conservative approach to nudity served the interests of both the show and HBO in presenting "tasteful" programming, provocative for defying both contemporary gay culture's and quality television's claims to the right to flaunt nudity and sex. In the context of a realist drama billed as "for us by us" (Lannan, Haigh, and lead actors Bartlett, Groff, and Russell Tovey, who plays Patrick's boss Kevin, are all out gay men) yet appearing on a cable network long associated with heteromasculinist discourse, that defiance risked displeasing both gay audiences and the straight viewership for quality television. Yet if, as McCabe and Akass posit, "part of the pleasure of HBO's original programming comes from how the institutional discourse works hard to tell us how the channel defies, resists and scandalises," *Looking* could seem either like a straitlaced opting out of such provocations or as a counterprogramming strategy whereby the very lack of sexual provocation serves as its mode of resistance.[112] *Looking*'s creative leads do not report the kind of encouragement toward showing nudity and sex that Louis C.K. encountered at HBO, nor is the show built around a sexually provocative premise (as were *Hung* and *Tell Me You Love Me*). Even if making its queer content palatable were the driving force shaping the show's representations,

Looking's branding as "tasteful" yet "real" reinvigorates HBO's early strategy for sexually themed programming. Marc Leverette describes that strategy as employing a visual and narrative aesthetic packaged as informational docudramas, with long-running series such as *Real Sex* (1990–2009) and *Taxicab Confessions* (1995–2010) conceived to distinguish HBO from then competitor Cinemax's soft-core approach.[113] To ensure its classy profile and commitment to showcasing "real sex," HBO was enticed by Lannan's collaboration with cowriter and director Haigh, whose 2011 film *Weekend* had received acclaim on the festival/art house circuit in large part for what was described as its reinvigoration of British social realism.[114]

As a result, the penis is a structuring absence in *Looking*. If, as I have been arguing, greater visibility by way of screening bodies and sex naturalistically works to disrupt the melodramatic/comic dyad and defuse the penis's phallic potency, what are we to make of *Looking*'s resistance to letting us look? Writing about *Looking* during its first season, *Slate*'s Justin Moyer proclaimed "the political necessity of seeing a gay man's erection on HBO." I find this entreaty less justified by Moyer's rationale that "the dick is the *raison d'être* of homosexuality" than by the risk that *Looking* would contribute to a representational history whereby gay male desire is sanitized and the penis retains the phallic mystique of the unrepresented.[115]

Before considering how *Looking*'s treatment of gay sex intervenes in that repressive record, I will briefly discuss the two instances of male full-frontal nudity included in season two of *Looking* (unlikely to appease those viewers in Moyer's camp). The first instance—featuring a head-on, well-lit glimpse of rugby players taking postgame showers—typifies HBO's tactic of using anonymous nudity by attractive background actors as enticing scenery (2.3, "Looking Top to Bottom"). Located in the representationally loaded milieu of the men's locker room shower, the scene queers (this being a gay men's rugby team) a space cinematically and culturally inscribed with homosocial anxiety. Centering its gaze on a burly man with a below-average-size penis in the foreground, with a side view of a more well-endowed man visible behind him, the scene's inclusivity supports the defetishization of penis size, something that *Looking*'s subsequent full-frontal shot cannot claim but that the series overall was at some pains to express. Though Patrick would be chided for asking the measurements of friend Dom's latest conquest in season one, *Looking* would occasionally betray its ambivalence around size—not unlike the social media app Mister did with a "How Big Is Your Favorite *Looking* Man?" advertising tie-in designed to play on curiosity about the show's never fully naked leads, in which characters' supposed penis size was correlated to less superficial aspects of personality.[116]

The second instance of full-frontal nudity features Agustín's second-season love interest, Eddie (Daniel Franzese), and so is noteworthy as *Looking*'s sole instance of a recurring actor appearing fully naked (2.8, "Looking for Glory"). Beyond its exposure of the penis, the casting of Franzese, an out gay man known for his memorable turn in *Mean Girls* (Mark Waters, 2004), in a role as an HIV-positive bear and LGBTQ+ youth activist, signaled the show's expansion of its representation of queer diversity and political engagement. Because the performer is also a self-professed "big dude," this full-frontal scene further makes visible an underrepresented contingent of gay male corporeality and gives eroticized representation to plus-size masculinity that, whether straight or gay, has been almost exclusively treated to pejorative fat figurations. Referencing HBO's growing reputation for showing bodies not typically seen on TV, Franzese proclaimed, "I'm going full Lena Dunham! I'm on HBO and I'll get naked."[117]

Though Moyer's plea to see a gay man's erection goes unsatisfied, Franzese's penis surfaces in a sexually intimate, if somewhat harrowing, setting. The scene shows Agustín and Eddie finishing sex with mutual masturbation. When Eddie's ejaculate shoots

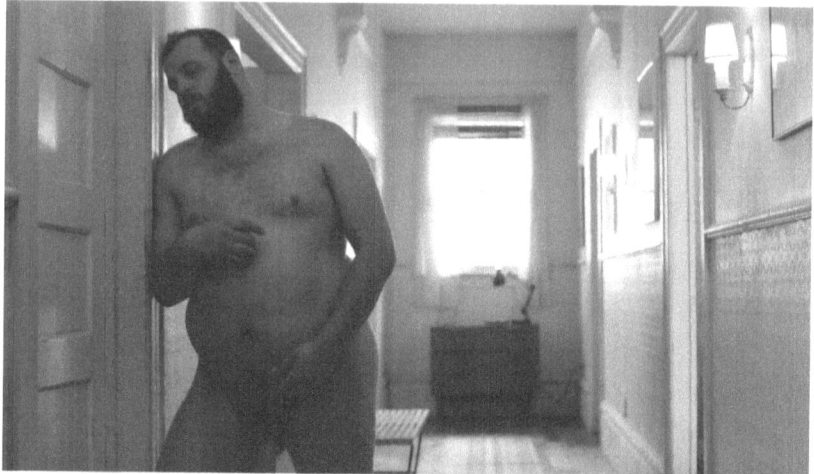

Fig. 2.7. Beyond the pale: Daniel Franzese as Eddie bringing full-frontal diversity to *Looking*.

into Agustín's eye, Agustín feigns calm but retreats to the bathroom. Eddie, still naked, gets up to go check on his boyfriend (see fig. 2.7). The full-frontal moment therefore is one that accompanies seropositive sex, and although it introduces a disquieting element in Agustín's reckoning with the sexual risk their relationship presents, the sequence is pitched in realistic rather than melodramatic terms. Interestingly, then, *Looking*'s two scenes of full-frontal male nudity are almost diametrically opposed, yet both diverge significantly from the melodramatic/comic binary as well as from heterosexist representations that elide or pathologize moments of gay eroticism.

As this sequence between Eddie and Agustín illustrates, the queer context of such images of full-frontal nudity needs to be considered in assessing *Looking*'s comparative visual modesty. To recall what was evidenced in *Stranger by the Lake*, the stakes for screening male nudity change when gay men's representation is concerned, given the way that gay men have been both demoted within the heterophallic regime and defined by its cultural imaginary through a reductionist fixation on sex acts that are rarely permitted to be screened. The gay male context demands a reconceptualization of "de-phallicization through representation."

Looking must contend with a directly homophobic visual economy controlling male nudity in contemporary quality television that (as Mueller's survey suggests) adopts its own dichotomy of invisibility or alignment with "surrender and humiliation." Considering the token gay characters of hypermasculine quality television, Mueller finds that, "when it comes to these characters having sex with a chosen partner, the camera often stays away," while the often-coercive male-male sex scenes that do make it on-screen are "more about a merciless establishing of hierarchies than they are about sexual gratification."[118] So where *Stranger by the Lake* appropriated stereotypes of gay promiscuity with its reaffirming and flaunting of sexually hedonistic displays, *Looking* opts for an overall less visually explicit but more diversified range of queer masculinities and male corp*orealities* of which Franzese's character and full-frontal scene serve as exemplar. Their respective politics of representation befits the aesthetic positioning of each. *Stranger by the Lake* portrays sex hypervisibly but with art cinema's narrative ambiguation, while the "writer's medium" of television leads *Looking* to articulate gay sexual intimacies through dialogue and scenario (though without capitulating to HBO's fondness for sexposition). "We made the choice to use sex as a storytelling tool," explains series creator Lannan. "It's not just: have sex for sex's sake."[119] Ironically, Lannan's justification serves implicitly to distinguish *Looking* from the ostensibly more prurient treatment of sex on HBO and, though he leaves it unnamed, from HBO's most notoriously salacious series, *Game of Thrones*.

Groff, who plays Patrick, further situates *Looking* as counterprogramming to HBO's erstwhile "soft-core" sex by praising the series' sexual realism: "Haigh does a really good job capturing the reality of sex instead of just the salaciousness of sex. So the sex scenes can be sexy but they also feel like real sex. It's not like you're watching perfectly shined, groomed bodies banging in soft lighting. You're seeing what's real. It's a little awkward. Kind of hot."[120] The borderline moralistic distinction among sex scenes, as conveyed by Lannan's and Groff's comments, belies the series' sex positivity, discussed below, even if *Looking* takes a less radical route toward visualizing gay sex than does *Stranger by the Lake*'s ubiquitous nudity and money shot inserts. It is telling that *Looking*'s opening sequence has Patrick fleeing his first attempt at cruising (in a wooded area not unlike *Stranger by the Lake*'s), anxious about being perceived as what he calls "one of *those* gays."

Much as the prudish Patrick eventually comes around to embrace (as will the show) a sex positivity grounded in realism rather than utopianism, it emerges that *Looking*'s distaste is not for gay men's sexual exploits (as some critics alleged) but rather for the rampant self-commodification that pervades "gay culture" (including "gay shows"). That self-commodification extends, in *Looking*'s logic, to the "sex for sex's sake" aesthetic that also privileges bodies conventionally deemed attractive and thus appropriate for looking at: white, able-bodied, fit, and young. Flouting that directive by presenting bodies like Franzese's, *Looking* also incorporates this sort of queer autocritique into story and dialogue. For example, Dom's birthday lament that, "At 40, Grindr issues you a death certificate," calls out the exclusionary ageism of social media–enabled contemporary gay sex cultures (1.6, "Looking in the Mirror").

While *Looking* never made it possible to look past the sex acts occurring among its gay characters, its first season tended to assume an in-the-know audience when referencing the mechanics of queer intimacy, thereby sidestepping some of the hoped-for visual confirmation. Such an approach, while redolent of the Motion Picture Production Code–style obfuscation that might be read as avoiding offending squeamish spectators, actually indicates how *Looking* initially addressed a gay audience while not rushing to explain its sexual or cultural rites to straight viewers. Without abandoning its heteroflexibility in this respect, by season two, *Looking* became more inclined toward explicitness, both verbally and graphically, in its articulations of gay sex.

To illustrate this evolution, consider first the most talked-about sex scene of season one, that between Patrick and his boyfriend-to-be, Latinx hairdresser Richie (Raúl Castillo), at the start of an episode in which they spend the day getting to know each other (1.5, "Looking for the Future"). The scene, which begins with Richie fellating Patrick just outside the frame, shows Patrick tense up and start to protest when Richie's face moves lower between his legs. "Relax, you just took a shower," Richie reassures him. Falling back in pleasurable submission, Patrick comes swiftly to orgasm. A short while later, sharing a postcoital brunch, Richie nonchalantly asks, "Did you have pineapple yesterday? I could still taste, um...." Though Richie's reference, like the sex scene itself, remains coy, the knowing spectator (as well as the wanting-to-know spectator) is given sufficient clues to infer the act being referenced—anilingus—without breaking from the dialogue's naturalism, as a more explicit effort to educate the straight and/or sexually vanilla viewer would require. The emphasis is on establishing the sex act's taking place and then considering its import at length as Patrick and Richie's conversation continues in veiled and not-so-veiled terms:

> PATRICK: Oh, c'mon! Seriously? I gave you the three second warning so you can't blame me.
> RICHIE: I don't think it's a bad thing, I'm just saying.... What, you don't do that?
> PATRICK: [*joking*] Not on purpose, and not on an empty stomach.... I just get nervous because it's not one hundred percent safe. I think that it's pretty safe, but you never know.
> RICHIE: Oh, you think I'm a *puta*?
> PATRICK: What is that?

RICHIE: A guy that fucks around with a lot of guys, swallows a lot of cum.

PATRICK: [*nervously*] Are you? I'm just paranoid. I sneeze and I think I've got HIV. I get tested all the time even though I'm incredibly safe.... You know, just to be one hundred percent sure.

RICHIE: My last boyfriend was positive. But don't worry, I'm not.

PATRICK: Weren't you freaked out, dating someone that, you know?

RICHIE: Yeah a little, but you know, I loved him, so . . . what're you gonna do? You just deal. I don't do that often, by the way.

PATRICK: Do what?

RICHIE: This morning . . . [*smiling cutely*] I don't know, I couldn't help myself.

The scene aims to disabuse straight and gay viewers alike of prejudices related to sex, race and ethnicity, and disease. With a callback to Patrick's previously expressed paranoia (in conversation with Agustín and Dom) about the prospect of coming into contact with an "uncut" penis (discussed below), another purportedly unclean act is absolved through Richie's show of intimacy and pleasure giving and is accompanied by his destigmatizing of seropositive relationships and (also to be discussed below) his salience as a queer man of color.

The visual coyness notwithstanding, *Looking*'s first-season sex scenes still function as instructive to a heteroflexible viewership. Groff recounts, for example, that straight friends reported having learned from the show that it is possible for gay men to have sex in the missionary position.[121] By season two, though the sex scenes remained relatively discreet, the ellipses and euphemisms gave way to more direct verbal descriptions. In the first sex scene of season two, Patrick lures his married boss, Kevin, to a Russian River rave, where their tryst in a wooded clearing is obscured by darkness and focuses mainly on facial close-ups. Yet any needed clarification is provided by Patrick's confessing to his friends the next morning that Kevin "fucked me in the butt against a tree" (2.1, "Looking for the Promised Land").

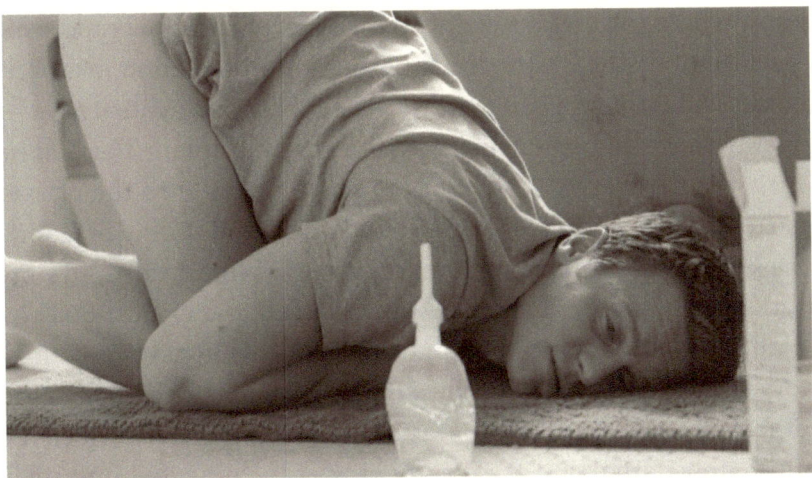

Fig. 2.8. Looking at the mechanics of gay sex: Patrick (Jonathan Groff) preparing for a date.

As the second season proceeds, the mechanics of gay sex become still more explicitly stated even as the need for such edification is cast in doubt, as exemplified by the plotline that has Patrick preparing for his second bout of anal sex with Kevin by purchasing and administering an enema (2.3, "Looking Top to Bottom") (see fig. 2.8).

> PATRICK: This is the most annoying part about being gay. Straight people never have to think about shooting water up their asses before sex.
> AGUSTÍN: Straight people are having butt loads of butt sex, trust me.

Though it may be justifiably accused of flattering straight(ish) viewers, this exchange also debunks the false dichotomy between gay versus heterosexual erotic practices (one whose clear political motives involve the condemnation of "bad sex," as Gayle Rubin observes). The scene ends with another line suggestive to anyone unsure why such preparation is necessary, as an embarrassed Patrick jokes to the pharmacy clerk ringing up his purchase, "And I'm not having a colonoscopy tomorrow." Her deadpan response, "Do you know where you are?" referring to their location in San Francisco's "gayborhood," the Castro district, brings the in-the-know joke back home while still proposing that queer sex has gone mainstream.

Whether alluding explicitly to the gay cult sitcom *The Golden Girls* (Susan Harris, NBC, 1985–92) or implicitly to the classic porn chestnut *Boys in the Sand* (in the 1970s stud styling of Dom), *Looking* pays homage to precursors it sees as significant and simpatico. In so doing, *Looking* positions itself as a critical text (in both senses—as important and as analytical) in gay screen history. What was perceived for some viewers as boring was for others intensely affecting, discomfortingly self-reflective, yet ultimately cathartic. "It's too fucking real," reflected one such critic-fan on the queer blog /bent, noting the series' melancholic tone and its probing of the characters' internalized shame and homophobia. And *The New Yorker* referred to *Looking*'s wallowing in "the new gay sadness," alluding to the lingering effects of an oppressive history.[122]

The post-closet, post-AIDS era of gay inclusion that makes *Looking* possible informs its moderate representational politics, just as the discourse challenging *Looking* displayed a post-queer assumption that LGBTQ+ cultural visibility was sufficiently assured as to obviate the need to protect and defend the sole US television show then airing whose central focus was the lives of gay men. In a plea to HBO to renew *Looking* past a second season, one critic noted, "*Looking* shows how rarely we get to see gay men together, let alone seeing them in bed together."[123]

Despite criticism of its muted sexual representations, *Looking* departs from the heterophallic visual economy of contemporary quality television, and HBO specifically, by challenging its association with the straight male spectator by reconfiguring its use of visual transgression as brand tactic (through *Looking*'s frequent prioritizing of the verbal). It also departs from the pattern Mueller observes whereby male nudity and male-male sex are linked to emasculation, violence, and physical vulnerability rather than emotional intimacy. In negotiating ways of representing gay male sex and nudity in a media industry that might seem to have achieved greater openness to a queer sensibility but is undeniably still subject to homonormativity, not to mention homophobia, *Looking* more broadly revises precedents for queer visibility and verisimilitude with its nonphallic politics of sexual and penile representation.

Regardless, *Looking* was canceled after its second season, presumably because the series had failed to generate a significant number of new subscribers or, barring that, sufficient fan and awards attention (it received no Emmy nominations) to make it the kind of high-profile property HBO prioritizes. With not just Showtime but newfangled provocateurs such as FX and Starz competing for audience share and cultural buzz, HBO is under pressure to maintain its longtime lead in premium cable subscribers. (Seemingly promoting quantity over quality, Amazon Prime Video, Hulu, and Netflix have not branded their original programming with the same degree of sexual provocation.)[124] Ultimately, *Looking*'s reverse provocation was not sufficient for what Tony Kelso argues is a business model in which "HBO is *forced* to take risks. If it relies on millions of everyday viewers to relinquish a few extra dollars each month for the opportunity to view programming they cannot get on commercial TV, then HBO simply must continually distinguish itself from broadcast and basic cable stations if it hopes to remain viable."[125]

The feature-length *Looking: The Movie*, written and directed by Haigh, was released on HBO in 2016, allowing for the story line's wrap-up and a final stage on which to confirm or protest its "boring" bona fides. Freed of the need to continue attracting viewers but mindful of its legacy, *Looking: The Movie* amped up the reflexive address to its critics and fans in both self-aggrandizing and self-defensive gestures. Its premise alone, instigated by Patrick's return to San Francisco from Denver (where he had moved) on the occasion of Agustín and Eddie's wedding, suggests the show's, like the happy couple's, wholesale transformation into what Agustín calls "Stepford Homos," in committing the series' queerest couple to state-sanctioned monogamy. "That televised gay angst should have anything to do with committed relationships is a victory for the mainstream gay-rights movement," wrote *New Yorker* critic Daniel Wenger about *Looking*'s supposedly "safe" queer politics.[126]

Yet as these characters will articulate in the pep talks, "maids of dishonor" toasts, and wedding vows to come, they are not buying into a heteronormative—or even homonormative—vision of marriage, but rather its queer reenvisioning. Fittingly, the engaged couple is toasted by legendary San Francisco LGBTQ+ activist Cleve Jones in a cameo. And they are married by a city hall justice of the peace played by Tyne Daly, famous as the more butch half of the crime-fighting duo *Cagney & Lacey* (Barbara Avedon and Barbara Corday, ABC, 1981–88), a network series subject to "de-gaying" and subsequently elevated to queer cult status.[127] *Looking: The Movie* goes so far as to mock, albeit lovingly, another "breakthrough" LGBTQ+ text while also calling out its own characters' homonormativity. The scene shows Dom and houseguest Patrick brushing their teeth side by side. "We're just like Annette Bening and Julianne Moore in *The Kids Are All Right*," jokes Dom, referring to Lisa Cholodenko's 2010 film about upper-middle-class lesbian moms (examined in chap. 4).

"I thought I'd be Keith Haring or Robert Mapplethorpe. Instead I'm Neil Patrick Harris, only not as cool because I can't tap dance." So laments Agustín to Patrick on the eve of his nuptials. Also joking but with more pathos, the reference to gay celebrity then (Haring and Mapplethorpe) versus now (Neil Patrick Harris) has Agustín coming to grips with the dissolution of his younger self's fantasy of queer radicalism in favor of homonormativity and implies that *Looking* may be part of a similar shift toward depoliticization in contemporary queer popular culture. When Patrick indignantly denies allegations by *Looking*'s most unpopular character, Richie's present boyfriend, Brady (Chris

Perfetti), of "femmephobia" (an aversion to effeminate gay men) and "giving [gay people] a bad name," it sounds like the show defending itself against allegations that its lead gay characters are too butch and apolitical.

Similarly, *Looking: The Movie* might have opted to dispense with sexual titillation altogether or to indulge in an erotic explicitness too risky when the show was still angling for renewal. Instead, though, the final sex scene offers another rejoinder to its critics by means of its most outré act yet. Significantly, the scene is between Patrick and a younger man he hooks up with after the bachelor party, showing Patrick and the series itself to have retreated from their previous tentativeness around casual intimacies (even as they both head toward a resolution that has Patrick reuniting with Richie). This time Patrick is shown performing, rather than receiving, anilingus. Told that he's "really good at that," Patrick replies, "I've been training." The narrative import of this and the couple's subsequent segue into anal sex is clear to regular viewers, confirming Lannan's remarks about the show's use of sex scenes as storytelling. At the start of the series, Patrick was an anal virgin with bottom shame (as Agustín tells him early in the show's run, "You still think getting fucked makes you the girl in the relationship"), who was paranoid about AIDS and neurotic about casual sex. Patrick's newfound versatility and self-acceptance go beyond erotic experience; nonetheless, his character's arc across the series is importantly traced through sex, with different acts functioning as key signposts along the way. *Looking* may have a dearth of full-frontal nudity and may not be, like *Queer as Folk*, "all about sex." But it is a lot about sex.

CODA: STILL LOOKING FOR THE NONPHALLIC PENIS OF COLOR

While I have been arguing that *Looking*'s strategy of keeping the penis mostly under wraps constitutes a "tell, don't show" form of provocation, this approach has made for a missed opportunity to screen nonphallic penises of color, especially given the show's multiracial cast.[128] The series' sole moment of openly confronting its and US culture's own racialized fetishization of the penis involves one of Patrick's most conspicuous instances of what I term (in chap. 4) "bad queer" behavior. When Agustín obnoxiously warns Patrick before his first date with "cholo" Richie that "he'll probably be uncut if he's a real Mexican," Patrick descends into a Googling tailspin of anxiety and winds up inappropriately blurting out his relief on discovering Richie to be circumcised, causing Richie to back away (1.2, "Looking for Uncut"). As Patrick laments to Agustín by phone afterward, "Everything was going fine until I acted like all I wanted to do was suck on his uncut cock, which it turns out he doesn't actually have. I think I may be racist as well." The episode-long exercise acts as a humiliating wake-up call for Patrick, but also addresses the broader complicity in cultural texts, gay and straight, with privileging white alongside otherwise normative (read: cisgendered, circumcised, and average-size or larger) penises.

Given this chapter's focus on a handful of films and television series from a mostly white Anglo-American context, some questions about nude male representation of men of color are regrettably unaddressed.[129] Yet to gaze on the rogues' gallery of male full-frontal nudity is to confront an extremely white lineup. That the penises on display in nonpornographic screen culture are almost exclusively white arises from the marginalization of men of color on-screen. They are rarely cast in leading roles and are alternately hypersexualized or desexualized in the roles that are available to them. The perceived hyperpotency or emasculation, respectively, of men of color seems to require concealment to maintain this disavowal of their ordinary manhood. In his landmark 1991 essay "Looking for My Penis: The Eroticized Asian in Gay Video Porn," Richard Fung contends that gay pornography, in keeping the Asian penis largely off-screen, confines Asian men to the role of passive, emasculated object.[130] Fung points to one extreme of a racialized dichotomy throughout cultural representation that privileges white heterophallicism and objectifies men of color and their penises in polarized terms of excess or lack. Of course, Fung's findings would need to be reevaluated to account for porn's explosion in the internet era and potential shifts in racialized representational norms in that context. But the pattern Fung observes seems both still present and, to a significant degree, applicable to nonpornographic and nongay contexts as well. As evidenced by the texts under discussion here, images of male nudity across a range of film and television enjoy white privilege comparable to that which Fung observes in gay hardcore pornography.

This paradigm is inextricably linked to the fact that the majority of screen images are created by and for white cishet men. Yet it also gestures at how, in the realm of representing male nudity and sex, anxiety about gazing on racialized and queer male bodies trumps the imperative to keep the phallic signifier of white heteromasculinist privilege veiled. Wesley Morris attributes the black penis's exclusion from the recent trend toward casual nudity in film and television to ongoing discomfort with black male sexuality; witness how Robert Mapplethorpe's infamous "Black Males" series, exhibited and published (by St. Martin's Press and titled *Black Book*) in 1986, retains the force of its provocation.[131] It seems the penis of color is profoundly destabilizing to white heterophallicism, exceeding the melodramatic/comic dichotomy's power to defuse the anxiety it produces. *The Crying Game* is a clear exception, but that its penis reveal (by the mixed-race performer Jaye Davidson) proved so excessively melodramatic—diegetically as well as paratextually, given its sensationalized referencing in the film's promotional campaign—clearly depends on Davidson's body being both trans and racialized.

While I would single out representations of male nudity as nonphallic masculinity that feature men of color by filmmakers such as Cui Zi'en, Ferzan Ozpetek, and Tsai Ming-liang, a final example from recent quality television provides a closing thought. In May 2017, the Starz series *American Gods* (Bryan Fuller and Michael Green, 2017–) based on Neil Gaiman's novel, depicted a sex scene between two Muslim men, one from Oman (a country where homosexuality is criminalized) and the other a genie-like mythical character who grants him his most desired wish (1.3, "Head Full of Snow"). *Vulture* estimated the scene to be "arguably the most erotic and explicit guy-on-guy sex scene ever aired on a mainstream American television show."[132] Though its portrayal of supernatural sex and its incorporation of computer-generated imagery to manifest its full-frontal displays (and the money shot that follows) adds a wrinkle to my argument in favor of naturalistic displays of male bodies and sex, this scene ultimately suggests that to represent male nudity as nonphallic masculinity—to make the penis more real—may involve diverging from the real. Alternatively, the scene might suggest that the taboo of screening full-frontal nudity and sex between men of color can only be transgressed through representation that is itself unreal.

NOTES

1. Three additional reality series premised around nudity premiered in 2013: Discovery Channel's survival series *Naked and Afraid*; TLC's *Buying Naked*, featuring nudists' search for real estate in Florida; and Syfy's *Naked Vegas*, about body painters working on the Vegas Strip; all use visual blurring to obscure genitalia. The male escort reality series *Gigolos* (Showtime, 2011–) and reality dating show *Naked Attraction* (UK Channel 4, 2016–) each feature unmasked full-frontal male (and female) nudity. Regarding the publicity around Bieber and Hamm, see Lauren Johnson, "This GIF Shows You Just How Photoshopped Justin Bieber's Calvin Klein Ads Were," *Adweek*, January 9, 2015, https://www.adweek.com/creativity/gif-shows-you-just-how-photoshopped-justin-biebers-calvin-klein-ads-were-162280/; Stephanie Marcus, "Jon Hamm Asks That You Please Stop Talking about His Penis," *Huffington Post*, April 23, 2014, https://www.huffpost.com/entry/jon-hamm-penis_n_5200589.

2. See Julie Miller, "Tom Hardy Is Filming a Period Adventure Drama in the Nude," *Vanity Fair*, February 9, 2016, https://www.vanityfair.com/hollywood/2016/02/tom-hardy-nude-taboo.

3. Ben Travers, "'The Leftovers' Longest Running Joke: A Timeline of Every Reference to Justin Theroux's Penis," *Indiewire*, May 29, 2017, https://www.indiewire.com/2017/05/the-leftovers-justin-theroux-penis-every-dick-joke-timeline-1201833541/.

4. Maria Elena Fernandez, "Why Full-Frontal Nudity Was All Over TV in 2015," *Vulture*, December 22, 2015, https://www.vulture.com/2015/12/full-frontal-male-nudity-was-all-over-tv-in-2015.html.

5. For an indication of how the penis's role was played up in the film's publicity, see Oliver Gettell, "Ryan Reynolds on the Man Who Made His 'Penis Look Perfect' in *Deadpool*," *Entertainment Weekly*, February 10, 2016, https://ew.com/article/2016/02/10/ryan-reynolds-deadpool-makeup-penis-look-perfect/.

6. For a history of the midcentury transformations in film censorship, see Jon Lewis, *Hollywood v. Hard Core: How the Struggle over Censorship Created the Modern Film Industry* (New York: New York University Press, 2002).

7. Peter Lehman, "Crying Over the Melodramatic Penis: Melodrama and Male Nudity in Films of the 90s," in *Masculinity: Bodies, Movies, Culture*, ed. Lehman (New York: Routledge, 2001), 27.

8. Peter Lehman, *Running Scared: Masculinity and the Representation of the Male Body*, new ed. (Detroit: Wayne State University Press, 2007), 125–26. Lehman's statement quoted in this chapter's epigraph appears on page 237.

9. Lehman, "Crying Over the Melodramatic Penis," 33.

10. Elizabeth Stephens, "The Spectacularized Penis: Contemporary Representations of the Phallic Male Body," *Men and Masculinities* 10, no. 1 (2007): 87–88.

11. Quoted in Lauren Rosewarne, *American Taboo: The Forbidden Words, Unspoken Rules, and Secret Morality of Popular Culture* (Santa Barbara, CA: Praeger, 2013), 189.

12. Lehman, *Running Scared*, 11.

13. Lehman cited in Stephens, "The Spectacularized Penis," 86.

14. The cable television programming under discussion herein all received a rating of TV-MA, or for mature audiences only, the equivalent of a film's R rating by the Motion Picture Association of America.

15. Lehman, *Running Scared*, 6.

16. Lehman, "Crying Over the Melodramatic Penis," 26.

17. See Maria San Filippo, *The B Word: Bisexuality in Contemporary Film and Television* (Bloomington: Indiana University Press, 2013), 152–201.

18. For analyses of the male buddy film cycle's transformation from the late 1960s forward, see Cynthia J. Fuchs, "The Buddy Politic," in *Screening the Male: Exploring Masculinities in the Hollywood Cinema*, ed. Steven Cohan and Ina Rae Hark (New York: Routledge, 1993), 194–210. See also Robin Wood, "From Buddies to Lovers," in *Hollywood from Vietnam to Reagan . . . and Beyond* (New York: Columbia University Press, 2003), 198–218.

19. Other bromances that venture into full-frontal male territory include *Borat* (Larry Charles, 2006), *Blockers* (Kay Cannon, 2018), *The Hangover Part II* (Todd Phillips, 2011), *Harold and Kumar Escape from Guantanamo Bay* (Jon Hurwitz and Hayden Schlossberg, 2008), *Unfinished Business* (Ken Scott, 2015), and *Walk Hard: The Dewey Cox Story* (Jake Kasdan, 2007).

20. Lehman, *Running Scared*, 129.

21. On the aim of belittling undersize penises, Lehman writes, "If pornography affirms the penis as the glorious phallus, penis-size jokes ridicule those penises that, although invisible in representation, fall short of maintaining the sight of the penis as a dramatic spectacle." Ibid., 237.

22. Peter Lehman and Susan Hunt, *Lady Chatterley's Legacy in the Movies: Sex, Brains, and Body Guys* (New Brunswick, NJ: Rutgers University Press, 2010), 161–66. The quote by Judd Apatow in this chapter's epigraph appears on page 161.

23. See San Filippo, *The B Word*, 199–201.

24. See, for example, Jada Yuan, "Adam Scott and Jason Schwartzman on Their Sundance Comedy *The Overnight* and Prosthetic Penises," *Vulture*, January 26, 2015, https://www.vulture.com/2015/01/scott-and-schwartzman-on-the-overnight-penises.html.

25. Lehman and Hunt, *Lady Chatterley's Legacy*, 23.

26. Lehman, "Crying Over the Melodramatic Penis," 33, 35.

27. Richard Corliss, "Sex and *Shame* in Venice: Michael Fassbender Is a Real X-Man," *Time*, September 5, 2011, http://content.time.com/time/arts/article/0,8599,2091805,00.html.

28. Alistair Fox, "The New Anglo-American Cinema of Sex Addiction," in *Transgression in Anglo-American Cinema*, ed. Joel Gwynne (New York: Columbia University Press, 2016), 21.

29. McQueen quoted in Alex Bilmes, "Inside Shame," *Esquire*, January 14, 2012, https://www.esquire.com/uk/culture/film/news/a965/the-long-read-inside-shame/. For discussion of Mulligan's nudity, see Kira

Cochrane, "Carey Mulligan: 'I Haven't Seen Myself in the Mirror for a Decade,'" *Guardian*, January 15, 2012, https://www.theguardian.com/film/2012/jan/15/carey-mulligan-naked-mirror-decade; Melena Ryzik, "Transforming a Body—And a Performance," *New York Times*, January 5, 2012, https://carpetbagger.blogs.nytimes.com/2012/01/05/transforming-a-body-and-a-performance/.

30. Quoted in Pamela McClintock, "Fassbender on Fire," *Hollywood Reporter*, January 18, 2012, https://www.hollywoodreporter.com/news/thr-cover-michael-fassbender-shame-nudity-dangerous-method-282859.

31. Lehman and Hunt, *Lady Chatterley's Legacy*, 124–25.

32. Lehman, "Crying Over the Melodramatic Penis," 37.

33. Alexandra Juhasz, "The Phallus UnFetishized: The End of Masculinity as We Know It in Late-1990s 'Feminist' Cinema," in *The End of Cinema as We Know It: American Film in the Nineties*, ed. Jon Lewis (New York: New York University Press, 2001), 211, 213.

34. References to television episodes throughout are cited with the season and episode numbers, separated by a period, and the title of the episode.

35. See So Mayer, "In Praise of Soft Cock," *cléo: A Journal of Film and Feminism* 5, no. 1 (2017), cleojournal.com/2017/04/20/praise-soft-cock/.

36. Linda Ruth Williams, *The Erotic Thriller in Contemporary Cinema* (Bloomington: Indiana University Press, 2005), 4. After first mention, I refer to L. R. Williams to distinguish her from Linda Williams, also quoted herein.

37. Douglas Keesey, "They Kill for Love: Defining the Erotic Thriller as a Film Genre," *CineAction*, no. 56 (2001): 46.

38. Nina K. Martin, *Sexy Thrills: Undressing the Erotic Thriller* (Urbana: University of Illinois Press, 2007), 6.

39. L. R. Williams, *The Erotic Thriller in Contemporary Cinema*, 193.

40. Ibid., 107.

41. See Mary Ann Doane, "Film and the Masquerade: Theorising the Female Spectator," in *The Sexual Subject: A Screen Reader on Sexuality* (New York: Routledge, 1992), 227–43; see also Linda Williams, "When the Woman Looks," in *The Dread of Difference: Gender and the Horror Film*, ed. Barry Keith Grant (Austin: University of Texas Press, 1996), 15–34.

42. *In the Cut* [unrated] DVD commentary by director Jane Campion and producer Laurie Parker, Sony Pictures Home Entertainment, 2003.

43. Lehman, *Running Scared*, 19.

44. Peter Lehman and Susan Hunt, "*Californication*: Trouble in Body Guy Paradise," *Flow*, 2008, www.flowjournal.org/2008/12/californication-trouble-in-body-guy-paradise-peter-lehman-arizona-state-university-susan-hunt-santa-monica-college/.

45. Lehman and Hunt, *Lady Chatterley's Legacy*, 6, 23.

46. Ibid., 69.

47. Sue Thornham, "'Starting to Feel Like a Chick': Re-visioning Romance in *In the Cut*," *Feminist Media Studies* 7, no. 1 (2007): 33–46.

48. See ibid.

49. *Stranger by the Lake* proved moderately successful not only on the art house circuit but with video-on-demand distribution via streaming platforms, particularly in the United Kingdom, where it received a near day-and-date release. A British Film Institute insight report found this to be an effective means of reaching the target LGBTQ+ audience (and, to lesser degree, a crossover audience), especially where sexually explicit material is concerned. See Peter Buckingham and Michael Gubbins (Sampo Media), "Insight Report: *Stranger by the Lake*," BFI, February 19, 2015, www.bfi.org.uk/sites/bfi.org.uk/files/downloads/bfi-insight-report-stranger-by-the-lake-2015-02-19.pdf.

50. The UK theater chain Cineworld canceled screenings of *Stranger by the Lake* just ahead of its planned premiere, only to reinstate them the next day after an ensuing social media protest. Of course, negative responses from gay-identified viewers to what was considered the film's retrograde politics did not go unsounded, though they came predominantly from the lower reaches of web comments and blog posts than from top-shelf gay publications. Anecdotally, in the discussion session that followed my presenting a paper on *Stranger by the Lake* at the 2016 Society for Cinema and Media Studies Conference, I was upbraided by an audience member who insisted the film is irretrievably homophobic.

51. Noah A. Tsika, *Pink 2.0: Encoding Queer Cinema on the Internet* (Bloomington: Indiana University Press, 2016), 91.

52. Susan Bordo, *The Male Body: A New Look at Men in Public and Private* (New York: Farrar, Straus and Giroux, 1999), 18.

53. Distributor Goldwyn Films reportedly cut the film's sex scenes (without consulting filmmaker Lee, whose protests on Twitter resulted in the scenes' restoration) in an attempt to increase visibility and thereby streaming revenue by bypassing Amazon Prime Video's block against making sexually explicit material available free of rental charge to subscribers. Zack Sharf, "'God's Own Country' Director Criticizes

Distributor for Censoring Gay Sex Scenes on Prime Video," *Indiewire*, May 20, 2020, https://www.indiewire.com/2020/05/gods-own-country-director-amazon-prime-censored-movie-1202232433/.

54. Gary Needham, "Closer Than Ever: Contemporary French Cinema and the Male Body in Close-Up," in *Mysterious Skin: Male Bodies in Contemporary Cinema*, ed. Santiago Fouz-Hernández (London: I. B. Tauris, 2009), 129.

55. See Liz Beardsworth, "What to Say about *Stranger by the Lake*," *Empire*, February 21, 2014, https://www.empireonline.com/movies/features/say-strangers-lake/.

56. See Peter Lehman and Susan Hunt, "From Casual to Melodramatic: Changing Representations of the Penis in Films of the 70s and 90s," *Framework* 40 (Spring 1999): 69–84.

57. Andrew Spicer, *Film Noir* (London: Longman, 2002), 89.

58. L. R. Williams, *The Erotic Thriller in Contemporary Cinema*, 125.

59. Martin, *Sexy Thrills*, 18.

60. Spicer, *Film Noir*, 90.

61. Max Cavitch, "Sex after Death: François Ozon's Libidinal Invasions," *Screen* 48, no. 3 (Autumn 2007): 313.

62. L. R. Williams, *The Erotic Thriller in Contemporary Cinema*, 1.

63. Richard Dyer, *Only Entertainment*, 2nd ed. (New York: Routledge, 2002), 142.

64. Linda Williams, "Cinema's Sex Acts," *Film Quarterly* 67, no. 4 (2014): 19.

65. Tsika, *Pink 2.0*, 103.

66. L. R. Williams, *The Erotic Thriller in Contemporary Cinema*, 33.

67. Wesley Morris, "After Normal: *Looking*, Michael Sam, and the State of Gay Culture," *Grantland*, February 21, 2014, grantland.com/features/after-normal/.

68. Tim Dean, *Unlimited Intimacy: Reflections on the Subculture of Barebacking* (Chicago: University of Chicago Press, 2009), 107.

69. Timothy Corrigan, *A Cinema without Walls: Movies and Culture after Vietnam* (New Brunswick, NJ: Rutgers University Press, 1991), 78.

70. In reading "erotic thrillers of the 1980s and 1990s [as] metaphors for the dangers of sex in the time of AIDS," Hirsch (like the film cycle he discusses) was concerned predominantly with hetero "sexually misbehaving characters." Foster Hirsch, *Detours and Lost Highways: A Map of Neo-Noir* (New York: Limelight, 1999), 189. Guiraudie's *Du soleil pour les gueux* (*Sunshine for the Poor*, 2001) also contains an allegorical reference to AIDS

in its protagonist's search for (mythical) animals she calls *"les ounayes,"* described as gentle creatures except when sick, when they briefly survive by feeding on human blood before dying young.

71. This remark was part of Kramer's address at Cooper Union Hall on November 21, 2004, published as the book *The Tragedy of Today's Gays* (New York: Tarcher, 2005). Until his death in 2020, the HIV-positive Kramer, who cofounded AIDS activist group ACT UP, had long been controversial for his outspoken derision of what he considered reckless sexual endangerment in the gay community.

72. Guiraudie leaves unresolved whether Michel's reluctance to extend his relationship with Franck past the lake's confines is due to his being closeted or disinclined to monogamy or both. The experimental documentary *Interior. Leather Bar.* (James Franco and Travis Mathews, 2013) aims at a similar decoding of *Cruising's* pleasures and perils for queer spectatorship.

73. José B. Capino, "Seminal Fantasies: Wakefield Pool, Pornography, Independent Cinema and the Avant-Garde," in *Contemporary American Independent Film*, ed. Chris Holmlund and Justin Wyatt (New York: Routledge, 2005), 155–56.

74. See Thornham, "'Starting to Feel Like a Chick.'"

75. Dyer, *Only Entertainment*, 146.

76. Dean, *Unlimited Intimacy*, 45.

77. L. R. Williams, *The Erotic Thriller in Contemporary Cinema*, 39; Tsika, *Pink 2.0*, 26.

78. Quoted in Ben Davies and Jana Funke, eds., *Sex, Gender, and Time in Fiction and Culture* (Basingstoke, UK: Palgrave Macmillan, 2011), 9.

79. Morris, "After Normal."

80. Quoted in Georges Bataille, *Erotism: Death and Sensuality*, trans. Mary Dalwood (San Francisco: City Lights, 1986), back cover.

81. Karl Schoonover and Rosalind Galt, *Queer Cinema in the World* (Durham, NC: Duke University Press, 2016), 216.

82. Gayle Rubin, "Thinking Sex: Notes for a Radical Theory of the Politics of Sexuality," in *Culture, Society and Sexuality: A Reader*, 2nd ed., ed. Richard Parker and Peter Aggleton (New York: Routledge, 2007), 152; Leo Bersani, *Is the Rectum a Grave? And Other Essays* (Chicago: University of Chicago Press, 2010), 34.

83. Lauren Berlant and Michael Warner use the term *sexual publics* to signify how sex and intimacy are regulated to maintain privacy and privatization for heterosexuality, whereas homosexuality is policed and punished according to justifications of public decency. See Berlant and Warner, "Sex in Public."

84. Dean, *Unlimited Intimacy*, 177; emphasis added.
85. Stephens, "The Spectacularized Penis," 94–95.
86. Quoted in Lee Edelman, *No Future: Queer Theory and the Death Drive* (Durham, NC: Duke University Press, 2004), back cover.
87. Ibid., 210.
88. Quoted in Beardsworth, "What to Say about *Stranger By The Lake*."
89. Janet McCabe and Kim Akass, "Sex, Swearing and Respectability: Courting Controversy, HBO's Original Programming and Producing Quality TV," in *Quality TV: Contemporary American Television and Beyond*, ed. McCabe and Akass (London: I. B. Tauris, 2007). Premium cable refers to subscription-based channels, whereas basic cable refers to commercial-dependent channels. In the United States, neither is under the domain of the Federal Communications Commission, which is empowered to regulate content and language on network channels and AM/FM radio.
90. See Marc Leverette, Brian L. Ott, and Cara Louise Buckley, eds., *It's Not TV: Watching HBO in the Post-Television Era* (New York: Routledge, 2008).
91. See Hannah Mueller, "'Jupiter's Cock!' Male Nudity, Violence and the Disruption of Voyeuristic Pleasure in Starz' *Spartacus*," in *The New Peplum: Essays on Sword and Sandal Films and Television Programs Since the 1990s*, ed. Nicholas Diak (Jefferson, NC: McFarland, 2017), 135–54.
92. Hannah Mueller, "'At Least Let Us See Them Before You Cut Them All Off!' The Gendered Representation of Nudity in Contemporary Quality TV," in *Contemporary Quality TV: The Auteur, the Fans, and Constructions of Gender*, ed. Ralph J. Poole and Saskia Fürst (Heidelberg: Universitätsverlag Winter, forthcoming). Steve Neale's work on another *Spartacus* turns up a similar pattern of the male body exposed only to be punished, finding it to be a homophobic response aimed at destroying the body's attractiveness to punish the viewer with visual displeasure. See Steve Neale, "Masculinity as Spectacle," *Screen* 24, no. 6 (1983): 2–16.
93. See, for example, Kelli Marshall, "The Anatomical Part Mysteriously Missing from 'Masters of Sex,'" *Alternet*, September 29, 2014.
94. See, for example, E. Alex Jung, "*Westworld*'s Simon Quarterman Thinks Every Actor Should Try Full-Frontal Nudity," *Vulture*, April 22, 2018, https://www.vulture.com/2018/04/westworld-season-2-simon-quarterman-interview.html.
95. Mike Hale, "'Euphoria' Review: HBO Raises the Stakes on Teenage Transgression," *New York Times*, June 14, 2019, https://nyti.ms/2Xbf4AB. *Euphoria* immediately came under fire for what the conservative watchdog

group the Parents Television Council alleged is "grossly irresponsible programming."

96. See Ralph J. Poole, "Wasting God's Gift? The Ruined City and the 'Melodramatic Penis,'" *Anglia* 132, no. 2 (2014): 310–35.

97. Lehman, *Running Scared*, x.

98. McCabe and Akass, "Sex, Swearing and Respectability," 70.

99. One additional instance of male full-frontal nudity occurs across the show's run, when Marnie's (Allison Williams) newlywed husband Desi (Ebon Moss-Bachrach) briefly appears naked, though because he's in the background of the shot and framed in Hannah's Skype screen as she talks to Marnie, it lacks the immediacy or bluntness of the moments featuring Tad Horvath and Chuck Palmer, respectively (5.3, "Japan"). Dunham's father, Carroll Dunham, is an abstract painter known for his cartoonishly exaggerated images of penises—a representational strategy opposite that of his daughter's, but one that I would argue offers a similar demystification of the phallus.

100. Quoted in Andrew Goldman, "Grumpus Maximus," *New York Times*, June 17, 2011, https://www.nytimes.com/2011/06/19/magazine/inside-the-bald-angry-head-of-louis-ck.html.

101. Quoted in Fernandez, "Why Full-Frontal Nudity Was All Over TV in 2015."

102. Quoted in ibid.

103. Quoted in Charlie Mason, "*The Leftovers*' Boss: 'There's No Excuse Not to Show More Dongs' on Television," *TVLine*, June 4, 2017, https://tvline.com/2017/06/04/the-leftovers-justin-theroux-naked-nudity-full-frontal/.

104. Kyle Buchanan, "Looking at 'Looking': How the HBO Series Reexamined Itself for Season 2," *New York*, December 29, 2014, https://www.vulture.com/2014/12/how-looking-reexamined-itself-for-season-2.html.

105. J. Bryan Lowder, "Why Is *Looking* So Boring?" *Slate*, January 21, 2014, https://slate.com/human-interest/2014/01/looking-hbos-gay-show-is-boring-and-bad-for-gays-straights.html; Tim Teeman, "Yes, *Looking* Is Boring. It's the Drama Gays Deserve," *Daily Beast*, January 24, 2014, http://www.thedailybeast.com/yes-looking-is-boring-its-the-drama-gays-deserve.

106. Lowder, "Why Is *Looking* So Boring?"

107. Rich Juzwiak, "*Looking*? Mmmmm, Maybe Another Time," *Gawker*, January 17, 2014, https://gawker.com/looking-mmmmm-maybe-another-time-1502622759.

108. Anthony Tommasini, "Looking for a Breakthrough? You'll Have to Wait," *New York Times*, January 14, 2001, https://www.nytimes.com/2001/01/14/arts/television-radio-looking-for-a-breakthrough-you-ll-have-to-wait.html.
109. Ibid.
110. Wesley Morris, "After Normal."
111. See Candace Moore, "Getting Wet: The Heteroflexibility of Showtime's *The L Word*," *Cinema Journal* 46, no. 4 (2007): 3–23.
112. McCabe and Akass, "Sex, Swearing and Respectability," 66.
113. See Marc Leverette, "Cocksucker, Motherfucker, Tits," in *It's Not TV*, ed. Marc Leverette, Brian L. Ott, and Cara Louise Buckley (New York: Routledge, 2008), 136–37.
114. See Clinton Glenn, "British Social Realism and Queerness in Andrew Haigh's *Looking* (2011)," *Journal of Interdisciplinary Studies in Sexuality* 1 (2013): 75–83.
115. Justin Moyer, "On the Political Necessity of Seeing a Gay Man's Erection on HBO," *Slate*, January 29, 2014, https://slate.com/human-interest/2014/01/why-doesnt-looking-hbos-gay-show-show-real-queer-sex-or-erections.html.
116. The ad circulated in advance of the season one finale. Mister bills itself as for those interested in finding long-term love, in opposition to hook-up app Grindr. See Matthew Tharrett, "How Big Is Your Favorite 'Looking' Man?" *Queerty*, March 7, 2014, https://www.queerty.com/how-big-is-your-favorite-looking-man-20140307.
117. Quoted in Jeremy Kinser, "Looking's Daniel Franzese on His HIV-Positive Bear Character, Being Completely Naked on Screen and Why He Came Out Publicly," *Queerty*, January 11, 2015, https://www.queerty.com/lookings-dan-franzese-on-his-hiv-positive-bear-character-being-completely-naked-on-screen-and-why-he-came-out-publicly-20150111.
118. Mueller, "'At Least Let Us See Them.'"
119. Quoted in Buchanan, "Looking at 'Looking,'" 90.
120. Quoted in Kevin Fallon, "How *Looking* Helped Jonathan Groff," *Daily Beast*, July 20, 2016, http://www.thedailybeast.com/how-looking-helped-jonathan-groff-learn-to-like-being-gay.
121. See ibid.
122. Peter Knegt, "'Looking' in the Mirror: Mourning the Loss of Television's Great Gay Catharsis," *Indiewire*, March 25, 2015, https://www.indiewire.com/2015/03/looking-in-the-mirror-mourning-the-loss-of-televisions-great-gay-catharsis-215569/; Daniel Wenger, "'Looking,'

Marriage, and the New Gay Sadness," *New Yorker*, March 22, 2015, https://www.newyorker.com/culture/culture-desk/looking-marriage-and-the-new-gay-sadness.

123. Brandon Norwalk, "HBO Should Renew *Looking*, Even Though Nobody Watches," *AV Club*, March 9, 2015, https://tv.avclub.com/hbo-should-renew-looking-even-though-nobody-watches-1798277314.

124. As of 2019, a year after the Motion Picture Association of America reported that the number of subscribers to streaming services had surpassed the number of cable subscribers globally, Netflix is in the lead with a reported 155 million subscribers worldwide. Deploying its over-the-top streaming service HBO NOW to contend with the cord-cutters and cord-nevers among the viewing populace, HBO reported having 142 million subscribers globally in 2018 and is vying chiefly with Netflix and Amazon, which reported 100 million Prime subscribers in 2018.

125. Tony Kelso, "And Now No Word from Our Sponsor: How HBO Puts the Risk Back into Television," in *It's Not TV*, ed. Marc Leverette, Brian L. Ott, and Cara Louise Buckley (New York: Routledge, 2008), 49; emphasis in original.

126. Wenger, "'Looking,' Marriage, and the New Gay Sadness."

127. Ironically, Daly gained legibility as the more butch-looking of the pair only after former costar Meg Foster, the performer originally cast as Cagney, was replaced by ABC studio executives concerned that she appeared too "dykey," alongside other changes made to tone down the lesbian connotations of the series. See Julie D'Acci, "Defining Women: The Case of *Cagney and Lacey*," in *Private Screenings: Television and the Female Consumer*, ed. Lynn Spigel and Denise Mann (Minneapolis: University of Minnesota Press, 1992), 168–201.

128. In addition to Latinx leads Frankie J. Alvarez and Raúl Castillo, *Looking*'s recurring cast features two Black actors, O-T Fagbenle (who plays Agustín's boyfriend Frank in season one) and Bashir Salahuddin (who plays Malik, the boyfriend of Doris [Lauren Weedman] in season two), along with Asian American actor Andrew Law (who plays Patrick's work buddy Owen).

129. For a study of male cinematic embodiment with a global scope and focus on ethnic/national identities, see Santiago Fouz-Hernández, ed., *Mysterious Skin: Male Bodies in Contemporary Cinema* (London: I. B. Tauris, 2009).

130. See Richard Fung, "Looking for My Penis: The Eroticized Asian in Gay Video Porn," in *How Do I Look? Queer Film and Video*, ed. Bad Object-Choices (Seattle: Bay Press, 1991), 145–68.

131. See Wesley Morris, "Last Taboo: Why Pop Culture Just Can't Deal with Black Male Sexuality," *New York Times*, October 27, 2016, https://www.nytimes.com/interactive/2016/10/30/magazine/black-male-sexuality-last-taboo.html?_r=0.

132. Abraham Riesman, "Bryan Fuller Demanded a Reshoot of *American Gods*' Gay Sex Scene Because It Wasn't Gay Enough," *Vulture*, May 14, 2017, https://www.vulture.com/2017/05/american-gods-gay-sex-scene-bryan-fuller.html.

PART II

Provoc*auteurs*

THREE

Art Porn Provoc*auteurs*

Feminist Critique through Corp*oreality* in the Work of Catherine Breillat and Lena Dunham

> There are certain things that are forbidden for women. I want to show these things, explore them beyond their limits.... If you consider that this is a provocation, this is what I do.
>
> Catherine Breillat

> My goal is to have a sexual verisimilitude that has heretofore not been seen.... I felt that the depictions of sex I had seen on television weren't totally fair to young women trying to wrap their brains around this stuff. I didn't do it to be provocative. I did it to be educational.
>
> Lena Dunham

AS EVIDENCED BY THE QUOTES ABOVE, Breillat's and Dunham's reluctance to describe their work as provocative speaks to the questionable connotations the term *provocation* has acquired.[1] However, these pronouncements also point to the possibility of reclaiming the term for feminist ends. As the eldest of the four provoc*auteurs* profiled in part 2, self-proclaimed "pariah of French cinema" Catherine Breillat may be viewed as a godmother of sorts, not only to (as I posit in this chapter) Lena Dunham but to many emergent women filmmakers.[2] Indeed, Desiree Akhavan, whose burgeoning career is examined in the next chapter, cites Breillat as a key influence.[3] Breillat greeted the millennium with the one-two punch of her controversial international hit *Romance* and long-delayed debut feature *Une vraie jeune fille* (*A Real Young Girl*, produced 1976), released in 1999 and 2000, respectively. The works compose part of what Breillat calls her "*décalogue*" of films devoted to exploring women's sexual experience.

American writer–filmmaker–television series creator Lena Dunham blazed a path beginning with the viral sensation of her 2007 YouTube video *The Fountain,* made while an Oberlin College undergraduate, which featured her clad in a bikini and bathing in a campus water feature. It continued with her postcollegiate inertia and squalid sex "in a pipe in the street" in breakout feature *Tiny Furniture* (2010); her frequent on-screen nudity and cringe-inducing sex scenes as Hannah Horvath on HBO's *Girls* (2012–17); her 2014 memoir's *Not That Kind of Girl*, which redefines the term *tell-all*; and her post-*Girls* penchant for public utterances that go viral on the strength of outraged callouts of her unexamined privilege.[4]

The concept of provocation has been central to the discourse on Breillat from the beginning; one would be hard-pressed to find a discussion of her that does not at some point characterize her work as provocative. Dunham has established herself as arguably the most provocative voice of her generation or, to echo the self-appellation of her *Girls*' alter ego, Hannah, while in an opium-induced haze of egomania in the series' pilot, as "the voice of my generation. Or at least, *a* voice of *a* generation." This was the first of many sound bites through which the creator was conflated with her character and the intended ironic self-critique was often overlooked. When I first set out to write on these women's dialogic relationship, the deluge of Dunham studies was not yet upon us, even if the word count devoted to *Girls* in the popular press was already formidable (and has continued to climb). Certainly these are the two figures who come up most consistently when I share this book's topic, with mention of Dunham (who is better known than Breillat in the English-speaking world) routinely eliciting a highly charged response from a broad range of people. As figures whose work consistently explores provocative sexual subjects and whose authorial signatures are indelibly associated with this courting of controversy, Breillat and Dunham embody par excellence my conception of the provoc*auteur*.

As a perusal of the literature on her indicates, Breillat divides audiences as radically as any filmmaker associated with the New French Extremity, the term coined by art critic James Quandt for films whose unflinching, arguably prurient treatment of sexual brutality dominated Gallic cinema at the turn of the 21st century.[5] The voluminous body of scholarship on Breillat reflects admiration of her bold commitment to cine-erotic exploration while also expressing concerns that the work's sexual obsessiveness renders it sensationalist and repetitive and risks reducing women's representation to their sexual selves. Particularly contentious is Breillat's play with imagery that invokes heterosexual pornography. John Phillips finds a "crudely staged and essentially phallocentric female gaze," whereas Gwendolyn Wells sees an "insist[ence] upon the inescapability of the realm of the visual, on the fundamentally gendered nature of the erotic imaginary, and on the complicity with which we inhabit our fantasmatic roles."[6] Such responses exemplify the impassioned dismissals and defenses of Breillat's work with regard to the question of feminism. It is a question frequently raised, including by Breillat herself, who asserts her reluctance to politicize representation with pronouncements such as, "I'm a feminist, but not in my films."[7] These conflicting critical responses to Breillat's work also gesture at its opacity. Helen Hester notes how "the director's explicitness continually turns away from its own apparent course and agenda," creating an "elusive and inaccessible" quality that is itself perverse.[8] What Hester proposes as a profound obstacle in interpreting Breillat's work I see originating in a provocatively nonprescriptive yet nonetheless feminist approach to representing women's bodies and sexual subjectivities—an approach that Dunham, in her different register, shares.

As has been cataloged (and decried) ad infinitum, *Girls* focuses on the messy lives of four expensively educated, underemployed, white, cisgender, (mostly) heterosexual twentysomethings in New York City. The characters include struggling writer Hannah, whose anxieties often vie with her aspirations; beautifully poised, if often for a fall, "gallerina" turned singer-songwriter Marnie Michaels (Allison Williams); flighty bohemian Jessa Johansson (Jemima Kirke); and Jessa's sexually naive cousin Shoshanna Shapiro (Zosia Mamet). Over its six-season run, *Girls* proved no less divisive than Breillat's work, enjoying Emmy-winning eminence and critical adulation alongside nonstop griping about the entitlement, self-absorption, and lack of diversity of its characters and perspective.

As with Breillat, Dunham's commitment to presenting women's subjectivity as not reducible to but importantly shaped by sexuality has been criticized for its ostensible complicity with sexually objectifying depictions and stereotypes of female masochism. Lamenting Hannah's allegedly regressive fixation on "non-fulfilling, awkward, degrading, and unprotected sex with [hookup-turned-boyfriend] Adam [Adam Driver] and her passive aggressive self-consciousness about her body," Serena Daalmans is one of many who deplore what other critics praise.[9] In *New Yorker* television critic Emily Nussbaum's estimation, Hannah is "raw and bruised, not aspirational."[10] I find furthermore that the portrayals of sex that *Girls* regularly features are deliberately anti-erotic, and posit that Dunham's choice to turn her fleshy torso and personal humiliations (sexual and otherwise) constitutes a feminist critique through corpo*reality*.

Such responses—positive and negative—disproportionately politicized the show and its creator, arguably to a greater extent than any other recent TV series or female celebrity.

Following attacks for assenting to (minimal) airbrushing for her 2014 *Vogue* fashion shoot, Dunham questioned whether hers was "an inherently political body."[11] As her quote at the beginning of this chapter implies, Dunham is more inclined than Breillat to acknowledge the political (or at least educational) intent and valence of her depictions of sex, yet she also, controversially and perhaps counterintuitively, uses supposedly negative and disempowering images of female (self-)degradation, such that a *Saturday Night Live* parody trailer for the second season of *Girls* featured a fake critic's blurb, "If this is feminism, then I'm confused" (39.15, "Lena Dunham/The National").

Against Phillips's and Daalmans's (and many others') criticisms of Breillat and Dunham, I suggest rethinking our approach to these provoc*auteurs*' work by understanding it as simultaneously feminist performance art and an (auto)critique of pornography. Paradoxically, Breillat is accused of being both a pornographer and an antiporn crusader who, in the view of one detractor, "portrays sex under patriarchy as particularly joyless and punitive."[12] Dunham is frequently assessed within frameworks of postfeminism, which is defined in multiple, often competing ways as following from, reacting to, and revising elements of second-wave feminism that are themselves not easily encapsulated. Breillat and Dunham both resist assimilation into any simple framework of contemporary feminism, aligning themselves with aspects of multiple feminisms that are in opposition. Both women defy the austerities of 1980s-style antiporn feminism by embracing strategies that employ women's sexualized bodies. But they do so in ways that run counter to postfeminism's politics of empowerment and autonomy—a politics that implicitly accepts masculinist individualism and whose aspirational striving toward "self-actualization" is at odds with what I will describe as Breillat's and Dunham's anti-aspirational "owning their abjection."

Their shared feminism might be characterized as one of sexual pragmatism, in that it acknowledges the inescapable effects of a culture dominated by women's sexualization and subordination (with conventional pornography as its extreme manifestation) and opts to work within that paradigm as a means to disrupt and critique its representational regime. Both provoc*auteurs*, in my view, aim to critique prescriptive feminism's denunciation of any form of sexual representation deemed negative alongside postfeminism's reconceptualization of sexual subjugation as a strategy of liberation and empowerment. Put another way, Breillat and Dunham point to what "feminist" and "porn" might be (if not what they typically are) in an egalitarian, sex-positive society. In bringing their nonprescriptive feminist ideology to bear on female erotic imagery and subjectivity, Breillat and Dunham stretch the definitional and representational boundaries of what is considered feminist as well as what is considered art and what is considered porn. Through examination of performative self-pronouncements and key works by both artists—Breillat's *A Real Young Girl, Romance, À ma soeur (Fat Girl,* 2001*), Sex Is Comedy* (2002)*,* and *Anatomie de l'enfer (Anatomy of Hell,* 2004) and Dunham's early video shorts, *Tiny Furniture,* and *Girls*—I aim to reveal how their complementary politics of screen representation and self-presentation of bodies and sex constitute a critical feminist art porn.

In their drive, as set out by their respective pronouncements at this chapter's start, to explore that which is forbidden for women and as such goes largely unrepresented on-screen, Breillat and Dunham invert pornography's "frenzy of the visible," the phrase Linda Williams adapts from Jean-Louis Comolli to characterize pornography's fixation with visualizing the ostensible truth of sexual pleasure.[13] As Williams demonstrates, heteronormative pornography obsessively fetishizes male ejaculation as the key signifier of truth, while porn's driving force, its asymptomatically disappearing goal, is the fantasy of capturing the far more elusive visual evidence of the female orgasm. In a related but not identical sense, this is Breillat's and Dunham's aim as well: not only to reveal, as Dunham calls it, "sexual verisimilitude" but to go further to document women's corpo*reality* in ways more visually and ontologically revealing than are typically achieved on-screen. Countering both Hollywood-style imagery and pornography, this critique through corpo*reality* humanizes rather than fetishizes women, revealing what goes unseen and unspoken in typical depictions of female embodiment and erotic intimacy. This chapter explores Breillat's and Dunham's complementary, if distinctive, approaches to defetishizing women through three provocative representational strategies: screening explicit sex to (auto)critique pornography; displaying abject embodiment overtly and affirmatively; and depicting women's self-formation through sexual self-degradation.

On the surface, Breillat's mannered stylization may seem incongruous with Dunham's irony-inflected naturalism. While Breillat often deliberately shapes characters and directs performances to be opaque and stilted, I will explore strategies through which she nevertheless engages spectatorial identification and affect, especially in her most sexually frank scenes. In so doing, Breillat disrupts the fetishizing visual pleasure of so much female embodiment on-screen and renders female sexual subjectivity in humanized, complex forms. In both oeuvres, viewers encounter a heightened form of self-inscription, with the off-screen Breillat's autobiographically informed screenwriting, frequent voicing of her characters' narration, and highly participatory approach to directing blurring the line between author and performer nearly to the same extent as Dunham. Much as Dunham and her *Girls'* alter ego, Hannah, display identical tattoos and other identifying features, Breillat also suggests a degree of nonperformance, or authenticity of character. She casts as her lead actors women who resemble her physically, conceiving them as conduits for her voice and embodied presence, even going so far as to physically arrange performers' body parts on set before shooting. "I am in their bodies," she has said of her performers.[14] The frequent nakedness of those performers, like that of Dunham on-screen, also encourages the audience's perception of their screen presence as a nonperformance. Nudity is seemingly a guarantor of authenticity, with both provoc*auteurs*' predilection for staging explicit sex scenes (rumored to be at times unsimulated in Breillat's case) only enhancing this sense.

The consonance between Breillat and Dunham also transcends, even as it is shaded by, their respective national and industrial contexts. Breillat's films are marketed as art cinema and released theatrically in art houses and are typically unrated due to her reluctance to make cuts demanded by ratings boards. In contrast, Dunham's television work inhabits the infamously permissive quality domain of premium cable channel HBO discussed in chapter 2. Despite the French government's subsidy system for homegrown cinema, known as *l'exception culturelle*, Breillat has complained that "it is never easy to drum up a budget or to find a distributor for my films in France," and her work has not achieved nearly the commercial reach of Dunham's, who, by age thirty, was a multiplatform power player who helmed a multiseason, award-winning US cable series and whose memoir scored a $3.7 million advance from Random House.[15]

No matter how bourgeois-defying, Breillat's and Dunham's provocations rely to a significant extent on their considerable privilege as socioeconomically secure, white, cis heterosexuals. Flaunting that privilege, both women are as well known for self-aggrandizing—and self-justifying—pronouncements as they are for their representational provocations. Breillat asserts unapologetically that, "as an artist, I don't have to be politically correct."[16] Dunham insists (often apologetically of late though still unyieldingly) that "there is nothing gutsier to me than a person announcing that their story is one that deserves to be told, especially if that person is a woman."[17] That both Breillat and Dunham become only more exemplary as provoc*auteurs* with every new dust-up means that to cover with any comprehensiveness their cumulative provocations would far exceed the constraints of one chapter. So while I discuss some of the written and spoken pronouncements that have indelibly informed both artists' provoc*auteur* signatures, I focus primarily on the sexual provocation in their screen representations.

To begin with the most blatantly provocative element of their respective oeuvres, a central concern for and about Breillat and Dunham is their work's relationship to pornography. Breillat in a number of ways encourages the comparison of her work to pornography. At the same time, she articulates in that work socially unacceptable forms of female desire, by implication revealing pornography to be structured by fundamentally socially conforming male-dominant logics. Her creation of genuinely transgressive scenes shows the extent to which, by contrast, the supposed transgressions of porn align with gendered norms. Dunham's relation to porn involves contesting its truth claims by representing forms of sexual realness that fall outside pornographic norms, whether those norms have to do with body type, the verbal accompaniments of intercourse, or the satisfactions or lack thereof that sex yields. In their mutually revisionist models of the gaze, Breillat and Dunham reveal the complicity between mainstream and pornographic modes of representation—a complicity denied by mainstream media.

PROVOKING PORN: SCREENING SEX AS FEMINIST CRITIQUE

"Exploring the nature of sex [allows] me to transcend the usual, horrible images that form the basis of porno films."[18] The openly antagonistic position vis-à-vis pornography Breillat expresses here and elsewhere is buttressed by her self-proclamation as a "sex entomologist."[19] The suggestion is that she seeks to bring to human sexuality the kind of detached gaze an entomologist turns on insects. Such assertions of her scientific power to reveal truth serve as defense of those aspects of her work that seem to some viewers indistinguishable from pornography. As scholars of pornography and its less censurable cousins soft-core and art film have demonstrated, the boundaries that fence off certain classes of films from others are crucially shaped by extratextual determinants of taste, market interest, and pressure from moralist organizations.[20] Breillat offers a succinct definition for a notoriously hard-to-define term: "It is censorship which defines pornography and sets it off from the rest of film."[21] Whereas the hard-core versus soft-core division rests on a determination of the film's degree of sexual explicitness, the division between porn and art cinema is factored aesthetically, with the latter perceived to be less contaminated by prurience or with loftier aspirations in style and meaning. The distinction turns not on what kind of sex can be shown but how it is shown. In Breillat's work, the representational markers of art cinema (experimental aesthetics, narrative ambiguity, and complexity) are intermingled with hard-core elements, making the distinction between art and porn purposely difficult to parse. Yet, as we will see, Breillat's films go further, not merely imitating but aggressively repurposing porn's aesthetic of realness in order to critique porn's sexual truth claims.

I adopt the more specific term *art porn* to signal Breillat's, as well as Dunham's, mode of representationally revisionist critique. In scrutinizing the ways that images construct and control female erotic desire, Breillat and Dunham position themselves in a sometimes uneasy relation to a mode they find troubling, whether for what Breillat describes as its "usual, horrible images" or what Dunham perceives as its worrisome ubiquity for men of her generation, characterized and addressed thusly: "Guys my age watch *so* much pornography. There's no way that you, young Jewish man from Chappaqua, taught this to yourself."[22] Recalling as well David Bordwell's characterization of art cinema as distinguishable from mainstream commercial cinema in its "commitment to both objective and subjective verisimilitude," the concept of a hybridized art porn signals a drive to represent sex and bodies without Hollywood-style sanitizing and masking, with the aim of reaching some greater truth about human desire and relationships.[23] Here, too, representational markers are used to signal opposition to the imitative approach characteristic of art cinema's "hard-core eroticism," with both provoc*auteurs* employing, though in revisionist ways, signifiers of authenticity typically associated with pornographic imagery in their shared quest to screen the truth of sex in the age of porn.[24] For these reasons, which I elaborate on below, I adopt the formulation *art porn* to signal how Breillat and Dunham's art explicitly references pornography's codes to appropriate porn for feminist use. In so doing, they invite (as do I) a questioning of assumptions about categorizations and uses of porn as well as a complicating of the values used to construct and contain art (cinema) and porn as cerebral and carnal, respectively.

The art versus porn debate has dogged Breillat since her first book, an erotic memoir titled *L'homme facile* (*A Man for the Asking*, 1984), was banned in France for readers under age eighteen on grounds of obscenity. In a much-noted irony, Breillat was seventeen at the time of its publication. Born in 1948 and raised in provincial southwest France, Breillat has described a repressively Catholic upbringing in which her parents pulled her and her sister out of school at puberty and confined them to the house, so concerned were they about their daughters' chastity in an era when the birth control pill was not yet available and abortion remained illegal.[25] Until Breillat moved to Paris at age sixteen, her only escape was the library, where she recalls having discovered the works of Bataille and Sade, whose influence is conspicuous throughout her oeuvre.[26] Breillat's notoriety was forged with her earliest films, most notably when the erotic drama *36 fillette* (1988) screened at the New York Film Festival. Featuring an underage girl and middle-aged man, the film received international attention when critics accused it of pandering to pedophilic impulses.[27]

In fact, Breillat had already begun desecrating fantasies of girlhood innocence with her first film, *A Real Young Girl*, based on her fourth novel *Le soupirail* (*The Opening*, 1974). The film was financed by André Génovès, a regular Claude Chabrol collaborator, with the goal of duplicating the commercial success of the French soft-core feature *Emmanuelle* (Just Jaeckin, 1974). Génovès subsequently suppressed *A Real Young Girl*'s distribution, fearing that it would be subject to a newly imposed tax on films classified with an X rating. When the company went bankrupt soon after, the lab retained possession of the negative.[28] There it languished until 2000, when the international recognition received by Breillat's breakout film *Romance* motivated *A Real Young Girl*'s long-overdue release. As indicated by the promotional image of its young protagonist sitting open-legged on railroad tracks, hand covering her exposed crotch, *A Real Young Girl* invites the comparisons that would earn Breillat the moniker "auteur of porn" even as the performer's defiant stare into the camera—a gaze repeatedly taken up by Breillat's female protagonists throughout her cinematic corpus—announces the film's confrontational stance and its disruption of complacent scopophilia (see fig. 3.1).

Openly courting comparison to hard-core pornography, *Romance* broke new ground in the representation of sex in art cinema with a scene of, rumor had it, unsimulated sex featuring, in a rare instance of crossover casting, hard-core performer Rocco Siffredi. Even among his hard-core cohort, this was a provocative choice. As one of the few male performers who can be said to have established a brand, the semiretired star of more than 1,300 films (according to Siffredi's Wikipedia page) is most associated with the "extreme anal" subgenre of heterosexual porn. More provocative still, Breillat reportedly did not reveal this casting decision to *Romance*'s cast and crew until shortly before Siffredi arrived on set, which reportedly unsettled the film's female lead, Caroline Ducey (who plays Marie).[29] Breillat would go on to cast

Fig. 3.1. The image of Alice (Charlotte Alexandra) used to promote *A Real Young Girl*.

Siffredi in her subsequent feature *Anatomy of Hell*, an adaptation of her 2001 novel *Pornocratie*, in a leading role written for him. Surmising about the commercially crippling, if publicity-potent, X rating given to *Romance*, "The X certificate was linked to the X chromosome," Breillat promoted the film with an image of a woman holding her hand between her legs with a red X obscuring the view.[30] She also retitled the film *Romance X* for its stateside release (where it received an R rating after the most explicit shots were masked with optical fogging). In Australian and Japanese markets, an uncensored *Romance* was denied classification and so was effectively banned, while Swedish feminists chained themselves to a theater door to prevent the film's being screened in Stockholm.[31] In the United Kingdom, *Romance* and *The Idiots* (Lars von Trier, 1998) were pivotal in inducing the British Board of Film Classifications to adopt a more liberal rule allowing "real sex" to be shown in eighteen-and-over releases.[32]

As Linda Williams observes, pornography's "frenzy of the visible" generates a focus on male ejaculation, "the money shot," as visual evidence of the immaterial pleasure of sex. Despite Breillat's having twice cast a performer from the straight porn industry known for his impressive endowment and the presence in her work of erect penises (often a key component in determining a film's classification as porn), Breillat's films contain none of the female performance of awe at the male member, a requisite response to phallic display in heterocentrist pornography. What attention the penis receives is in the form of scrutiny (or its opposite, studied inattention), both by the female protagonists and Breillat herself. This reversal of the gaze on the part of a woman director results not in objectification of the male member, a simple inversion of mainstream cinema's treatment of the female body, but in its defetishizing. As discussed in chapter 2, this strategy, given the penis's bifurcated representational history as either hypervisible (in porn) or masked (in most other cinematic modes), can work by means of both veiling and revealing. Breillat characteristically opts to show the penis, but in ways that render it absurd (as with the daughter's imagined sight gag of her father's flaccid penis poking out of his pants in *A Real Young Girl*), or fabricated (as with the prosthetic penis crafted for The Actor, played by Grégoire Colin, in *Sex Is Comedy*), or farcical (as with the banana his female director substitutes as a prop in the same film) (see fig. 3.2). In so doing, Breillat compromises the phallus's power as heteronormative signifier. The latter scene confers on Breillat's surrogate, Jeanne (Anne Parillaud), the power to disarm The Actor, who has been jokingly using the prosthetic to undermine her directorial authority. As Douglas Keesey notes, "Jeanne's gaze here is aggressive (devouring), facetious (his penis is but a banana) and possibly desirous (fellation) ... [but] Jeanne's ultimate goal is to see beyond male sexual aggression, to break through machismo and reach the human underneath, to playfully antagonize the other until he becomes worthy of her desire."[33]

In *Anatomy of Hell*, the penis is shown to be unnecessary, and not even particularly conducive, to the female orgasm. In the

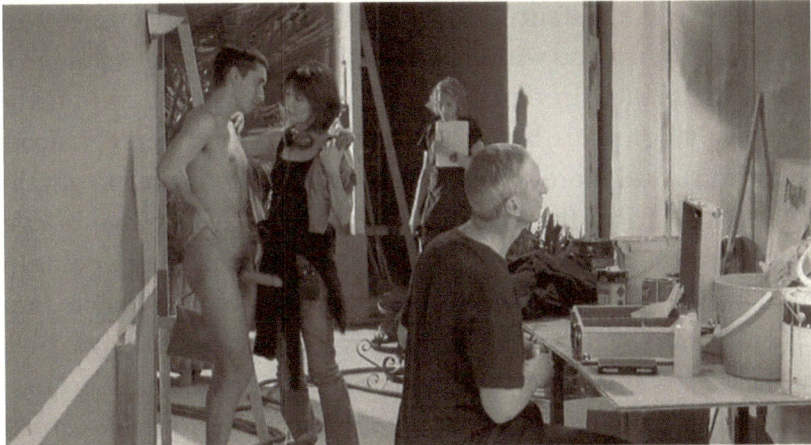

Fig. 3.2. Director Jeanne (Anne Parillaud) supervises The Actor's (Grégoire Colin) prosthesis fitting in *Sex Is Comedy*.

four nights of intimacy shared by Siffredi's character, known only as The Man, and The Woman (Amira Casar) who pays him to accompany her home, the only instance in which she climaxes involves his manipulating a stone dildo inside her while she masturbates. "The Italian Stallion's" (as Siffredi is known in the porn world) manhood has been rendered expendable, as empty a signifier as the inanimate dildo (and less adequate at getting the job done). Breillat's divestiture of the penis from phallic authority and from female pleasure begins playfully enough, with The Man intent on the woman's sexual satisfaction (albeit in return for financial compensation). Over the course of this difficult film, which Breillat conceived as "a real frontal attack on pornography," Breillat repeatedly puts the penis on display to undermine and trouble its connotations of phallic authority.[34] Whereas Siffredi's penis is erect, at its most "porn-like" appearance, during a sadistic rape scene, in a moment of intimate connection between the two, his penis appears covered in her menstrual blood.

At the same time, Breillat offers a further reversal on straight porn's frenzy of the visible by rendering female pleasure as palpably as possible. For instance, a close-up shows fingers inserted into a woman's vagina and withdrawn coated in clear viscous fluid in a scene in *Romance* in which Marie is being pleasured, again without involving a penis, by her boss and older lover Robert (François Berléand). Still more provocatively, given its reference to youthful sexualization, Breillat uses editing to create a visual bridge between a flashback image of young children playing doctor in *Anatomy of Hell* that cuts to The Man inserting his fingers into The Woman's vagina and withdrawing them, again making visible what is typically elided, even in female full-frontal nude scenes: a more up-close and authenticated—even if performed—study of women's sexual anatomy and arousal. Whereas female sexual pleasure is at best unconvincingly pantomimed and at worst nonexistent in straight porn and mainstream sex scenes, Breillat typically recasts male bodies (Siffredi's in particular) nonphallically, making them serve women's fantasies and pleasures.

Breillat extends the French tradition of "philosophy in the bedroom" by injecting female-voiced self-reflection into sex scenes, a strategy that purposefully alienates viewers from such scenes' visual pleasure. In *Romance*, a lengthy monologue is delivered by an introspective Marie during her tryst with pickup Paolo (Siffredi)—a technique that Eleri Butler finds reminiscent of docuporn, "a reality-based entertainment genre that takes pornography as its subject and offers sexual display and sexual talk as its key attractions" (see fig. 3.3).[35] So, too, the viewer's appreciation of women's nude forms is disrupted and their bodies individuated by means of voiced self-examination (as performed by the undressed protagonists of *A Real Young Girl* and *Fat Girl* as they stare at their mirrored reflections). Most uncanny is the way in which Breillat's films, as is the norm in pornography, take place largely "with[in] a space of eroticism removed from everyday reality," as Emma Wilson notices, thus prompting discord between the familiar (exaggeratedly hermetic sex) and the unfamiliar (Breillat's privileging of female subjectivity and her

Fig. 3.3. Philosophy in the bedroom: Marie (Caroline Ducey) and Paolo (porn star Rocco Siffredi) in *Romance*.

defetishizing aesthetic) that disrupts the pleasurable immersion that porn offers.[36]

Against both conventional porn's proffering of realness and Hollywood-style cinema's own brand of highly manipulated "realism," Breillat explicitly reminds us of the illusoriness of images, going so far as to begin *Anatomy of Hell* with this disclaimer: "A film is an illusion, not reality-fiction or a happening; it is a true work of fiction. For the actress's most intimate scenes, a body double was used. It's not her body; it's an extension of a fictional character." Admittedly, this statement was contractually foisted on Breillat by actor Amira Casar to prevent her from being perceived as having had unsimulated sex with Siffredi, yet the intentionally vague language Breillat scripted blurs the question of when precisely the body double was used.[37]

Ironically, since Casar's mandate required shots that obscured the use of a body double, the female form ends up fragmented much as the "meat shots" (genital close-ups) of conventional pornography do. Helen Hester finds Breillat's critique of porn "to some extent compromised" by Breillat's framing of female genitals in extreme close-up even as she notes these shots' "affecting oddness and illegibility." Yet it is precisely the "asignification and disorientation" effect that Hester observes which marks Breillat's opposition to porn, in which such shots aim at an extreme visibility designed to reassure rather than jar the voyeuristically positioned viewer.[38] Breillat's appropriation of porn's meat shots works, then, to defamiliarize their erotic signification. The shots work also, as Martine Beugnet observes, to defamiliarize their gendered signification: "The function and use of the close-up in particular mark a desire to do away with the usual binarisms and blur the frontiers between the inside and outside, masculine and feminine, figurative and abstract, sensory and conceptual, subjective and objective."[39]

Yet another disruptive strategy involves juxtaposing these porn-like close-ups in visual alignment through montage with nonerotic images—for example, ejaculate landing on Marie's stomach followed by a squirt of gel in preparation for an ultrasound examination in *Romance*, a film that ends with a quick succession of provocative, rhymed images: glory holes, beaver shot, a baby crowning during birth. Kelley Conway notes that this montage "underscores with admirable economy, and humor, even, a link between two 'institutions'—porn and medicine—both of which are shown here to render the female body passive, acted upon, and in need of investigation."[40] As with Alain Guiraudie's venture into screening female nudity in *Staying Vertical* (mentioned in chap. 2), here and elsewhere Breillat refuses to uncouple the erotic from the gynecological in representing female embodiment, suggesting the challenges of doing so for real women.

The request made by *Anatomy of Hell*'s The Woman to The Man to "watch me where I'm unwatchable" is tantamount to that which Breillat makes of her audience. Indeed, this film's premise is self-reflexive, in staging a scene predicated on voyeurism, with

The Man acting as the viewer's surrogate in gazing on (but forbidden to touch) a woman laying herself bare. When The Woman undresses and masturbates at length, never breaking gaze with The Man and, by means of the camera's positioning for direct address, we viewers, Breillat robs us of the distanced voyeurism on which narrative cinema's staging of sexual fantasy depends. Breillat also distances the audience from pleasurable immersion in sexual scenes by filming them with discomforting, defetishizing scrutiny and duration. In doing so, Breillat borrows porn's predilection for the long take, well suited for capturing the cinéma vérité of real sex acts. Yet she deploys it less in the service of authentication than distanciation, and the result radically compromises the visual pleasure in sexual performance that porn delivers.

The most memorable long takes in Breillat's oeuvre, two sobering scenes in *Fat Girl* (the first lasting twenty-five minutes, the second five minutes) of virginal teenager Elena (Roxane Mesquida) goaded into anal and then vaginal penetration by the smooth Fernando (Libero De Rienzo), several years her senior, reveal the complex interplay between Breillat's formal strategies and her performers. In the lead-up to the first scene of seduction, as Fernando boasts of having abandoned another woman as punishment for her sexual voraciousness, he balances an ashtray on Elena's prone torso in a telling signal that he regards her merely as an object. In both scenes of sexual intercourse, Breillat abruptly cuts away from the static long take on the fully naked Elena to the tearful face of younger sibling Anaïs (Anaïs Reboux), who is suffering silently on both sisters' behalf across the room, in a visual suggestion of the distance that now separates the two (see fig. 3.4). The combined effect of two atypical elements—the shock cut disrupting Breillat's signature static long take and the emotive moment in Reboux's otherwise impassive performance—encourages audience identification with both sisters. Breillat's careful manipulation of camerawork, editing,

Fig. 3.4. Anaïs (Anaïs Reboux) crying as her sister loses her virginity in the background in *Fat Girl*.

and performance here and elsewhere balances distancation and identification, such that it precludes our (simply) deriving visual pleasure from the scene even as the spectatorial experience is one of affective realism, intensely conveying the sisters' shared suffering. Though it must be stated that what I (and the artists themselves) characterize as deliberately anti-erotic rendering of sex scenes arises from complex artistic motives and, given that arousal is an effect rather than a property of a work, makes any blanket judgment difficult.

Breillat's *Sex Is Comedy* offers a fictionalized reenactment of the making of *Fat Girl*, ostensibly for the purpose of justifying the unorthodox measures Breillat herself takes as a director. Her alter ego Jeanne alternately coaxes and commands the actors into performances she insists are about intimacy rather than titillation. "A 'nude scene' as they say—I hate that expression—always frightens [the actors]," says an exasperated Jeanne, "even though paradoxically it's what made them want to do the film!" Both self-searching and self-serving, the flippantly titled *Sex Is Comedy* ends with an immensely difficult scene in which, again in real time, the actor Roxane Mesquida, playing herself, reenacts the coercive deflowering endured by her *Fat Girl* character. That both scenes are simulated qualifies without nullifying the toll it takes on Mesquida, billed as The Actress, who is (Jeanne reminds her shell-shocked crew) a readily consenting adult and amply compensated but also understandably shaken by the experience. The film closes on Jeanne embracing the sobbing actress in a poignant moment that transcends the film-within-a-film distancing, permitting our identification with the character despite the way in which the film's reflexive techniques restrict our immersion in the diegetic world. The empathy provoked by this scene is a nonmoralizing yet effective means of reminding the audience of the cost of creating such images, even as their creation, Breillat implicitly argues, remains necessary so long as oppressive pornographic images and real-life sexual coercion persist.

Yet given that Asia Argento, star of Breillat's *Une vieille maîtresse* (*The Last Mistress*, 2007), has described Breillat as "the most sadistic and downright evil director I've ever worked with" (in response to Breillat's own impugning of Argento's sexual and professional ethics), Breillat's tactics demand a fuller exploration.[41] Mesquida describes Breillat's directorship in positive terms, saying "I have such confidence in her that I completely let myself go, because I know very well that she will not abandon me." Breillat's remarks convey her own sense of the complexity of the director's role in creating sexually explicit cinema: "I had wanted to show that a film shoot is the pleasure of torment ... when you go to the end of an intimate scene, the actors take an enormous pleasure from it, as does everyone on the set, even if, afterward, no one wants to admit it. We are in a society where you don't want to acknowledge your pleasure. You have to mortify yourself, to say it's not my fault, they pushed me into doing it. Certainly, you have to be pushed into doing it and I am there for that."[42] Breillat's flagrant, if vaguely worded, admission to a directorial approach bordering on (or even constituting) sexual coercion courts controversy to a degree that might be damaging to her provoc*auteur* brand in a culture where consent, defined as freely given and fully and repeatedly articulated, has become the gold standard for distinguishing between acceptable and unacceptable forms of sexual activity. While it raises a complex set of issues that this chapter cannot fully explore, Breillat suggests that the discourse of consent (which one might see as fundamentally connected to free market ideology) might not be fully adequate as a framework for questions of sexual ethics.

Where Breillat provokes consideration of the ethics of creating sexually explicit images in terms of its effects on performers, Dunham's focus is on the ethics of disseminating such images in terms of their effects on viewers and society. Dunham puts questions of consent, and the relations between those questions and the impact of omnipresent pornography, at the center of her work. The frequently discomforting sex scenes in *Girls* probe how porn's normalization and internalization may cloud consensual boundaries between partners and in women's own sexual psyches. As with Breillat's distanciation strategies, Dunham denies the viewer untroubled immersion in these scenes by direct references to their being inspired, and provoked, by porn. An example can be found in the much-discussed dirty talk between Adam and Hannah during *Girls'* first on-screen sex scene. Adam narrates, "I knew when I found you that you wanted it this way. You were a junkie and you were only eleven. And you had your fuckin' Cabbage Patch lunchbox. You're a dirty little whore and I'm going to send you home to your parents covered in cum" (1.2, "Vagina Panic"). Trapped beneath him, Hannah's game yet unconvincing attempt to follow his lead, pleading "Oh, don't do that. They're gonna be so angry," followed by her response to his order to "Touch yourself"—"It's a little hard from this angle"—prove as disruptive to spectatorial immersion (if not to Adam's focus) as that of the midcoitus monologues of Breillat's female protagonists. Afterward, when Hannah jokingly references their role-play, she is met with a blank stare. It is unclear whether Adam is uncomfortable acknowledging his dirty talk outside the moment or whether he feels no need to palliate his fantasy life through ironic dismissal. In this and other scenes of characters' sexual role-play, *Girls* mocks porn's ludicrous scenarios while also signaling how the attraction of its fantasies of the forbidden and the misogynistic demands disavowal. Among the main characters in *Girls*, Adam most fully embodies the effects on Millennial men of porn's proliferation, while Hannah represents women's internalizing of its sexual performances, informed by Dunham's own experience. As she relates, "I got good at performing: back arched, hair flying, assuming attitudes I thought were desirable to a partner who watched either porn or foreign films."[43] This chapter's final section will parse how *Girls* stages scenes of sexual role-play to confront questions of consent, power, and self-knowledge.

As Elaine Blair points out in an early essay on *Girls*, Dunham uses pornographic convention to counter Hollywood's lack of interest "in even hinting at the ways that people actually reach orgasm, [an omission] that is disheartening above all for female viewers.... A dose of porn, judiciously applied by an extremely intelligent director, can save cinematic sex."[44] In connecting *Girls'* sexual naturalism to pornography's aesthetic of realness and arguing for its value to female viewers, Blair encapsulates my own conceptualization of Dunham's work as feminist art porn. This mode made for a highly effective means of situating *Girls* in its HBO milieu, where it clearly aligned with the channel's "sex, swearing and respectability" brand yet also distinguished itself with its awkwardly honest depictions of sex.[45]

Though *Girls* was frequently compared to *Sex and the City* (Darren Star, 1998–2004) in early promotional discourse, the earlier series approached sex in markedly different terms. As Meredith Nash and Ruby Grant note, "For a show that was supposed to more accurately represent single women, viewers rarely, if ever, saw any of the female characters fumble in the bedroom. Sex never involved smudged makeup and the lighting was always perfect. Viewers never saw bodily fluids, stained sheets, or genitals... it is unrealistic that viewers [of *SATC*] never saw the characters in an uncomfortable sexual situation or expressing feelings of ambivalence or guilt about declining sex or more broadly."[46] Along with their more authentic take on urban women's sexual adventuring, the sex scenes in *Girls* also stood apart from those associated with HBO's popularizing of sexposition. Rather than the device of using sex scenes as a titillating backdrop during otherwise visually uninteresting scenes of narrative exposition, Hannah's resistance to "play[ing] the quiet game" during sex (as Adam says in an attempt to silence her in the middle of her explanation of why she declines his request for anal sex, in the series' pilot) operates similarly to Breillat's leading women philosophizing in the bedroom. It creates ironic distance while verbally critiquing the sexual and sexpositioning norms propagated by the pornification of popular culture.

As discussed in chapter 2, at the time that *Girls* was green-lit, HBO was seeking to expand its brand beyond its associations with alpha males and barely clad female eye candy while maintaining its reputation for uncensored irreverence. Clearly, *Girls* proved a boon for the latter, to such a degree that the aforementioned "It's Not Porn, It's HBO" parody ad featured an unmistakable reference to one of *Girls*' many "raw and bruised, not aspirational" (recalling Nussbaum's summation) sex scenes. The show's grrrl-power politics of representation, then, served Dunham's and HBO's rather different goals. The female ensemble of *Girls* broached the walls of HBO's boys' club, providing much-needed diversity beyond the network's roster of "difficult men."[47] As *Looking* would do subsequently for queer male representation, being both of and apart from HBO permitted *Girls* to pivot between the channel's artistic profile and its heterophallic norms, placing the series in much the same liminal space between art cinema and pornography occupied by Breillat's work.

Like Breillat, Dunham's critique of porn targets its heterophallic assumptions, as expressed in her widely retweeted response to the 2013 Hustler hard-core feature *This Ain't Girls XXX*, in which Dunham explained her top three objections to the film:

1. Because *Girls* is, at its core, a feminist action while Hustler is a company that markets and monetizes a male's idea of female sexuality.
2. Because a big reason I engage in (simulated) onscreen sex is to counteract a skewed idea of that act created by the proliferation of porn.
3. Because it grosses me out.[48]

The performer who plays the Hannah-styled character in *This Ain't Girls*, Alex Chance, shares with Dunham an average-size body type and has expressed finding Dunham's celebrity inspiring. Chance responded with a defense articulated in terms of consent: "If I'm in control of what's happening, I don't see any wrongness."[49] Writer-director Stuart Canterbury took a more assertive tack: "It is interesting that Ms Dunham and her supporters are so quick to condemn a movie that nobody has seen yet.... To say that all pornography is anti-feminist is a tired cliché which undermines the right of free sexual choices that a liberated women [sic] can make for herself."[50]

What might have turned into a Twitter storm ended there, but the episode raises the question of the fairness of Dunham's judgment, based as it was entirely on the Hustler brand's reputation for not being female consumer–friendly, and of how different her response would have been had the film been made by a feminist or queer porn producer. Dunham's out-of-hand dismissal of Hustler's parody might seem to mitigate against categorizing her work as art porn, yet her comment clarifies that Dunham, like Breillat, objects not to the existence of porn but to the distorted, antifeminist nature of so much of it and its domination of our sexual imaginary. Dunham's concern stems from a sense that creating sexually explicit images puts one simultaneously in a position of responsibility, given the power of those images, and disempowerment, given one's lack of control over their subsequent manipulation and circulation, particularly in the digital era in which sampling and meme culture alongside rampant piracy work to normalize the re-contexualization of sexually explicit material. Whether legally permissible (as in the case of Hustler's *Girls* parody) or unlawful (as in the recent case involving the BBC Three/Hulu limited series *Normal People* [Lenny Abrahamson and Hettie Macdonald, 2020] and Pornhub), this type of redistribution is in some cases tolerated or even welcomed by the work's original creator(s)—chapter 2's discussion of *Stranger by the Lake* featured one such instance—or are evidently judged not sufficiently favorable to the original work's profitability or reputation to be tolerated.[51]

Dunham would find herself even more directly implicated in this sort of decontextualized reuse of graphic material when the instantly infamous shot, in *Girls*' season four premiere, of Marnie receiving anilingus from boyfriend Desi was turned into a GIF animation that spread virally online on the eve of Allison Williams's star turn as Peter Pan in a live TV special (4.1, "Iowa"). This and another plotline in season five turn on the question of proprietary rights to sexually explicit imagery, suggesting both were tuned in to the outcry at the time around the hacking and posting online of private nude photographs of female celebrities including Selena Gomez and Jennifer Lawrence. In a season five episode, the blanket objection to porn that Dunham made in response to the Hustler parody is displaced onto the male feminists of the show. When Hannah discovers that her boyfriend Fran (Jake Lacy) masturbates to ex-girlfriends' naked selfies, she asks why he would "not just use porn like a normal human male" (5.3, "Japan"). Fran's reply—"Porn is disgusting. Those girls, they're underage, they're on drugs. Many of them have been abused. So, no, that doesn't really get me hard"—appears noble, yet is undercut by Hannah's discovery of his predilection, which she equates with "killing someone then keeping their shrunken head as a trophy." Though clearly not equivalent to the sometimes exploitative practices of porn production or to the phenomenon of "revenge selfies" increasingly making news, Fran's questionable assumption that both former and present girlfriends would consent to his use of these images undermines his antiporn position and leaves him open to Hannah's mockery for having "taken this radical antiporn stance like he's Andrea fucking Dworkin," alluding to the most outspoken hard-liner in feminism's antiporn faction.

Between these two extremes a more moderate viewpoint is voiced, albeit with sarcasm, by Ray (Alex Karpovsky), even as he concedes to Hannah the unseemliness of Fran's habit: "So he's opposed to the enslavement and trafficking of young women. What a monster. The moral underpinnings of your argument are at best, at very best, extremely unclear. But for the record, I think it's very gross." In one of many such moments through *Girls*' run, the show addresses contemporary debates and mores around the production and consumption of sexually explicit images, signaling the link between textual and paratextual discourse through Ray's callback to Dunham's earlier condemnation of Hustler's "gross" parody. This chapter's final section examines how the later seasons of *Girls* often structured plotlines as a means of talking back to critics and viewers. But through repeated references to conventional porn, the series from its start provocatively addressed a fraught cultural fixation with its own apparent obsession with staging explicit sex.

While many of *Girls*' heterosexual sex scenes are deliberately anti-erotic, even farcical, I would ascribe its limited and rather cavalier treatment of lesbian sex not to heteronormativity alone but to an interest in disrupting conventional straight porn's (and that of mainstream media outlets, and especially prestige cable's) fetishization of girl-on-girl scenes. Rather than risk reproducing such scenes' heterophallic address and inauthentic presentation of lesbian eroticism, *Girls* opts to keep its portrayal of intimacies between women focused on female friendship. Scenes that might seem pitched toward lesbian titillation, such as a season two moment in which Jessa joins Hannah in the bathtub, are instead rendered as endearingly comic moments of (over)friendly familiarity. In this case, Hannah confesses to "peeing in every bathtub I've ever been in," and Jessa retaliates with shooting a "snot rocket" in Hannah's direction (2.4, "It's a Shame about Ray"). In a rare instance of explicitly referencing Sapphic eroticism, *Girls* teasingly leads up to and then ruptures straight porn's fantasy of the three-way, in a season one sequence in which Marnie and Jessa kiss under financier Thomas-John's (Chris O'Dowd) lecherous gaze. His attempt both to direct and to get in on the action provokes an indignant Jessa to whisk Marnie out the door, promising their dumbstruck host, "I'm going to go eat her cunt on the sidewalk right now" (2.3, "Bad Friend").

The show's only other instances of lesbian sex—between Jessa and a woman she meets at rehab in season two and Hannah's seduction by a yoga teacher at a spiritual retreat in season five—both end prematurely. The latter, in particular, is pitched in a tone of broad comedy. In both cases, the presumed intention to mock viewer expectations for girl-on-girl action risks appearing to mock lesbianism itself. Although these scenes are in little danger of playing into porn's lesploitation, they could be accused of overcorrecting by never offering viewers the defetishized, naturalistic treatment of lesbian sex that the show regularly gave heterosexual sex. Though it came late and was an exceptional occurrence in the show's run, the season five sex scene between Elijah (Andrew Rannells) and boyfriend Dill (Corey Stoll) accomplished precisely that for male-on-male sex. The scene was particularly noteworthy for the men's face-to-face positioning, which is unusual for mainstream representations of gay male sex (5.4, "Old Loves"). Given the different stakes for screening lesbian versus gay sex, here the show found it more suitable to adopt an affectionate tone that gave gay male eroticism the intimacy it is elsewhere denied. It also harkens back to the show's depictions of the also culturally underrepresented intimacies of female friendship.

Disrupting conventional dichotomies of art versus porn by displaying yet defetishizing the female form in sexualized contexts, Breillat and Dunham foreground women's humanity and sexual subjectivity in opposition to the objectifying norms of conventional pornography and Hollywood-style nudity and sex. Their defamiliarizing strategies for presenting sex on-screen ensure that Breillat's and Dunham's work can be, but is never simply, titillating for the creator or viewer. Breillat's and Dunham's mutual referencing of how porn conventions shape perceptions of women's sexual subjectivities illuminates another key shared characteristic: neither reviles pornography unequivocally or imagines that one could inhabit some unsullied space outside its cultural influence; rather, they both seek to expand and revise its representational contours to feminist ends. My characterization of these provoc*auteurs*' bodies of work as art porn signals my understanding that both artists foreground their critique of porn without denying their own creation of images that share some characteristics of the pornographic. Through the concept of art porn, I hope to contribute to troubling the boundaries between these categories and to demonstrate the ways that these provoc*auteurs* appropriate, (auto)critique, and reshape the erotic energies that fuel both pornography and their own work.

OWNING ONE'S ABJECTION: NUDE PERFORMANCE AND EMBODIMENT

In parallel to their revisions of both pornographic and Hollywood-style models of the gaze and its objects, Breillat and Dunham challenge dominant modes of representation by depicting and affirming women's bodies and desires at their most "unladylike." Kathleen Rowe Karlyn observes that the "unruly woman" of screen comedy subverts patriarchal authority through her anarchic humor and/or excessive (bodily) performance.[52] Dunham's early short films, posted on YouTube and later included as special features on the Criterion Collection DVD of *Tiny Furniture*, preview the performances of bodily abjection, sexual exhibitionism, and self-satire to come. In *Pressure* (2006), filmed in her college library, Dunham's character listens curiously as two female friends discuss orgasms before interjecting to describe a childhood habit of jiggling her finger in her nose in order to experience the subsequent relief of sneezing. Her friends, looking disdainful, desert her in a remote section of the stacks. After a furtive look around, she repeats her cherished ritual and, after a satisfying sneeze, the screen goes to black. This sly nod to the 1894 film *Fred Ott's Sneeze*, the first surviving motion picture to be copyrighted (by its producer Thomas Edison), announced Dunham's penchant for self-exhibitionism aiming at unseating gendered and artistic codes of propriety and preeminence.

Hooker on Campus (2007) has Dunham tarted up in fishnet stockings and a bustier, asking bemused passersby on Oberlin's placid Midwestern campus, "Want to have a good time?" What follows alternates improvisatory interactions with evidently unsuspecting participants and those clearly staged to satirize the privileged environs and liberal hypocrisy of the collegiate bubble. Dunham's "sex worker" gets nowhere with venturing, "If you hear of any people who want a roommate, the dorms look really nice," and "Do you think you could maybe swipe me a meal?" She is then assertively approached by a young woman who says with scripted earnestness, voicing the type of PC feminism that *Girls'* Hannah would go on to violate, "I couldn't just walk by you. I'm a gender studies major. Could I take you to a safe place? Your body is a temple."

Most prophetic of Dunham's future work is her viral YouTube video *The Fountain*, in which she undresses down to her bikini, stomach bulge prominent, in a burbling campus fountain

Fig. 3.5. Lena Dunham's public performance of private acts in her 2007 video *The Fountain*.

(see fig. 3.5). She then proceeds to meticulously set out toiletries and bathe herself in a matter-of-fact manner devoid of Anita Ekberg–style frolicking. A guard appears and awkwardly requests that she vacate the fountain and that her camera operator stop filming. "They don't allow it in other fountains on campus," the guard reports. It seems unlikely that the response by onlookers in the virtual world beyond campus—those who treated her to a barrage of rebukes in YouTube's comments section—would have been quite so punitive had her actions been less banal or her unclothed body more conventionally perceived as camera-ready. Dunham got the last laugh when, after the video was featured by YouTube's curator and attracted a reported million views overnight, her career was launched—although so, too, was the cycle of appreciation and abuse her work seems destined to provoke.

These short films exemplify Dunham's insistence on bringing the private into the public, both in flaunting a body type that popular media mandates must stay concealed and in exposing the intimate female acts of everyday self-maintenance and (given *Pressure*'s reference to onanism) self-pleasure. *The Fountain*'s humor in particular is produced by the apparent lack of performance. In casually, unabashedly going about her ministrations as if alone in her bathroom, Dunham dispenses with any feminine masquerade. Her indifference to public scrutiny provokes the guard's consternation and the YouTube haters' ire. She concedes to the guard's order, though not without drolly noting the fountain's male statuary: "No one's telling *him* not to be naked in public." Following this abbreviated shoot, Dunham debates her penchant for being naked in public with her boyfriend, who joins her on-screen. "If there are ten people is it public or private?" she presses him. "You want to be naked in front of people who don't really want to see you naked," he concludes just before consenting to a kiss for the camera.

Dunham would extend this precedent for physiological and sexual exhibitionism in her subsequent career, bringing embodied acts usually relegated to the private sphere (from using the bathroom to food bingeing to sex) into the public to raise explicitly feminist questions about the separation of those domains. The satirical publication *The Onion* parodied Dunham's delight in the disgusting with an article titled "Next Episode of 'Girls' to Feature Lena Dunham Shitting Herself During Gyno Exam While Eating a Burrito."[53] The joke raised a question central to Dunham's practice: Why, for women, do eating and reproductive realities fall into the same not-to-be-seen category as the excretory? By the time Dunham hosted *Saturday Night Live* in 2012, she could joke in the opening monologue about "the old saying that if you're nervous about giving a speech just imagine the audience naked—or at least imagine they haven't seen you naked," then fend off cast members approaching to ask her for advice about their sex lives and bodies. Already, self-exposure had effectively become Dunham's brand (39.15, "Lena Dunham/The National").

"You should be on *Saturday Night Live*," Charlotte (Jemima Kirke) tells Aura (Lena Dunham) in *Tiny Furniture*, presciently enough. "Or maybe something more early Yoko Ono, where you're just moving through a gallery and everyone's watching you." As Dunham has explained, "A lot of my parents' friends were performance artists, so I think I just understood that the body could be a tool in that exploration."[54] One such influence is clearly Dunham's mother, photographer Laurie Simmons, an important figure in the 1980s feminist art scene. In scrutinizing the ways that images construct and control women's sense of themselves and their desires, Dunham's influences extend beyond Breillat to encompass a tradition of women artists using nude self-performance to articulate a feminist politics of embodiment—a strategy that predictably came under attack by some feminist factions. "The woman who displays her own body as her artwork seems to me to be travelling in the tracks of an outworn tradition that spirals downward and inward to nothingness," Germaine Greer pronounced in 2008.[55] Whatever their revisionist intentions, Greer sees these women artists as continuing the patriarchal artistic tradition of fetishizing the female nude, perhaps in a bid to make feminism more palatable to mainstream sensibilities. Her consternation, though, seems importantly connected to its being, in Greer's words, "beautiful bodies" that are on display. Body performance artists of the 1970s and 1980s such as Marina Abramović, Carolee Schneemann, and Hannah Wilke were conventionally beautiful and slender, qualities without which they might not have been able to command the positive attention and critical response they did. Their conformity to beauty norms limits and even undermines their work's impact, especially when viewed in a contemporary context.[56]

Though Greer's concerns are not without merit, I find it important to distinguish Dunham from those earlier pioneers of embodied performance in that hers is not one of the "beautiful bodies" (at least not according to prevailing beauty standards) and to note that her nude performances are never silent—as with Breillat's protagonists, the female voice literally interjects. Greer's implication that the nonideal female form is the more effective, if no less exhibitionistic, tool for the creation of feminist art suggests that Dunham's work should be seen as both adapting and critiquing, rather than simply imitating, this feminist tradition of nude performance art. Moreover, where those earlier artists performed their "body work" in the rarefied domain of art-world institutions, Dunham's milieu is the contemporary internet-enabled popular culture landscape—ranging from cable television and Indiewood, to YouTube and Instagram, to red carpet appearances and TMZ. In all these places, her body type stands out conspicuously. As feminist blog Hello Giggles notes, "Dunham's body is what women see in dressing rooms, in locker rooms, and in the mirror. But seeing it in a space typically reserved for stick-thin starlets seems somehow avant-garde."[57] Or as Schneemann herself puts it more piercingly, Dunham's presence among the emaciated and surgically enhanced bodies of Hollywood constitutes an "ideal of normal" in a sea of "deformed" women's bodies.[58]

I connect Dunham to a more radical vein of body art performed by women artists such as Eleanor Antin, Catherine Opie, Orlan, Cindy Sherman, and Annie Sprinkle, who flaunt their ostensibly "grotesque" bodies—whether merely average sized (in the case of Antin); tattooed, pierced, and gender nonconforming (Opie); surgically or cosmetically manipulated (Orlan and Sherman); or gynecologically exposed (Sprinkle)—in resistance to cultural beauty norms and expectations of femininity.[59] What the alternately supportive and denigrating response to Dunham, parsed below, ultimately establishes is the political potency of her strategy of what Ross Singer calls *spectacular self-subjugation*—"an activist tactic by which the body is given up temporarily to an exploitative system as a means of staging carnivalesque resistance against that system before a mainstream audience."⁶⁰

However intentionally "spectacular" Dunham's performative embodiment may be—the term sits uncomfortably with what I characterize as her defetishized, naturalistic self-representation—the outsized reverberations of the discourse around *Girls* have ex post facto endowed Dunham's body with the force, if not spectacle, of symbolism. Precisely because we were—and still are, despite her pioneering efforts and that of other average- and plus-size women celebrities that followed—so unaccustomed to seeing bodies like Dunham's flaunted in visual culture, her image mobilizes a carnivalesque defamiliarization of our culture's beauty standards and gender roles. Dunham's frequent exposure of her (by *Playboy*/Hollywood standards) small breasts, for example, normalizes a wider range of women's bodies, linking her with the coalition that includes comedian Tig Notaro's topless appearance, post–double mastectomy, during her 2014 "Boyish Girl Interrupted" tour and that of other women who publicly brandish their breasts (or lack thereof) in fights for lactivism, breast cancer awareness, sexual equality, and LGBTQ+ rights.

Given that Dunham's body baring, which admittedly then functions as spectacle, may elicit a gaze uncomfortably akin to gawking at a freak show attraction, I find it critical to emphasize her self-subjugating agency as provoc*auteur*. Dunham's agency is crucial not only to ensuring her performance's subversive feminist potential but also for its direct acknowledgment of her cultural privilege, to which her body's legible markers of whiteness and class attest. That visible privilege must be taken into account when registering Dunham's ability to resonate powerfully with (especially female) viewers of HBO, large numbers of whom enjoy bodily agency comparable to Dunham's. For those women viewers, Dunham's self-display creates a sense of identification that precludes Othering. This balancing of defiant self-love and courageous self-mockery constitutes what I describe as Dunham's "owning her abjection."

In Julia Kristeva's feminist theoretical formulation, abjection is a heteropatriarchal tool for coercing female bodies into regulated social subjects, alienating women from their bodies and one another. "And yet," Kristeva notes, "from its place of banishment, the abject does not cease challenging its master."[61] Thus, Kristeva proposes a strategy of seizing abjection from the patriarchal arsenal, reappropriating it for feminist activism: "The abject is perverse because it neither gives up nor assumes a prohibition of rule or a law, but turns them aside, misleads, corrupts, uses them, takes advantage of them, the better to deny them."[62] If shame is the coerced response to revealing that which gendered or sexual hegemonies dictate must remain hidden, then to apply this Kristevan tactic of owning one's abjection is to defy that coercion and to transform self-disgust into self-affirmation. This is not to propose a simple resignification of shame as positive rather than negative, but rather to acknowledge the shared experience of shame that connects us. Queer theory has developed a related reimagining of the productive, politically and sexually liberating potential of transforming and surrendering to specifically queer experiences of shame.[63] Dunham's work aligns with feminist and queer theory's repurposing of abjection and shame, preferring their revisionist use to the politics of empowerment and aspiration with which postfeminism reproduces heteromasculinist norms.

Breillat's work similarly calls for feminist and queer framing of its preoccupation with abject anatomies. Assessing Breillat's films, Liza Johnson finds that, "while not homosexual, [they] seem to me most certainly queer in their polymorphous, autoerotic, or otherwise truly nonnormative erotics."[64] Concurring, I would place Breillat's feminist and queer explorations of abjection and shame at the center of her cine-erotic imaginary. As Adrienne Angelo notes, for Breillat's female protagonists, abjection "is exemplified by [their] vomit, urine, and vaginal fluids, which signify a body whose own borders are unstable and threaten to erupt or transgress proper codes of feminine conduct."[65]

36 fillette, the first release in Breillat's unofficial "virgin trilogy" (with *A Real Young Girl* and *Fat Girl*) initiates this depiction of young women's struggle to fulfill cultural expectations that they be simultaneously chaste and desirable, and the experience of abjection that those contradictory mandates create. Fourteen-year-old Lili (Delphine Zentout), intent on losing her virginity, moves to fellate the man she has chosen for her first sexual experience, only to gag and throw up in his crotch. The moment serves as a literal and figurative manifestation of her inexperience and inner turmoil.

In *A Real Young Girl*, Breillat employs surreal elements and much blurring of fantasy and reality sequences to convey the disorienting, uncanny experience of pubescent sexuality. Fourteen-year-old Alice Bonnard (played by then twenty-year-old Charlotte Alexandra) grapples internally with a changing body and surging libido and externally with the conflicting lust and shame directed her way by adults, peers, Catholicism, and popular culture. In two protracted sequences, Alice watches televised musical performances by imitation French pop stars in the mold of Johnny Hallyday and Françoise Hardy, popular figures in the early 1960s, when *A Real Young Girl* is set. The songs, with lyrics by Breillat, reflexively stage contrasting performances of heteromasculinity and heterofemininity for the instruction of adolescent spectator Alice. The male singer's sweaty, sneering boasting of sexual conquests is juxtaposed with a demure young woman wearing a white frock and stroking a daisy while coyly singing, "Am I a little girl? I don't know, I don't know. Or a big girl? Only you can know for me." The film's depictions of Alice's real and fantasized reveling in her abjection convey a savage retort to this idealized performance of sexually pure, submissive girlhood.

The brazen Alice, whose name and blue headband recall Lewis Carroll's fantasy tale of another sexually alluring innocent, signals her intractability with her opening lines, "I don't like people. They oppress me." Unlike heteromasculine fantasies of adolescent girlhood, our look at this *real* young girl (the French title's idiomatic meaning is "virgin"), does not omit Alice's curious inspection of her bodily fluids and her imaginary staging of fantasies evoking animalistic urges and self-humiliation. The film contains some of the most provocative scenes in Breillat's oeuvre and include Alice cavorting with chicken feathers stuffed up her rear (inspired by an earlier shot graphically depicting her mother disemboweling a chicken but also, Douglas Keesey notes, referencing *poule* as French slang for prostitute) and submitting to having an earthworm placed on her pubis.[66] These scenes of distasteful (if fantasized) degradation, which made this film one of Breillat's most divisive, implicitly critique romanticizing and fetishizing images of adolescent girlhood, paradoxically employing fantasy sequences to render bodies and sex with an unflinching, defetishized realism.

For all its perversity, *A Real Young Girl* stands as one of Breillat's most amusing works. The sequence in which Alice stumbles home with her knickers around her ankles (apparently enjoying reveling in sordidness), her feigning nonchalance while inserting a sticky spoon into her vagina under the dinner table, and her blatant spying on hunky townie Jim (Hiram Keller) share a deadpan, off-kilter tone that comically undercuts the perversity of the action. A similar sensibility is evident not just in Dunham's abject alter egos but in the veritable genre of surrealism-tinged films about girls' sexual awakenings that *A Real Young Girl* initiated. The most Breillatian among them include *Attenberg* (Athina Rachel Tsangari, 2010), *Feuchtgebiete* (*Wetlands*, David Wnendt, 2013), and *La niña santa* (*The Holy Girl*, Lucrecia Martel, 2004).

The performance of owning one's abjection functions similarly in other Breillat films to defetishize bodies and sex so as to humanize female characters. During a postcoital conversation between Marie and Paolo in *Romance*, the latter expresses disgust at used condoms, which Marie likens to the shame women are made to feel about tampons.

> PAOLO: Once they've been used, they're revolting. Not very pretty.
> MARIE: They are rather disgusting. It's like a Tampax. To screw, you take it out discretely, hide it under the bed so the guy's not turned off. Guys are easily disgusted. Later, you have to get it back. I quite like disgusting things.

Such a detailed discussion of prophylactics and feminine hygiene products departs from both Hollywood-style cinema and straight porn's sexual fantasy realms, where condoms are thought to break the mood for characters and viewers alike and menstruation is unmentionable. In *Anatomy of Hell*, The Man is shown a bloody tampon by The Woman, who claims the applicator device must have been invented by a man "who feels protective and superior ... who doesn't like or understand us" and who is intent on prohibiting women's exploration of their own bodies. "It's because of this blood that [women] are called impure," she continues, "The truth is, [men] are afraid of this blood which flows without there being any wound." She then dips it teabag-like into a glass of water, from which both drink. By film's end, The Man has moved from visual discomfort at getting menstrual blood on his hands to appearing unfazed upon withdrawing his blood-covered penis after sex. He has overcome his fear of and disgust at the reality of female bodies—an effect that the film, through its repeated presentation of that reality, has presumably had on the viewer.

In using menstrual blood to signal women's humanity, Breillat's work positions itself in a feminist artistic tradition reaching from Judy Chicago's 1972 *Menstruation Bathroom* piece to Chilean artist Carina Úbeda's 2013 installation "Cloths." Though menstrual blood has been used to both horrifying and pitiable effect in cinema, most famously in Brian De Palma's *Carrie* (1976) and in *Superbad* (Greg Mottola, 2007), its inclusion in sex scenes provokes (diegetic and nondiegetic) discomfort that is importantly gendered in its evocation of women's shame and men's anxiety and disgust. Jessa's pregnancy scare in season one of *Girls* turns on just such a scene, when, much to her relief, she starts menstruating mid-conquest with a young man who (presumably like some viewers) is unnerved by the sight (1.2, "Vagina Panic"). More recently, *I Love Dick* (Sarah Gubbins and Joey Soloway, Amazon, 2016–17) ended its eight-episode run with a cliffhanger of coitus interruptus, when the eponymous love object played by Kevin Bacon withdraws his hand from between the legs of protagonist Chris (Kathryn Hahn), his confidence at making her repeat "You make me so wet" falling flat when he discovers that his hand is coated in blood, leading him to hastily retreat to the bathroom. Another gynophilic show, Netflix's *Glow* (Liz Flahive and Carly Mensch, 2017–), also includes in its premiere season period sex offered up as proof of emotional intimacy by recovering-chauvinist director Sam Sylvia (Marc Maron) to his girlfriend Rhoda (Kate Nash), though she breaks up with him regardless (1.8, "Maybe It's All the Disco"). We might view such moments as a trickle-down effect from the Breillat universe, where the brandishing of used condoms and tampons displaces straight porn's frenzy of the visible, finding another outlet for the frustration caused by the impossibility of visually evidencing the female orgasm. As Helen Hester notes of Breillat's screening of extreme sex and bodily abjection, "The most remarkable thing about these scenes is that, despite advocating explicitness, they also draw our attention to the unavoidable constraints faced by the practice of *making visible*."[67]

Perhaps the key feature uniting Breillat's leading women is their striking lack of self-shaming, their freedom from looking at themselves through others' (namely, men's) eyes. In this sense, *Fat Girl*'s Anaïs is the Breillat hero par excellence. Although *A Real Young Girl*'s Alice is played by a shapely, pretty blond, and Breillat's other female leads are slender and delicately feminine in appearance, Anaïs's bulk is put singularly on display. Yet Anaïs appears immune to external or internalized shaming, especially in comparison with her sister's hunger for male approval, as evidenced by the unabashed relish with which Anaïs devours food despite others' visual disapproval. Breillat has confessed to modeling *Fat Girl*'s sisters on the relationship between herself, who "did nothing but eat," and sibling Marie-Hélène, thirteen months older and, according to Breillat, an anorexic model and actor who posed for adult magazines *Lui* and *Playboy*.[68] Whereas her sister Elena's good looks attract the amorous attentions of an older Italian man, food serves as Anaïs's substitute for the sensuality denied her even as it serves to protect her from the sexually manipulative Fernandos of the world. At their first meeting, Fernando and Elena amorously embrace while across the table Anaïs lovingly attends to a banana split. Whereas Elena is never shown eating (only serving a plate to her boyfriend, just as her father receives food from his wife), the food Anaïs constantly consumes is no less clearly a sexual substitute than her emotionally neglected mother's (Arsinée Khanjian) chain smoking. Anaïs's mother's self-denial is contrasted with the corpulence of Fernando's mother (played by Fellini and Pasolini muse Laura Betti). Not until vacation's end, en route back to Paris sans her already departed husband, do we see Anaïs's mother gorging along with Anaïs on gas station sandwiches. In addition to her character's defiant overeating, Reboux's expressions and gestures establish Anaïs's femininity-resistant armor. She is never seen smiling, and the glowering looks she gives the camera (most notably in the closing freeze-frame) spurn diegetic and nondiegetic gazes even as she defies the invisibility foisted on "fat girls" in scenes that foreground her awkward, unflatteringly attired inhabitation of what her sister Elena deems her "lumpy" body.

Putting her own body on unclothed display, despite its more closely resembling Anaïs's than Elena's, Dunham continues Breillat's tradition of screening and performing female corp*oreality* while adapting it to an American millennial context defined by beauty-standard denialism—which "puts the onus on individual women to improve their self-esteem instead of criticizing societal beauty standards writ large"—and beset by competing discourses of feminist empowerment and anti-aspirationalism.[69] What so many Dunham haters have dismissed as passive-aggressive exhibitionism I read rather as a radical refusal of (self-)disciplinary regimes that engender women as what Michel Foucault, in describing our culture's internalized modes of social regulation, termed "docile bodies."[70] Such regimes have only been intensified by a reactionary postfeminist discourse that forgives and even encourages women's physical and sexual self-subjugation through consumerist practices of diet, exercise, fashion, cosmetics, depilation, and body augmentation.

In one of the more vicious press attacks during her early years of fame, after she wore what appeared to some to be a pants-less outfit to a 2012 industry event, Dunham called out the double standard of expectations that conventionally attractive women bare all while heavier women stay covered up: "If [actor] Olivia Wilde had gone to a party in ... little shorts, she might have been on a 'weird dressed list' or been told her outfit was cute. I don't think a girl with tiny thighs would have received such no-pants attention.... My response is, get used to it because I am going to live to be 100, and I am going to show my thighs every day till I die."[71]

Not long after, on a January 2013 broadcast of his satellite radio show, Howard Stern said of Dunham, "It's a little fat girl who kinda looks like Jonah Hill and she keeps taking her clothes off and it kind of feels like rape.... I don't want to see that." Phrasing his response to seeing Dunham unclothed as an experience bordering on sexual assault attests to the extreme anxiety her brand of corporeal defiance provokes. Following Dunham's Golden Globe wins for *Girls*, Stern recanted with the backhanded remark, "Good for her. It's hard for little fat chicks to get anything going," which Dunham then good-naturedly joked to David Letterman she wanted engraved on her tombstone.[72] Though Dunham may count a few missteps among her public pronouncements, she has remained unflappable amid the barrage of public body shaming, steadfastly continuing to flaunt her nakedness in defiance of social norms that insist that heavier women should stay covered up, express discontent with or apologize for their larger form, and actively abstain in an effort to "improve" themselves.

The put-downs hurled in response to Dunham-as-Hannah's body-baring on *Girls* are telling for demonstrating, as Brett Lunceford notes, that "taboos on nakedness do more than reign [sic] in sexuality; controls on nakedness function as controls on the body itself—how one can appropriately use one's own body."[73] In another early moment of Dunham-shaming, *The Wrap*'s Tim Molloy directed the following objection to Dunham at a 2014 Television Critics Association panel: "I don't get the purpose of all of the nudity on the show. By you particularly. I feel like I'm walking into a trap where you go, 'Nobody complains about the nudity on *Game of Thrones*,' but I get why they are doing it. They are doing it to be salacious and, you know, titillate people. And your character is often naked just at random times for no reason."[74] What Malloy's remark reveals, apart from his overlooking of more progressive potential uses of nudity than mere titillation, is his chief grievance: Dunham's choice to perform the majority of the female nudity herself in the face of a public and press known to mock her as "blobby" and worse.[75]

But despite Dunham's valiant public rebuttals and the reassurances her female characters provide one another—in direct contrast to the often negative judgments voiced by their male counterparts—neither she nor her alter egos feign imperturbability in the face of cultural policing and its negative effects on female body image. When *Tiny Furniture*'s Charlotte, reading aloud haters' comments to Aura's YouTube videos (actually lifted from those provoked by *The Fountain*), asks, "You can't possibly take these seriously?" Aura admits, "I do sometimes," echoing Dunham's own admission to internalizing shame. "Sometimes I think, 'Boys were mean to me in high school, so I can take whatever.' Of course that doesn't mean you can handle five thousand commenters saying you're fat, but it does prepare you for feeling like a weirdo."[76] Through our engagement with such performances of (self-)shaming, writes Liza Johnson, "shame can be understood as a type of enabling knowledge by which to see and feel desires and attachments, even weird ones, with a kind of singularity that demands neither identification nor repulsion, that functions, perhaps, more like empathy."[77] Like Aura and Dunham herself, *Girls'* Hannah also acknowledges the inevitable sting and internalization of social shaming, which enables the knowledge and empathy that Johnson describes by revealing the process by which women learn to be their own harshest critics. As Dunham explains, she chooses to shoot Hannah from unflattering angles and in poor lighting, playing up her physical imperfections, because "that's how the character sees herself." As Hannah reveals in an outburst, "No one could ever hate me as much as I hate myself, so any mean thing someone's gonna think of to say about me, I've already said to me, about me, probably in the last half hour" (1.9, "Leave Me Alone").[78]

A key to Dunham's provocation in performing as Hannah is her character's self-described "baby's body" and accompanying penchant for dressing like a very young girl, albeit one who is decidedly not nymphet-like (3.10, "Role Play"). Hannah's childish gestures and actions (she's often shown pouting with face in hands, and she spends inordinate amounts of time in the bathtub and in bed) emphasize her character's arrested development, while her often sloppy comportment and graceless movements (sloped shoulders, belly pooching out of ill-fitting clothes, clomping down stairs) assert a petulant defiance of edicts to "grow up" or "clean up." Hannah is affirmed in her abjection by permissive Jessa. In the season one finale, they steal a moment in the bathroom during Jessa's surprise wedding. Sitting on the toilet, Jessa tells Hannah, "I love you. You're so fucking gross lying on the bathroom floor" (1.10, "She Did"). Hannah's body becomes still more unruly in refusing to conform to expectations of how women should look and act. Like Dunham herself, Hannah is frequently chided for not wearing pants, and few women performers save *Fat Girl*'s Reboux have been filmed eating so often and with such gusto. The first season of *Girls* begins with a close-up of Hannah forking pasta mouthward and ends with her stuffing herself with wedding cake in a scene she would later parody in the opening skit for the 2012 Emmy Awards telecast. In a culture that effaces and shames women eating in the same way it prohibits the display of "unladylike" bodily processes, not to mention "unseemly" sexual appetites, to begin and end *Girls*' first season with Hannah blissfully chowing down is audacious, as is a defiant Dunham's willingness to appear in a TV broadcast bingeing on cake while sitting naked on a toilet. Each act comprises a shift away from shame and toward owning her abjection, en route to rejecting the regime of docile bodies that regulates gender performance and body image through exacting modes of submission and self-denial.

In the series pilot, when Adam asks about her abundant tattoos, Hannah recounts her motivation as a teenager: "Truthfully, I gained a bunch of weight very quickly and I felt very out of control of my own body and it was this riot grrrl idea, like 'I'm taking control of my own shape.'" When he presses her about whether she has tried losing weight, she shoots back defensively, "No, I have not tried a lot to lose weight because I decided that I was going to have some other concerns in my life!" This self-reflexive tactic articulates Dunham's own determination to remain imperviously self-affirming in the face of public denigration. Dunham's efforts to create a purposeful and distinctly feminist "voice of a generation" frequently exceed the diegetic frame to engage with her critics.

An exemplary instance of this is the two dreamy, sex-filled days Hannah spends in a well-appointed brownstone with handsome doctor Joshua (Patrick Wilson) in a season two stand-alone episode (2.5, "One Man's Trash"). Told that she's beautiful, Hannah is surprised. "Don't you think you are?" asks Joshua, to which she replies with a tentative "Um . . . yeah, it just isn't always the feedback I've been given." This moment provoked a spate of cuttingly indignant responses (not all by anonymous internet trolls) that took "the especially and assertively ugly" Dunham to task. Having described Dunham thusly, two *Slate* staff writers alleged this was an unrealistically self-flattering premise, asking, "Why are these people having sex, when they are so clearly mismatched—in style, in looks, in manners, in age, in everything?"[79] It is a safe bet that these writers are not composing this sort of think piece each time a new sitcom featuring a portly male performer married to a thinner, younger, hotter female performer debuts. Staff writers for both *Entertainment Weekly* and *Esquire* surmised about the episode that the likeliest explanation was that it was all a dream.[80] Patrick Wilson's real-life wife, actor Dagmara Domińczyk, issued a rebuttal via Twitter: "Funny, his wife is a size 10, muffin top & all, & he does her just fine.""[81] A chorus of feminist bloggers, critics, and scholars joined in to defend Dunham, many of them concurring with Hannah Mueller's view that *Girls* "single-handedly managed to expose the double-standard ruling the public discourse on quality television: Masculine drama shows relying on the continuous display of beautiful naked women dismiss criticism on behalf of authorial vision; whereas a show that represents female nudity as realistically diverse is criticized as inauthentic."[82]

The female nudity on display in *Girls* is dominated by "imperfect" female bodies, chiefly Dunham/Hannah's, consistently and insistently presented as if to affirm their beauty and right to visibility and pleasure. Notably, the only breasts besides Hannah's that are shown in season one are those of her middle-aged mother, Loreen (Becky Ann Baker), during a shower tryst with husband Tad (Peter Scolari) that turns tragicomic when he slips and falls (1.6, "The Return"). As was discussed in chapter 2, *Girls* is bookended by shots of male full-frontal nudity (the first being this scene's naturalistic view of a naked, humiliated Tad), whereas women's pubic areas chalk up a few more equally significant glimpses. The only woman seen fully naked apart from Hannah during the show's first few seasons is Adam's intensely neurotic sister Caroline, played by the often-naked and proudly hirsute performer Gaby Hoffmann. That this shot involves a startling moment of self-hurting exemplifies *Girls'* use of female nudity to reveal women's naturalistic embodiment and emotional nakedness, as opposed to its typical eroticization (3.3, "She Said OK").

Echoed by these unconventional female nude scenes with Loreen and Caroline (which continue during Caroline's season four pregnancy), Hannah's own nudity operates in nontitillating registers of (tragi)comedy, naturalism, and emotional vulnerability that function to defetishize even the sexualized female body. Some of Hannah's (semi)nude scenes take place during and after sex with Adam or position her naturalistically in mundane moments (changing clothes, in the bath). But many others show Hannah flaunting a body that onlookers (both diegetic and nondiegetic), influenced by our society's exacting and highly gendered standards of attractiveness and decorum, are primed to criticize. The sheer confidence with which Dunham-as-Hannah, regardless of social milieu, brandishes her voluptuous backside, love handles, and small breasts creates an effect paradoxically combining absurdist incongruity and banal naturalism. With Dunham herself directing and editing the unflattering setups and shock-cuts, the surprise of seeing this representational rarity—an "unsightly" woman undressed—may initially provoke a comic effect, yet characterization and performance ultimately render these displays irreverent and self-affirming rather than mocking and self-shaming. In making the "chubby girl/

sidekick" formerly relegated to the narrative margins into the central character, employing a naturalistic approach that encourages spectatorial identification, and tethering her character so closely to her public persona, Dunham humanizes Hannah in a way that ensures she will not be rendered invisible (as the "unappealing" girl often is) and that her looks do not constitute the sum total of her character.

In contrast to the passive-aggressive questioning and sometimes outright cutting comments directed at Hannah's bodily appearance and comportment by the straight male characters on *Girls* (not to mention Dunham's real-life critics), Dunham's women costars regularly provide positive reinforcement about Hannah's body image and, in the case of regular collaborator Jemima Kirke, model for her how to own one's abjection. "You've got the greatest little tits—like a 1960s porn star," Kirke's Charlotte tells Dunham's Aura in *Tiny Furniture*, before enticing her to crash, sans pants, a gathering of gaping high-schoolers. "Haven't you been to the beach?!" Charlotte asks them flippantly. In *Girls* as well, Hannah and Jessa both display a penchant for casual nudity and physical intimacy with friends, as in their aforementioned scenes set in bathrooms. Never one to be outdone, Jessa would eventually join Hannah (and Caroline) in appearing bottomless, in a postcoital shot, noticeably next to never-nude Adam Driver (5.10, "I Love You Baby"). Even when it goes unshared, Hannah's unabashed nakedness around her girlfriends furthers Dunham's feminist critique of women's visual fetishization as it detaches female nudity from women's heterosexualized desirability, repositioning it instead in contexts of naturalism and female intimacies.

More conventionally attractive and slender women actors appeared seminude on *Girls* (though neither of the other recurring female leads Zosia Mamet or Allison Williams, who refused to sign HBO's nudity clause, did so). But the imperfect, naturalistic female body remained at the show's representational forefront, and by season five, *Girls* refocused the self-reflexive lens on Dunham's corp*oreality*, upping the ante as if daring the internet's body police to respond. Finding day-to-day intimacy with Hannah discomforting, boyfriend Fran informs her that it is too distracting to engage in argument while "your fucking bush is hanging out." Hannah, who is still conciliatory at this point, replies, "If it's making you uncomfortable, I will cover my bush" (5.2, "Good Man"). Fran's outrage here recalls the complaints (also frequently voiced by young white men) about Dunham's penchant for nudity in public discourse around the show. With Fran's subsequent attempts to police Hannah's boundaries, Hannah (and perhaps some viewers) begins to suspect that Fran is only superficially, as Marnie insists, "the nicest guy you've ever dated." Indignant at learning that Fran prefers masturbating to his ex-girlfriends' nude selfies rather than her own (admittedly "goofy") ones, Hannah laments, "I worked very, very hard to overcome the challenges of my nontraditional body type and accept myself for who I am. And I'm not gonna be edged out of my own life by girls who don't even have any interesting fat deposits on them. Until this happened, I was basically [swimsuit model] Kate Upton to myself" (5.3, "Japan"). Hannah here asserts both her sense of self-improvement and self-worth while admitting her vulnerability to external scrutiny. But in keeping with *Girls'* avoidance of the Hollywood fantasy of unlikely personal transformation and of the self-blame inflicted by beauty-standard denialism, what materializes here and over the course of six seasons is neither an unlikely bounty of self-acceptance nor endless self-flagellation.

Hannah's desire to create some more conventionally alluring images for Fran's spank bank serves as an occasion for more full-frontal nudity and self-reflexivity, with Ray, who Hannah has deputized as photographer, saying (in a sly reference to Dunham's *Vogue* shoot), "You're going to thank me later for using the special lens" (see fig. 3.6). Fran and Hannah come into further conflict

Fig. 3.6. Hannah's (Lena Dunham) photo shoot in season five of *Girls*.

over the question of nudity after Hannah borrows a showstopping move from Sharon Stone's character in *Basic Instinct* (Paul Verhoeven, 1992) to escape an interrogation from the principal at the school where she is a substitute teacher.

> HANNAH: Honestly, men are so afraid of the female vagina, we should be, like, galvanizing and using this tactic to literally win wars. I also think it helped that my bush is at full capacity right now, which I'm sorry about.
> FRAN: Showing your vagina to your boss is not an okay thing to do. Do you really not get it? Are you that broken? Like, how damaged is your thought process? As an adult, you should know, taking your genitals out—
> HANNAH: Stop, okay? Literally stop. I didn't do anything that bad. I'm not like Bill Cosby or something.
> FRAN: At the very least, I would hope that you would know I would never want you to show your vagina to anyone but me.
> HANNAH: Oh, so now I'm not supposed to show my vagina to anyone but you, Fran? It's about to be summer! (5.7, "Hello Kitty")

Whether treated naturalistically, with pathos, or with tongue firmly in cheek, these and other moments when Dunham's characters bare all reflexively critique the male gaze's mechanisms for containing female embodiment through its narrowly defined norms of erotic display. The irreverent, humanizing displays of female nudity in Breillat's and Dunham's work effect unruly subversions of patriarchal authority and convey a heightened register of embodied corpo*reality*, of the mundane activity and fleshy materiality of the body against the photoshopped unreality of mainstream image making.

CARNAL KNOWLEDGE: SELF-FORMATION THROUGH SEXUAL SELF-DEGRADATION

Also connecting Breillat and Dunham is their shared understanding of the role that sexual experience plays in owning one's abjection. For the characters they create, self-knowledge and self-acceptance are arrived at through conscious acts of sexual self-degradation. As with their appropriations of porn and their corporeal exhibitionism, these depictions of physically and emotionally "raw and bruised" sex have proven divisive for critics and scholars. Ginette Vincendeau judges that Breillat's "obsessive focus on sexuality, notwithstanding its intellectualization, means her women are purely carnal rather than social beings" and finds "most disturbing . . . Breillat's suggestion that to be raped is a potentially liberating experience."[83] Liz Constable, by contrast, terms Breillat's female protagonists "unbecoming" women to identify their rejection of women's imperative to be appealing—a rejection that enables a reconstruction of female subjectivity. Constable sees these women enacting surrender—the choice to take pleasure in sexual pain and humiliation, not merely in service to another's desire but in a way that is individually transformative and also yields "a possibility of reciprocity generative of intimacy" within a couple: "This surrender, *unbecoming* as it might at first appear, is nevertheless often significant to the transformative process of *becoming* a sexual subject for women, and to the articulation of desire *without* masochism for women."[84] In depicting her leading women as self-determining in choosing submission (or, to use Constable's term, surrender), Breillat depathologizes women's sexual self-degradation and frees these socially stigmatized acts from the pressures of moral or political prescriptions. Breillat suggests that to open oneself and trust another so deeply as to risk losing one's dignity enables one to achieve a greater sense of self-worth and self-awareness. Thus, the only thing deemed shameful in Breillat's diegetic world is the silencing and repressing of desire.

This quest for self-knowledge through carnal knowledge reaches its apotheosis in sequences that have Breillat's leading women characters responding to experiences of sexual violence with little of the expected victimization and stigmatization. In *Romance*, Marie invokes the *Pretty Woman* (Garry Marshall, 1990) rule and, with it, a form of prostitute role-play. Refusing to kiss Paolo, she says, "I don't care who stuffs my cunt. But I can't kiss someone I don't love. It's too intimate." She agrees to give Paolo oral sex, dictating the circumstances under which she will do so, and then brings the same authority to bear in defining her role and aim in penetrative sex: "I want to be a hole. The more gaping, the more obscene it is, the more it's me, my intimacy. The more I surrender ... that's my purity." Like a woman-directed retelling of *Looking for Mr. Goodbar* (Richard Brooks, 1977) minus the moralizing tragic ending, the ironically titled *Romance* tells the story of a kindergarten teacher, spurned by her male model boyfriend Paul (Sagamore Stévenin), whose search for erotic fulfillment and personal liberation through this extreme self-subjugation (as in her wish to be an obscene "hole") is not altogether effective. Neither is Marie's subsequent encounter, in *Romance*'s most argued-over scene, with a stranger who first propositions and then violently penetrates her. Though left crying and clearly shaken, the words she hurls upon his retreat ("I am not ashamed, asshole!") declare Marie's refusal to regard the instance as shaming. The oral sex The Woman gives The Man at the start of *Anatomy of Hell* works similarly. As Douglas Keesey notes, the close-up of semen dripping from her mouth "would be 'obscene' in a pornographic film in which the viewer is excited by female degradation, but Amira's [sic] glowing face and defiant look show her struggle to transcend feeling sullied or shamed."[85]

In Marie's more successful encounter with school principal Robert, she finds bondage a productive route to satisfaction and freedom: "Tying me up without tying me down was the secret of his ritual," she reflects. Ultimately, their pleasurable intimacy becomes figuratively procreative when Robert steps in as father to Marie's baby by her now ex-boyfriend Paul. In a departure from Eleni Butler's aforementioned characterization that Breillat "portrays sex under patriarchy as particularly joyless and punitive," Marie and Robert's bondage scenes are pleasurable for the participants as well as amusing, in their droll enactment of elaborate role-play, for viewers (and were intended to be such, according to Breillat).[86] Though they are few and far between, good men in Breillat's films—among whom I would count *Romance*'s Robert and Paolo—are those who can occupy both masculine and feminine positions in sexual as well as emotional terms and who are able to recognize and accept in any individual woman aspects of both mother and "whore," nurturing and desiring, pure and impure.

As contentious for its rape connotations as the scene in *Romance* described above, *Fat Girl*'s final sequence works similarly to provoke consideration of women's agency to control their self-narrative, if not always their experience. The sequence is thought by some to be an ironic fantasy fulfillment of Anaïs's preternaturally mature pronouncement, "The first time, I'd like it to be a man I don't love." Responding to police questioning after a violent sexual attack at the hands of the axe murderer who killed her mother and sister, Anaïs denies having been raped. "Don't believe me if you don't want to," she obstinately tells the officers.[87] Electing to deny victimhood and its requisite shaming, Anaïs defines the experience for herself with the same willful self-determination that Breillat and Dunham (and her namesake, the erotic diarist Anaïs Nin) bring to their (self-)images while inviting concerns about women's rape fantasies, about rape's discursive erasure, or even (as in Vincendeau's remark above) about rape's liberating potential.

Emily Fox-Kales interprets the scene metaphorically, finding "this sadomasochistic merging of pleasure and pain that marks the sexual experience of Breillat's female protagonists" as projecting how, "particularly for the adolescent girl, sexual desire and danger are inextricably linked, often embodied by the figure of an unknown male attacker who mysteriously appears to initiate her into experience."[88] The same might be said for Marie's denial as well, for although not adolescent, she remains caught up in the same culturally imposed and individually internalized dynamic as Anaïs—which entices women to eroticize their own subjugation and disarticulation and which recalls Vincendeau's observation that "Breillat explores with great lucidity the traps [for women] of conventional heterosexuality."[89] In a culture of sexuality dominated by heteromasculine desire, scenarios such as those Fox-Kales references in Breillat's work follow, if mockingly, erotic literature and film's leading women's narrative trajectory that Gwendolyn Wells calls "ascent through degradation"—a tradition spanning Pauline Réage's *The Story of O* (1954) to Adrian Lyne's *9½ Weeks* (1986) to E. L. James's *Fifty Shades of Grey* (2011). Breillat clarifies, however, that *Romance*'s Marie "goes through scenes of masochism and learns to free herself—exactly the opposite of *The Story of O*, which posits the norm is pleasure through masochism and through being dominated."[90] In her women characters' venturing into these gray areas of sexual experience, Breillat suggests that in a world saturated by toxic heteromasculinity, it becomes extremely difficult to understand what actually constitutes consent, what is a genuine affirmation of women's right to define their own experience, and the standards by which we should judge representations of women's desires.

Where Wells locates Breillat's work in *The Story of O* lineage, Emily Nussbaum traces Dunham's portrayal of postadolescent but still foundering female sexuality to a literary tradition reaching from Mary McCarthy to Mary Gaitskill in "stories about smart, strange girls diving into experience, often through bad sex with their worst critics."[91] From Dunham's first feature, *Creative Nonfiction* (2008), in which her character Ella endures a sexless relationship with an unhoused male classmate using her for her bed, to the similar encounters Aura suffers with apartment-crashing moocher Jed (Alex Karpovsky) and in having sordid sex "in a pipe in the street" with cheating coworker Keith (David Call) in *Tiny Furniture*, Dunham positions her characters on the receiving end of sexual humiliation.

The relationship between Adam and Hannah in early episodes of *Girls* extends this dynamic, with Hannah consciously (if at first naively) framing her interactions with Adam less in terms of her being a girlfriend than as stations on the path to her becoming a sexually mature woman and professional writer. "I do explore," Hannah assures ex-boyfriend Elijah about her current love life. "Right now, I'm seeing this guy, and sometimes I let him hit me on the side of my body" (1.3, "All Adventurous Women Do"). The self-delusion in her statement vies with self-agency as she undertakes the process of sorting out which are Adam's desires and which are her own. Though a male writer profiling Dunham for *Rolling Stone* claims that "Hannah clearly gets off on being degraded ... and [Adam is] into *doing* the degrading," it is not at all clear that she actually orgasms during, or even enjoys, these sessions.[92] In an interview with *Fresh Air*'s Terry Gross, Dunham described her intention in shaping these scenes: "A phenomenon that Hannah experienced—and Hannah experienced it because I experienced it—was the sense that if you were a girl who didn't have an ideal body, what you had to offer was your willingness to please, your openness to adventure and your desire to do it all. ... 'I'm a fat girl, just do it—I'm down for anything. I'm not like those skinny girls. I can't say no.' ... You don't have to, obviously, be chubby to feel this, you just have to feel an essential sense that you yourself are not enough."[93]

When enacted "safely, sanely, and consensually," as the subculture's ethos goes, the practices associated with BDSM work to stage and perform power relationships in a way that delegitimizes their ostensible naturalness. Hence, the admonitions that come from Hannah's confidantes concern the nature of the relationship rather than sexual degradation itself, suggesting that such acts are not inherently degrading but become so in the absence of commitment, intimacy, or honesty, or in a context of power imbalance. Upon hearing Hannah's report of more "hooker stuff" with Adam, Marnie chides, "Hannah, Adam is not allowed to do that to you; he's not your boyfriend." And a woman coworker, upon seeing the dick pic Adam intends for someone else but mistakenly sends to Hannah, tells her, "You need to have a little self-respect" (1.4, "Hannah's Diary"). Spurred by this, Hannah divulges to Adam that she wants to be with someone "who wants to hang out all the time, and thinks I'm the best person in the world, and wants to have sex with only me." From this point forward, Hannah's sexual subjugation will be increasingly more self-imposed, occurring on her emotional terms and under her authorship and agency.

Adam's command, "You should never be anyone's slave except mine," though hardly a conventional oath, announces this shift into a paradoxically more egalitarian and committed relationship. Yet Adam grows increasingly obsessive, crossing lines of consent (in one scene, he urinates on Hannah without warning), and Hannah begins to chafe at his physical dependence on her (he is bedridden after an accident resulting from stepping into traffic during an argument). Asserting her authority to leave him nonetheless, she says, "It's not your choice. It's my choice." She appears to have turned over a new leaf when she tells new squeeze Sandy (Donald Glover), "I used to like any guy who liked me and so now I'm really being thoughtful about this and taking the time to figure out what I'm looking for in a romance relationship." With Sandy, Hannah feels reassured that "when we have sex there's no part of me that wishes I didn't exist." But this lack of shame comes at the expense of radically different values (Sandy is politically conservative), and they break up soon thereafter.

Estranged throughout season two, Hannah and Adam independently explore their personal motivations and gendered determinants for degrading sex, coming to understand its volatility and potential for inducing mortification and regret—and eventually real emotional pain—when practiced in unsafe contexts. In one instance, Hannah attempts dirty talk during a hookup with a hometown friend who forcefully protests her "I'm tight like a baby, right?" come-on (1.6, "The Return"). In another scene, in "One Man's Trash," Joshua shuts down after Hannah reveals, "Once I asked someone to punch me in the chest then come on that spot. That idea came from my brain. What makes me think I deserve that?" Hannah finds these partners less willing than she to acquiesce to role-play scenarios and to find fantasy abuse narratives a turn-on in a way that links sexual subjugation to gender and (recalling her comment to Terry Gross) body image.

Endowed with greater power as both the sexual dominant and as a man in a patriarchal culture, Adam's explorations with degradation apart from Hannah have still more disturbing repercussions, as seen in his destructive dynamic with his new girlfriend Natalia (Shiri Appleby). Shutting down his attempts to denigrate her with words, she informs him, "I can like your cock and not be a dirty whore," asserting a feminist stance against the sexual self-degradation eroticized by porn culture (2.10, "Together"). In their next encounter, after trustingly following Adam's orders to crawl on all fours across his squalid apartment before reluctantly submitting to his ejaculating on her breasts, Natalia tells him afterward, visibly pained, "I don't think I liked that . . . I didn't like that" (2.9, "On All Fours"). As with Fran's disavowal that naked selfies of ex-girlfriends are exploitative, this scene's cum shot—a mainstay of porn but extremely rare even on cable television—references hard-core as a means to reveal the blurred line between consent and coercion. What Natalia endures here, and perhaps also what Hannah experiences in some of her assignations with Adam, is what comedian Amy Schumer riffs about in her 2012 stand-up special: "We've all been a little raped . . . there's a gray area of rape," referring to the spectrum of borderline and not fully consensual sexual experience in women's lives, much of which goes unacknowledged. Fittingly, it is Schumer, playing Natalia's friend, who pushes her to confront Adam when they encounter each other in a coffee shop after he ghosts her following their distressing encounter. Addressing a horrified Hannah as a rapt Ray look on, Natalia delivers a scathing diagnosis of Adam's impulse toward sexual degradation: "You know what you have on your hands here, right? You have an off-the-wagon, Neanderthal sex addict sociopath who's going to fuck you like he's never met you and like he doesn't love his own mother." Turning to Adam, Natalia says, "And then you're going to cry, because that's what you do" (3.1, "Females Only").

The encounter hangs heavily over Adam and Hannah's reconciliation at the start of season three. It goes unaddressed until Hannah, tired of being treated "like an ottoman with a vagina," attempts to enliven a sex life stalled by monogamous routine and Adam's preoccupation with preparing for his first Broadway role. They try enacting a role-play scenario that Hannah concocts, but Adam interrupts her midcoitus, upset by her authorial direction. Their resulting argument allows Hannah to voice the ambivalence she (and *Girls* viewers) have felt around the dynamic of degradation that constituted her and Adam's early sexual exchanges, and her confusion about its dissolution. She tells him, "You used to have all these ideas about me being a little street slut or an orphan with a disease.... I was just trying to do it the way we used to, the way that sex always was for us" (3.10, "Role Play"). Appearing surprised at her outburst, Adam denies any "creepy" connotations to be drawn from ideas "just coming to us in the moment" and reproves her for being "outside your body watching everything." But Hannah insists incredulously, "I don't have ideas like that," finally articulating her own lack of desire for that vein of sexual self-degradation. In saying this, Hannah forces Adam into an awareness that, although she was often complicit, it was (and is) exclusively his desires dictating their sexual dynamic, and not until the power imbalance outside the bedroom is rectified can their dominant-submissive role-play be mutually pleasurable. Over *Girls'* third season, Hannah and Adam's relationship gradually transforms into a more reciprocal, if by no means untroubled, sexual and emotional coupling. The pair lack the emotional honesty that would make their role-play mutually pleasurable and connective rather than hurtful and distancing, though the show makes clear it is not sexual degradation intrinsically but its misuse under nonconsensual or emotionally conflicted circumstances that is to blame. *Girls'* discourse on (self-)degradation illuminates the burdensome cultural silence, and thus ignorance, around sexual desire's differential experience by opposingly socialized women and men. One could argue it is this emotional distance, aggravated by their literal distance from each other in season four, that ultimately leads Adam and Hannah to end their relationship.

Where Hannah too long subordinated her desires silently to Adam's, Jessa from the series' start modeled a mode of sexual self-degradation perhaps more like Breillat's in its refusal of shame and its nonprescriptively feminist aim toward self-formation. When prim Shoshanna reads from a manual similar to *The Rules* that "sex from behind is degrading," Jessa rejects the dictum angrily: "What if I want to feel like I have udders? This woman doesn't care about what I want.... I'm offended by all the supposed-tos. I don't like women telling other women what to do or how to do it or when to do it. Every time I have sex it's my choice" (1.2, "Vagina Panic"). So long as her choice is freely made, Jessa embraces sexual submission in a way that understands it as a pleasurable performance rather than an oppressive position, even if it runs counter to dominant feminist scripts around comportment and empowerment. Nonetheless, during the show's early seasons, Jessa's performance of submission is not always done with the "safe, sane, and consensual" edict in play, as in the fevered make-out in a bar bathroom when Jessa's latest conquest tentatively asks, "Is that okay?" to which she responds, "Don't ask me that again ever" (1.2, "Vagina Panic").

The role-play sex Adam and Jessa (both by then sober) have in season five better serves to counter what was unspoken and hence nonconsensual between him and Hannah. Starting out with an assurance by Jessa that she's using protection, she requests that Adam pretend to be a high school jock who fails to pull out in time and so risks impregnating her. His stellar performance ("Oh, God, what am I gonna tell my parents? What the fuck am I gonna tell Coach? He'll never let me borrow his car again. I'm gonna lose my scholarship!") leaves a laughing Jessa satisfied and praising him, "You're brilliant!" (5.5, "Queen for Two Days"). Fittingly, it is Jessa who dispels the shame of sexually transmitted diseases with her mantra about contracting HPV: "All adventurous women do" (1.3, "All Adventurous Women Do"). And it is Jessa who urges Hannah to turn inappropriately touchy-feely treatment from her season one boss to her advantage, saying, "Fuck him for the story, Hannah!" (1.4, "Hannah's Diary).

The impulse to sexual self-subjugation in Dunham's oeuvre is ascribed to several factors: culture's pornification; women's socialization for submissiveness; and a postfeminist condition, diagnosed by Katie Roiphe in her writing about *Girls*, in which "theatrical fantasies of sexual surrender offer a release, a vacation, an escape from the dreariness and hard work of equality."[94]

Dunham's alter egos, however, experiment with sexual self-degradation first and foremost with the motive of becoming writers. As Sean Fuller and Catherine Driscoll observe, "Sex is a part of Hannah's relationship to the world that she worries she has not experienced enough, and the way she takes up and takes part in sexual fantasies is less escapist than it is part of her ambition to 'feel all the things' that a real writer should know about."[95] These socially shameful acts that catalyze self-formation in Dunham's hands, as in Breillat's, involve both the kinds of scenes discussed in this and the previous section, which reveal the corpo*reality*—the awkward, the messy, the humiliating—of bodies and sex, and scenes that explicitly and reflexively link shame and (self-)degradation to characters' writing.

Also simpatico with Dunham's work, Breillat's films are often diaristic, involving confessional interior monologues in voice-over (often voiced by Breillat herself). In a surreal (seemingly fantasized) scene evincing Breillat's self-inscription, *A Real Young Girl*'s Alice vomits on herself and then uses her vaginal secretion to write her name on a mirror's surface ("an almost literal *écriture féminine*," notes Liza Johnson) as she intones, "Liberated by the vomit's warmth, disgust makes me lucid."[96] Breillat makes ingenious use of the discontinuity wrought by *A Real Young Girl*'s postsynchronized sound (Alice's and Mme. Bonnard's voices are dubbed by Breillat's sister and mother), and the resultant out-of-body effect and heightened interiority enhance our sense of Alice's alienated, subjective perspective. Despite the Lewis Carroll allusion, Breillat's autobiographically inspired depiction of Alice's stultifying home life and surveillance by parents and villagers (including Shirley Stoler as a scowling storekeeper) make her world seem less wonderland than prison. Rather than giving in to the attempts by those around her either to sexualize or infantilize her, Alice takes control of her body and identity. "It was at that very moment that I decided to write [in] my diary," she announces, her soiling of her otherwise feminine frock proving (as she says) metaphorically liberating. *A Real Young Girl* exemplifies how sexual fantasy and writing the self provides female adolescents specifically an escape from the shaming and submissiveness enforced by society, perhaps particularly overbearing in the Pompidou-era provinces in which Breillat's debut film takes place, but even in the present undeniably oppressive.

Just as critics took umbrage at Breillat's audacity in publishing her first memoir at age seventeen, Dunham was similarly chastised for releasing hers at the relatively ripe age of twenty-eight, and for chronicling in its pages a discomforting account of her childhood sexual experimentation with her younger sibling.[97] Self-formation is closely tied up with writing for Hannah, and the previously discussed pattern of Dunham reflexively addressing her body-shamers is mirrored by Hannah's struggle throughout *Girls* to maintain her professional integrity and authorial voice in the face of external feedback. Believing one's own life makes for superior subject matter but also scorned for her solipsism and fixation on sexual experiences, Hannah is briefly deterred in a season one episode that has her attempting and failing to base an essay on the weighty but impersonal topic of death (1.9, "Leave Me Alone"). "What could be more trivial than intimacy?" always-cynical Ray asks, disdaining the topic of her work in progress with a dismissal that recalls how women's writing (on the page and for the screen) is stigmatized for its supposedly feminine, frivolous preoccupations.

After she experiences another surge of self-doubt in season two, Hannah's book editor (John Cameron Mitchell) orders her to retrieve her self-revealing authorial voice: "Did your hymen grow back? Where's the sexual failure? Where's the pudgy face slick with semen and sadness? More Anaïs Nin, less Jane Austen!" (2.9, "On All Fours"). Hannah heeds his words and finishes her memoir with stories drawn from her own, often abject, romantic and sexual experiences. The TED-style talk in which Mimi-Rose (Gillian Jacobs), Hannah's replacement in Adam's affections, proclaims her determination to subordinate romantic relationships to her creative pursuits seems intended to make Hannah reevaluate her own priorities, though it is unclear whether it is her flair for self-destructiveness or her reliance on romantic drama for creative material that prevents Hannah from taking the advice (4.9, "Daddy Issues").

Throughout the series, the paradox that painful life experiences make for good material is repeatedly explored, and the season four narrative in which Hannah temporarily moves away from Adam to attend the Iowa Writers' Workshop indicates how work and romance ultimately vie for priority even as the two feed each other. Though short-lived, Hannah's trials in this graduate-school environment ruled by politically correct virtue signaling provide Dunham once again with a forum in which to reflexively address criticisms about *Girls*, particularly its controversial play with sexual (self-)degradation, timely given the release of Dunham's memoir (with its detailed account of her college sexual assault) between season four's production and broadcast.[98] Workshopping a short story in a fiction-writing seminar, Hannah issues the class a trigger warning before reading aloud a graphic description of an encounter in which her character is sexually dominated. "The goal was not to say no," she reads. "In my choicelessness, I was free for a moment" (4.2, "Triggering").

In response to this articulation of precisely what Dunham (and Breillat) aim for in their screen enactments of liberating self-degradation, Hannah's classmates echo Dunham's real-life detractors: "It's about a really privileged girl deciding that she's going to let somebody abuse her." A fellow student's comparison of the essay to *Fifty Shades of Grey* suggests how the sex scenes in *Girls* have been superficially and unfairly conflated with the conventional fantasy of male dominance and female submission presented by E. L. James's neo-Gothic romance. Moreover, Hannah's male cohort's ascription of "literary merit" to male writers describing blow jobs pointedly alludes to the difference in response to sexual explicitness as screened elsewhere on HBO, which receives favorable treatment from critics and audiences alike, as opposed to the litany of complaints about *Girls'* ostensibly excessive sexual displays. As allegations mount that Hannah's short story is offensive to those who have suffered abuse and that the very experience of reading it proves traumatizing to her classmates, their professor offers a voice of reason that would be well extended to our contemporary culture of fear around disturbing ideas in and out of the classroom: "Everyone here is an adult and can make their own choices."[99]

Still another rebuke comes as a result of Hannah's presumed taking of autobiographical liberties, with many nods of agreement in reply to one classmate's vexed question, "How are we supposed to critique a work which is very clearly based directly from the author's personal experience?" As was Breillat's aim with *Sex Is Comedy*, this sequence (and Hannah's experience overall in Iowa), however self-serving, provides an irresistibly satisfying means for Dunham to rebut critics who obsessively politicize *Girls*, moralize about its sexual displays, and reductively conflate fictional and nonfictional personae. A response from her sole defender in the class, "We can't squash her voice," all but echoes Dunham's own defense, quoted early on in this chapter, of having "prematurely" written a memoir: "There is nothing gutsier to me than a person announcing that their story is one that deserves to be told, especially if that person is a woman." Opting to leave Iowa before completing her first term, Hannah proceeds to trespass teacher-student boundaries in her next gig as a high school substitute teacher. She is fired after the *Basic Instinct* incident, though by the end of season five she has found a more suitable outlet for her confessional overshares at an open-mike for the radio storytelling show *The Moth*. Dunham, meanwhile, continues to provoke her critics with self-performances that are defiantly feminist in their personal-is-political oversharing and body flaunting.

Girls' final season features a stand-alone episode that extends season four's debates at the Iowa Writers' Workshop to address a more literal form of sexual exploitation by a writer, fictionally embodied by eminent novelist Chuck Palmer (Matthew Rhys). The novelist finds himself facing down a young woman's allegations (made on Tumblr, no less) that he pressured her to give him oral sex during a hotel room liaison while on a book tour (6.3, "American Bitch"). While the episode deflects some of Dunham's own bad press onto, as Hannah terms him, "a male writer I love [who] reveals himself to be a heinous sleaze bag," here, too, the show incisively grapples with sexual power dynamics by reflexively addressing issues of privilege, consent, public shaming, and the question of separating artist from art. Reminiscent of David Mamet's two-hander *Oleanna*, though with Hannah as a writer who reports the story rather than the alleged victim, the episode unfurls in real time as Chuck invites her to his apartment for what he claims is a desire to tell his side of the story. The two swap reflections on feeling exploited and silenced by others, and, with their rapport intensifying, he asks her to lie with him on his bed. "But I'd encourage you to keep your clothes on to delineate any boundaries that feel right to you," he says, shortly before unzipping his pants to expose his penis (played on-screen by a prosthetic)—the third and final instance of male genital exposure on *Girls*. A disbelieving Hannah briefly grasps it before recoiling with indignation, at which moment they are interrupted by Chuck's preteen daughter arriving home. The episode ends with Hannah appearing to soften as she watches Chuck entranced at the sight of his progeny practicing the flute.

To judge by its ending, "American Bitch" seems to withhold a verdict on sexual consent versus coercion in favor of acknowledging the asymmetrical vagaries of so many sexual encounters, the frequent injustices arising from such encounters being tried in the court of public opinion, and the lumping together of sexual predators and sexual opportunists. Chuck defends his actions as "invitations" without threats or strings attached ("Did I put a gun to her head? Did I offer her a job?"), though he admits leading women on by raising ultimately unfulfilled expectations of future contact. He is, in his own estimation, "stupid, but not evil." The episode seems to call for a reasonable acknowledgment of those gray areas of consent that exist in certain sexual encounters—especially those confused by "the power imbalance" that Hannah ascribes to this one—before going on to question Chuck's assertion that his life was "destroyed" by noting his well-appointed surroundings and the rave *New York Times* review for his latest book.

Even as Hannah schools a disbelieving Chuck on what a nonconsensual blow job would look like, she warms to the narrative possibilities: "It would be very choky. It would involve somebody sort of holding someone else's head down and kind of, you know, maybe holding them by the hair, by the pigtails." Pouncing on this, Chuck's view that his assignation with the young woman provided her with "something to write about. She has a story. She has an experience," is both rationalizing and self-aggrandizing—even if he is then subject to a humiliating description of the encounter as recounted on Tumblr: "He made sad noises while I sucked him off."

In referencing Hannah's own faltering writerly ethos since her attempt in season one to follow Jessa's "fuck him for the story" advice and seduce her handsy boss, her debate with Chuck five seasons later is intended as Hannah's self-reckoning (and perhaps Dunham's as well), with "experience . . . the way people crave it and the way people use it," as Chuck puts it. Hannah will propose that it was less the story than the young woman's desire "to feel like she exists" that drove her into an intimate encounter with an esteemed man paying her attention. To this, Chuck proposes yet another theory: that she and other women use sex defensively, as the means by which they "resisted being known, guessing instead that the man they were standing across from wanted something or someone else entirely." This brings him to disclose his actual rationale for summoning Hannah: so "I can ask you where you're from, what you want, who you are. I can show you you're more to me than just a pretty face." Yet on the heels of this apparently sincere interest in seeing her comes another opportunity to scold, however deservedly ("You thought you knew everything, but you didn't. You listened to one source and then you flapped your lips"), to indoctrinate ("You can't let politics dictate what you write or who you fuck"), and with his final power play, to challenge her into seizing (so to speak) an opportunity that will make for another clickable story.

Despite its morally nonprescriptive treatment of fraught subject matter on the eve of the #MeToo moment, not to mention its provocative (albeit prosthetic) full-frontal reveal, the episode garnered greater critical appreciation than any other in *Girls*' later seasons, as if in agreement with Hannah's Iowa classmates on the advice Dunham herself might appear to have taken: "It would be much more interesting if there was a complex examination about the real ways that people challenge each other sexually" (2.4, "Triggering").

To Chuck's hand-wringing that "your world can be destroyed by something called 'Tumblr' without an 'e,'" Hannah responds, "That's why the internet is so cool, because it takes all the voices that have been marginalized." Chuck bursts back, "Some might argue it's a monster we've created that will ultimately kill us." While both are likely correct, over the course of the episode, the suggestion becomes that because technology-enabled contemporary media so often distorts truth, a deeper understanding of context and rationale demands face-to-face discussion.

The first season of Joe Swanberg's Netflix anthology series *Easy* (2016–19) features a similar storyline in which Marc Maron plays Jacob, a successful graphic novelist who thinks little of exposing his personal life on the page until he sleeps with young fan Alison (Emily Ratajkowski), a self-described "selfie artist" who turns their encounter into the subject of an art show (1.5, "Art and Life"). Jacob's enraged public confrontation over what he perceives as an invasion of his privacy ("Privacy is dead," Alison informs him) leads to his subsequent mauling on social media, though ultimately they arrive at an understanding of the way each callously weaponizes old and new media respectively.

Intent on voicing both sides of the story, these two one-off episodes give empathetic and even-keeled—if perhaps ultimately equivocal—treatment to an issue that would shortly thereafter explode with revelations about sexual harassment and assault by Harvey Weinstein and many more men in the entertainment and publishing industries. Chuck Palmer in *Girls* is clearly meant to resemble literary lothario Philip Roth, whose early novel *When She Was Good*—his only work with a woman protagonist—Hannah delights in finding on Chuck's bookshelf. "I know I'm not supposed to like him because he's a misogynist and he demeans women," she laments. Chuck encouragingly gives her the autographed copy, only to have her throw it back at him in disgust following his transgression. Roth's novel (whose reputed original title provides the episode's name and whose protagonist is said to have been inspired by his first wife) is about an emotionally damaged woman whose moralistic attempts to reform the men in her life ultimately prove self-destructive.[100] It echoes Chuck's entreaties to Hannah "to tackle subjects that matter. . . . Are you really gonna use all this skill to write for some shitty website, being paid a meaningless fee to slam some guy [for] getting head in some sterile hotel room in Rhode Island?" But these men's narratives also appropriate a woman's voice without permission for personal gain. In other words, they do precisely what Chuck and Maron's Jacob allege to have been subjected to. What both episodes further underscore is the effectiveness of provocation, whether at selling copies or getting clicks, building careers or making money. Such works might be "depthless," as Jacob alleges, but he nevertheless admits, "I think we're selling a few books."

CODA: NASTY WOMEN

Breillat and Dunham represent sex as an often ambivalent and ambiguous exchange, befogged by murky lines of consent and power dynamics, and subject to one's own self-writing and the repercussive experience of sexual assault. Like Breillat before her, Dunham was criticized for her explicit depictions of women's sexual (self-)subjugation, and Dunham courted censure on different grounds when she elected to end two seasons of *Girls* in ways that, as Adam's girlfriend Mimi-Rose would say, reinforce "constructs of romantic discourse": Adam's storybook rescue of Hannah in the season two finale and the equally magical coda at the end of season four that flashes forward to Hannah's newfound bliss amid a New York winter wonderland with her boyfriend Fran.

Unsurprisingly, Dunham's choice to end *Girls* on another retreatist note, with Hannah choosing to become a single mother rather than terminate her unplanned pregnancy, incited a still more fractious response that made good on the series' final opportunity to generate controversy. This ending is daring in opting not to endorse reproductive rights more assertively by having Hannah choose abortion—an unexpected development both because of the show's progressive politics and because Hannah, at this point in the show's narrative, seems strikingly ill-suited for motherhood. To suggest that Hannah could parent sufficiently seems as fancifully wish fulfilling and narratively conventional as Adam's shining knight rescue and the happily ever after (for a time, at least) with Fran. That the final episode concludes open-endedly but optimistically, at the moment latching is accomplished and the bond between mother and infant forged, violates the series' stronger inclination toward resisting progress. As Philip Maciak insightfully points out, to have Hannah magically transformed by motherhood buys into a dangerous biological determinism.[101] Or perhaps the prophetic words

Natalia hurled during her confrontation with Adam and Hannah at the start of season three will be realized: "You're going to end up with a baby that you can't fucking care for. You're going to kill that kid!" (3.1, "Females Only").

Having suffered a stroke in 2004 that left her partially paralyzed and hospitalized for four months, Breillat subsequently underwent significant financial loss at the hands of notorious swindler Christophe Rocancourt, the very subject whom she was researching for a new film project.[102] Breillat's necessary circumscription in the wake of these coupled events has proven productive against all odds. Since then, she has completed four films: *The Last Mistress*; two feminist-inflected retellings of sexual cautionary tales, *Bluebeard* (2009) and *The Sleeping Beauty* (2010); and *Abus de faiblesse* (*Abuse of Weakness*, 2013). The latter was adapted from a book Breillat wrote recounting her experiences with Rocancourt and features an exacting performance by Isabelle Huppert. Yet none of these works projects the same degree of sexual provocation as those examined above. And although Breillat was reported in 2014 to be planning her first English-language film, a story of a love affair set in 1960s Japan, no news has emerged of it since.[103]

Apart from Dunham, Breillat's cine-erotic legacy of extreme intimacy and sexual abjection has been taken up mostly by other provoc*auteurs* of French cinema, compatriots such as the already discussed Abdellatif Kechiche and Alain Guiraudie as well as Gaspar Noé (*Love*) and François Ozon (*Swimming Pool*, 2003), along with expatriates working in France such as Michael Haneke (*The Piano Teacher*, 2001) and Paul Verhoeven (*Elle*, 2016). Such films' ability to stimulate discussion and stand out from the clutter of millennial watercooler movies derives from their continuation of Breillat's mission to revise porn and Hollywood conventions of sexual representation into an art porn hybrid. While Breillat's industry presence seems confined for now to her post as professor of film at the European Graduate School in Switzerland (where she was named head of the international competition jury at the 2019 Locarno Film Festival), we need look no further for evidence that she retains the potential to provoke than her remarks in March 2018 on the culture podcast Murmur, which may prove the most controversial utterances of her career to date. In an interview that was taken off Murmur's website after a day, Breillat questions the strategy of the #MeToo and #BalanceTon-Porc movements, echoing the "old school" French feminism of other detractors, including actor Catherine Deneuve, in deploring those movements' alleged rhetoric of victimhood: "When you're 25 or 30 and you go to a man's hotel room, you know the game," she asserted.[104]

Since completing *Girls*, Dunham's creative work has included founding the feminist newsletter *Lenny* and a publishing imprint at Random House, producing two documentaries and two forthcoming scripted series for HBO, appearing as Valerie Solanas on *American Horror Story* (Ryan Murphy, FX, 2011–) and as a Manson Family member in *Once Upon a Time ... in Hollywood* (Quentin Tarantino, 2019), and creating with her producing partner Jenni Konner the HBO comedy series *Camping* (2018). But all this work has been largely overshadowed by her presence online and in the public eye. Like Breillat, Dunham has found herself in hot water over her response to #MeToo. Her defense of a *Girls* writer-producer accused of sexual assault struck many as at odds with her exhortations, in the wake of the allegations against Harvey Weinstein, that women "do not lie about rape." (She later apologized for the statement she issued in her colleague's defense.)[105]

Dunham has only become increasingly infamous, and reviled by many, for such tone-deaf public comments as "No one would be calling me a racist if they knew how badly I wanted to fuck [actor-musician] Drake," and for an ill-judged recounting in print of having imagined professional football player Odell Beckham Jr. to be sexually appraising her when the two were in proximity at the 2016 Met Ball. The remarks, received as presumptuous and racially offensive, were widely clucked over in online commentary ("peak white entitlement," *The Huffington Post* judged), even as they provoked their own presumptuous reading of Dunham's conclusions, as in the *HuffPost* writer's translation: "You're not interested in me, so you're just like all the other misogynistic black rappers who I can't connect with."[106] Another apology from Dunham followed, and soon after a "Lena Dunham Apology Generator" appeared on Twitter.

Writing about the first cycle of promotional discourse around *Girls*, Faye Woods notes that Dunham's confessional social media posts produced a blurring of her with her character that enhanced the perception of intimacy and authenticity that served to brand her authorial voice.[107] In her apologetic explanation on Instagram for yet another comment that provoked offense, Dunham directly acknowledged her self-performance and invited its conflation with her on-screen alter egos: "My words were spoken from a sort of 'delusional girl' persona I often inhabit—a girl who careens between wisdom and ignorance (that's what my TV show is, too) and it didn't translate."[108] Her precipitating gaffe, uttered during a discussion of Planned Parenthood on her "Woman of the Hour" podcast, that "I wish I had" an abortion was intended to convey her preference for a more firsthand appreciation of the importance of reproductive rights. The comment, while unfortunate, was somewhat understandable given podcasting's call for verbal extemporaneity; nonetheless Dunham's explanatory post elicited reprisals as bluntly personal in their insults as those received since career's start. Yet Dunham's "wish" here also speaks to that thread linking her and Breillat, discussed in the last section, in valorizing painful or shaming experiences as valuably self-forming (not to mention making for good material). Characteristically, Dunham has responded creatively and self-reflexively to this latest callout by cocreating and cohosting *The C Word* (for premium podcast start-up Luminary), a project devoted to reexamining the historical record on women regarded by society as "crazy."

Without dismissing Breillat's taunts and Dunham's blunders, it deserves noting that as the locus of controversy has shifted from the actual watercooler to its millennial incarnation in cyberspace, conversations around provoc*auteurs* threaten to become shallower and more purely reactive. Whereas the watercooler is precisely a place of processing and reflection—where we think through, in a collective way, a provocation—social media is often mobilized as an attention-seeking space where one blasts out one's own opinion with the goal of being the first and/or most extreme voice. It is also important to remember that creators like Breillat and Dunham are used to embedding their provocations in a dense and complex narrative context that they control; in contrast, social media is thin on context, making it easy to lose control of the narrative. Neither Dunham nor Hannah were by any means universally embraced when *Girls* erupted onto the cultural scene in 2012. Indeed, "hate watching" remained a potent driver of viewers to *Girls* into its final season, as indicated by a *Vulture* article titled "Hannah Horvath: Why Do We (Still) Hate Thee So?"[109] Though Dunham claims always to have intended Hannah's inappropriate behavior to be a subject for derision, by *Girls*' final season, the conflation of Dunham's public persona with the character of Hannah had grown so outsized as to seem self-caricaturing both on-screen and off-. As Hannah declares in a fervent attempt to put herself over at a job interview, "I give zero fucks about anything yet I have a strong opinion on everything—even topics I'm not informed on" (6.1, "All I Ever Wanted").

Amid nonstop denunciations of *Girls*' "all-consuming narcissism and entitlement" and problematic postfeminism, pushback against "Dunham fatigue" in feminist media studies, and increasing resistance from Millennial and Gen Z students to her inclusion on syllabi, appreciation of Dunham, however qualified, has become its own form of provocation. Thus, there is a general imperative to tread carefully in discussing her in whatever public forums. Writing about her dust-ups, *Vanity Fair*'s James Wolcott posits that each cycle of outrage "erodes the value of Dunham's persona and creative brand."[110] Given both Breillat's and Dunham's ill-received remarks of late, and judging from the deflating trajectory of both Breillat's career and *Girls'* critical acclaim and fandom over its six seasons—perhaps inevitable, given the hyperbolic embrace the series enjoyed at its outset—it remains to be seen whether these provoc*auteurs'* brands have been irreparably compromised. I will return to this question of provocation that goes "too far" at the end of this book, where I will further size up some of its gendered determinants.

To speculate on Dunham's legacy when she is in her thirties befits her precocious celebrity, though there is doubtless much more of her to come. Her "nasty woman" attributes extend beyond body image to encompass a thoroughly unladylike, impressively anti-aspirational protagonist.[111] Though the audacious images of her splinter-embedded rump, tits-out mesh top, *Spring Breakers*-worthy string bikini, and love handles aplenty seem as likely to foster a feminist legacy as the Capris and pantsuits worn a half-century earlier by Mary Tyler Moore, as Laura Petrie on *The Dick Van Dyke Show* (Carl Reiner, 1961–66) and later as Mary Richards on *The Mary Tyler Moore Show* (James L. Brooks and Allan Burns, 1970–77)—the latter fittingly the show Hannah and roommate Marnie stay up late watching in *Girls'* pilot.

Although average-size rather than plus-size, Dunham's corpo*reality* has already proven its indelible import for popular culture in promoting not-thin women into leading roles (even if they remain rare as romantic leads) and in making awkward, naturalistic sex a mainstay of women-created TV comedies such as *Broad City* (Ilana Glazer and Abbi Jacobson, 2010–11; Comedy Central, 2014–19) and *Fleabag* (Phoebe Waller-Bridge. As J. Soloway (co-creator of *I Love Dick* and *Transparent* (2014–19), remarked in the wake of Waller-Bridge's much-awarded triumph at the 2019 Emmys, "Phoebe wouldn't be there without Lena and I wouldn't be there without Lena."[112] Dunham's owning of her abjection also has had effects in welcoming into mainstream representation an acknowledgment of the libidinal drives of adolescent females, as with the "lustful middle school girl" protagonists of *Eighth Grade* (Bo Burnham, 2018) and *PEN15* (Maya Erskine and Anna Konkle, 2019–), and a fad for what Soraya Roberts names "the new female grotesque" of (especially older) women performers such as Olivia Coleman in *The Favourite* (Yorgos Lanthimos, 2018) and Nicole Kidman in *Destroyer* (Karyn Kusama, 2018). These portrayals embody "the unacceptable woman pushing her unacceptability to its limits," though, Roberts notes, such grotesqueries are permissible only "as long as you're a symbol of virtue or remain appealing out of costume."[113]

Though working in an American system far less financially or critically supportive of sexual provocation than that of France, Dunham's refusal to stand down even after much media scolding, whether of her exhibitionist self-displays or culturally insensitive pronouncements, offers continuing testament to Emily Nussbaum's reinterpretation of the grievance so often directed at Dunham: "But *Girls* also suggests that entitlement can be a superpower: It's the strength to believe, even when no one is listening, that you do have something to say."[114] Going further, Dunham's unfiltered admissions can be credited with creating teachable moments in which the dynamics of unexamined privilege have been laid bare and subject to valuable cultural debate in the virtual classroom of the online mediasphere. Whether greeting *Girls*' final season by flaunting cellulite-studded flanks on the cover of *Glamour*'s all-women-produced February 2017 issue, or introducing herself at the 2016 Democratic National Convention as "Hi, I'm Lena Dunham and according to Donald Trump, my body is probably, like, a two," or chronicling on social media in consummate oversharing form her struggle with endometriosis that resulted in her decision to have a hysterectomy at age thirty-one, Dunham stands out for her refusal to cover up, slim down, or shut up.

I have suggested a way of understanding Breillat's and Dunham's work through the lenses of feminism and porn, even as their work pushes and revises those concepts as well. Breillat and Dunham mobilize body performance to construct naturalistic rather than fetishistic representations of nudity and sex that enable and empower female subjectivities, though again by pointing provocatively to (self-)degradation as the route to self-knowledge. When Brett Lunceford posits that "to perform nude embodiment is to make explicit the performance of self," he gestures at the individualism that is written on the body, stripped of certain social signifiers, yet also reduced to others—namely, gender and race.[115] More than their controversial play with degradation, it is these clinging significations that ultimately limit the political power of body performance by Breillat, Dunham, and other provo*cauteurs* of corpo*reality*, as they shift cultural meanings that remain tied to bodies rather than untying them altogether. Yet ours remains for now a culture of "bodies that matter," to reference Judith Butler's seminal text.[116] Thus, we carry on the imperative to examine identity-inscribed bodies and sexual acts as they continue to define and confine our social subjectivities. And so it is of urgent importance that Breillat and Dunham, in defiantly and mindfully owning their abjection, wield their bodies as weapons for change.

NOTES

1. Breillat quoted in David Durnell, "Woman's Body as an Anatomy of Hell: Nihilism, Recursion and Tragedy in Breillat's *Anatomy of Hell*," *OffScreen* 10, no. 7 (July 2016), https://offscreen.com/view/anatomy_of _hell; Dunham quoted in Ryan Lattanzio, "'Girls' Creator Lena Dunham Poses for Playboy and Answers 20 Questions," *Indiewire*, March 14, 2013, https://www.indiewire.com/2013/03/girls-creator-lena-dunham-poses-for -playboy-and-answers-20-questions-198982/. Dunham did, in fact, appear in *Playboy*, though while wearing no less clothing than she typically wore on *Girls* (an oversize T-shirt reading "I Posed Today").

2. Quoted in Benjamin Secher, "Catherine Breillat: 'All True Artists Are Hated,'" *Telegraph* (London), April 8, 2005, https://www.telegraph.co.uk/culture/film/starsandstories/3672302/Catherine-BreillatAll-true-artists-are-hated.html.

3. Akhavan references Breillat's influence in So Mayer, *Political Animals: The New Feminist Cinema* (London: I. B. Tauris, 2015), 147.

4. See Lena Dunham, *Not That Kind of Girl: A Young Woman Tells You What She's "Learned"* (New York: Random House, 2014).

5. Other key figures of the New French Extremity include Virginie Despentes and Coralie Trinh Thi (*Baise-moi*, 2000), Bruno Dumont (*Humanité*, 1999), and Gaspar Noé (*Irreversible*). See James Quandt, "Flesh and Blood: Sex and Violence in Recent French Cinema," *Artforum*, February 2004, https://www.artforum.com/print/200402/flesh-blood-sex-and-violence-in-recent-french-cinema-6199.

6. John Phillips, "Catherine Breillat's *Romance*: Hard Core and the Female Gaze," *Studies in French Cinema* 1, no. 3 (2001): 140; Gwendolyn Wells, "Accoutrements of Passion: Fashion, Irony, and Feminine P.O.V. in Catherine Breillat's *Romance*," *Sites* 6, no. 1 (2002): 65.

7. Quoted in Michael Nordine, "Catherine Breillat Says Asia Argento Is a 'Traitor,' Harvey Weinstein Isn't That Bad, and She's Against #MeToo," *Indiewire*, March 29, 2018, https://www.indiewire.com/2018/03/catherine-breillat-asia-argento-harvey-weinstein-jessica-chastain-me-too-1201945040/.

8. Helen Hester, "Perverting the Explicit: Catherine Breillat's Visual Vocabulary of Desire," in *Tainted Love: Screening Sexual Perversion*, ed. Darren Kerr and Donna Peberdy (London: I. B. Tauris, 2017), 48.

9. Serena Daalmans, "'I'm Busy Trying to Become Who I Am': Self-Entitlement and the City in HBO's *Girls*," *Feminist Media Studies* 13, no. 2 (2013): 360.

10. Emily Nussbaum, "It's Different for 'Girls,'" *New York*, April 2012, nymag.com/arts/tv/features/girls-lena-dunham-2012-4/index1.html.

11. Lena Dunham, "Retouched by an Angel," *Lenny*, letter no. 24 (March 8, 2016), https://www.lennyletter.com/story/lena-dunham-doesnt-want-her-photos-retouched. Feminist website Jezebel offered $10,000 for the untouched photographs and then published them.

12. Eleri Butler, "Catherine Breillat: Anatomy of a Hard-Core Agitator," in *Peep Shows: Cult Film and the Cine-Erotic*, ed. Xavier Mendik (London: Wallflower, 2012), 83.

13. See Linda Williams, *Hard Core: Power, Pleasure, and the "Frenzy of the Visible*," expanded ed. (Berkeley: University of California Press, 1999).

14. Quoted in Kevin Murphy, "Hell's Angels: An Interview with Catherine Breillat on *Anatomy of Hell*," *Senses of Cinema*, no. 34 (February 2015), http://sensesofcinema.com/2005/on-recent-films-34/breillat_interview/.

15. Quoted in Secher, "Catherine Breillat."

16. Quoted in Nordine, "Catherine Breillat Says."

17. Dunham, *Not That Kind of Girl*, xvi.

18. Quoted in Geoffrey Macnab, "Sadean Woman," *Sight and Sound* 14, no. 12 (2004): 22.

19. Quoted in Nick James, "Looks That Paralyze," *Sight and Sound* 11, no. 12 (2001): 20.

20. See, for example, Jon Lewis, *Hollywood v. Hard Core: How the Struggle over Censorship Created the Modern Film Industry* (New York: New York University Press, 2002).

21. Quoted in Linda Williams, *Screening Sex* (Durham, NC: Duke University Press, 2008), 296.

22. Quoted in Frank Bruni, "The Bleaker Sex," *New York Times*, April 1, 2012, https://www.nytimes.com/2012/04/01/opinion/sunday/bruni-the-bleaker-sex.html; emphasis in original.

23. David Bordwell, "The Art Cinema as a Mode of Film Practice," in *Film Theory and Criticism*, 7th ed., ed. Leo Braudy and Marshall Cohen (New York: Oxford University Press, 2009), 652.

24. L. Williams, "Cinema's Sex Acts," 15. This objective of screening sexual truth is ideologically complementary to, if stylistically distinct from, other varieties of feminist and queer porn of the instructional sort produced by sex educators-performers and "altporn" auteurs such as Lorelei Lee, Tristan Taormino, and Courtney Trouble—"Porn that doesn't fake it!," as Trouble's self-proclaimed "radical porn" site No Fauxxx's tagline promises—or in the "dyke" and "genderqueer" vein of films by producer-performers such as Shine Louise Houston and Jiz Lee. See Feona Attwood, "Art School Sluts: Authenticity and the Aesthetics of Altporn," in *Hard to Swallow: Hard-Core Pornography on Screen*, ed. Claire Hines and Darren Kerr (London: Wallflower, 2012), 42–56; Tristan Taormino et al., ed., *The Feminist Porn Book: The Politics of Producing Pleasure* (New York: The Feminist Press, 2013).

25. Douglas Keesey, *Catherine Breillat* (Manchester: Manchester University Press, 2015), 13–14.

26. Ibid., 3–5.

27. Keesey proposes that *36 fillette*'s lothario Maurice (Etienne Chicot) was inspired by director Maurice Pialat's obsession with actor Sandrine

Bonnaire during the filming of *À Nos Amours* (*For Our Loves*, 1983). Breillat was on set to observe the film, and I discuss the film elsewhere as displaying a hypersexualized visual fixation on its youthful star. Ibid., 6, 32. See Maria San Filippo, "A Tale of Two Suzannes: *À nos amours* (*For Our Loves*, 1983) and *Suzanne* (2013)," *Senses of Cinema*, no. 77 (December 2015), sensesofcinema.com/2015/feature-articles/a-nos-amours-and-suzanne/.

28. Keesey, *Catherine Breillat*, 6, 11.

29. Ducey maintains that the sex was simulated, Siffredi claims it was unsimulated, and Breillat has maintained her customary vagueness on the topic. For Ducey's response, see E. Butler, "Catherine Breillat," 81. See also Saul Anton, "Interview: Catherine Breillat Opens Up about 'Romance,' Sex and Censorship," *Indiewire*, September 23, 1999, https://www.indiewire.com/1999/09/interview-catherine-breillat-opens-up-about-romance-sex-and-censorship-82059/.

30. Quoted in Brian Price, "Catherine Breillat," *Senses of Cinema*, no. 23 (December 2002), sensesofcinema.com/2002/great-directors/breillat/.

31. Keesey, *Catherine Breillat*, 7.

32. Mattias Frey, *Extreme Cinema: The Transgressive Rhetoric of Today's Art Film Culture* (New Brunswick, NJ: Rutgers University Press, 2016), 94–106.

33. Keesey, *Catherine Breillat*, 68–69.

34. Quoted in Keesey, *Catherine Breillat*, 135. *Anatomy of Hell* is assuredly Breillat's most disdained film, and I might be tempted to exclude it were it not so constitutionally provocative. The elements that I find most contradict my feminist framing of Breillat's work concern a scene in which The Man anally penetrates The Woman (with a backhoe handle) in such a way that seems neither presented for critique (as in *Fat Girl*) nor as consensual (as in *Romance*) nor a fantasy sequence (as in *A Real Young Girl*). Also questionable is the choice to make Siffredi's character gay, which undermines our ability to read the film as a critique of heteropatriachal relations between men and women and affixes a homophobic conflation of misogyny to male homosexuality. Breillat claims the film was inspired by her first marriage (to a gay man, François Wimille) as well as by Marguerite Duras's 1982 novella *The Malady of Death*, itself thought to be inspired by Duras's relationship to a gay man. See Keesey, *Catherine Breillat*, 144.

35. E. Butler, "Catherine Breillat," 82.

36. Emma Wilson, "Deforming Femininity: Catherine Breillat's *Romance*," in *France on Film: Reflections on Popular French Cinema*, ed. Lucy Mazdon (London: Wallflower, 2001), 147.

37. See Victoria Best and Martin Crowley, *The New Pornographies: Explicit Sex in Recent French Fiction and Film* (Manchester: Manchester University Press, 2008), 69–70.

38. Hester, "Perverting the Explicit," 53–54.

39. Martine Beugnet, *Cinema and Sensation: French Film and the Art of Transgression* (Edinburgh: Edinburgh University Press, 2007), 107–8.

40. Kelley Conway, "Sexually Explicit French Cinema: Genre, Gender, and Sex," in *A Companion to French Cinema*, ed. Alistair Fox, Michel Marie, Raphaëlle Moine, and Hilary Radner (Malden, MA: Wiley-Blackwell, 2015), 468–69.

41. Breillat had previously stated, when asked about Argento's charge that she was raped by Harvey Weinstein, that she found the charge unwarranted and the actor to have been "motivated by self-interest—it was a kind of semi-prostitution." Quoted in Nordine, "Catherine Breillat Says." In 2020, Weinstein was found guilty of sexual assault and rape and sentenced to twenty-three years in prison. Argento's responding tweets, posted on March 30, 2018 and since deleted from her Twitter account, are quoted in Ariston Anderson, "Asia Argento Fires Back after Catherine Breillat Defends Harvey Weinstein," *Hollywood Reporter*, March 31, 2018, https://www.hollywoodreporter.com/news/asia-argento-fires-back-catherine-breillat-defends-harvey-weinstein-1098829. In addition to condemning Breillat's directorial methods, Argento decried Breillat for having collaborated as co-screenwriter of David Hamilton's 1977 soft-core film *Bilitis*; the former fashion photographer Hamilton was accused by multiple women of having raped them when they were underage; he committed suicide in 2016, shortly after four women's accusations went public. Argento has since been accused by a male former costar of sexual assault when he was underage.

42. Mesquida and Breillat quoted in Keesey, *Catherine Breillat*, 9, 55–56.

43. Lena Dunham, "One of a Kind," *Lenny*, letter no. 72 (February 7, 2017), http://independentonlinenewsreporter.blogspot.com/2017/02/lena-dunhams-sexual-healing.html.

44. Elaine Blair, "The Loves of Lena Dunham," *New York Review*, June 7, 2012, https://www.nybooks.com/articles/2012/06/07/loves-lena-dunham/.

45. See Janet McCabe and Kim Akass, "Sex, Swearing and Respectability: Courting Controversy, HBO's Original Programming and Producing Quality TV," in *Quality TV: Contemporary American Television and Beyond*, ed. Janet McCabe and Kim Akass (London: I. B. Tauris, 2007), 62–76.

46. Meredith Nash and Ruby Grant, "Twenty-Something *Girls* v. Thirty-Something *Sex and the City* Women," *Feminist Media Studies* 15, no. 6 (2015): 982.

47. This reference is to Brett Martin's *Difficult Men: Behind the Scenes of a Creative Revolution: From The Sopranos to The Wire to Mad Men and Breaking Bad* (New York: Penguin, 2013). Although the book focuses on the importance of the (male) auteur-showrunner for authoring HBO's hit shows and rebranding effort, it effaces the pivotal role *Sex and the City* played in laying the groundwork for what has been called TV's new golden era.

48. @lenadunham, Twitter posts, May 24, 2013, 12:21 a.m., https://twitter.com/lenadunham/status/337785477824401408; 12:23 a.m., https://twitter.com/lenadunham/status/337785858356826113; 12:24 a.m., https://twitter.com/lenadunham/status/337786057695318016.

49. Quoted in Esther Zuckermann, "The 'Girls' Parody Porn Stars Just Want Lena Dunham to Understand," *Atlantic*, May 31, 2013, https://www.theatlantic.com/entertainment/archive/2013/05/girls-parody-porn-stars/314687/.

50. Quoted in Anna Breslaw, "Director of *Girls* Porn Slams Lena Dunham for Being Too Conservative," *Jezebel*, June 1, 2013, https://jezebel.com/director-of-girls-porn-slams-lena-dunham-for-being-too-510837480.

51. A twenty-two minute "super cut" compilation of intimate scenes from *Normal People* appeared first on Pornhub and quickly spread to other sites; at the behest of the series' executive producer, Pornhub took down the clip and verified such actions were not in compliance with site policy. It has become par for the course for sex scenes from films and television shows to be illegally uploaded to porn hosting sites, and it is largely incumbent on the copyright holder to request such material's removal. See Zack Sharf, "'Normal People' Producer Slams Pornhub for Circulating Sex Scenes: 'Deeply Disrespectful,'" *Indiewire*, May 21, 2020, https://www.indiewire.com/2020/05/normal-people-producer-sex-scenes-pornhub-1202232767/.

52. See Kathleen Rowe (now Kathleen Rowe Karlyn), *The Unruly Woman: Gender and the Genres of Laughter* (Austin: University of Texas Press, 1996).

53. "Next Episode of 'Girls' To Feature Lena Dunham Shitting Herself During Gyno Exam While Eating a Burrito," *The Onion*, March 14, 2013, https://www.theonion.com/next-episode-of-girls-to-feature-lena-dunham-shitting-h-1819574677.

54. Quoted in Simon Hattenstone, "Lena Dunham: 'People Called Me Fat and Hideous, and I Lived," *Guardian*, January 10, 2014, https://www

.theguardian.com/culture/2014/jan/11/lena-dunham-called-fat-hideous-and-i-lived.

55. Germaine Greer, "The Connection between Art and Exhibitionism," *Guardian*, January 28, 2008, https://www.theguardian.com/artanddesign/artblog/2008/jan/28/theconnectionbetweenartand.

56. For a historical contextualization of Dunham's work in relation to these feminist body performance artists, see Saroya Roberts, "Naked If I Want To: Lena Dunham's Body Politic," *Salon*, February 9, 2013, https://www.salon.com/2013/02/09/naked_if_i_want_to_lena_dunhams_body_politic/. The connection to Schneemann is valuable for the way in which her work also benefits from consideration of its feminist dialogue with porn, which Jennifer Moorman parses insightfully in "Women on Top: The Work of Female Pornographers and 'Sexperimental' Filmmakers" (PhD diss., University of California, Los Angeles, 2014), 50–135.

57. Michelle Konstantinovsky, "Why Lena Dunham's Body Matters (And Why It's Ridiculous That It Does)," *Hello Giggles*, April 26, 2012, https://www.huffpost.com/entry/why-lena-dunhams-body-matters_n_1458765.

58. Quoted in Roberts, "Naked If I Want To."

59. I am thinking in particular of Antin's work *Carving: A Traditional Sculpture* (1972), 148 black-and-white photographs documenting her loss of ten pounds over 37 days; Opie's tattooed and pierced "dyke mother" self-portraiture; Orlan's theatricalized documenting of her multiple plastic surgeries throughout the 1990s; Sherman's "society portraits" from 2008 of herself in the guises of aging matriarchs; and Sprinkle's "Public Cervix Announcement" performance, in which she invites audience members to view her cervix with speculum and flashlight. Though not as radical in form or content, the (semi)nude photographic self-portraiture produced by Francesca Woodman during the 1970s, before her suicide at age 22, seems a likely inspiration for Dunham as well in its uncomfortably intimate yet playful depictions of female embodiment and the transgressive blurring of private and public spaces. It would also not surprise me were Dunham to have seen Chantal Akerman's early works, particularly *Je Tu Il Elle*, in which the filmmaker incarnates a similarly exposed but coy presence on-screen.

60. Brett Lunceford, *Naked Politics: Nudity, Political Action, and the Rhetoric of the Body* (Lanham, MD: Lexington Books, 2012), 6.

61. Julia Kristeva, *Powers of Horror: An Essay on Abjection*, trans. Leon S. Roudiez (New York: Columbia University Press, 1982), 2.

62. Ibid., 15.

63. Such experiences include the queer child's subjectedness to what Eve Sedgwick calls "painful individuation" or the gay Asian male's relegation to racialized and feminized bottomhood that Hoang Tan Nguyen elucidates. See Sedgwick, *Touching, Feeling: Affect, Pedagogy, Performativity* (Durham, NC: Duke University Press, 2003), 37; and Nguyen, *A View from the Bottom: Asian American Masculinity and Sexual Representation* (Durham, NC: Duke University Press, 2014).

64. Liza Johnson, "Perverse Angle: Feminist Film, Queer Film, Shame," in "Beyond the Gaze: Recent Approaches to Film Feminisms," ed. Kathleen McHugh and Vivian Sobchack, special issue, *Signs* 30, no. 1 (Autumn 2004): 1371.

65. Adrienne Angelo, "Sexual Cartographies: Mapping Subjectivity in the Cinema of Catherine Breillat," *Journal for Cultural Research* 14, no. 1 (2010): 47.

66. Keesey, *Catherine Breillat*, 23.

67. Hester, "Perverting the Explicit," 51; emphasis in original.

68. Quoted in Keesey, *Catherine Breillat*, 51.

69. Amanda Hess, "'I Feel Pretty' and the Rise of Beauty-Standard Denialism," *New York Times*, April 23, 2018, https://www.nytimes.com/2018/04/23/movies/i-feel-pretty-amy-schumer-beauty.html?login=email&auth=login-email.

70. See Michel Foucault, *Discipline and Punish: The Birth of the Prison*, trans. Alan Sheridan (New York: Pantheon, 1978) and *The History of Sexuality*, vol. 1, *An Introduction*, trans. Robert Hurley (New York: Random House, 1978).

71. Quoted in Courtney Hazlett, "Lena Dunham Explains Her Thighs—And the 'No-Pants' Look," *Today*, October 9, 2012, https://www.today.com/entertainment/lena-dunham-explains-her-thighs-no-pants-look-1C6358990?franchiseSlug=todayentertainmentmain.

72. Stern and Dunham quoted in Kimberly Nordyke, "Howard Stern Apologizes to Lena Dunham, Says She's Not 'Just a Talentless Little Fat Chick' (Audio)," *Hollywood Reporter*, January 15, 2013, https://www.hollywoodreporter.com/news/howard-stern-apologizes-lena-dunham-412824.

73. Lunceford, *Naked Politics*, 8.

74. Quoted in Alyssa Rosenberg, "5 Productive Ways to Ask Lena Dunham about the Nudity on 'Girls,'" *Think Progress*, January 10, 2014, https://thinkprogress.org/5-productive-ways-to-ask-lena-dunham-about-nudity-on-girls-67253fdcf72a/.

75. "Blobby" was the term used by journalist Linda Stasi, who called Dunham "a pathological exhibitionist, in "New 'Girl' on Top," *New York Post*, January 24, 2013, https://nypost.com/2013/01/04/new-girl-on-top/.

76. Quoted in Ross McCammon, "Lena Dunham Is Building an Empire," *Esquire*, November 13, 2012, https://www.esquire.com/news-politics/a16688/lena-dunham-interview-1212/.

77. Liza Johnson, "Perverse Angle," 1382–83.

78. Quoted in Meghan Daum, "Lena Dunham Is Not Done Confessing," *New York Times*, September 10, 2014, https://www.nytimes.com/2014/09/14/magazine/lena-dunham.html?_r=0.

79. David Hagland and Daniel Engber, "Was That the Worst Episode of *Girls* Ever?" *Slate*, February 10, 2013, https://slate.com/culture/2013/02/girls-on-hbo-one-man-s-trash-episode-5-of-season-2-reviewed-by-guys.html.

80. Tracie Egan Morrissey, "What Kind of Guy Does a Girl Like Lena Dunham 'Deserve?'" *Jezebel*, February 11, 2013, https://jezebel.com/what-kind-of-guy-does-a-girl-who-looks-like-lena-dunham-5983437.

81. @Dagword, Twitter post, February 12, 2013, 7:48 a.m.

82. Hannah Mueller, "'At Least Let Us See Them Before You Cut Them All Off!' The Gendered Representation of Nudity in Contemporary Quality TV," in *Contemporary Quality TV: The Auteur, the Fans, and Constructions of Gender*, ed. Ralph J. Poole and Saskia Fürst (Heidelberg: Universitätsverlag Winter, forthcoming).

83. Ginette Vincendeau, "Sisters, Sex, and Sitcoms," *Sight and Sound*, December 2001, reprinted in *Fat Girl* DVD liner notes, Criterion Collection.

84. Liz Constable, "Unbecoming Sexual Desires for Women Becoming Sexual Subjects: Simone de Beauvoir (1949) and Catherine Breillat (1999)," *MLN* 119, no. 4 (September 2004): 679, 690–93; emphasis in original.

85. Keesey, *Catherine Breillat*, 138.

86. E. Butler, "Catherine Breillat," 83; see Breillat quoted in Robert Sklar, "A Woman's Vision of Shame and Desire: An Interview with Catherine Breillat," *Cineaste* 25, no. 1 (December 1999): 25.

87. Breillat has said that this ending was an allusion to Robert Bresson's *Mouchette* (1967), whose tortured heroine refuses to give in to gossips wanting to confirm her rape by the town tramp so she claims he is her lover. See Stéphane Goudet and Claire Vassé, "One Soul with Two Bodies: An Interview with Catherine Breillat," DVD notes on *Fat Girl*, Criterion Collection. Original interview appeared in *Positif*, no. 481 (March 2001): 26–30.

88. Emily Fox-Kales, "A ma soeur! Erotic Bodies and the Primal Scene Reconfigured," *Journal for Cultural Research* 14, no. 1 (2010): 23.

89. Vincendeau, "Sisters, Sex, and Sitcoms."

90. Wells, "Accoutrements of Passion," 53; Breillat quoted in E. Butler, "Catherine Breillat," 68–69.

91. Emily Nussbaum, "Hannah Barbaric," *New Yorker* (February 11 and 18, 2013): 100.

92. Brian Hiatt, "Girl on Top," *Rolling Stone*, February 28, 2013, https://www.rollingstone.com/movies/movie-news/lena-dunham-girl-on-top-237146/; emphasis in original.

93. Lena Dunham, "Lena Dunham on Sex, Oversharing and Writing about Lost 'Girls,'" interview with Terry Gross, *Fresh Air*, NPR, September 29, 2014, audio, 44:59, https://www.npr.org/templates/transcript/transcript.php?storyId=352276798.

94. Katie Roiphe, "Working Women's Fantasies," *Newsweek*, April 4, 2012, https://www.newsweek.com/working-womens-fantasies-63915.

95. Sean Fuller and Catherine Driscoll, "HBO's *Girls*: Gender, Generation, and Quality Television," *Continuum: Journal of Media and Cultural Studies* 29, no. 2 (2015): 8.

96. Liza Johnson, "Perverse Angle," 1377.

97. See Dunham, *Not That Kind of Girl*.

98. See ibid.

99. For an incisive discussion of the perils of mandating against potentially triggering ideas in academic forums, see Laura Kipnis, "Sexual Paranoia Strikes Academe," *Chronicle of Higher Education*, February 27, 2015, https://www.chronicle.com/article/Sexual-Paranoia-Strikes/190351/. For a testament to the generative potential of teaching challenging sexual material that is particularly relevant to this chapter, see Katariina Kyrölä, "Squirming in the Classroom: *Fat Girl* and the Ethical Value of Extreme Discomfort," in *Unwatchable*, ed. Nicholas Baer, Maggie Hennefeld, and Laura Horak (New Brunswick, NJ: Rutgers University Press, 2019), 317–22.

100. In 2017, shortly before Roth's death, his much-younger former lover Lisa Halliday published a novel titled *Asymmetry*, which gives a fictionalized account of their relationship.

101. Philip Maciak, "The *Girls* Finale," *Los Angeles Review of Books*, April 24, 2017, https://lareviewofbooks.org/article/the-girls-finale/#!.

102. The project, an adaptation of Breillat's 2007 novel *Bad Love*, was to have starred actor-model Naomi Campbell.

103. Inkoo Kang, "Catherine Breillat to Make First English-Language Film," *Indiewire*, May 20, 2014, https://womenandhollywood.com/catherine-breillat-to-make-first-english-language-film-3c87fa5fccaa/.

104. Quoted in Nordine, "Catherine Breillat Says."

105. See "Lena Dunham Apologises for Defending *Girls* Writer Accused of Sexual Assault," *Guardian*, November 19, 2017, https://www.theguardian.com/culture/2017/nov/20/lena-dunham-apologises-for-defending-girls-writer-accused-of-sexual-assault. See also Lena Dunham, "Harvey Weinstein and the Silence of Men," *New York Times*, October 9, 2017, https://www.nytimes.com/2017/10/09/opinion/harvey-weinstein-lena-dunham-silence-.html. Dunham reported having told Hillary Clinton, on whose campaign she was an active ambassador, that major donor Harvey Weinstein was a rapist well in advance of the story's breaking.

106. Zeba Blay, "The Way Lena Dunham Talks about Black Men Is Peak White Entitlement," *HuffPost*, September 6, 2016, https://www.huffpost.com/entry/the-way-lena-dunham-talks-about-black-men-is-peak-white-entitlement_n_57cecdfde4b0e60d31e00ebc. Dunham's remarks comprised part of her interview with Amy Schumer in the September 6, 2016, issue of *Lenny*.

107. Faye Woods, "*Girls* Talk: Authorship and Authenticity in the Reception of Lena Dunham's *Girls*," *Critical Studies in Television* 10, no. 2 (Summer 2015): 42–43.

108. @lenadunham, Instagram post, December 20, 2016.

109. Kathryn VanArendonk, "Hannah Horvath: Why Do We (Still) Hate Thee So?" *Vulture*, April 13, 2016, https://www.vulture.com/2016/04/hannah-horvath-why-do-we-still-hate-thee-so.html.

110. James Wolcott, "Ms. Dunham Regrets," *Vanity Fair*, February 2018, 36.

111. "Nasty women" is the term then candidate Donald Trump used in reference to opponent Hillary Clinton during the third presidential debate on October 19, 2016, which was subsequently taken up by Clinton supporters and feminists more widely as an emblem of pride.

112. Quoted by Kathryn Hahn, interview by Jesse Thorn, *Bullseye*, Maximum Fun, December 6, 2019, audio, 31:14, https://maximumfun.org/episodes/bullseye-with-jesse-thorn/kathryn-hahn/.

113. Amanda Hess, "The Lustful Middle School Girl Rises," *New York Times*, February 22, 2019, https://www.nytimes.com/2019/02/22/movies/pen15-eighth-grade-middle-school-girls.html; Soraya Roberts, "Hollywood and the New Female Grotesque," *Longreads*, December 2018,

https://longreads.com/2018/12/17/hollywood-and-the-new-female-grotesque/. See also Mary Russo, *The Female Grotesque: Risk, Excess, Modernity* (New York: Routledge, 1994).

114. Nussbaum, "It's Different for 'Girls.'"
115. Lunceford, *Naked Politics*, 142–43.
116. Judith Butler, *Bodies That Matter: On the Discursive Limits of "Sex"* (London: Routledge, 1993).

FOUR

Inbetweener (In)Appropriations

"Bad Queer" Provoc*auteurs*
Lisa Cholodenko and Desiree Akhavan

I've always been interested in what makes people attracted to each other. How do people negotiate their needs? And where do sexual attraction and power and intimacy come into the mix for better and not better?

Lisa Cholodenko

I don't use language appropriately. I am always using the wrong words . . . "dyke" is one of those words. I use it with love, and I think it's a great word. I love the way it rolls off the tongue. Have I earned the right to use it as a bisexual woman? In the eyes of some people, no. . . . It's tricky, actually. Right now I'm editing something, and one of the characters uses the word "fag." A lesbian uses the word. And I had a real discussion today about, you know, what are we going to think about that woman who uses that word? And is that appropriate? And this is the stuff that my life is built around. I'm really fascinated by the language people use and who's able to say what word.

Desiree Akhavan

A 2015 INDIEWIRE BLOG POST ASKED, "Is this the end of the model gay character?"[1] The impetus for the question was the commercial underperformance of *Freeheld* (Peter Sollett, 2015), the fictional adaptation of a true story about a lesbian couple's legal battle over domestic partner benefits, starring Julianne Moore and Ellen Page. The film's screenwriter, Ron Nyswaner, publicly protested against what he felt had been a "de-gayed" project, suggesting that *Freeheld*'s box office fizzle was, paradoxically, a result of the same sort of "idealized" and "normalized" gay characterizations that had been previously ascribed to the crossover success of Nyswaner's best-known project, *Philadelphia* (Jonathan Demme, 1993). Granted, *Freeheld*'s failure to gain traction was greeted as far less shameful than that of that season's other hoped-for crossover film about LGBTQ+ history, *Stonewall* (Roland Emmerich, 2015). That film's cisgendered whitewashing of the landmark uprising (which had been led largely by trans people of color) incited a boycott campaign and scathing reviews.

Freeheld's and *Stonewall*'s shared lack of appeal suggests a degree of disillusionment with the representational tenets of "palatability" and "universalism" once touted as the path to uniting straight and LGBTQ+ audiences. Whatever one's ideological vantage point, these films seemed both too gay—their pride (or pandering, in *Stonewall*'s case) emblazoned too earnestly on their sleeve—yet not radical enough in aesthetic, sexual, or political terms to seem verifiably queer. In academic discourse, the last two decades' embrace of the term *queer* as a critical praxis has entailed at least a partial rejection of the term *gay*. Associated with New Queer Cinema's progenitor, the Gay New Wave of 1970s–80s feel-good, commercially minded films such as *Desert Hearts* (Donna Deitch, 1985) and *Making Love* (Arthur Hiller, 1982), *gay* came to be equated with identitarian and visibility politics and traditionally defined "positive images" that appeared archaic by century's end, when Lisa Henderson noted: "Positive no longer means portraying members of historically marginalized groups in mainstream or high-status positions, or simply rewriting the rules about who can and cannot be represented as a member of the social and symbolic club."[2]

Thereafter *queer* evolved in academic circles as the more progressive term, the hallmarks of which Arlene Stein and Ken Plummer formulate as follows:

1. A conceptualization of sexuality and gender as socially constructed and discursively reinforced
2. The problematization of sexual and gender categories, and of identities in general
3. A rejection of civil-rights strategies in favor of an anti-assimilationist politics of carnival, transgression, and parody
4. A willingness to interrogate areas which normally would not be seen as the terrain of sexuality or gender.[3]

Yet as demonstrated by the debate over *Freeheld* and *Stonewall*, *gay* did not directly give way to but rather took up a place in contention with *queer*, to voice an ongoing attraction to mainstream visibility. Harry Benshoff finds reason to defend this attraction: "Several queer critics have suggested that the new images of 'nice gays'—overwhelmingly white, asexual, and removed from the queer community—have worked to create a new demonization of 'bad queers'—people who have the kinds of sex and sexual politics that clash with white picket fences. . . . However, such mainstreaming is an important development in the history of queer representation because it affords not just a *quantitative* difference in queer representation (i.e. more and more images) but also a *qualitative* difference: the greater number of images being produced also allows for a greater diversity and complexity of images."[4] Nonetheless, *Freeheld* and *Stonewall* relied on a representational politics perceived, from a queer perspective, as dated and even damaging for its commercial co-optation and ideological complicity with heteronormative hegemonies. Thus the "de-gaying" to which Nyswaner objected would be more fittingly termed a "de-queering." Even as criteria for evaluating "queer but not gay" representational politics has coalesced, dissatisfaction continues to be voiced by those for whom the term *queer*, which had once connoted ACT UP–era radicalism, has come to signify contemporary LGBTQ+ politics' premature retreat from the activist barricades and queer culture's co-optation as an "anything goes" lifestyle choice and commodification as a brand label. As a 2016 *New York Times* article asking "When Everyone Can Be 'Queer,' Is Anyone?" points out, "The radical power of 'queer' always came from its inclusivity. But that inclusivity offers a false promise of equality that does not translate to the lived reality of most queer people."[5]

In sum, *queer* has become a contested term for its ontological, representational, and political valences, provoking concerns that the subversive power it once wielded has been diluted. Acknowledging divisions of taste alongside tensions in the queer community may prove more of a test for political advocacy than a facade of all-inclusiveness and positivity. But what pushes this mounting divisiveness to a cultural tipping point is its coinciding with and compounding the 21st century imperative to cut through the clutter of an oversaturated screen mediascape. This imperative is met, I will argue, by provoking controversy through voicing an oppositional radical sensibility and tapping into that of its likeminded niche audience—a creative and critical sensibility that I name (in a callback to Benshoff) "bad queer."

To consider how these drives to re-radicalize, or perhaps "re-queer," representational and political discourse connect at the point of sexual provocation on 21st century screens, this chapter singles out a cross-generational pairing simpatico in their shared authorial signatures as bad queers: New Queer Cinema pioneer Lisa Cholodenko and Millennial media creator Desiree Akhavan. Where Catherine Breillat's and Lena Dunham's provoc*auteurism* shares strategies of feminist critique through performances of corpo*reality*, discussed in chapter 3, Cholodenko and Akhavan mutually construct bad queer self-inscriptions through what I will characterize as their "inbetweener" positioning vis-à-vis sexual and representational politics. To be a bad queer in this sense is to stand outside what *queer* currently affirms or legitimates—as determined by a sometimes testy negotiation between what one such bad queer, novelist and cultural critic Bret Easton Ellis, snarkily refers to as the "healthy mainstream values mirroring The Culturally Correct Gay Elite" and academic queer theory's drive (as enumerated above by Stein and Plummer) continually to redefine the boundaries of subversion.[6]

Queer-identifying figures take up, or are consigned to, bad queer positioning when their enunciation or performance of queerness runs counter to currently prescribed tastes or norms—a position Ellis and two of his fellow godfathers of queer culture, drag performer RuPaul and filmmaker John Waters, have occupied, whether temporarily or perennially, and one they wear with pride. While RuPaul presides over one of the most commercially successful LGBTQ+ cultural products in history, the reality competition series *RuPaul's Drag Race* (LOGO, 2009–16, VH1, 2017–), his dismissiveness toward pronoun policing and other controls on language usage (witness the flaps over his use of the terms *tranny* and *shemale*) rankles those who call out his cis privilege and hostility to trans community members whom he designates "fringe people who are looking for story lines to strengthen their identity as victims."[7] So, too, is Waters—"The Pope of Trash"—regularly praised or chastised, respectively, for being "a beacon of sanity in an overly PC world" or "the worst kind of transphobic bigot."[8] Waters's (past) gleefully trashy sensibility and (present) inclination to make fun of trans celebrity Caitlyn Jenner have increasingly come in for questioning, less on aesthetic grounds of being "in poor taste" (an allegation Waters embraces) than on political grounds as being insensitive to the trans community. Ellis, the most consistent bad queer of the bunch, long maligned for the notoriety of his novels *Less than Zero* (1985) and *American Psycho* (1991), now uses his podcast to excoriate what he regards as the middlebrow sanctimony of such LGBTQ+ critical darlings as *Moonlight* (Barry Jenkins, 2016). Ellis regularly scuffles with the media watchdog group GLAAD over its "new gay fascism" of Hollywood self-patronizing (in both senses) disguised as cultural sensitivity.[9] Or as Waters put it in his 2014 appearance on RuPaul's YouTube interview series *RuPaul Drives...*, "Just because it's gay doesn't mean I have to like it" (WOWPresents, 2.6, 2.14, "RuPaul Drives...John Waters").

Given their shared age demographic, this bad queer oppositionality might seem to reflect intergenerational rivalry between old and new LGBTQ+ politics. But as bad queer Millennial Akhavan demonstrates, the divide is cross-generational, and as the bad queer triad's comments above suggest, the bad queer's stance is by no means apolitical. In eschewing identitarianism, so-called virtue signaling, and supposedly sympathy-grabbing narratives (of victimhood, for example), bad queer comprises an ideological counterposition that is simultaneously less separatist and less assimilatory than the civil rights–informed rhetoric of mainstream LGBTQ+ politics. At the same time, bad queer dispositions chafe at academic queer theory; even if they ultimately share a commitment to unthinking cultural norms, the bad queer swerves from that critical orientation's tendency toward stringent policing against assimilation and its energetic self-positioning as subversive.

Cholodenko's *The Kids Are All Right* (2010) and Akhavan's web series and first feature film are their most consummately bad queer works to date in their impudent play with mainstream LGBTQ+ and queer aesthetic tastes, cultural values, and rhetorical rules. In pushing back against whatever *queer* is determined to be at a given moment by whichever queer cultural authority (whether GLAAD or *GLQ*), the bad queer violates standards of homonormative respectability politics and the (unacknowledged) boundaries of queer theory. In so doing, these bad queer figures and texts remind us that, just as the fiercely policed constraints of heteronormative culture can produce rigidities and narrowness, queer cultural institutions and logics can also produce demands for conformity around and narrow definitions of what is acceptable or progressive. Reacting against restrictive definitions originating in both the activist and the academic realms, bad queer oppositionality endeavors to "re-queer" queer—to further radicalize our conceptualization of queer with the aim of realizing a more transgressive futurity. This project enacts the consistently self-critical reassessment that feminist literary critic Barbara Johnson proclaimed necessary: "Any discourse that is based on the questioning of boundary lines must never stop questioning its own."[10] While a bad queer oppositionality is not guaranteed to be either progressive or transgressive, it engages in "the transformative practice of queer politics" that queer critical theorist (and *GLQ*'s cofounder) David M. Halperin, by way of Foucault, describes as "an experiment we perform on ourselves so as to discover our otherness to ourselves."[11] To adopt a bad queer perspective is to defamiliarize queerness, in other words—a tricky proposition, given that queer already signifies strangeness and obliqueness. This is precisely why the modes employed by the bad queer provoc*auteurs* explored in this chapter are disruptive and revealing.

Such provocations might be seen less as critiques of specific elements of call-out and cancel culture and more as reflecting a general urge toward claiming artistic freedom and insisting on a space for self-reflexive humor (effectively placing the provocations within, rather than against, sex and gender radicalism). Or they might be seen simply as attempts to restore the libidinal charge of humor and fun to an enterprise that threatens to become locked into a one-dimensional mode of censoriousness and policing. In appropriating Benshoff's term "bad queer" to identify this resistance to imperatives to instrumentalize representation and advocate for assimilation, I also nod appreciatively at cultural critic Roxane Gay's self-presentation as a "bad feminist," who is "flawed and human ... [with] interests and personality traits and opinions that may not fall in line with mainstream feminism."[12] Drawing on Gay's avowing of traditionally feminine, politically indefensible proclivities and eschewing of relentlessly positive role models in favor of "flawed and human" figures, I regard as bad feminists those women provoc*auteurs* and their protagonists explored in chapter 3, for whom aspirational feminism often runs aground on lived realities, and who, in response, manifest "regressive" acts and "retreatist" values. To condemn those as bad feminist choices is to ignore how choice itself is drained of meaning in a context lacking sufficient options for access and agency. Although this chapter focuses on my related formulation of the bad queer, both Cholodenko and Akhavan as well as their alter ego protagonists are identifiable as bad feminists in embodying the conflict generated by contemporary neoliberal feminism's promise of freedoms (sexual and otherwise) that are irreconcilable with gendered inequities, systemic barriers, and internalized obstacles.

This bad queer formulation is inspired as well by cultural theorist Eve Oishi's conception and coinage of an analogous figure of racialized representation, the "bad Asian": "Any Asian American who makes noise, acts nasty, or in any way flouts the expectations of racist stereotype is a Bad Asian. Bad as in 'badass.' Bad as in anyone who does not covet white patriarchal approval; anyone who challenges racism, class oppression, sexism, homophobia; anyone who talks candidly about sex and desire."[13] A key textual element that signals what I refer to as bad queer representation is the refusal of what Kobena Mercer has termed, in the context of racial imagery, "the burden of representation" afflicting minority-authored and minority-reflecting images, the expectation that they convey positive characterizations and uplifting narratives.[14] The badly behaving or antiheroic character remains a province permitted almost exclusively to white men—see, for example, the disproportionate fury directed at the mere brats of Dunham's *Girls* (who themselves get away with a lot because of their white upper-middle-class privilege) versus the admiring embrace given the sociopathic protagonists of *The Sopranos* (HBO, 1999–2007),

Breaking Bad, *Mad Men* (AMC, 2007–15), and *Game of Thrones*. As we will see, Akhavan's irreverence, and that of her on-screen alter egos, proves sufficiently disruptive to the burden of representation to qualify her as both bad Persian and bad queer.[15]

The bad queer sensibility emanates, I suggest, from a perspective of (non)belonging—a simultaneous inhabiting of insider and outsider positions in relation to a designated group, be it one composed around an identity formation, political or theoretical coalition, or professional ecosystem. In using *inbetweener* as a descriptor of the sexual identity of Cholodenko's and Akhavan's characters (and of the bisexually identified Akhavan herself), I am referencing the term's use in queer culture to signify a position or movement between binary constructions that disrupts and resists such binaries. *Tweener* (its shortened form) designates someone whose sexuality and/or gender identity is nonbinary—neither gay nor straight, neither masculine/butch nor feminine/femme. Inbetweener, as I use it to refer to Cholodenko's and Akhavan's professional positioning in the screen media industry, refers to their working across media platforms (film, television, web series) and, in Akhavan's case, transnationally (she started in the New York independent film scene, lived in London from 2015–19, and currently is Brooklyn based). For these women, inbetweener also refers to their racialized positionality as Jewish American and Iranian American, respectively. Inbetweener refers furthermore to both artists' circulation across the often-overlapping LGBTQ+ and indie distribution and festival circuits. It refers to Cholodenko's crossing over into a realm of mainstream recognition as a result of the commercial success and awards prestige of *The Kids Are All Right* and the HBO miniseries *Olive Kitteridge* (2014). Akhavan seems poised to traverse a similar path, having won the US Grand Jury Prize at Sundance for her second feature, the young adult adaptation *The Miseducation of Cameron Post* (2018), and for being among those movie industry figures invited in 2019 to join the Academy of Motion Pictures

Arts and Sciences. Cholodenko's and Akhavan's positioning as sexual and industrial inbetweeners permits a queer parallax of sorts—a distinctive "third space" perspective that underwrites their bad queer sensibility.

I use bad queer not to suggest that we no longer need queer as a conceptual or coalitional formation (far from it, in light of the current political climate). Rather, I follow David V. Ruffolo's formulation, in *Post-Queer Politics*, of the provocative term in his book's title, as a means to trouble the queer/heteronormative dyad. For Ruffolo, this deterritorialization of queer is necessitated by the contemporary complexities of neoliberal capitalism and globalization, which he argues render untenable queer theory's notion of discursively bound "subjugated subjectivities." He offers instead a concept of "dialogical becomings" that are better able to account for the pluralities, materialities, and virtualities of bodies and lives in today's world—a world that "no longer individualize[s] bodies amongst each other but dividualize[s] them within themselves."[16]

While Ruffolo's project attends to contemporary politics more broadly and more intensively than I do here, his post-queer praxis resonates with what I find to be the inbetweener determinants of Cholodenko's and Akhavan's self-inscriptions as provoca*teurs*. Ruffolo's concept of the dividualized self and my notion of the inbetweener align in their attention to the intersectionalist determinants that mutually and complexly inform identities and that, as legal scholar Kimberlé Williams Crenshaw demonstrates, compound one's societal privilege or oppression.[17] Intersectionality comes to bear for Cholodenko and Akhavan in the relations between their relative privilege and cultural capital as first-world, educated, financially secure, and cisgender and the simultaneous disenfranchisement they experience as a result of their queer identities and their status as "not quite white" (to borrow Sharmila Sen's formulation) queer women in a white heteropatriarchal industry and culture.[18] While Cholodenko's

Jewishness goes unexplored on-screen save a notable scene in her debut feature *High Art* (1998), discussed below, Akhavan has, through her on-screen alter egos, given increasing prominence to relating her experience as a second-generation Iranian American to that as a queer woman. In my consideration of Akhavan's debut feature *Appropriate Behavior* (2014) below, I locate the primary source of narrative conflict in the entanglement of these two facets of Akhavan's identity. As I take up elsewhere, Akhavan's 2018 UK Channel 4/Hulu series *The Bisexual* (about an American in London who, after ending a decade-long relationship with her girlfriend and business partner, starts dating men) gives the complications of reconciling with one's ethnic heritage a degree of narrative emphasis second only to questions of sexuality, but arguably conveying even more emotional weight.[19] The discrepancy between Cholodenko's and Akhavan's work with regard to issues of ethnic identity and (given the current climate of rising antisemitism and pervasive Islamophobia) racialized status raises interesting questions about generational difference in their representational politics. Both women draw on their respective privilege to enact bad queer representations that are themselves intersectionally inscribed by the highly specific, individuated perspectives of the artists themselves—representations that resist rhetorical containment through LGBTQ+ community narratives, party-line politics, or queer theory trends.

To encapsulate, my exploration of these provoc*auteurs*' self-inscriptions and their screen representations' challenging of gay and queer scripts finds Cholodenko and Akhavan articulating inbetweener identifications that originate in an insider/outsider sensibility of (non)belonging and intersectionalist determinants of subjectivity. Such articulations are provocative first in their resistance to LGBTQ+ identity politics' push for positive images and progressive narratives. They are provocative furthermore for their sidestepping of queer theory's tendency (despite its ostensible commitment to an antifoundationalist perspective) to capitulate to a relatively coherent notion of queer subjectivity and, by extension, to reconstitute a queer/heteronormative binary. Like the empirical grounding queer theory has a tendency to elide, the resulting individualized (or dividualized) perspectives may be more telling—and more inconvenient and hence inappropriate—than gay or queer sexual and representational politics can encompass.

In the course of her career, Cholodenko has defied the "healthy mainstream values" that Bret Easton Ellis disparages at the same time that she has incited the ire of queer critics and scholars in her shift from New Queer Cinema provoc*auteur* toward more mainstream and arguably homonormative projects—particularly in her crossover success *The Kids Are All Right*. Though she has not (yet) been subject to the same hostility from queer critic-scholars, Akhavan has arguably gone further in signaling a bad queer self-inscription through her performance, akin to that of Lena Dunham, as her self-proclaimed "superficial, homophobic" alter ego in her most prominent works to date, the web series *The Slope* (2011–12), made with then partner Ingrid Jungermann, and her debut feature *Appropriate Behavior*. Both women therefore embody, through their work and professional self-inscription, the (post)queer theoretical notion of *disidentification* as both a rhetorical practice and a personal negotiation of (non)belonging.

Queer scholar José Esteban Muñoz formulates disidentification as a mode of queer critique that "both exposes the encoded message's universalizing and exclusionary machinations and recircuits its workings to account for, include, and empower minority identities and identifications."[20] Cholodenko's and Akhavan's shared practice of disidentification stems from this position of (non)belonging—a simultaneous insider/outsider betweenness—in dominant (straight) culture, in the mainstream LGBTQ+ culture to which Bret Easton Ellis refers, and in the self-proclaimed radically queer vanguard. It thus works to expose and revise the limiting, prescriptive narratives of each.

BAD CROSSOVER QUEER: LISA CHOLODENKO

As suggested by Cholodenko's quote at the beginning of this chapter, from the outset of her career, her screened and spoken reflections reveal a logic of desire too sharply attuned to material contingencies and interpersonal dynamics to comply with any fixed, transparent notion of sexual orientation or preference.[21] Owing to this perspective's divergence from the politically expedient narrative of sexuality as innate and immutable—that which made Lady Gaga's "Born This Way" an LGBTQ+ anthem—it is not the lesbian-identified Cholodenko's personal-authorial credentials but rather her representational politics that are perceived as being (increasingly) in need of queer verification. Even so, as this chapter asserts, Cholodenko's textual inscriptions should be regarded as demonstrably queer not on account of their lesbian authorship but for the reason feminist-queer theorist Teresa de Lauretis posits: "A text is queer, regardless of the queerness of its authorial persona, if it carries the inscription of sexuality as something more than sex."[22] Such an anti-identitarian yet politically inflected definition of queer correlates to Cholodenko being ever mindful of sex(uality) as bound up with, as she puts it, negotiations around need (material and otherwise), structures of power, and competing forms of intimacy. Across the span of her two-decade career to date—from the Fassbinder-inspired excess of queer signification in her debut feature *High Art* to the alleged homonormativity of crossover hit *The Kids Are All Right* to the distance she has lately maintained from explicitly queer material—the direct, unapologetic instrumentalizing of sex and sexuality by Cholodenko's characters and within her own self-inscription has continually landed her in the critical crosshairs as a bad queer.

With *High Art*, Cholodenko achieved art house notoriety among a new wave of women filmmakers aiming to provoke both with their dark, sexually charged subject matter and in their troubling of industrial and critical designations such as "indie," "feminist film," and "gay cinema." Looking back at *High Art* some two decades after the 1990s New Queer Cinema moment, critic B. Ruby Rich (who devised the historical label) singles out the film for having "defied all prior taboos of contemporary lesbian cinema by showing the dark side of lesbian society and having the nerve to go for an unhappy ending."[23] Lesbian independent filmmaking in the wake of New Queer Cinema had ventured little in style or number beyond those produced at the height of the moment, the most commercially successful of which were the romantic comedies *Go Fish* (Rose Troche, 1994) and *The Incredibly True Adventures of Two Girls in Love* (Maria Maggenti, 1995). *High Art* departs radically from those films' lo-fi aesthetics and feel-good story lines with its lushly filmed yet grittily depicted portrait of an affair between an ambitious aspiring art critic and a heroin-addicted has-been photographer cut short by the latter's death from a drug overdose. Cholodenko's subsequent feature, *Laurel Canyon* (2002), is less bleak and less identifiably queer, though it, too, focuses on a professionally driven young woman who experiences personal—and sexual—awakening in her encounter with an older, accomplished, but (self-)destructive woman.

The arrival in 2010 of Cholodenko's third feature, *The Kids Are All Right*, amid nationwide debates over marriage equality, caused a stir nearly as resounding but far more clamorous as had *Philadelphia* and *Brokeback Mountain* before it. Its comparable commercial and critical success was simultaneously hailed as evidence of progress in mainstream LGBTQ+ visibility and acceptance, and of homonormativity's stranglehold over queer cultural production. The narrative traces Nic (Annette Bening) and Jules (Julianne Moore) and their two teenage children as their tenuous domestic harmony is threatened after meeting their sperm donor, Paul (Mark Ruffalo). The story is autobiographically informed by Cholodenko's mothering of a child with her long-time partner Wendy Melvoin, a guitarist in Prince's backing band The Revolution and later one-half of the duo Wendy and Lisa. Yet Cholodenko's collaboration on the screenplay with Stuart Blumberg, known for scripting conventional Hollywood rom-coms (and a straight man, no less), raised eyebrows. Also perceived by some as a betrayal of her queer/indie roots was the film's ostensible promotion of bourgeois values and allegedly phallocentric sex scenes, which sparked a much-read blog-post critique by queer scholar Jack Halberstam titled "The Kids Aren't Alright."[24]

In revisiting these alternately laudatory and dissenting responses to *High Art* and *The Kids Are All Right*, and considering the underdiscussed *Laurel Canyon* and Cholodenko's recent television work, I explore the inbetweener positioning that characterizes Cholodenko's career and films and shapes her bad queer provoc*auteur* signature. Cholodenko's work takes a defiantly inbetweener stance in its troubling of sexual binaries at the same time that it stakes out an inbetweener position among entertainment industry categorizations that regulate notions of art versus commerce and film versus television and those that reinforce classifications of LGBTQ+ cinema and women's cinema. Cholodenko's career disrupts the boundaries established by an ideologically and industrially heteropatriarchal hierarchy, and thus valuably models an inbetweener route for (queer) women practitioners in the contemporary US independent media sphere.

I argue also that Cholodenko's individual works reflexively stage negotiations of her extradiegetic concerns as a sexual/industry inbetweener, focusing specifically on the politics of queer representation (*High Art*), the mediation between art and commerce (*Laurel Canyon*), and creative engagement with sociopolitical issues (*The Kids Are All Right*). With characters who resist sexual categorization as much as she herself resists ideological and industrial categorization, Cholodenko's work provocatively probes the fluidity of desire as well as the complexities of identity both personal and professional. Cholodenko's output thus increasingly reflects digital-era trends in its mobility across media platforms and narrative modes and in its illustration of online forums' growing significance for determining discourse, whether in the form of critical blogging in response to *The Kids Are All Right* or social media's send-up of her 2015 network TV miniseries *The Slap*. If not to the same degree as Millennials Dunham and (as we will see) Akhavan, Cholodenko's brand has accrued its bad queer associations through such channels' power to amplify and disseminate ever more expediently the provoc*auteur* self-inscription she has established since her career's start.

HIGHS AND LOWS

For a fiftysomething commercial director whose debut feature appeared in 1998, Cholodenko's output advanced at a relatively modest clip. In addition to (co)writing and directing the three aforementioned films and two miniseries, in her career's first two decades she directed just one additional feature-length work (the 2004 Showtime film *Cavedweller*, based on a Dorothy Allison novel and starring and produced by Kyra Sedgwick) and a handful of television episodes (*Homicide, Hung, The L Word, Six Feet Under*). Cholodenko clarifies that this intermittency had been not by choice: "I've had years that have been horribly depressing and scary and I've been *that close* to applying to work at Whole Foods," she confesses.[25] It is testament to the vicissitudes of American low-budget filmmaking after the 1990s indie boom that a director whose first feature won the Waldo Salt Screenwriting Award at Sundance and whose subsequent features found mounting commercial success would be driven to contemplate such a professional demotion.[26] Certainly other filmmakers (Gregg Araki, Cheryl Dunye, Tom Kalin, Rose Troche) with whom Cholodenko shared the New Queer Cinema spotlight have sustained lags in creative output, with only Todd Haynes and Gus Van Sant maintaining consistently active directing careers. Haynes and Van Sant provide interesting counterpoints to Cholodenko for the way all three have reshaped US queer cinema's contours toward more commercially and narratively expansive ends, though we might speculate that Haynes's and Van Sant's higher productivity stems from the male privilege that still affords (even gay) men disproportionate access to directing work both in Hollywood and on its margins. Cholodenko's gender and out lesbianism surely has something to do with her erratic employment and qualified recognition in the industry. What also seems relevant is her inbetweener resistance to being professionally as well as sexually "pigeonholed"—a term uttered by both female protagonists, with similar inflection, in *High Art*.

Cholodenko's debut feature is a bad queer bildungsroman that self-reflexively confronts these gendered and sexual determinants of success as it tracks a focused young woman's professional rise and auspicious emergence upon editing a spread for eminent photography magazine *Frame*. From its opening sequence of Syd (Radha Mitchell), an assistant editor who is expected to run demeaning errands for her higher-ups, assiduously working after hours, *High Art* proves attuned to how women's labor is devalued and exploited even in the ostensibly nurturing, noncorporate art world. *High Art* challenges feminism's frequently hollow invocations of female solidarity as the route to women's professional success through its portrayal of the taut professional triangle comprised by three forceful figures: on-the-rise Syd; *Frame*'s imperious executive director, Dominique (Anh Duong); and Lucy Berliner (Ally Sheedy), Syd's upstairs neighbor and a once-famous photographer who takes Syd as her editor, muse, and lover before succumbing to a fatal overdose. *High Art* inaugurates a narrative framework that informs each of Cholodenko's feature films: women's navigation of a postfeminist professional landscape in which their success is nominally encouraged but beset by external and internal modes of containment that prompt them to explore alternative forms of fulfillment, artistic and otherwise.

High Art's interest in scrutinizing the gendered contours of women's career building and self-fulfillment is signaled by the casting of Sheedy, known both for her youthful career as one of the "Brat Pack" and for retreating from Hollywood prematurely because, as she describes, "I just needed to get out. I was really unhappy. I needed to find something different for myself."[27] Her comeback role in *High Art*, for which she won a National Society of Film Critics Award, dovetails with the self-exiled character she plays, in one of several reflexive layers in the film. Confiding in Syd in the refuge of her darkroom, Lucy rationalizes her spiral into burnout obscurity by claiming to have felt "pigeonholed" by the art world as her career took off. "There just stopped being a line between me and work. People were glomming on to something I was doing then, and I just got trapped." Defending her and her employer's mutual interests in resuscitating Lucy's career, Syd replies, "The people at *Frame* think you're an amazing photographer. I don't think they want to trap you; I think they want to support you." Dominique pushes Syd to use her influence with Lucy to solicit a new piece, but *Frame*'s maven is dissatisfied with Lucy's initial offering of stylized underwater portraits of her girlfriend, Greta (Patricia Clarkson). Pushing Lucy to "revisit some of your older themes ... an examination of your friends and your life," Dominique decrees that the "cultural currency" of Lucy's work resides in the "rigor" and "realism" that characterized her early focus on "the intimacy and desolation of her subjects." That early work, which catches Syd's discerning eye when she sees it hanging in Lucy's apartment, depicts a druggy, sexually debauched milieu recalling Nan Goldin's *The Ballad of Sexual Dependency* (exhibited 1985; published 1986) and other controversial chronicles of New York's heroin-chic, No Wave downtown scene.

Though Syd's superiors veil their demands in euphemism, it is evident that Lucy once more risks being pigeonholed as an image maker of explicitly queer eroticism. The underwater portraits are denounced by Dominique for having "no context." She scoffs at Syd's defense of their quality: "Lucy Berliner has been invisible for ten years. The public has a five year memory and that's it." Echoing her, associate editor Harry (David Thornton) says, "If a best-selling crime writer disappeared for ten years and came back peddling love poems, how do you think it would do? It's a business, Syd." Noting Cholodenko's allusion to R. W. Fassbinder's high-camp lesbian ménage in *The Bitter Tears of Petra von Kant* (1972), Lee Wallace sees *High Art*'s Sapphic triangle (in which Lucy is torn between Greta and Syd) as a standoff between two artistic alternatives tethered to old world and new: German actor "Greta's claim to the Fassbinder aesthetic, which ties together homosexuality, artistic intensity, and an unchecked impulse to self-destruction" versus the sober, industrious, American careerism Syd represents.[28] The inbetweener space that *High Art* occupies, unmistakably drawing on European art film but emerging from the grassroots 1990s American filmmaking (including that of New Queer Cinema) that would by decade's end evolve into Indiewood, suggests a third way that, had she lived, Lucy would find through her productive, profitable, and less entrapping partnership with Syd.

Such a partnership, while not codependent, still threatens to be co-optative. The naive optimism with which Syd regards the art world's interest in reviving Lucy's career is challenged once Syd comes to have a personal stake in the images to be circulated and consumed. Syd's ultimate choice to turn over the photographs Lucy had taken of her during a weekend spent together constitutes a public coming-out as a queer woman, given that she served as Lucy's model for the intimately composed images to be featured in *Frame*. Intrigued but confused upon examining the proposed layout, Dominque says, "I don't understand. Are you her sitter?" To Syd's uneasy response, "Not exactly," Dominque seizes on the images' potential for titillation and asks, with barely contained elation, "Are you her lover?" Syd, after a beat, answers in the affirmative. Having first clarified that she was not acting merely as Lucy's model, Syd distinguishes here between artistic versus authentic performance; the photographs exhibit the truth of her lesbian desire. Lucy's urging Syd to use these photographs defers to Syd's superiors' (and, by extension, the art world's) imperative that queer-identified artists such as Cholodenko make queerness explicitly visible in their work, preferably in established representational paradigms such as the mise-en-scène of erotic decadence suffusing Lucy's famous images.

In comparison, Lucy's new portfolio of images for *Frame* reflects the less sensationalistic, (literally and figuratively) sober reality of her current life and relationship with Syd. It still satisfies Dominique's (and the public's) desire to peer voyeuristically into explicitly queer spaces but allows Lucy and Syd to retain creative and editorial control and give clear-headed, full consent. The images they select for the spread highlight this reflexive gesture whereby Cholodenko connects and revises photographic and cinematic gazes. The first image shows Syd looking directly into the camera, confronting the viewer with the same knowingness she brought to bear on Lucy, at the point in the narrative when the photograph was taken, regarding her drug use. Also included are a series of shots in which Syd is seen sleeping, then groggily waking up to face the camera, then joined in the frame by Lucy, who (having set the self-timer) lies atop and nuzzles her as Syd continues to look into the camera (see fig. 4.1). Collectively, the images are strikingly intimate, yet, by virtue of their reflexive techniques of direct address and author-as-subject, they are also resistant to allowing the viewer's immersion into a fantasy realm. Though offering up their sexual involvement for visual pleasure, Lucy and Syd revise their queer self-representation with an inbetweener approach that seeks not to destroy that pleasure but to engage the spectator in a recognition of the sexual/visual economy that (re)produces queerness for financial profit, career advancement, and political containment. In much the same way, Cholodenko's

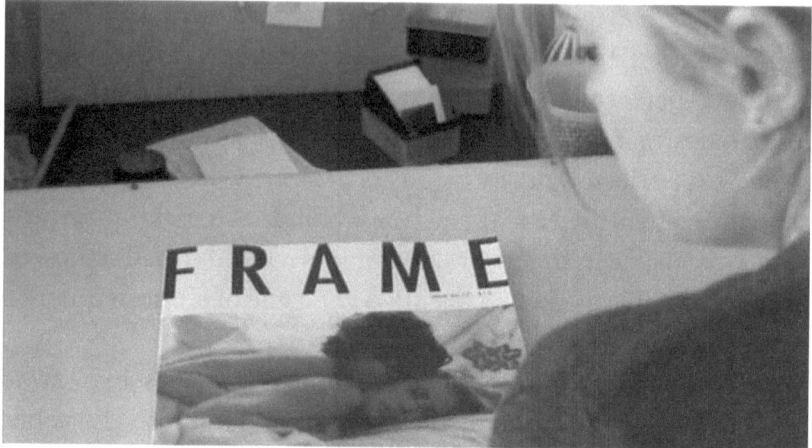

Fig. 4.1. *High Art*'s Syd (Radha Mitchell) surveying the cover image photographed by her lover Lucy (Ally Sheedy), also used to promote the film.

handling of queer material in her work is attuned to its own inevitable self-commodification. Fittingly, Lucy and Syd's artistic collaboration produces a cover shot for *Frame* that also served as the main promotional image for Cholodenko's film, signaling Lucy as being the director's on-screen surrogate, as another bad queer provoc*auteur* weighing art versus commerce and reconciling the projection of a professional persona with personal privacy.

Lucy also serves as Cholodenko's on-screen surrogate in terms of their shared (if lightly touched on) inbetweenness as "not quite white." In a subtle yet unmistakable instance in *High Art*, Cholodenko fleetingly refers to her own Jewishness—a sufficiently compelling component of her heritage that she lived in Jerusalem for eighteen months after college, but one that she has not elsewhere incorporated into her work. In a scene late in the film, Lucy visits her austere mother's refined home to announce her intention to leave town for a while, ostensibly to seek treatment for her addiction. Hearing that Lucy has just returned from the country with her "friend" Syd, her mother perks up. "Syd? That's a man's name." Lucy's reply, "She's definitely not a man," leaves her mother visibly deflated but still hopeful. "Is she Jewish?" "I don't know, Ma," Lucy replies wearily. During the stilted exchange that follows, Lucy's mother bitterly refers twice to Greta as "the German," demanding to know "What did she do to you?" "Nothing. I did it to myself," Lucy resolutely responds. Saying stiffly, "I can't help you with that," her mother stands and exits the room, ignoring Lucy's imploring "Don't walk away from me, Ma." The confluence of signifiers evident, in however veiled a form, throughout their exchange—Lucy's moneyed background and Jewish heritage, the apparent lack of any other living family, the maternal disavowal of her sexuality—suggest that Lucy struggles to reconcile the divisions in her life arising from her familial estrangement and personal choices and is fated (given her fatal overdose thereafter) not to succeed. Inbetweenness here is rendered as an intractable state that leaves a queer daughter irreconcilably at odds with her familial expectations and heritage as a result of her intercultural (even interracial) border crossing. Whereas this brief but lingering scene remains Cholodenko's sole probing of the tensions connected to her own racialized and queer positionality, Akhavan puts similar tensions between ethnic and queer identities at the center of her work, albeit in a more seriocomic register.

Where Lucy seems to be Cholodenko's stand-in as an embodiment of industrial inbetweenness and not quite whiteness, Syd signifies the sexual inbetweenness, if not of Cholodenko herself (who came out as lesbian at age seventeen), then of the logic of desire across Cholodenko's body of work. The impulse to read Syd as autobiographically inspired relates to the industrial as well. With her first commercial directorial outing, Cholodenko faced the challenge of entering the film industry while bearing the "lesbian director" label and managing the expectations that label entails. "I think there are always going to be gay characters and themes in my work. [But] I don't want to be in a ghetto; it's time for us to transcend those borders," Cholodenko stated in 1998.

"This New Queer Cinema thing was very specific and very important in a moment, [but] I'm not sure it's all that relevant now."[29]

Just as Cholodenko would confound those expectations by straying from New Queer Cinema toward more mainstream projects, her characters—starting with Syd—defy what I named, in *The B Word, compulsory monosexuality* to claim a sexual inbetweenness subject to unpredictable vicissitudes of desire and multiple determinants of libidinal attachments.[30] Syd's confession to Dominique fails to conform to the classic coming-out narrative that fixes sexual identity as static, discursively bound, and thus politically containable. Her admission that she is Lucy's lover (rather than, for instance, a lesbian) remains in the realm of the behavioral, personal (more than political), and fluid. While such a conception of sexuality aligns with queer theory's antifoundationalism, *High Art*'s defiance of the teleological narrative drive toward coming out and "choosing a side" makes it a complex, deliberately provocative product for gay cultural consumption.

In signaling the contingency of sexuality, Syd unsurprisingly becomes vulnerable to diegetic aspersions that, casting her (unnamed as such) bisexuality in pejorative terms, ironically serve to disavow bisexuality as a viable identity. This happens, for example, when Greta, in what surely is an intentional linguistic slip, accuses Syd of being a "psychophant" out to seduce Lucy with the goal of advancing her own career. *High Art* regards Syd with the shrewd understanding that her sexual desire is inseparable from her professional desire. Responding to her boyfriend James's (Gabriel Mann) disparagement, Syd proclaims her professional desire in terms that invite us to understand it through, though not to conflate it with, her analogous attraction to the queer world that Lucy represents: "If you weren't so fixated on putting me in a box, on *pigeonholing* me ... no matter what I do, you can't stop telling me it's wrong. I'm trying to get somewhere, all I get from you are these slurs about my job and the people that I've met and how pretentious and meaningless and idiotic it is, and—you know what? It's not meaningless to me. This is what I care about."

Yet Syd's attraction and ambition remain conflated by characters and critics alike, with Maria Pramaggiore positing, "The central theme of the art world's exploitation of artists is inextricably bound to Syd and to her bisexuality: Syd is the channel through which Lucy becomes vulnerable again to the expectations of commodified art making." Pramaggiore views Syd rather more harshly than the film seems to, and she overlooks the less exploitative industrial inbetweener position that I see Syd and (with her comeback) Lucy occupying. Pramaggiore goes on to note *High Art*'s affiliation between bisexuality and art: "As an erotics of refusing distinctions, bisexuality acts as a metaphor... for the promiscuous blending of high art and low entertainment." I agree with this assessment, but I would cast the relationship in more affirmative terms, where sexual/industrial inbetweenness enables a move beyond such binarisms.[31] Cholodenko seems not simply to blend but to disidentify altogether with markers of high/low and straight/gay—a blurring of boundaries that is extended in her subsequent feature films.

CALIFORNIA DREAMIN'

Like *High Art*, Cholodenko's next two features, *Laurel Canyon* and *The Kids Are All Right* (hereafter, *Kids*), can be read as industrial allegories of her negotiation of an inbetweener path between professional worlds—queer filmmaking and mainstream (heterosexual) cinema—and between the expectations of compulsory monosexuality that those two worlds mandate. Jodi Brooks finds that Cholodenko's films ponder "what it is to live and move—and to choose—between worlds."[32] Yet the women protagonists of *High Art* and *Laurel Canyon* refuse the imperative to choose between, and instead find productive ways to inhabit both worlds and indeed reveal their porous overlaps.

After all, *Laurel Canyon*'s titular fantasy world is one of privilege that is dependent on the commercial infrastructure of the entertainment industry that supports it. Cholodenko's resistance to conjuring the (literally and figuratively) queer spaces of her films in utopian terms, and indeed her willingness to confront the escapism they enable, suggests a similarly unidealized vision of the space of queer cinema. Bohemian music producer Jane (Frances McDormand) admits, "I like capitalism as much as the next guy," though she balances commerce and creativity with an ethical stance that parallels the way she conducts her emotional life. Jane's estranged son, Sam (Christian Bale), newly arrived in Los Angeles for his medical residency, avoids their interpersonal tension by working long hours. His fiancée, Alex (Kate Beckinsale), is struggling to complete her dissertation and finds herself inexorably drawn to the studio where Jane and her significantly younger rocker-boyfriend, Ian (Alessandro Nivola), are working to finish a record. Soliciting Alex for input, Jane describes her métier in terms suggestive both of Cholodenko's openness to working in more mainstream (i.e., popular) realms of the entertainment industry and of Jane's fluid logic of desire: "Anyone with instincts knows about popular music. That's why it's popular. You strike me as someone with strong instincts. Well, you know when you're repulsed and when you're turned on, right? That's all it is. Either it pulls you in or it leaves you cold." The photographic legacy of her accomplished career that layers her home's walls, and which Alex pores over, establishes Jane as a kindred soul to *High Art*'s Lucy, but one who survives and flourishes by way of the compromising moderation with which she keeps the bohemian spirit alive.

Jane manages her erotic life with a similarly open-minded but clear-eyed realism. Her bisexuality is presented in passing, almost as a given, when Sam inquires about an ex-girlfriend. "Veronica and I stopped having sex after the third month," Jane replies in a foreshadowing of the "lesbian bed death" cliché that angered critics of *Kids*. I find Jane's comment more objectionable than the parallel implication in *Kids*, where the same-sex couple's near-celibacy seems attributable to long-term monogamy rather than lesbianism. Otherwise, *Laurel Canyon*'s treatment of Jane's sexual fluidity resists heteronormativity ("Why do you want to spoil this with domesticity?" she asks Ian when he proposes moving in) while loosening associations of bisexuality with hedonistic amorality by having Jane ultimately abstain from a ménage à trois with Ian and her future daughter-in-law, Alex. "Sublimation," as Sam refers to it when fighting the urge to similarly act on his attraction to alluring coworker Sara (Natascha McElhone), is sometimes necessary to avoid emotional damage, the film suggests. With this realistic but not moralistic view, Cholodenko again throws cold water on the voyeuristic expectations held by characters and viewers alike. As in *High Art*, Cholodenko seems at first to conform to "lesploitation" convention. Amorous cavorting among Alex, Jane, and Ian in a swimming pool is followed by a hotel room rendezvous, re-creating the heterophallic trope of a two-girls-and-one-guy threesome centered on male pleasure. Jane's interruption of this scenario constitutes a cockblock of the straight male fantasy that Ian and the film's viewers anticipate.

Not unlike Jane's professional straddling of commerce and art, Cholodenko herself embodies inbetweenness in making this film. While hardly devoid of Hollywood wish fulfillment, *Laurel Canyon*'s dreamy setting and romanticization of the entertainment world still clearly displays Cholodenko's indie-style creative vision. That vision is exemplified by the character of Jane, who is exceptional for being a strong *and* sexy, grounded *and* flawed, middle-aged female protagonist. As with *High Art*, it is also possible to see shades of Cholodenko in *Laurel Canyon*'s younger female protagonist. Not unlike the filmmaker (who, though she was raised in California and attended college there, relocated to New York to attend Columbia University's graduate film program), Alex is an East Coast Ivy Leaguer who goes west to Hollywood and is caught up, for a time, in its seduction. Just as Syd in *High Art* establishes a middle way between Lucy's self-destructive path and Dominique's exploitative one, Alex, by the end of *Laurel Canyon*, acknowledges how the experience "really opened me up" but appears back on track with both her dissertation and her relationship with Sam. There is certainly something recuperative about *Laurel Canyon*'s denouement, with its heterosexual, age-appropriate couple reunited at film's end (prefiguring the much-complained-about restoration of monogamous coupling at the end of *Kids*). However, Cholodenko suggests that emotional commitment does not preclude sexual temptation but provides a worthwhile reason for its sublimation. Thus, I would challenge *Cineaste*'s view of the Cholodenko female protagonist as an "interloper within a bohemian milieu with aspirations toward being an insider."[33] Unlike *Kids*' Paul, whom lesbian mom Nic berates for having invaded her domestic sphere, *Laurel Canyon*'s Alex as well as *High Art*'s Syd seek to redefine themselves not by upsetting the balance of the queer space they enter but by unbalancing their rigidly conventional selves.

The sexual fluidity that permeates Cholodenko's first two features arises again in *Kids* through an inbetweenness that acknowledges how emotional bonds (rather than normative values) are determinants of desire as well as, occasionally, reasons to sublimate those desires. Like Syd and Alex, Jules in *Kids* is drawn by a complex skein of desire into an affair with her children's biological father. But just as *High Art* and *Laurel Canyon* resist the conventional path of the coming-out narrative, *Kids* plays with but ultimately rejects the Hollywood paradigm of lesbianism undone by the arrival of a straight male interloper exemplified in films such as *The Fox* (Mark Rydell, 1967) and *Personal Best* (Robert Towne, 1982). Though Jules has enjoyable (far too enjoyable, to some critics) sex with Paul, she is not shown to doubt her sexual identity. When Nic learns of the affair, she asks, "Are you straight now?" Jules responds with a defiant "No! That has nothing to do with it." She then tells Paul with equal vehemence, "I'm gay!"—deflating any fantasy Paul might entertain as a straight man who "loves lesbians" of lesbianism as always susceptible to replacement by heterosexuality.

While bisexuality again goes unspoken, Jules's affirmation of her lesbian identity seems less a knee-jerk endorsement of essentialism than a reclaiming of her impulse, and right, to identify as she chooses despite having had (enjoyable) sex with a man. Paradoxically, Jules's unwavering self-identification as lesbian—much like Cholodenko's own—testifies to the film's affirmation of sexual inbetweenness, wherein personal and political identity does not preclude erotic and emotional desire. In keeping with Cholodenko's aim to probe the rules of attraction, as stated in her quote at the beginning of this chapter, this recognition of sexual fluidity acknowledges that desire is often steered by circumstance and emotional need ("to be appreciated," as Jules tearfully tells Nic). Yet the sticky suggestion that Jules is irresistibly drawn to Paul, in some primal urge prompted by seeing her children's faces in his expressions, uncomfortably links female sexual attraction to mothering—one in a litany of criticisms aimed at the film. Cholodenko's implied urging here that we consider the possibility that the biological father of Jules's children might elicit in her some particular libidinal urgency provocatively cuts against the grain of LGBTQ+ parenting politics and of contemporary feminism.

DISCIPLINING *KIDS*

The unwieldy financing (despite its modest budget) of Cholodenko's third feature led to a protracted development phase of five-plus years, such that she could not have foreseen that setting this film about lesbian partnership and parenting in present-day Los Angeles would make it ground zero when the anti–marriage equality ballot Proposition 8 passed in the November 2008

California state elections. The would-be amendment was almost immediately appealed, and ultimately ruled unconstitutional by the California Supreme Court in 2010, the year of *Kids*' release. This degree of diegetic, if neither explicit nor didactic, political engagement is in keeping with Cholodenko's handling of controversy: courting it in her choice of subject matter while disavowing it through representational treatments that avoid taking radical positions. At the time of the film's release, Cholodenko made this promotional statement: "Our intention wasn't overtly political. The subversion, as we saw it, was to be nonpolitical, and just to make this human story that was about a family that people could relate to, no matter what your identity or your sexual preferences were."[34] Yet, as Fiona Cox perceptively notes, the film's "ostensibly apolitical tone . . . is in fact its most political aspect."[35] Certainly the choice of promotional tagline—"Nic and Jules had the perfect family, until they met the man who made it all possible"—seems designed to provoke ire with its cheeky literalism narrowly disguising a decidedly un-queer nod to biological determinism.

Kids definitively established Cholodenko's status as an industry inbetweener. With an estimated production budget of only $4 million, made possible by leads Bening and Moore working for scale, *Kids* is one of a dying breed of "middle-class movies," so named by filmmaker Mark Duplass for their falling into the ever-widening gap in film production between studio-backed blockbusters and microbudget indies.[36] This sweet spot that *Kids* occupies financially parallels the inbetweener positioning that the film achieved by virtue of crossing over. Investment in the project was not so large that there was a risk of losing creative control, but it was enough to avoid the stringencies involved in an ultra-low-budget production. "It felt a little like making *High Art* except we didn't exploit people," as Cholodenko put it.[37]

Kids' critical reception contributed to the extradiegetic discourse that locates Cholodenko as an inbetweener vis-à-vis constructions of straight/mainstream (that is, heteronormative or homonormative) versus queer filmmaking. Suzanna Danuta Walters indicates how *Kids*' public relations campaign and approving critics "went down the well-worn universalist track" of emphasizing broadly "relatable" characters, a poignant story line, and assimilationist gay family values, in order "to have its homosexual difference and contain it too."[38] Given these (mostly white cishet) mainstream critics' apparent obliviousness to those universalizing and normativizing aspects that queer viewers found objectionable, it was apt and appropriate that so many feminist-queer voices weighed in against the film's widespread acclaim, though I would express some reservations about blogged responses by noted scholars Jack Halberstam and Lisa Duggan. Both have long and distinguished careers as queer cultural commentators, and their expectations of the film, given its import for contemporaneous LGBTQ+ politics, are understandably rigorous. Yet in denouncing the film's ostensible attempt to prove its lesbian bona fides, both scholars risk making *Kids* a whipping boy while voicing judgments about its lead actors' unglamorous styling (Halberstam terms Moore "dowdy," lamenting that she "loses her looks!") and critiquing the film's lesbian representation from a position of insider knowledge (Halberstam questions why Nic, rather than Paul, isn't the BMW motorcycle enthusiast, "classic beemers [being] a popular queer choice of motorcycle, in fact").[39] Agreeing heartily with Halberstam, Duggan's response decries what she calls Cholodenko's "absolutely vile" direction of a "dyke-face minstrel show." Duggan's comments are worth quoting at length for their fixation on visible markers of lesbianism:

> Annette Benning's [sic] Nic was a cartoon andro[gynous] dyke (they clearly didn't try for butch). Not just her scripted role as a priggish, controlling, condescending asshole, but . . . her gestures, her facial expressions and the way she held her mouth, her stance, her movements. These, one may argue, are questions of acting—perhaps Annette Benning just tried too hard and turned herself into a caricature? But she had a lesbian director (!) who

finally guided her gestures and expressions and movements and decided which versions and edits would make it into the film. But if Benning's Nic was bad, Julianne Moore's Jules was horrifying, offensive and repulsive (I could add more adjectives, but maybe that's enough?). As the somewhat more femme partner, she nonetheless manufactured the same cartoon mouth thing that was supposed to look "dykey," similar gestures and movements and ... they made her look really bad in order to make her lesbian. (My pal [Kathryn Bond] Stockton began to fear coming home to her lovely girlfriend Shelley White in overalls and a bad sun hat.) Has Cholodenko never seen Wanda Sykes move or Portia de Rossi smile?[40]

Whatever fault one can find with Nic's domineering parenting and partnering and with *Kids'* participation in a representational tradition that softens and effaces female masculinity, Halberstam's and Duggan's comments posit that lesbianism is something verifiable by means of visible indicators. Assuming that lesbianism must be manifested in a set of sanctioned looks and behaviors that conform to gendered expectations, whether macho (riding motorcycles) or feminine (not wearing overalls), runs the risk of reinforcing the very stereotypes that Halberstam and Duggan disparage in the film. Halberstam further asserts that, "by not making much of a gender distinction between Nic (vaguely butch) and Jules (vaguely femme)," *Kids* disservices real lesbian couples.[41] Again, this heteronormative positioning of a supposedly insufficiently butch-femme pair as unbelievable and unappealing devalues Cholodenko's disidentification with binary-reproducing norms of gender and sexuality. One can understand the heat-of-the-moment intensity of these immediate responses without sharing their sense that Cholodenko was obligated to conform to a specific set of parameters when imagining a lesbian couple on-screen.

Also drawing the ire of these and other critics was the film's invocation of "lesbian bed death," as contrasted with orgasmic heterophallic sex (see fig. 4.2). One may resist these academic

Fig. 4.2. Jules (Julianne Moore) "genuflecting" before Paul's (Mark Ruffalo) penis in *The Kids Are All Right*.

bloggers' zeal for holding the film's representations to a severe standard of lesbian legitimacy without veering to the opposite extreme of giving the film a pass on its insensitivities and missteps. A presumptuous claim in *Cineaste* notes, "Of course, only the incorrigibly politically correct will find [Jules and Paul's] brief romp, which is played mainly for laughs, objectionable."[42] Those who take Cholodenko to task for having, as Walters puts it, "Jules genuflect[] before Paul's penis" fail to note that in their subsequent sexual encounter, Jules sits astride Paul demanding he pull her hair as she slaps his face until she orgasms—rather queer sex, one might say.[43] Cholodenko defended her omission of a lesbian sex scene that she claims to have filmed but left out during editing because "it somehow felt disingenuous. To play it that way would have been to pander—a political maneuver."[44] Instead, Cholodenko makes two references to lesbian cunnilingus that, though "tastefully" veiled or euphemized, are unmistakable: Jules under the covers pleasuring Nic and her joking that, after first meeting Nic, her "tongue started working again." After confronting her son Laser (Josh Hutcherson) when he is caught with his moms' stash of gay porn, Jules's honest explanation of why she and Nic would not prefer to "watch two women doing it" implicitly defends the film's omission of a lesbian sex scene as well: "You would think that. But in most of those movies, they've hired two straight women to pretend and the inauthenticity is just unbearable."

Queer scholars Jasbir Puar and Karen Tongson, in a refreshingly cool-headed entry in the blogging blitz, offer a reading of Cholodenko's intentions that aligns with my own: "[Cholodenko's films] never featured who anyone would call 'likeable' characters. All of her films' protagonists have been white, privileged, pretentious and undeniably fucked up ... [whom Cholodenko] ... softly, but also scathingly satirizes [as] the denizens of queer(ish) urbanity, primarily in Los Angeles."[45] Echoing their sentiment, I would respond to critics who find that Nic and Jules's partnership replicates the terms of conventional straight marriage—from breadwinner Nic rebuking submissive Jules in front of others to Jules going down on Nic—by stressing that the film hardly endorses their marriage as equitable and conflict-free. Several scenes are devoted to Jules expressing her frustration with their marital status quo and her need for greater professional and personal, more than sexual, fulfillment.

On the topic of what Halberstam calls *Kids*' "casual racism," clearly the film does not invite us to applaud—through neither does it condemn—Jules for her (as Jules herself calls it) "fucked up" treatment and abrupt dismissal of Latinx gardener Luis (Joaquín Garrido).[46] Nor are we invited to look past Tanya's (Yaya DaCosta) rightful fury when Paul informs his younger black employee and casual sex partner, that in "need[ing] to start thinking about having a family," he must end their extracurricular trysts. From Tanya's first appearance on-screen, when Paul refers to her as "Foxy"—alluding to Pam Grier's leading role in the blaxploitation classic *Foxy Brown* (Jack Hill, 1974)—we are made aware of Paul's hypersexualization of her as someone he regards not as mother material. In contrast, Jules is—to use the word she chooses, and he repeats, in describing her vision for his home landscaping project—the "fecund" mother of his children.

Although I take issue with these attempts to discipline, from both ideological directions, *Kids'* representational options and our responses to them, much of the feminist-queer critique of *Kids* hits home. Collectively these readings illuminate what is genuinely troubling about *Kids*: its homonormative endorsement of marriage and family values and the right to defend them at any cost, alongside its complicity in a Hollywood-designed representational system that glosses over questions of class and race. As Puar and Tongson conclude, *Kids* is less "an ugly film" than it is a film that "reveals the ugliness at the heart of queer and bourgeois-bohemian fantasies about being different." The film is compelling precisely because of "how uncomfortable it makes us feel when we actually *do* experience the tiniest moments of self-recognition within these characters."[47]

Kids ventures the same risky maneuver as Lena Dunham's *Girls* in flaunting its characters' flaws, made riskier still through the slippage between authors and characters that Cholodenko and Dunham invite. While their shared aim may be to reveal human ugliness of the sort Puar and Tongson observe, both of these provoc*auteurs* often elicit responses predicated instead on disavowal and disidentification with characters judged to be visually unappealing, insufficiently sensitive on matters of diversity, and oblivious to their privilege. In both cases, online forums—websites and blogs featuring feminist-queer media commentary—act as incubators for these highly personal, near-real-time responses to screen representations that themselves seemed in conversation with contemporaneous debates around sexual politics, and that even used self-reflexive gestures to issue self-justifications or mea culpas, in service to their authorial prerogatives. Though Cholodenko's detractors alleged she was playing it safe with *Kids'* homonormativity, the film has proven to be her career peak in provocation to date. Nonetheless, the projects that followed have continued both to convey an awareness of Cholodenko's bad queer brand construction and to underscore the growing importance of online forums for eliciting critical talkback.

CHOOSING SECURITY BUT STILL COURTING CONTROVERSY

Though it was rumored that *Kids* was to be developed as an HBO series, instead Cholodenko ultimately brought a different project to fruition at the prestige cable channel: a four-part limited series adapted from an acclaimed story collection focused on an aging matriarch living in a coastal Maine enclave.[48] Based on Elizabeth Strout's Pulitzer Prize–winning work, *Olive Kitteridge* was Cholodenko's second collaboration with performer Frances McDormand, who bought the rights to Strout's book and developed the project. McDormand hired playwright-screenwriter and out lesbian Jane Anderson to adapt and chose Cholodenko as director. Depicting the second and third acts of the lengthy marital union of spouses Olive (McDormand) and Henry (Richard Jenkins) Kitteridge, the film expands *Kids'* contemplation of long-term monogamy across a longer temporal structure. The stories focus on, as Delphine Letort characterizes it, "the containment of desire and the efforts a couple make to preserve marriage 'till death tears us apart.'"[49] In effect, Cholodenko addresses the same age-specific determinants that critics of *Kids* found her using as a smokescreen to avoid Nic and Jules's sex life and breakup (the latter seemingly an impossibility, given that they're "too old" in the estimation of son Laser, who voices the film's final lines and thus has the last word on the matter). Whether Cholodenko was retreating into safer territory or testing the double standard applied to same-sex couples' representation, the sexual and marital sedateness of *Olive Kitteridge*'s heterosexual marrieds was unsurprisingly not subject to the same insinuations of effacing eroticism or endorsing dysfunctional couple dynamics that were directed at *Kids*.

McDormand plays Olive with a New Englander's exacting resolve and impatience with sentiment and silliness. Her character aligns with Clara Bradbury-Rance's characterization of the gendered landscape of Cholodenko's work as "exhibit[ing] many of the outlined traits of postfeminist culture that seem by their very nature to be pitted in opposition to feminist and queer convictions: female temporal anxiety; demonization of purportedly overbearing mother figures; the ultimate privileging of familial—if not biological—relations over friendship-based communities; the girling of femininity and the glorification of youth and naivety; and the representation of older women (who defy that girlification) as jaded." But as Bradbury-Rance is quick to concede, "Representation does not equate to complicity."[50] Here, as in *Laurel Canyon*, any impulse Cholodenko may have had to "demonize" the mother figure as unforgivably inappropriate or "overbearing" is undone by McDormand's winning star persona and the script's shift in point of view. In Strout's stories, the point of view is dispersed among townspeople; here it sits squarely with Olive and so reveals her more sympathetically than would an outsider's perspective. Not unlike *Laurel Canyon*'s Jane, McDormand's Olive is a strong-willed, literally unapologetic woman who defies social propriety and gendered dictates of decorum and deference, giving Olive's "inappropriate" behavior queer resonance.

Letort's examination of the novel-to-screenplay adaptation points to the series' reshuffling of Strout's narrative structure to present as the opening scene one in which Olive trashes a Valentine's Day greeting card from her husband, seeing it as a worthless sentimental commodification of love. Letort further observes that *Olive Kitteridge*'s temporal structure, spanning twenty-five years over its four episodes, "resists the decline narrative associated with 'ageism', using Olive Kitteridge's self-conscious character to question cultural images that undergird discrimination against older people on grounds of age."[51] Letort points to the intersectional concerns that characterize Cholodenko's work even in the absence of explicitly queer content that takes on queer meaning nonetheless. A concern with the analogous abjection resulting from ageism is thematically central to *Olive Kitteridge*, and desire and visibility are treated as embedded in social and material relations. As regards the latter, this project maintains Cholodenko's ongoing interest in probing how need and attraction coalesce. Much as Syd's attraction to Lucy is bound up in professional ambition, and Jules's desire for Paul is predicated on a confluence of familiar and strange, Olive finds longevity and security to be inextricable factors in figuring desire.

The "female temporal anxiety" that Bradbury-Rance notes in Cholodenko's leading women gnaws at Olive as she watches her only son grow up and move away and the family pharmacy sold to a corporate chain. Olive's attitude is mournful but not a denial of aging, such as her husband Henry demonstrates in flirting with helpless-acting younger women (whom Olive views with derision). As if still in character, McDormand's stern countenance throughout the 2015 Golden Globes ceremony (where she surprisingly failed to win the Best Actor award for which her *Olive Kitteridge* performance was nominated) was disparaged with a social media meme likening her to "Grumpy Cat." The incident indicated the extent to which women celebrities are judged harshly for not exhibiting girlish charm even as they are berated when found not to be "acting their age."[52] By the 2018 Academy Awards telecast, amid the upheaval wrought by the Time's Up and #MeToo movements, McDormand's star persona commanded an equally viral response when, having won an Oscar for her role in *Three Billboards Outside Ebbing, Missouri* (Martin McDonaugh, 2017), she used her acceptance speech to rousingly advocate for gender parity in Hollywood. Despite the political tide turning from snark to applause, McDormand's "angry feminist" affect has unfolded over a career in which she has shunned sexually exploitative roles and spoken out against cosmetic surgery—twin symptoms of what she has referred to as the "cultural illness" of ageism.[53]

Olive proves to be as assailable a role model as Cholodenko's other bad queer protagonists. Made lonely by her husband's death and son's absence, Olive connects with irascible Republican widower Jack Kennison (Bill Murray) in the tellingly titled fourth and final installment of the miniseries, "Security." In a first date dinner conversation that turns divisive when Jack reveals that he has not spoken to his daughter in two years because she has chosen to live with another woman, Olive is forced to contend with balancing her desire for companionship with her rejection of bigotry. As with all her work, Cholodenko integrates discussion of sexual alternatives into even those narratives not explicitly or primarily queer-themed. The couple's conversation, and date, ends when Jack accuses Olive of being as judgmental as he is. The allegation inaccurately equates bigotry with Olive's strong pronouncements, which never stem from superficial markers of race, class, or sexual orientation. In choosing to reconcile with Jack, Olive privileges emotional and perhaps (given Jack's wealth) financial security over her misgivings about his character. It is a vexing conclusion given that we have admired Olive's principled self-sufficiency, but it is also courageous and truthful in its portrayal of Olive as entirely human in her need. It is ultimately akin to other Cholodenko protagonists in balancing the thrill of liberation with the safety of security.

Cholodenko, in her next project, took on an even more diminished authorial role, executive producing and directing the first episode of the eight-part NBC miniseries *The Slap* (2015). The ensemble drama was adapted from a best-selling novel by Greek Australian writer Christos Tsiolkas and adapted for American television (after success in its initial incarnation on Australian television) by playwright-screenwriter Jon Robin Baitz, both openly gay writers.[54] The narrative focuses on the aftermath of an adult's slapping a young boy at a gathering of family and friends. The boy's parents press charges, and those who witnessed the incident find themselves pressured to take sides. Though its potential for provocation goes largely unrealized, at least in the US version, *The Slap* interestingly mobilizes the assumption that the physical discipline of children is impermissible as a springboard for assessing less clear-cut forms of inappropriate behavior. *The Slap*'s initial provocation is, in violation of liberal norms condemning corporeal punishment, that both the screenplay and Cholodenko's direction encourage viewers not to side entirely with the disciplined child and his indignant parents. More provocative still is *The Slap*'s thematizing of various modes of adult exploitation (including financial and sexual) of youth, which it does not always treat with the expected sympathies. The narrative conceit of relaying the unfolding tale through eight different politically inscribed character perspectives, and the inducement through its tagline "Whose side are you on?," clearly aimed to stoke cultural conversation. While proving too labored for most critics, the ploy allowed the series to be at once discursively divisive and demographically all-inclusive, and its accompanying hype as network TV "event viewing" attempted to reheat retrograde strategies of broadcasting (as opposed to narrowcasting) and watercooler-worthy live (as opposed to time-shifted) spectatorship that more recently found its first sizable payoff, then scandalous fallout, with ABC's 2018 *Roseanne* revival. What traction *The Slap* gained involved "hate viewing," incited by withering critical reviews and snark-filled viewer comments online, and circulated through social media platform Twitter and in IMDb comment boards.[55] The critical response ultimately earned *The Slap* a higher profile than it likely would have achieved absent this chorus of derision.

Though bearing less of her direct creative imprint, *The Slap*'s themes echo those of Cholodenko's self-scripted films. Enlisted to document the festivities where the punitive incident takes place, budding photographer and gay teen Ritchie (Lucas Hedges), a victim himself of homophobic cyberbullying, becomes a key witness given his roving camera's panoptical perspective. Wrestling with how much of one's personal life should be submitted to public scrutiny, forced to confront people he both admires and sees as flawed for engaging in behavior that endangers their loved ones, Ritchie's consternation and ultimate surrendering of "pictures of these people who I love trying hard to make it through a day" mirrors Syd's conflicted handing over of photographic proof of her queer desire. It speaks as well to Cholodenko's interest in representing the ugly humanity that Puar and Tongson note is put on (self-)revealing display in *Kids*. In its focus on the multicultural ensemble's conflicting customs, *The Slap* continues Cholodenko's exploration of alternative family formations and its complex wrangling of security, tradition, and acculturation in a society that remains heteropatriarchal. Though her defiance of patriarchal presumptuousness is not as showstopping as *Kids'* Nic telling Paul she needs his observations on parenting "like I need a dick in my ass," *The Slap*'s Anouk (Uma Thurman), a proudly single and childless executive producer on a television series, refuses to be manhandled by the wealthy, hot-blooded Harry (Zachary Quinto), who is facing indictment as a result of the slap. "You come from a place where men can get away with whatever they want," Anouk informs the second-generation Greek American turned Westchester County warrior, "but the world has changed." Given Anouk's professional role (changed from the novel and Australian miniseries, in which the character was a television writer), alongside her denunciation of male privilege, we might locate in her another stand-in for Cholodenko, presciently giving voice to what Time's Up and #MeToo advocates would articulate a few years later.

As *The Slap*'s premise demonstrates, Cholodenko remains attracted to controversy, and although her projects have become increasingly mainstream, her work proves anything but conflict-averse. It might seem deflating to register the trajectory of Cholodenko's career from her initial breakout as New Queer Cinema cause célèbre to her recent retreat into producing others' work for premium cable and network television, and most recently Netflix, with arguably tepid results.[56] Without doubt, this is a familiar path for American women directors, from Claudia Weill in the 1970s to Angela Robinson in the 2000s, who both faced difficulty sustaining momentum after their first features and subsequently found a toehold in the relatively impersonal business of directing episodic and series television. Weill did not make another film after the studio-sabotaged sophomore feature *It's My Turn* (1980), and Robinson spent a decade in development on her 2017 film *Professor Marston and the Wonder Women*. Yet Cholodenko's segue seems suggestive of what Mark Duplass, in his keynote address at the 2015 South by Southwest Film Festival, heralded as a transitional moment: "As the death of the middle class of film has happened, it has been re-birthed in television. The way you used to make really awesome $5 million movies that didn't have movie stars in them and had really great, cool original content, that's happening in cable TV right now."[57] Moreover, Cholodenko challenges the artistic and political devaluation of her smaller-screen projects, *Olive Kitteridge* and *The Slap*, in leveraging her career and that of other women and queer artists across borders of media, audience, and nation.

This cross-cultural (self-)promotion forged through mutual provocation promises to be further heightened by Cholodenko's current project, a Paramount Studios–financed adaptation of festival sensation *Toni Erdmann* (Maren Ade, 2016). This story of a workaholic woman personally and professionally unhinged by her prankster father's intrusion into her life resumes Cholodenko's focus, most prominent in *High Art*, on women's navigation of a postfeminist professional landscape. Already provocative for being a Hollywood remake of a critically revered European art film, speculation has run high as to how Cholodenko and star Kristen Wiig will handle two decidedly provocative scenes in the original version. One scene involves the female lead's ingestion of a cum-coated petit four as a come-on to her coworker/casual sex partner, and the other is an audacious scene of excruciating length featuring the female lead hosting a work party fully naked. Unsurprisingly, the remake's announcement fueled much online advocacy for fidelity to the original, a prime example of the long-tail watercooler effect enabled by online forums.[58] That Lena Dunham and her former writing and producing partner Jenni Konner were initially attached as screenwriters creates yet another link among the provoc*auteurs* profiled here and signifies the potency and currency of these self-inscriptions of sexual provocation in the contemporary mediascape. Indeed, a comparably provocative combination is in the works, as it was subsequently announced that Cholodenko would again team up with her *Kids* writing partner Stuart Blumberg on the screenplay. At present, the project is delayed in development after Jack Nicholson (who was to have costarred, after a decade-long hiatus from the screen) dropped out, yet with Wiig still attached and producers Adam McKay and Will Ferrell on board.

My opening contention that Cholodenko models an industrial inbetweener route for women practitioners in the contemporary US media sphere must be qualified by an acknowledgment of the extent to which institutional and ideological barriers to entry and experimentation remain, as evidenced by Cholodenko's sporadic output and recent turn to less personal projects. Yet Cholodenko's authorial signature remains distinct in offering an inbetweener vision that looks beyond regulatory regimes governing both professional and personal identity. Observing how Cholodenko's disidentification from agreed-upon criteria for queer cinema "risks her reputation of integrity in [the] queer community," Bradbury-Rance astutely points to how Cholodenko's films "promote queerness in yet another way, by rejecting the idea of a perfected self and a goal-oriented (read: future-oriented) narrative/life."[59] Alongside this embrace of human complexity and the present, Cholodenko similarly affirms desire's incorrigible logic without granting it free rein. As Jules counsels Laser in *Kids*, "Sometimes human sexuality is counterintuitive." To build fulfilling lives and relationships and to sustain emotional security necessitates a degree of compromise with regard to desire, such that sexual inbetweenness sometimes is harder to perceive but remains irrevocably present in Cholodenko's films and characters. Their and her queer sensibility, though representationally muted and politically modulated, is articulated through the industrial inbetweenness that Cholodenko engages to remain productive and personal. Embracing the middle road, Cholodenko's work remains reflexive and provocative in its questioning of artistic integrity and representational politics and in its negotiations of the culture industry and her position in it.

"THE BISEXUAL, PERSIAN LENA DUNHAM": DESIREE AKHAVAN

In her 2014 feature film debut, *Appropriate Behavior*, Akhavan stars as alter ego Shirin, a twentysomething Brooklynite bisexual not out to her Iranian American family and emotionally adrift after breaking up with her girlfriend. Indebted, by her own admission, to elder provoc*auteurs* Breillat as well as Cholodenko, Akhavan has also shared cultural space with her contemporary, Lena Dunham. Dunham provided a blurb for *Appropriate Behavior*'s advertising campaign ("Audacious and Funny and Unique") and cast Akhavan in season four of *Girls*. Fittingly, Akhavan's three-episode arc as Chandra, Hannah's piously PC classmate at the Iowa Writers' Workshop, suggests their shared affinity for provocative modes of self-inscription even as it illuminates the politics of sexuality, race, and ethnicity that define and divide them. Hannah's wildly inappropriate overshare, on their initial meeting, "No one ever thinks I'm legal, like, in the bedroom," is quickly weaponized by Chandra in the fiercely competitive space of their creative writing workshop. As Hannah's story comes up for discussion, Chandra asks their writing professor, "How are we supposed to critique a work which is very clearly based on the author's personal experience? I had the opportunity to speak with Hannah yesterday and she is very much this character" (4.2, "Triggering"). The ensuing debate over the BDSM elements in Hannah's story, as discussed in chapter 3, functions as an autocritical means for Dunham to address the conflation and condemnation of herself and her alter ego Hannah in cultural discourse around *Girls*. In an ironic twist on her own flouting of appropriate behavior and the invitation issued by her work to blur her on-screen roles with her real life self, Akhavan as Chandra plays the part of PC police that Akhavan herself eschews. Chastising Hannah for circulating a written defense (disguised as an apology) of her right to offend, Chandra haughtily informs Hannah, "Those cubbies are sacred spaces. They are meant for sharing art and not spewing hate." To Hannah's protest that her classmates' response has brought on writer's block, Chandra sarcastically turns the accusation back with a charge of "So you're saying it's our fault you can't write" (4.4, "Cubbies"). When Hannah retaliates with her own allegations, it is Chandra's (and, by extension, Akhavan's) questionable claim to spokeswoman status for ethnic diversity that is playfully, if pointedly, addressed. "You were blessed with an exotic name and now you get to be the first and foremost authority on third world issues here in Iowa," pronounces Hannah (4.3, "Female Author").

For all their fictional ribbing of each other, Akhavan's claim that in her alter ego screen roles she is performing "the worst aspects of my sexuality" resonates with Dunham's own self-assessment of what motivates Hannah's bad behavior.[60] Where Akhavan's and Dunham's mutual appreciation is suggested through their creative collaboration and reinforced by their cross-referential branding, Akhavan singles out Breillat as stimulating her artistic and political energies: "When I saw [Breillat's *Fat Girl*], it was such an incredible moment of thinking: This is what filmmaking is, this is how you fuck with the medium. I see the way that sex is depicted in films as a feminist pursuit of mine . . . and that's something Breillat has done in all her work."[61] As we will see, Akhavan approaches filmmaking and sex scenes in particular with a feminist ethic that shares both Breillat's and Dunham's penchant for blurring the boundaries between art and pornography while defetishizing the female body.

As with Breillat and Dunham, that defetishization turns on Akhavan's naturalistic deployment of nudity and "spectacular self-subjugation," the purposeful use of the body to resist exploitation that was discussed in chapter 3. Evident connections between Akhavan and Dunham on that count are their willingness to appear naked or unflatteringly attired on-screen and the small breasts that both flaunt. After a screening of *Appropriate Behavior* at the Provincetown Film Festival, an audience member told Akhavan that she was brave. Akhavan recalls, "I thought he was saying I was brave for being an Iranian bisexual. But he said, 'You have the smallest tits ever, but you show them, and I think we need to see different kinds of breasts in movies.' I couldn't stop laughing, but I said, 'You're right, and I'm starting a revolution.'"[62] In the scene referenced here, Akhavan's character Shirin embarks on a threesome with a girl-guy couple that is at first arousing (for the participants and potentially the audience) but devolves into awkwardness and wilted libidos (instigated by Shirin's "inappropriate" dig at the male half of the couple, which I examine below for its bad queer implications). In so doing, Akhavan performs the prov*auteur* strategy of referencing heterophallic pornography only to expose its illusory aspects. Showing how sexual adventure can swiftly sober into uncomfortable reality, the scene balances eroticism and awkwardness as effectively as *Girls* and renders a ménage à trois with the same levity as does Cholodenko in *Laurel Canyon*.

Akhavan sees herself and her screen alter egos occupying an inbetweener position that she explicitly names bisexual, even as she shares with Cholodenko a predilection for troubling the boundaries of identity. That I paired her with Cholodenko before learning that Akhavan counts *High Art* as her favorite LGBTQ+ film (followed by *The Kids Are All Right*) and claims it was an inspiration for *Appropriate Behavior* speaks to their simpatico sensibilities as sexual and industry inbetweeners. Akhavan said of *High Art*, "That film undid me a little. . . . It satisfied the cinephile in me and the homo."[63] Akhavan also reports having betrayed her own mandate to cast only Iranian actors in the roles of Shirin's family members by casting Spanish Vietnamese actor Anh Duong as Shirin's mother, in homage to her role as haughty boss Dominique in *High Art*.[64] In singling out *High Art* for praise, Akhavan alludes to its exceptionality among so many gay-themed indie films for both its aesthetic quality and its politically incorrect daring.

Like Cholodenko, Akhavan deliberately evades the usual desiderata of LGBTQ+ representation, with their shared signature as inbetweeners (sexual and otherwise) proving particularly difficult to pigeonhole within conventional identity markers. The first to admit, "I'm very politically incorrect and always have been," Akhavan's discussion of sexual identity frequently diverges from LGBTQ+ cultural scripting in ways that insist on the unruliness of both desire and self-understanding.[65] While Cholodenko's breakout film conflated lesbianism with heroin addiction (hardly an assimilationist tactic) and *Kids* incited queerer-than-thou ire with its perceived homonormativity, *Appropriate Behavior* has been treated far less harshly despite its snarky derision for the earnestness and rigidity of some LGBTQ+ discourse—though, as I will discuss below in regard to this and Akhavan's earlier, even more provocative web series, both her use of ironic comedy and her (self-) racialized status serve as buffers that are unavailable to bad queers Bret Easton Ellis and John Waters, or (arguably) to Cholodenko.

Much as Cholodenko engages in reflexive self-examination of women's place in the art industry, Akhavan's debut work thematizes her own burgeoning self-definition as a filmmaker and the precarious labor it involves. We might see Akhavan's alter egos resembling Cholodenko's young women protagonists, *High Art*'s Syd and *Laurel Canyon*'s Alex, not only in being sexual inbetweeners but in their struggle to find their footing in a professional world that seeks to pigeonhole them. Like Cholodenko's movement from New Queer Cinema experimentalist to crossover filmmaker, Akhavan's aesthetic and commercial niches escape easy categorization—an inbetweener positioning that, as with Cholodenko, has generated both praise and provocation.

While the edgy lesbian drama and the crossover gay hit were still rare enough commodities in their different moments that *High Art* and *The Kids Are All Right* made waves, at the time of *Appropriate Behavior*'s release in 2014 Akhavan was faced with cutting through a far denser thicket of competing product. As Rebecca Beirne notes of lesbian film distribution in the digital age, innumerable indie releases go unnoticed as a result of their impractical attempts to emulate Hollywood's online distribution norms, much less the theatrical release model that these days rarely accommodates such low-budget niche fare.[66] *Appropriate Behavior* circumvented this self-contained lesbian film ecosystem by using two other productive routes to building authorial brand and audience: the web series (discussed later in this chapter) and the film festival circuit.

Appropriate Behavior further straddled the infrequently broached divide between festivals organized around identity (such as LGBTQ+ and people of color groupings) and those programming a broader range of independent releases. The film was well equipped to span these divides given Akhavan's "bisexual Persian" imprimatur and its audience pull as a festival crowd-pleasing edgy romantic comedy. *Appropriate Behavior* premiered at Sundance and was nominated for an Independent Spirit Award (for Best Screenplay); it was picked up for UK distribution by queer film specialist Peccadillo Pictures; it received another screenwriting award at Outfest; and it won the Grand Jury Prize at the San Diego Asian Film Festival. It earned sufficient word-of-mouth and critical praise to stay aloft after its festival run, something few films manage to do given the imbalance of festival premieres in relation to distribution deals and streaming views. Its pre-VOD profile, then, permitted *Appropriate Behavior* sufficient LGBTQ+ credibility to snag what Beirne terms is "the queer stamp of approval for consumers navigating a sea of pseudo-lesbian sexploitation films" (and, I would add, bland lesbian rom-coms).[67]

Moreover, *Appropriate Behavior* was able to occupy multiple indie niches by virtue of its creator's branding, however reductive, as "the bisexual, Persian Lena Dunham." Yet Akhavan has commented on the limited currency of this hook on both production and exhibition ends of the filmmaking process in ways that suggest her dissent from the norms of positive representation has not gone unnoticed. Remarking on the difficulty of sourcing funding from cultural nonprofits as opposed to private equity (which eventually financed *Appropriate Behavior*), Akhavan acknowledged the drawbacks of her brand of sexual provocation: "The people who tend to love the film, at least in the states, have been 30-45 year old men, straight men.... I have not received that kind of love and affection from women's organisations, or grants. I just don't think I fit the mould of what you want for your Persian grant, or your women's grant or your gay grant."[68] Akhavan's remarks here compel a questioning of how cooperative grassroots networks for women's and queer film production mandate certain norms with which provoc*auteurs* fail to comply.

Akhavan's being branded the new Lena Dunham, however high concept, did not catapult her past the velvet rope that circumscribes contemporary theatrical exhibition. While Akhavan's appearance on *Girls* undoubtedly encouraged analogies to

Dunham, it also underscored how critical sexuality and ethnic/racial qualifiers are in determining and delimiting the two women's respective paths as provoc*auteurs*. "On the indie film circuit and in the film festival world, it's very attractive to be a gay, Iranian film," observes Akhavan, "but then in the theatrical setting to get a distributor and a release, it's not."[69] Acknowledging the drawbacks to this intersectional persona and brand, the qualifiers *bisexual* and *Persian* suggest just how distinctive and revisionist a perspective Akhavan brings. To begin parsing that, I first consider Akhavan's provoc*auteur* mobilizing of queer adaptation in *Appropriate Behavior*'s narrative in her allusion to Woody Allen's 1977 Academy Award-winning romantic comedy *Annie Hall*.

"A GAY *ANNIE HALL*"

Unlike her designation as the next Lena Dunham, it was Akhavan herself who referred to her debut feature as "a gay *Annie Hall*" while it was still in the script development stage.[70] I would propose more precisely that *Appropriate Behavior* is both a feminist and queer retelling of *Annie Hall*, a film that was groundbreaking in its narrative and formal rupturing of rom-com and cinematic conventions alike. To begin my consideration of *Appropriate Behavior* at the moment when its central couple fatefully meets signals its shared narrative nonlinearity with *Annie Hall*, where the equivalent initial meeting occurs a third of the way into the film's running time and well after the opening sequence has revealed the couple's breakup to come. In rom-com parlance, the "meet-cute" refers to the narrative trope whereby the couple-to-be initially encounters one another in a way that signals their compatibility and foreshadows their ultimate union. Befitting *Appropriate Behavior*'s also being an uncoupling comedy, on first chatting up girlfriend-to-be Maxine (Rebecca Henderson) on a Brooklyn stoop outside a New Year's Eve party, Shirin's lack of gay political correctness both sparks their repartee and foreshadows some of the difficulties with which their relationship will struggle.

> SHIRIN: I love dykes.
> MAXINE: You know that word is incredibly offensive.
> SHIRIN: Oh, I'm bisexual so it's okay.
> MAXINE: Still offensive.
> SHIRIN: You know how I meant it.
> MAXINE: Doesn't matter how you meant it.
> SHIRIN: Tomato-tomahto.

Shirin's allusion to the Gershwin tune "Let's Call the Whole Thing Off," immortalized on-screen first by Astaire and Rogers and then by Harry and Sally, combines with the New Year's Eve timing to create a wink to rom-com convention while announcing Akhavan's disruption of such (neo)traditional notions of opposites attracting for better rather than worse. Getting the final word but no acquiescence otherwise, Shirin's dismissal of the distinction as one of small differences challenges Maxine's insistence on the opposing position, that no contextual rationales exist for using traditionally homophobic language—one wrangled over continually in LGBTQ+ spaces and (recalling Akhavan's quote at the beginning of this chapter) by LGBTQ+ media creators.[71] At the time of *Appropriate Behavior*'s release, Akhavan marked her own position as aligning with Shirin's: "The more that you are uncomfortable with these labels, the more you ghettoise them. It's up to us to decide what these labels mean, and to reclaim these terms for ourselves. It's like people referring to themselves as dyke—I decide what a dyke looks like, I decide how to re-appropriate a term."[72]

The meet-cute dialogue between Alvy (Woody Allen) and Annie (Diane Keaton) in *Annie Hall* is memorably comprised of fatuous mansplaining (on Alvy's part) and feigned self-composure (on Annie's), leaving so much unspoken that it requires subtitling to expose their unguarded interior monologues (Annie: "I'm not smart enough for him"; Alvy: "I wonder what she looks like naked"). Shirin and Maxine's is the more authentic exchange because it allows for the acknowledgment of and debate over Shirin's use of bad queer language, where Annie's oblivious microaggression in telling Alvy "You're what Grammy Hall would call a real Jew" elicits only an eye roll of disbelief in response. While such cultural and, by extension, ideological division will prove as decisive a thorn in the couple's side as that of *Annie Hall*'s odd coupling between Jew Alvy and WASP Annie, Maxine relents to a smile when Shirin continues, "I like girls like you. You know— manly, but also a little bit like a lady." Out of their willingness to speak revealingly emerges the meet-cute's signal that they are destined to bond in their mutual misanthropy. Maxine, ranting about "Brooklyn parties and everyone talking about their Kickstarter campaigns," asks furiously, "Did you see that guy with the waxed Dali mustache? I mean, what the fuck is that guy's problem? Who the fuck does he think he is?" An enraptured Shirin responds, "I find your anger incredibly sexy. I hate so many things too." The kiss they exchange just shy of midnight, sealed by their common cynicism and contempt for the outrages of 21st century urban life, serves as rebuttal to the romantic comedy genre's valorization of screwball couples with their sunny comportment and playful camaraderie and of latter-day rom-com's manic pixie dream girls with their vacuous positivity and life-embracing outlooks.

Moreover, Shirin and Maxine's shared negativity establishes and revises the meet-cute bonding that convinces us of the couple's (however short-term) compatibility. After their breakup, Shirin's attempt at sexual healing leads her to an OkCupid date with good-looking but vapid "BrooklynBoy82" (James C. Bristow). A close-up on his profile page, where his self-summary begins, "I like a lot of things," provides a telling reveal that Shirin's search for a casual encounter with the anti-Maxine promises to disappoint. That those "things" include "good movies...indie stuff, like Goddard [*sic*] and Tarentino [*sic*]," offers another sly jab at Brooklyn poseurs and introduces what will be a reflexively employed running joke about *Appropriate Behavior*'s distinction from, and opposition to, such indie and LGBTQ+ sanctimony. Making small talk on the way to seducing him, Shirin struggles to suspend disbelief when learning that he performs "a combo stand-up/folk music act." "I have never heard of that," Shirin replies, deadpan. "My art defies labels," he proclaims proudly. "Why does comedy always have to be so mean, at somebody's expense? I want to use my comedy to bring attention to social justice issues." Though she remains respectfully poker-faced, letting the previously glimpsed profile page make the joke at his expense, this invitation to viewers to chuckle at his earnestness conveys just how unsuitable a match he is for the sharp-tongued Shirin—and how preferable is Akhavan's "mean" mode of comedy. Their exchange having none of the ironic banter of her and Maxine's meet-cute, "BrooklynBoy82" proves equally vanilla as a sexual partner, so tentative (or perhaps just tipsy) as to be incapable of rough sex even after Shirin invites it, leaving her to fantasize about Maxine's topping her in a flashback sequence that wistfully recalls their (for a time) dialogic and erotic chemistry.

Appropriate Behavior continues to signal its embrace of irony and politically incorrect pleasures through reflexive self-referencing, even if not running the gamut of distanciation techniques that are employed in *Annie Hall* (ranging from split screen to direct address to Marshall McLuhan appearing as himself). In both films, these references to artistic creation and the creative potential to be mined from romantic failure are at once self-deprecating and self-aggrandizing. Alvy's attempt to turn his life into art with a play based on his relationship with Annie comes off as self-indulgent and humorless—qualities that *Annie Hall* avoids. Shirin's job teaching filmmaking to Brooklyn preschoolers (based on Akhavan's former gig at an organization called Video Kid Brooklyn) functions similarly to mock artistic pretension in favor of humor and humility. Undercut by coteacher Tibet (Rosalie Lowe), under whose tutelage the advanced class (composed entirely of girls) is improbably creating a shot-by-shot remake of Hitchcock's *The Birds* (1963), Shirin struggles to control her own hyperactive brood of (all) boys. Unable to get them to sit still for the duration of Thomas Edison's minute-long film *The Kiss*, and with one boy protesting "That's not 'propriate for our age!" Shirin finally gives in to their collective vision: "To make a movie about farts!" At the screening that concludes Shirin's teaching stint, after the advanced class's virtuously multicultural montage filmed in "artful" black and white, the "not-advanced class" lets loose with their flatulent antics. That a chaste kiss is deemed "not 'propriate" where farting zombies and women-terrorizing birds are acceptable provides a subtle yet sly dig at the cultural hypocrisy of celebrating vulgarity and misogyny while censoring adult sexuality.

Much as *Annie Hall* endorses its own melancholy resonance over and above the mawkish amateur theatrics of Alvy's play-within-a-film, *Appropriate Behavior* indulges the lighthearted irreverence of animal comedy over the pompously self-important art film. While *Appropriate Behavior* falls somewhere in the middle on this "art versus farts" continuum, in maintaining its bad queer opposition to the saccharine toothlessness of so much gay rom-com, it refuses the temptation of fantasy wish fulfillment that Alvy references when he asks, "You know how you're always trying to get things to come out perfect in art because it's real difficult in life?" Observing how queerness has been ideologically conflated with failure—of heterosexuality, of reproductive futurity, of bourgeois capitalism—Jack Halberstam notes, "The queer body and queer social worlds become the evidence of that failure, while heterosexuality is rooted in a logic of achievement, fulfillment, and success(ion)."[73] In embracing the creative potential of failure that *Annie Hall* enacts while redressing Alvy's—and, to some degree, the film's and by extension Allen's—failure to see beyond cishet male privilege, *Appropriate Behavior* models Halberstam's notion of the queer art of failure.

Fig. 4.3. Annie (Diane Keaton) reading up on feminism, much to Alvy's (Woody Allen) sexual frustration.

Clearly we are encouraged to view as self-serving the nebbish Alvy's Pygmalion-like desire to mold Annie in his own loftily held (if self-hating) image, as he instructs her on worthwhile adult education ("Just don't take any course where they make you read *Beowulf*") and other cerebral pursuits (Bergman and Fellini films, Ernest Becker's *The Denial of Death*). Where the film's feminist awareness more forcibly registers is in Annie's gradual resistance to Alvy's teachings and worldview. She turns to reading material of her own, whether Simone de Beauvoir's feminist tract *The Second Sex* or the conservative periodical *National Review* (see fig. 4.3). The latter prompts Alvy's derision and the memorable line referencing its longtime editor, in response to Annie's late-night plea to be rescued from an intruding insect, "Why don't you get William F. Buckley to kill the spider?" Though opinions may vary (especially among contemporary viewers contending with controversies over Allen's personal life), Alvy's quick wit and quirky charm does not ultimately dissuade viewers from the perception that Annie's eventual choice to leave him shows good sense.

The question of whether Shirin is better off with or without Maxine is a thornier one, hinging less on women's liberation than on the tensions between good and bad queer politics. *Appropriate Behavior* flashes back to a bookstore scene early in their relationship in which Maxine insists on educating Shirin much as Alvy had tried to transform Annie, plying her with canonical LGBTQ+ texts to (as she says) "broaden her horizons" despite Shirin's demurral, "Oh, I don't need new reading material. I'm only up to book two of the *Twilight* series." Taking in the sober cover of *Stone Butch Blues*, Leslie Feinberg's pre-Stonewall memoir of working-class dyke life, Shirin echoes Annie's line from forty years earlier, "This is some pretty serious stuff here." "I'm asking you to read some books. You don't need to get your septum pierced—yet," is Maxine's sardonic response. Where Annie is pressured to adopt Alvy's pessimism ("I feel that life is divided into the horrible and the miserable"), Shirin faces the expectation, tellingly signaled through Maxine's joking, that she become "more gay."

Both Alvy and Maxine participate in the cultural (self-)constructions of their respective identity groups; Alvy plays up the world-weariness of cultural Jewishness, and Maxine promotes the LGBTQ+ narratives of prideful self-acceptance and performative coming-out. As Alvy, Allen gives voice to the inbetweenness of midcentury American Jews whose bourgeois liberal identity was nonetheless marked as not quite white. Alvy makes recurring references to ethnicity, highlighting the disconnect in worldviews between the privileged, racially unmarked Annie and the still-racialized Alvy. *Appropriate Behavior* signals its appropriation of *Annie Hall*'s ethnic culture clash with blatant irreverence in showing Shirin's oversexed pal Crystal (Halley Feiffer) flirting with an underage Hasidic boy in a wry nod to Alvy's visual projection of how Annie's Midwestern granny, "a classic Jew hater," imagines him in Orthodox suiting and sidecurls. Alongside Crystal's "inappropriate" toying with intergenerational and cross-cultural taboos, *Appropriate Behavior* will undercut Maxine's gay pride values, whose clash with Shirin's bad queer sensibility echoes *Annie Hall*'s Jew/WASP cultural divide.

Early in the film but (given its nonlinearity) post-breakup, Shirin feigns queer consciousness in an attempt to win back her ex. "You're not the only one who cares about gay rights," she says after crashing Maxine's reading group that is focused on, its facilitator announces, "the criminal justice system and its bias against the queer community." Soon Shirin and Maxine's bickering is drowning out a middle-aged gay man lamenting the "consensual sex with my sixteen-year-old boyfriend" that branded him an eighteen-year-old sex offender. With their myopic disregard for the afflictions of others and their mutual negativity, Shirin and Maxine's shared bad queer sensibility evinces, at least at their relationship's start, their compatibility—to such a degree that Maxine takes advantage of the solemn moment when she and Shirin prepare to exchange in unison their first I-love-yous to joke that she is "thinking of transitioning to a man."

Alongside mockery directed toward such ostensibly off-limits topics as religious piety, statutory rape, and gender confirmation surgery, *Appropriate Behavior* pokes fun at the self-important excesses of contemporary queer culture's sex radicalism. Before embarking on what Maxine devises as some decidedly unsexy role-play involving a tax auditor and a small business owner, Shirin proposes *safeword* as their safeword ("Let's cut out the middleman, 'cause what happens if you forget your safeword?"). When Maxine, despondent at "killing the sexy," admits, "I'm vanilla," Shirin responds in horror, "Don't say that!" In the lead-up to the aforementioned threesome she attempts post-breakup, Shirin will again burst out inappropriately, dumbfounded that the (unappealing to her) cishet man in the couple should own a latex outfit to use at play parties, "That sounds horrible!" Maxine and Shirin's failure in these moments to embrace queer sex-positivity bonds them initially, much like their shared revulsion for hipster posturing, but that only Shirin sticks to this bad queer sensibility determines their ultimate incompatibility. After their breakup, Maxine aggravates Shirin with a smug embrace of the gentrified Brooklyn affectations she previously derided, boasting that her new girlfriend "goes to her West African dance class religiously." "Is she Black?" Shirin asks disparagingly. The answer, naturally, is no—and yet Shirin's satisfaction is short-lived when the girlfriend turns out to be the insufferable coteacher Tibet.

The most pronounced bad queer aspect of *Appropriate Behavior* arises at a point of maximum divergence from *Annie Hall*, in which neurotic narcissist Alvy, the character with whom we are most closely aligned, attempts to indoctrinate Annie. Here Shirin occupies the pupil's position but proves not so pliable as Annie initially is shown to be, even as Maxine works to inculcate Shirin in much the same way. Just as Frank Krutnik assesses that Alvy and Annie "cannot find common ground without risking a damaging loss of self," to succumb to Maxine's gay pride script would be inauthentic to bad queer Shirin.[74] In both films, the coupling grows strained when the all-important appreciation of irony that fueled their respective meet-cutes is overpowered by Jewish Alvy's and lesbian Maxine's shift from comic to tragic registers in regarding their cultural oppression. The discrepancy between Alvy's irony in referencing his Jewish alterity with dark jokes about pogroms ("My Grammy never gave gifts, she was too busy being raped by Cossacks") and his increasingly monomaniacal obsession with going to see Marcel Ophüls's four-hour documentary about French collaboration with the Nazis, *The Sorrow and the Pity* (1969), is what ultimately makes their cultural difference burdensome to Annie. To viewers as well, in the context of 1970s upper-middle-class Manhattan, Alvy's self-victimizing ("I distinctly heard it ... 'Jew eat yet?'") seems paranoid in a way that it would not have been in 1940s Europe or even, given antisemitism's alarming reemergence, today. This is why the joke lands, and why our sympathies lean toward the put-upon Annie rather than the uptight Alvy.

The self-characterization rings similarly when Shirin expresses disbelief that her thirty-three-year-old brother is engaged, only to have her mother remind her, "I was only nineteen when I married your father." Shirin's sarcastic response ("Well, this isn't the Islamic Republic of Iran, Mom. Do you see a hijab on my head?") is viewed as merely bratty, because the actual reality of arranged marriage—which Akhavan's own parents may well have had—seems so remote in Obama-era Brooklyn. Even as Akhavan has recalled former Iranian president Mahmoud Ahmadinejad's notorious denial of homosexuality in his nation resonating sharply with her young adult self (he made the remarks during a visit to Columbia University in 2007, around the time that Akhavan was coming out), its perverse denialism could be regarded more simply as preposterous from the relatively safe vantage point of an America on the verge of *Obergefell v. Hodges*.[75]

Where Maxine is initially charmed by Shirin's bad queer political incorrectness and occasionally reveals some of her own (joking about gender transitioning, for example), her increasing virtue-signaling and humorlessness regarding her gay alterity gradually erodes their compatibility. Maxine's preference for re-reading *Stone Butch Blues* over sex with Shirin provokes exasperation on par with that Annie expresses at having to endure Alvy's *The Sorrow and the Pity* marathons (see fig. 4.4). Admonishing Shirin that "the only aspect of gay culture that's okay with you is drag," Maxine conveys her refusal to regard LGBTQ+ oppression with the camp humor and distancing that the drag queen embodies. While Shirin's inappropriate pronouncements are often elitist (she sizes up the patrons at a gay bar with, "These people don't look like they went to college"), they also debunk the narrative of LGBTQ+ community solidarity and take aim at the LGBTQ+ party-line politics that she, like RuPaul, dismisses for its focus on victimhood. Maxine's insistence that "my friends are my family—you don't know what it's like," reiterates another narrative of LGBTQ+ exceptionalism in needing to form

Fig. 4.4. Maxine (Rebecca Henderson) opting for *Stone Butch Blues* over sex with Shirin (Desiree Akhavan) in *Appropriate Behavior*.

alternative relationships as a result of necessary, rather than elective, estrangement from biological kin. It also provokes Shirin's insensitive, if bracing, reply: "Enough of the lesbian orphan propaganda! We all have shit families. Of course it's a choice."

Ultimately, it is Shirin's prolonged reluctance to come out to her family that most significantly undermines her and Maxine's relationship. Maxine condemns Shirin's evasions as "don't ask, don't tell," referring to the infamous Clinton administration policy regarded as capitulating to the US military's (and electorate's) institutionalized homophobia. Shirin's defense, "They know, and I know they know. You think I'm a bad person because I'm not coming out on your terms," might be a self-serving attempt at avoidance. But we also might read this conflict as less about the importance of coming out and more about Shirin's resistance to Maxine's attempts to reshape her and her desire to assert her own agency over the terms of her life. Though sparing us the self-satisfaction of Alvy counting it as "a personal triumph" when he runs into Annie improbably taking a new boyfriend to see *The Sorrow and the Pity*, Shirin does come to understand that

Maxine's exacting standards are grounded in their own "never again" ethos. This gradual recognition on Shirin's part is signaled in a shot of her, now-single, finally reading *Stone Butch Blues*.

Shirin's failure to come out on Maxine's terms, and on her schedule, fuels the queer theoretical import yielded by *Appropriate Behavior*'s nonlinear narrative structure—the clearest evidence of its debt to, and reworking of, *Annie Hall*. Allen's film was exceptional for its time as a self-billed "nervous romance" that failed to deliver the expected couple (re)formation and happily ever after. *Appropriate Behavior* borrows the earlier film's frequent use of flashback, circular structure, and open-endedness but goes further to posit a more pointedly nonteleological trajectory that has distinctly queer connotations. In their antiprogressive inclination to move backward and resist growth, flashbacks resist the teleological imperative toward progress and futurity's pull. Alongside its other queer aspects, *Appropriate Behavior*'s nonlinearity resists what Elizabeth Freeman terms *chrononormativity*, the institutionally and ideologically enforced temporal manipulations by which social subjects are regulated for maximum productivity and conformity. Together with what Dana Luciano terms the *chronobiopolitical* forces that shape "'the sexual arrangement of the time of life' of entire populations," this imposed timeline functions to construct normative subjects and lifestyles, and operates through the overvaluation of temporal markers, or milestones.[76]

Queer theory's deconstruction of temporality reveals time as a social construct, naturalized to those whom it privileges and in its own elevation of linearity, continuity, and progression along with such attendant chronobiopolitical discourses as progressivism, reproductive futurism, and neoliberalism. Whitney Monaghan points to (white cishet) male reviewers' criticisms of *Appropriate Behavior*'s nonlinearity (something *Annie Hall* was not criticized for) and insightfully formulates its significance as both inbetweener and queer: "By positioning Shirin as a figure caught between these two identities, Akhavan uses the question of 'appropriateness' to challenge the temporality associated with teleological and progressive/progressing milestones. Akhavan's film suggests that it is not enough to substitute heteronormative milestones with 'queer' ones. Rather, it suggests that we must critique the politics of value underpinning the supposed necessity of attaining these milestones."[77] As Monaghan notes, Shirin's recombination and revaluation of gay/straight milestones enable her inbetweener navigation of and deviation from heteronormative and homonormative temporal paths. Claire Perkins points, moreover, to how this "in-between sensibility manifests as a commentary on the difficulty—and undesirability—of 'achieving' the social and temporal expectations of a range of intersecting identities."[78] Embedded in, and enabled by, this antiteleological mode of queer resistance, *Appropriate Behavior*'s compulsive lapse into flashbacks comprising the heartbroken Shirin's memories subsumes us in her subjectivity, offering a heightened mode of identification with the rarely seen or heard experience of being a bisexually identified woman of color.

BRAVING "THE B WORD"

As I explore in *The B Word*, given bisexuality's history of discursive effacement and representational deniability, Akhavan's explicitly and specifically bisexual voice stands out even from that of Cholodenko and other kindred bad queers.[79] So rare is it to find a cultural text that explicitly identifies its protagonist as bisexual and that centrally thematizes bisexuality, I was both elated to discover *Appropriate Behavior* and regretful that the film was not released in time to discuss it in *The B Word*. While bisexual representation is on the rise in popular culture, Akhavan remains exceptional in her shaping of a provoc*auteur* signature informed by the inbetweener sensibility I trace to bisexual alterity.[80] Readers familiar with my previous book will recall bisexuality's ability to provoke—a quality that, paradoxically enough, results from both its troubling blurring and its alleged reinforcement of the sexual binarism. Just as latter-day feminism posits that the one universal quality to womanhood inheres in the experience of misogyny and sexism, it would seem that for bisexuals a unifying experience, alongside that of biphobia, is the hiding-in-plain-sight sense encapsulated by Akhavan's observation that "it's the one sexuality where you're defined by whoever your partner is at that moment."[81] An inbetweener conceptualization would instead characterize bisexual subjectivities as different from monosexual subjectivities, and as distinct (though not disassociated) from other queer subjectivities, by their deprioritization of gendered object choice as determinative.

Fittingly, one of the images used to advertise *Appropriate Behavior* places Shirin in just such an inbetweener position, framed by the couple with whom she has the ill-fated threesome. *Appropriate Behavior*'s inbetweener status is apparent in its purposefully dual address to, and accommodation of, queer and straight audiences. An important signal of this dual address is the film's choice to explain the meaning of the term *gold star* (a lesbian who has never slept with a man). An explanation with a similar purpose occurs in a scene in Cholodenko's *Kids* when Jules explains lesbians' predilection for gay male porn. Such a use of dual address aims to accommodate the straight audience without alienating queer viewers, employing a representational strategy distinct from an in-the-know address aimed at a queer audience.

This kind of insider/outsider divide can be observed in a comparison of references to lesbian sex in two 1990s US independent films: *Chasing Amy* (Kevin Smith, 1997) and *Go Fish*. In the former, the lesbian lead gives her straight guy pal a demonstration, complete with visual aids, of fisting. His astonishment at, and subsequent education in, the mechanics of lesbian sex mirrors that of the presumed straight audience for this film. In contrast, a scene in *Go Fish* shows a butch/femme couple beginning their first date with an extended scene of nail cutting that goes wholly unexplained and presumably not understood by straight viewers, whom this lesbian-authored and -acted film declines to acknowledge, let alone educate. Befitting its own bisexual protagonist, *Appropriate Behavior* adopts *Chasing Amy*'s mode of dual address, which constitutes a form of code-switching that is advantageous in "having it both ways" (to reappropriate a common slur about bisexuals). Yet, as if embodying its protagonist's bisexual liminality, the film is never fully at home in gay or straight camps.

Though Akhavan has noted the need for more bisexual role models ("There's Tila Tequila and Anne Heche; we're not doing great," she lamented in 2015), she appears more intent on conveying with immediacy and complexity the experience of bisexual alterity to dispel the simplistic conceptualizations and representations it has long endured.[82] Doing so requires overcoming the culturally imposed shame and misperception that disproportionately hangs over the B word, as Akhavan suggests: "Saying you're bisexual is like saying 'I'm a huge slut.' It's so uncomfortable, and I feel very taboo calling myself bi, but it is what I am and every time I say it I'm winning a tiny victory for myself, I am going to dictate what this means, and it doesn't mean I can't make up my mind or I'm confused."[83] Akhavan's comment echoes those of Breillat's and Cholodenko's female protagonists in their insistence on the right to self-definition, which is seen in the rejection of the role of rape victim asserted by *Romance*'s Marie and *Fat Girl*'s Anaïs and the resistance to sexual pigeonholing by *High Art*'s Syd and *Kids*' Jules. Having first begun to self-identify as bisexual while an undergraduate at Smith College ("a good place to be a lesbian, a terrible place to be bisexual," she recalls), Akhavan has continued to proclaim herself bisexual in an era, and among a generation, suspicious of labels for their propensity to reinscribe binarisms, whether of sexuality or gender.[84] Asked why she did not fit in among her undergraduate queer community, Akhavan recalls, "Because I wasn't gay enough! I didn't have a half-shaved head and a pierced septum."[85]

Being on the receiving end of this cultural perception that bisexuality is inadequately queer further informs Akhavan's inbetweener sexual and representational politics. Similar to Dunham's strategy of spectacular self-subjugation, Akhavan leans into this semi-exclusion from the queer club that would not have her as a member, flaunting the bad queer moniker projected onto bisexuals and resignifying it as inappropriately rather than inadequately queer. Whereas Akhavan's own statements straightforwardly assert her bisexual identity, her fictional alter egos again share with those of Dunham their manifestation as what Akhavan admits to being "the worst aspects of my sexuality."[86] With *Girls*' Hannah, such exaggeratedly inappropriate announcements as the aforementioned "barely legal" remark self-satirize Dunham's own flagrant exhibitionism, while Shirin's embodiment of bisexuality demonstrates both that the cultural stereotypes it bears are not entirely off base and that they nonetheless fail to reveal the whole story.

Rather than affirming bisexuality through positive or relatable representation, Akhavan's bad queer provocation reveals bisexuality in all its personally and politically assailable having-it-both-ways messiness, endowing it with human complexity. In *Appropriate Behavior*, the centrality of Shirin's subjectivity and its narrative positioning between opposing poles of denial and distrust from Persian and queer communities alike cultivate empathy for the ways bisexuality contends with suspicion from all camps. Having demonstrated that Akhavan's irreverent approach to bisexual self-inscription survived her professional transition to making feature films, this chapter's last section will examine the web series *The Slope*, Akhavan's highly provocative first foray into ironic takedowns of contemporary queer culture, including bisexuality.

The relationship between Shirin and Maxine, however, does not transcend bisexuality's associations with passing and equivocating—on which *Appropriate Behavior* gazes sympathetically but not entirely forgivingly. Akhavan gives her fictional family prominent placement in *Appropriate Behavior,* to such a degree that Maxine accuses Shirin of being "a grown woman in a completely codependent relationship with your parents." This gestures at the significance of her Persian heritage in her self-identification, as discussed below, but also depicts how bisexuals navigate a complicated terrain both akin to and distinct from those not out as gay or lesbian. Again, its complications stem partly from bisexuality's negative cultural associations as well as from its inbetweener (in)visibility.

In her exploration of these aspects of bisexual alterity, Akhavan pays particular attention to the role played by language. That the language of the closet often relies on double meanings suggests its kinship with irony. When Shirin's father (Hooman Majd) asks, "How's your love life—any boys?" Shirin responds cagily, "No boys at all." Not always so deft, Shirin later slips up in her attempt to respond in accord with heteronormative assumptions. Helping with her post-breakup move into a grim Brooklyn loft shared with a stone-faced Goth couple, Shirin's mother says optimistically, "At least you have a sexy roommate." "Felicia? I find her a bit terrifying," Shirin answers, to which her mother confusedly responds, "No, I meant the guy!" Shirin similarly stumbles when her father asks why her apartment with Maxine has only one bed, offering up a conspicuously improbable excuse.

> SHIRIN: It's European and thrifty. There are a lot of benefits. I have an Italian friend named Cecilia and she and her best friend shared one bed for years, and they saved so much money on rent that they were able to afford very big weddings to their boyfriends. Also, in the movie *Beaches,* these two best friends shared a bed, and it was very inexpensive.
> FATHER (IN FARSI): Italians are weird.
> SHIRIN (IN FARSI): You're right.

With only a few lines in the film spoken in Shirin's parents' native language and translated through subtitles, this moment recalls *Annie Hall*'s meet-cute in revealing to viewers these characters' inappropriate sentiments, and uses language to hide meaning from—in this case—the uncomprehending Maxine. Alongside the reference to representational effacement of lesbianism (in *Beaches*), this emphasis on the evasiveness that language permits speaks to another facet of passing that Shirin and Akhavan embody as women whose gender presentation is femme. As the casual slippage into Farsi indicates, so too do Shirin and Akhavan embody an inbetweener position as not quite white.

That Shirin straddles a cultural divide between queerer-than-thou Brooklyn hipsters and the comparably biphobic norms of her family's Persian community—where women can openly dance together but lesbianism is verboten—provides a sense of bisexuality's uniquely adaptive yet, as a result, maligned, (in)visiblity. This (in)visibility can be advantageous in allowing Shirin to avail herself of femme privilege in relying on her girlfriend's chivalry in buying them drugs ("You're lucky I veer butch," says Maxine). But it can also be maddening in moments such as when Shirin runs into Maxine and her new girlfriend Tibet at a party.

> SHIRIN: Maxine and I used to be together, can you believe it?
> TIBET: Nope.
> SHIRIN: Why not?
> TIBET: I thought you were straight.
> SHIRIN: Fuck you.

That Tibet's presumption provokes such anger in Shirin suggests another pent-up aspect of bisexual alterity: the assumption that femme equals straight—so pervasive, irritatingly enough, to be voiced by a lesbian so femme as to be a former hair model (as she makes a point of informing Shirin at their first meeting). Akhavan had earlier acknowledged this dissonance when, after being introduced as part of a lesbian couple in *The Slope*, she feels compelled to add "even though I don't look gay" (1.5 "It Gets Better"). Notably, however ironically this pronouncement is meant to be taken, the conflation of sexuality and gender goes a step further (in referring to herself as gay) to indicate her own internalized impulse to efface bisexuality—an impulse that similarly characterizes Shirin's coming-out sequence, discussed below.

But where Shirin is partially delineated according to bisexual stereotype—in being femme and not fully out—in other ways Akhavan diverges from stereotypical representations of bisexuality. For example, it is Maxine who cheats on Shirin, and she does so with a man. The incident, which happens in a drunken moment late into a night of Pride partying, is sexually insignificant in that it neither progresses past kissing nor undermines Maxine's lesbian identity. As she explains, with seemingly unintended perversity, "It was a man; it was like kissing a baby, just lips touching." Yet the scene is representationally significant for countering cultural expectations that it will be the bisexual woman who proves promiscuous, adulterous, and inevitably "led astray" by a man. At the same time, Akhavan steers clear of a falsely egalitarian view of bisexuality as always involving attraction to men and women in equal measure. It is clear during the threesome sequence that Shirin has a far more intense connection with the woman than with the man, this being one of three heterosexual encounters within the film all of which characterize Shirin as being (in her own words) a "boner killer."

Notwithstanding its heroine's pining for an ex-girlfriend and clear interest in foregrounding lesbian over straight sex, *Appropriate Behavior*'s validation of bisexuality is hinted at even before Shirin is so identified. And, again, it is articulated in a way that demonstrates how language places judgment on bisexuality that Akhavan's ironic yet humanizing treatment works to undo. Reassuring Shirin that she was right to end it with Maxine, Shirin's friend Crystal reminds her, "She wasn't even fucking you towards the end." Shirin offers the weak protest, "Maybe it was a phase."

Here the café table between them provides a visual bridge to the nightstand on which an unused strap-on dildo sits in *Appropriate Behavior*'s first flashback, in which Shirin and Maxine attempt their mood-killing sexual role-play. Though on first viewing the memory appears triggered visually, it is in fact Shirin's turn of phrase that provides the aural callback we register only later. For Shirin has just inadvertently echoed the words with which Maxine ends their final fight: "Don't bother telling your parents about us. I know you, and the more that I think about it, this is probably just a phase." Maxine's stinging dismissal of bisexuality as "just a phase" becomes the tipping point past which their coupling cannot recover.

At the same time, Shirin resists pressure from the other side of the aisle to stay closeted, as when she works up the nerve to come clean with her brother Ali (Arian Moayed):

> SHIRIN: My old roommate Maxine and I were in a relationship.
> ALI: Ah, so you're a lesbian.
> SHIRIN: I was pretty into all the guys I was with, so I think I'm bisexual.
> ALI: And that's a thing?
> SHIRIN: I'm afraid so. How do you think Mom and Dad are going to take it?
> ALI: You're not gonna tell them now that it's over?!

Though sibling rivalry as much as outright biphobia informs this exchange, Ali's response repeats monosexist presumptions (that bisexuality is really lesbianism, nonexistent, and just a phase) and earns Ali's appraisal of her as a "sexually confused narcissist."

Having regularly taught *Appropriate Behavior*, I find the current generation of college undergraduates largely sympathetic to Shirin's dissembling around coming out, and opposed to Maxine's insistence on her doing so—at least on a timetable that Maxine dictates. Less concurrence greets the question of whether Shirin's being closeted fatally undermines Shirin and Maxine's viability as a couple. While Shirin manages to come out by film's end, it is partially and to only one parent and not in time to save her relationship with Maxine. It does not, in other words, have the pivotal or revelatory weight typically conferred on it by the coming-out narrative—one that, with its teleological imperative, rarely accommodates bisexuality. Fittingly, Shirin chooses deliberately ambiguous wording when she confesses to her mother, "Mom, I'm a little bit gay." Her mother responds in Farsi, "No, you're not," in another momentary crossing of language for the purposes of denying queerness. Shirin insists, "Yes I am, and I was in love with Maxine." Her mother merely shushes her, no longer trusting language to keep the truth veiled. The scene ends there, its indeterminacy left unresolved. Even if Shirin suspects, as she goes on to tell Crystal, that her mother "knows for sure what's up," the coming-out process is treated as an ongoing, always incomplete one that does not necessarily result in the extreme displays of rejection or acceptance presented in more conventional versions of the coming-out narrative. Rather than emphasizing coming out, with its connotations of choosing a side, the film's teleology remains focused on the couple's breaking up and so withholds the gendered object choice deployed as determinant of monosexual identity.

At the same time that *Appropriate Behavior* validates Shirin's bisexuality in a way that those around her refuse to do, the legitimacy of her lesbian relationship with Maxine is signaled through the bookending shots of Shirin first failing then succeeding in disposing of the strap-on dildo that was her gift to Maxine (and which Maxine returns when they break up). The strap-on here acts as signifier of queer authenticity—not unlike the nail-cutting scene in *Go Fish*. In finally managing to dispose of the strap-on, Shirin is not repudiating lesbian sex or desire, but changing the object's signification to symbolize her uncoupling. She lets go not of same-sex desire but of her resistance to acknowledging the end of the relationship. In this sense, the strap-on is a substitute for the heteronormative (or homonormative) couple's engagement diamond and wedding band, and its triumphant disposal constitutes a queering of rom-com's clichéd scene of the newly (or not so newly) single person unshackling herself from a relationship now over.

BEYOND (BI)SEXUALITY

Akhavan's recent series for UK television's Channel 4 and US streaming service Hulu, titled *The Bisexual* and cocreated with *Appropriate Behavior* collaborator Cecilia Frugiuele and producer Rowan Riley, furthers her project of bisexual representation and provocation. In the series, Akhavan plays a woman who, following a breakup with her long-term girlfriend, begins dating men. Yet for all the centrality of bisexuality in Akhavan's body of work, she is quick to note, "So much of my life has nothing to do with being bisexual."[87] Owing in part to bisexuality's (in)visibility, certainly for Shirin and presumably for Akhavan as well, far more visible to those around them is their Middle Eastern origins, as signaled through name and appearance. Addressing the tokenism involving her Iranian American identity in her professional life, Shirin complains to Crystal that she is quitting her journalism job because, "The only reason they hired me in the first place is 'cause they wanted a Middle Eastern person. Now that Yavah's in editorial, everyone's gushing over how Syrian she is." During her interview for the job teaching filmmaking to children, Shirin is again on the receiving end of ethnicity fetishism when middle-aged hipster Ken (Scott Adsit), on hearing that she is Iranian, enthuses about a *Vice* article on Tehran's underground hip-hop scene, asking eagerly, "So you're part of that?" Shirin's response, that her yearly trips to Iran are spent "watching Disney videos with my grandmother while she untangles jewelry," clearly disappoints Ken, who will go on to mistake her name on every attempt until finally, at the end of the film, he manages to address her correctly.

Although its treatment of these microaggressions remains lighthearted (Ken being a sympathetic if feckless character),

Appropriate Behavior's referencing of Shirin's Middle Eastern roots works in tandem with that of bisexuality to critique the exoticizing of both. When Maxine accompanies Shirin to a celebration of Noruz, the Iranian New Year, Shirin playfully calls Maxine out on her fascination with the "beautiful ritual" of fire jumping. "Ew, you are totally having one of those 'I'm dating an immigrant' moments," Shirin teases her. "Like, 'Isn't learning about other cultures so fun and enriching!'" Yet the more biting undercurrent of Shirin's response acknowledges that Maxine's enthusiastic acceptance of Shirin's ethnic heritage stems from its posing no threat to Maxine's whiteness, whereas Shirin's closeted bisexuality troubles Maxine's lesbian self-perception and politics. In fact, Shirin's ethnicity and sexuality are inseparable— knowledge Maxine resists in taking a superficial view of Persian identity that celebrates its pageantry while overlooking its prohibitions.

When Maxine accuses Shirin of "playing the Persian card" as justification for not coming out to her parents, Shirin responds, "I'm sorry, what country is it that you get stoned to death if you're convicted of being gay? Oh, yeah. Wait, I know. It's Iran. The country that my entire family comes from!" Shirin's remark is clearly self-serving in associating her homeland with violent oppression of homosexuality, when her parents' age and secularism identify them as being among the generation of Persians to have left Iran precisely because of the postrevolutionary theocracy whose persecutions Shirin references.

Even as Shirin uses familial disapproval as a crutch (if not a false concern, given the disavowal with which her mother greets her coming-out), *Appropriate Behavior* emphasizes how cultural heritage and family ties are not easily extricated from the process of identifying and coming to terms with one's sexuality. This inextricability is audiovisually signaled in the shot described earlier of a lovesick Shirin finally reading *Stone Butch Blues* as Persian music prompts the narrative's segue back to the

Fig. 4.5. *Stone Butch Blues*' reappearance signals Shirin's coming to terms with her compartmentalized identities.

Noruz celebration Maxine attends (see fig. 4.5). The shot forms a seamless fusion of past and present temporalities and queer and ethnically marked spaces. As mentioned earlier, this shot is momentous for suggesting how Shirin eventually comes to regard her compartmentalizing of her queer and Persian selves as untenable and her semicloseted equivocations as shameful without negating her understandable reluctance to come out in a culture in which Akhavan recalls, "You don't talk about ugly things ... you just turn your head the other way. So I didn't even hear of one Iranian homosexual my whole life. And when I came out, it was like saying—it was like coming out as a leprechaun or a unicorn. It was like a fictitious thing."[88]

These considerable powers of deniability are on display at the Noruz gathering, where Shirin assuages Maxine's concern about "being in enclosed spaces where I can't detect any visibly gay people" by sharing her suspicion that an uncle is "harboring some bi-curious tendencies." When Maxine asks whether they have talked about it, Shirin replies, "Of course not. Persians communicate mostly through gossip." Her derision at the way that community constructs itself against the open expression of nonnormative desire is borne out a short time later. A quartet of young women briefly engage Shirin and Maxine in a conversation that ends abruptly when Shirin ventures emotional honesty. "What just happened?" Maxine says confusedly. Shirin explains that their encounters follow an identical script every Noruz.

As visual illustration of this "don't ask, don't tell" protocol, the sequence's shot–reverse shot structure permits Shirin and Maxine a frame of their own so long as they remain platonic and gender-conforming (Maxine, there as Shirin's "white friend," having been enticed into wearing a dress) and even permits them the culturally approved same-sex dancing. Yet the alternately framed shot during this exchange between "appropriate" and "inappropriate" female groupings sets off Shirin as a "bad Persian" for her failure to assimilate among her hyperfeminine peers, just as an earlier sequence showed Shirin sharing the frame with her parents opposite their "good Persian" son and his fiancée, both successful surgeons.

Shirin's perceived failure as a Persian is visually and narratively intertwined here with her queer failure to conform to mature biological and capitalist dictates of reproductive futurism. Whereas the American New Year serves as a launching pad for Shirin and Maxine's relationship with its queering of rom-com's meet-cute, the Iranian New Year first provides Shirin cover for her queer coupling, but, a year later, the event spurs her (however partial, and partially acknowledged) coming-out. Shirin's queer appropriation of these milestones disrupts their traditional markers of midnight kisses between heterosexual couples and platonic dancing between women. Thus these tandem new years are another means by which the film's cyclical narrative structure departs from the chrononormative teleology that Shirin, and Akhavan, resist.

In *Appropriate Behavior*'s final scene, Shirin and Crystal, sitting next to each other on the subway, voice disbelief at the "appropriate" timeline dictated by (neo)traditional rom-com, with its entreaties to women to remain sexually chaste until they "put a ring on it"—or at least until after a few dates. Having expressed interest in having a threesome of her own (with Shirin's Goth roommates), Crystal muses, "There are people in this world who go on dates that are perfectly great, and then they wait awhile before they engage in sexual contact." "That's disgusting," Shirin responds, deadpan. "I'm pretty sure it happens outside New York," says Crystal, agreeing. As the film's final words of dialogue, their ironic mockery of the sexually conservative logic that condemns "promiscuity" as practiced by "urban elites" as "disgusting" gains extra weight. Rejecting both the desexualized quality of so many gay romances and the homonormative culture that produces them, *Appropriate Behavior* presents as the film's final coupling (platonic) girlfriends who identify as bi (Shirin) and heteroflexible (Crystal), but whose mutual logic of desire is decidedly queer.

One further revisionist twist on rom-com's conventional couple formation follows, as the camera angle narrows to isolate Shirin in the frame, continuing to hold on her as the diegetic sound gives way to a musical track that continues to play over the end credits (see fig. 4.6). It becomes the sight of a single woman's uncoupling that provides *Appropriate Behavior*'s final image. The shot invokes unconventional romantic comedies of the women's liberation era, including *Annie Hall, Girlfriends* (Claudia Weill, 1978), and *An Unmarried Woman* (Paul Mazursky, 1978). These films all rejected rom-com's requisite delivery of happily-ever-after coupling. Yet by virtue of its framing and duration, this final shot alludes even more directly and knowingly to the iconic last image of *The Graduate* (Mike Nichols, 1967), in which the runaway couple rides off into an indeterminate sunset to the strains of Simon & Garfunkel's "The Sounds of Silence" (see fig. 4.7). The track chosen to close *Appropriate Behavior*, Electrelane's "To the East," is equally evocative, not only for being the work of a queer female act but in employing lyrics that undermine any confidence

Fig. 4.6. *Appropriate Behavior*'s final shot.

Fig. 4.7. The iconic final shot of *The Graduate*.

that narrative resolution has been reached. The song carries the refrain, "I want to be with you. I'm just waiting until you say these words; Come back, come back, come back to me."[89]

Just as the expected rom-com (re)coupling is thwarted, the pat ending of so much conventional gay narrative is rejected, both in leaving work still to be done with Shirin's coming-out and in suggesting that her heartbreak, though muted, is far from fully exorcised. Alongside its queer rewriting of another canonical (and straight male–authored) rom-com, to conclude with Shirin traveling alone to her own uncertain future circles back to the film's start, when she was riding the rails but crying and not nearly out of the tunnel, so to speak. A fitting ending for a film that has resisted chrononormative teleologies, *Appropriate Behavior*'s open-endedness suits queer conceptions of sexuality as constantly in flux, as becoming rather than being.

In the time between *Appropriate Behavior*'s release and the start of production on her second feature, Akhavan co-starred in *Creep 2* (Patrick Brice, 2017). This sequel to "mumblegore" streaming sensation *Creep* was produced by the Duplass Brothers, Mark and Jay, and starred Mark as a serial killer who lures his victims by means of Craigslist's Gigs ads. Like her appearance in *Girls*, the role offered Akhavan another opportunity for ironic self-inscription as a provoc*auteur*. As largely improvised found-footage horror films in the mold of *The Blair Witch Project*, *Creep* and *Creep 2* satirize the "horror" of unguarded personal encounters for Millennials for whom ubiquitous screens enable solipsism and social estrangement, but who nonetheless are pushed by economic precarity into such risky gig economy ventures as that which leads *Creep*'s videographer victim into a deadly lair. In *Creep 2*, it is less financial desperation than naked ambition that stirs Sara (Akhavan), a struggling filmmaker so intent on upping views of her YouTube series *Encounters* that she violates her own safety protocol in an attempt to provide a stirring finale to an otherwise tepid season of episodes featuring her "casual encounters" with eccentric Angelenos. Referencing both the web series (discussed in the next section) that launched Akhavan's career as well as the Craigslist-inspired odyssey for the eponymous purple La-Z-Boy that inspired the Duplasses' breakout feature *The Puffy Chair* (2005), Sara's show also parodies the extreme measures taken by the enterprising would-be stars of YouTube to stand out among the channel's crowded ranks.

This conceit of a web series within an indie film also self-reflexively stages a generational and gendered face-off between the alter egos of Mark Duplass and Akhavan. The game-changing episode that Sara imagines becomes a moxie-testing dare that Duplass's character, Aaron, describes to Sara as "a murder film where the pupil fells the king, because I know you well enough to know you'll do anything to make a great piece of art." Like Duplass himself, Aaron is on the cusp of turning forty and confesses to finding his "killer instincts" dulled by the monotony of routine. His bid to lure Sara into a cinematic collaboration (wherein he promises not to kill her in the next twenty-four hours to provide them mutually satisfying material) carries the same vampiric connotations of Syd's bosses in *High Art*, if more playfully conveyed in what is at heart more schlock than straight horror.

The early 2000s revival of microbudget indie filmmaking facilitated by digital technologies particularly benefited women filmmakers red-lined from studio directing, though they were nonetheless largely written out of the era's mumblecore legend that consecrated male filmmakers like the Duplass Brothers and paved the way for their current prominence as indie incubators. Claire Perkins aptly sums up *Appropriate Behavior* as "transpos[ing] the emotional awkwardness of Mumblecore from the terms of male anxiety and egotism to those of a queer female subjectivity."[90] Akhavan, who cites the Mark Duplass–starring mumblecore film *Hannah Takes the Stairs* (Joe Swanberg, 2007) as inspirational for being "the first time I saw a film that was lower budget," might be regarded as belonging to a mumblecore 2.0 generation more open to acknowledging women's authorship. But despite enjoying festival and critical embrace, Akhavan did not wholly avert the second-film slump that frequently befalls women filmmakers (especially those working in or on the margins of Hollywood).[91] In an *Indiewire* interview, Akhavan called the industry out on its refusal to grant second-time women filmmakers the franchise-bestowing "Colin Trevverow moment."[92] She was referring to Trevverow's being entrusted with helming the megabudget tentpole *Jurassic World* (2015) after the Sundance success of his indie first feature, the Duplass-produced *Safety Not Guaranteed* (2012).

In both reaping the benefits of the mumblecore boys' club while collaborating with women filmmakers like Katie Aselton (wife of Mark) and Lynn Shelton, the fraught alliance that the Duplass Brothers offer for emergent provoc*auteurs* like Akhavan receives disarming self-recognition through *Creep 2*'s table-turning confrontation between filmmaker and subject. Addressing the double standard head-on, if with tongue in cheek, Aaron strips fully naked to expose himself to Sara and the audience as testament to his artistic resolution to be self-revealing. That Sara's reciprocal undressing keeps her lower half off-screen serves to counter the gendered disproportionality of on-screen nudity that prevails in both mainstream and indie production, the focus of chapter 2. Here it prefigures the authorial control that Sara/Akhavan will maintain despite temporary testing by Aaron's entreaties that "I can be a fucked up guy and give you everything you want as an artist."

Intent on provoking her subject into a click-worthy on-camera display, Sara cannily inveigles Aaron by flattering his own artistic self-regard, asking, "What would Francis Ford Coppola do?" The question references Aaron's earlier extolling of the "great man's" ability to fight off midcareer decline, though when one assesses Coppola's failure to live up to his early moviemaking achievements, the allusion proves both falsely self-aggrandizing and predictive of Aaron's imminent fall. It is *Creep*'s cynical premise that nothing short of a snuff film can seize the attention and satisfy the skepticism of today's jaded viewers. In contrast, *Creep 2* sees Sara fighting back "final girl"–style to retake hold of the camera and with it authorial control. Refusing the role of muse to which Aaron attempts to consign her—pausing in his grave-digging preparations for her body's disposal to say, "You inspired me like Coppola"—Sara rears back to life, monster-like, and unceremoniously kills him with a shovel to the head.

Creep 2 ends with a coda depicting Sara walking a New York City street, far from the West Coast woods she managed to escape, then entering the subway. The film's final shot, showing her seated en route to an unknown destination, is all but identical to *Appropriate Behavior*'s opening, suggesting her alter ego's survival is akin to Akhavan's own emergence out of YouTube's throngs. To address those origins, I take a cue from *Appropriate Behavior*'s nonlinearity to end this chapter by discussing Akhavan's first and still most irreverently bad queer foray as provoc*auteur*, the web series that served as her breakout project.

SUPERFICIAL, HOMOPHOBIC LESBIANS: *THE SLOPE*

In 2010, NYU Graduate Film classmates-turned-couple Desiree Akhavan and Ingrid Jungermann teamed up to make a web series set among the lesbian bourgeoisie of Park Slope, Brooklyn, with the premise, "What if we filmed us talking smack about gay people?"[93] Through the safe remove of their (as the tagline promised) "superficial, homophobic" alter egos, Desiree and Ingrid (as I will refer to their on-screen personae) express their creators' sense of marginalization from and even opposition to mainstream LGBTQ+ rhetoric. Conceived as a class assignment, *The Slope* proved pivotal both as a career launching pad for the then couple as well as a personal jumping-off point for Akhavan. "It's how I came out to most people in my life," she recalls.[94] Released on Vimeo as two seasons of eight episodes apiece, *The Slope* found patronage from alt-comedy impresario Michael Showalter (their NYU professor and a season two guest star). Akhavan and Jungermann were named among *Filmmaker*'s 25 New Faces of Independent Film and appeared on *Out*'s annual *Out100* list, accolades that suggest how Akhavan was already forging an inbetweener positioning that would accommodate her straddling of indie and LGBTQ+ industry niches. Indeed, it points to what I have suggested is the increasing coalition between indie and bad queer audience sensibilities that are put off by more commercial-minded LGBTQ+ cultural products and politics.

Emerging on the heels of straight-friendly soap *The L Word* and contemporaneously with crossover hits *Glee* (Ryan Murphy, Brad Falchuk, and Ian Brennan, Fox, 2009–15) and *Modern Family*, *The Slope* was at the vanguard of a new wave of internet-distributed works that elsewhere I collectively call "bad queer women's comedic web series."[95] These series spoke to viewers dissatisfied with what became known as the "gaystreaming" strategies of first Showtime and then LOGO, and with network TV's broadly comic, caricature-reinforcing "gay minstrel shows"—so named by bad queer Bret Easton Ellis.[96] Two key progenitors of the bad queer women's comedic web series even took *The L Word* as their explicit target of parody: *The D Word* (Dasha Snyder, 2005), six short episodes produced for cable access show *Dyke TV*, which were legally prevented from being aired, and *The F Word*, a live theatrical show chronicling the "real" lesbians of Framingham, Massachusetts, recorded in 2008 and circulated on creator Faith Soloway's website and later on YouTube.[97] Offering an irreverent alternative to LGBTQ+ content perceived as mainstream (read: earnest and anodyne) or Millennial (read: all-embracing pansexuality and endless gender variance), these bad queer web series express the plurality of the imagined queer community and expose political contestations in its ranks. In so doing, they serve as brand differentiation for a new generation of queer media producers.

Seeing legacy TV as inimical to the development of nuanced, sustained LGBTQ+ characters and narratives, creators gravitated to the web series, where the affordability of production combined with the proliferation of crowdfunding mechanisms such as Kickstarter (which supported *The Slope*'s second season) and video-hosting sites like Vimeo and YouTube opened new opportunities for creation and distribution—particularly to queer/women/of color most impeded by the media industry's exclusionary practices. These technological and financial drivers coincided with the growing nichification, or narrowcasting, of media content, which segmented a consumer population hitherto reductively regarded by advertisers and content providers as one monolithic LGBTQ+ community.

Aymar Jean Christian terms these new forms of series production *open TV*, crediting them with "model[ing] the kind of open, and diverse, TV ecosystem the deregulated landscape was intended to fertilize, before corporations purchased distribution channels, increasing the scale of production but not always wages, creative freedom or audience and brand input."[98] As open TV's preeminent mode, the web series in its first generation offered an edgier, less filtered version of LGBTQ representation than legacy TV afforded. Without positing a utopian/dystopian dichotomy between the two, we can view their distinct creative hierarchies and financial demands as respectively encouraging or discouraging bad queer rhetoric in a rejection of the palatable and universal in favor of the provocative and individuated. With *The Slope* leading the way, these bad queer web series emerged online alongside a post–*L Word* wave of corporate-supported queer programming on television and streaming services. These series included Freeform's *The Fosters* (Brad Bredeweg and Peter Paige, 2013–18), Amazon's *Transparent*, and Netflix's *Orange Is the New Black*, whose June 2013 debut served as the most prominent piece of evidence for the assertion that "lesbians are having the best summer ever on TV."[99] Just as online blogging provided a key forum for queer critics and scholars to sound off on the provocative politics of Cholodenko's *Kids*, the newfound ease of making, distributing, and promoting web series enabled a voluble response to LGBTQ+ norms (of representation and otherwise) by content creators themselves. Yet even if the combined industrial, aesthetic, and ideological deregulation of the online platform encourages the kind of bad queer representational politics largely absent from FCC-regulated, corporate-controlled TV, it is also the case that web series are designed to attract views and ad revenue. Thus, they serve as launching pads for their creators (and sometimes the series themselves) into the commercial film and TV realm—raising the possibilities, respectively, that these series will chase clicks with provocation for provocation's sake or, alternatively, that their irreverence will require tempering.

What is most noteworthy about *The Slope*'s snarky oppositionality, and that of its bad queer web series sisters, is its turning inward to address as the object of its satire not heteronormative culture but homonormative and queer culture. These bad queer sexual and representational politics are contrarian both in resisting the assimilatory values of the "corporate PC fascism" that Bret Easton Ellis views as enforcers of homonormativity, and in their ironic distance from the uber-progressive logics and prescriptive politics of queer Millennial culture.[100] Put another way, this bad queer sensibility is one nostalgic for a queer past less tainted by assimilationism, but that also cannily registers the contradictions and historical myopia of contemporary queerdom's admixture of umbrella inclusiveness and PC policing.[101] We might read *The Slope* as aligned, though only facetiously, with the gay conservative critique of "queer snowflakes," Millennials supposedly too fragile to face down the kind of questioning or hostility that once was a predictable consequence of publicly articulating a queer identity. I would orient *The Slope* more precisely as emanating from latter-day queer theory's antisocial turn to reclaiming cultural texts and artifacts of queer negativity and failure. Such queer cultural products and narratives, Jack Halberstam finds, "refuse triumphalist accounts of gay, lesbian, and transgender history that necessarily reinvest in robust notions of success and succession," and so acquire an ally in these bad queer web series' provocations.[102]

Moreover, and to again point at how Akhavan's provoca*teur* signature bridges queer and indie cultural zones and blends their taste profiles, *The Slope* (and the bad queer web series that followed it) re-creates for the small screen the cinematic sensibility that Jeffrey Sconce refers to as the "smart film." Writing about 1990s US independent filmmakers like Alexander Payne and Todd Solodnz, Sconce characterizes this sensibility as an ironic distance from mainstream culture and the sociopolitical values it embodies. Sconce argues that such an approach should be viewed as neither apolitical nor nihilistic. Rather, "in its refusal of conventional terms of debate, irony can be a brutally honest rhetorical strategy . . . a strategic disengagement from a certain terrain of belief, politics and commitment."[103] Related to the inbetweener view that I have attributed to Cholodenko and Akhavan, irony's critical distancing enables a queer sight line that defamiliarizes contemporary LGBTQ+ discourse. *The Slope*'s skeptical (self-)appraisals of "superficial, homophobic lesbians" and the alternately homonormative and "queer snowflake" environs they cohabit thereby function as ironic metacommentary to critique "model gay" assimilationist values and representational tropes alongside queer ideologues' policing of identity and party-line politics.

The entirety of *The Slope*'s debut episode (1.1, "Miserable Animals") stages this drama of LGBTQ+ community in-fighting as it plays out around the same issue broached in *Appropriate Behavior*'s meet-cute sequence and puzzled over by Akhavan in the quote at the beginning of this chapter: the question of (in)appropriate language. The episode starts in the middle of a quarrel, as Ingrid protests Desiree's ostensibly homophobic "use [of] the term 'gay' to mean both homosexual and lame."

> DESIREE: How many homophobes do you know . . . hanging out with their super-dykey girlfriends?
> INGRID: But people who aren't homophobic don't call their girlfriends super-dykey.
> DESIREE: I see your point, only if you weren't plagued by so much internalized homophobia, you'd have reclaimed the term "dyke" by now and you'd be wearing it as a badge of honor.

INGRID: That's only if I say it about myself.
DESIREE: You can't reappropriate a term and then not let me use it.
INGRID: You're bisexual.
DESIREE: I prefer bi-curious.... I don't think gay people are lame, I just think you are acting lame when you're being so super gay, and by that I mean when you're making me feel bad because you don't think I'm as gay as you are. And it really hurts my feelings that you're saying this because how much gayer could I get having a huge public fight in the park with my super gay girlfriend?
INGRID: I'm sorry, I didn't mean to hurt your feelings.
DESIREE: Let's not fight again. We're both super gay.

As someone who is bisexual (or "bi-curious"), Desiree already embodies the bad queer through her alliance with a maligned identity habitually rendered as both not-gay and not-queer. Bisexuality, as I note in *The B Word*, is disavowed as an identity even as it (ironically) is perceived to reinforce identity categories that queerness seeks to undo.[104] Desiree moreover distances herself from gay codes of discourse in her weak defense of the politically incorrect use of *gay* to mean lame (the ableist slur goes unremarked by both characters) and, as in *Appropriate Behavior*, in her ostensibly inappropriate use of *dykey*. Though Ingrid, in response, attempts to teach Desiree that such terms are only selectively permissible, her rules of discourse are undermined by Desiree's more radically queer (if self-serving) conceptualization of language as unfixed, context-contingent, and available for anyone's appropriation. Neither's position is endorsed or refuted, and clearly the two are intent on one-upping each other, but together they question assumptions underlying queer discourse and challenge its cultural scripts.

In an *AfterEllen* profile from 2012, Akhavan pleads with fans of *The Slope* to spread the word for fear that otherwise "we are all going to be stuck with Whitney from *The Real L Word* [Ilene Chaiken, Showtime, 2010–12] as the voice of our people."[105] Referring to the most noxious character in the widely reviled reality-style spin-off series, Akhavan takes aim at then-contemporary queer programming as a means of oppositional branding. Singling out *The Real L Word* for further derision in the season one episode "Queer Programming," Ingrid resists Desiree's entreaties to view the show: "I don't even like that it exists. I'm not going to watch an episode." Desiree responds, "I don't like it either but I'm obligated to watch because it's the only queer programming. It's also really broadened my vocabulary because now I know what a 'soft butch' is." When Desiree's cell phone rings a moment later, it emits the earworm from *The L Word*'s opening credits track. With this debate over the lose-lose alternatives of avoiding or indulging in pandering programming, *The Slope* slyly promotes its own niche-filling potential as the superior alternative. *The Slope* further distinguishes itself from the queer ethnographic approach attributed to *The Real L Word* by failing to translate "soft butch," declining the opportunity to educate viewers through the type of translating characteristic of crossover media (including, as noted earlier, *Appropriate Behavior*).

Upping the stakes from gay TV's guilty pleasures to LGBTQ+ activism, *The Slope*'s fifth episode, titled "It Gets Better?" parodies the "It Gets Better" public service campaign aimed at LGBTQ+ youth. Desiree and Ingrid's entry into the viral video series is prompted by their resistance to its appeals. As Ingrid notes, "Not only are they really dramatic, they're not really helpful." Adopting the videos' testimonial form of address, Ingrid admits to having evaded youthful bullying, saying, "I wasn't out in high school. I mostly dated athletic black men." Desiree confesses she was "most definitely" bullied, not because of her sexuality but "because I was very ugly, and a little bit fat.... Nobody really gave a shit about my sexuality." She concludes, "There is a way to be out, gay and happy in high school and it's if you are a hot girl." "Or a colorful gay guy that has a boa and a catchphrase," Ingrid adds. In relating their own experiences in terms that counter the dominant script, the couple challenges the "It Gets Better" campaign's characterization of high school politics as founded on heteronormativity—suggesting rather that factors such as social affiliation, athleticism, lookism, and charisma may matter more. They present a checklist as a substitute for the "vague advice" they find the campaign disseminating, "for kids who want to *make* things better" (with tenets ranging from "Don't be fat" to "Don't do theater"). The video ends with a final admonition from Desiree, spoken with a campy inflection that emphasizes its tongue-in-cheek deflation of both the self-dramatizing of gay youth alongside the "It Gets Better" campaign's inducements to them: "Don't kill yourself, because suicide is super gay."

What saves their critique of contemporary LGBTQ+ activism's earnestness from sounding self-righteous is the couple's admission to their own self-absorption and political apathy. When a canvassing do-gooder asks them, "Do you have a moment for gay rights?" they respond, automatically and in unison, "No" (1.2, "Pretty People"). Also in bad queer fashion, Desiree and Ingrid defy the imperative to validate preferred labels for self-identification. Professing ignorance at the LGBTQ+ addendum "and questioning," Desiree is informed that it refers to those unsure of their sexual leanings, which she dismisses as their "just having some bi-curious Katy Perry moment." "Pretty recently you had your own bi-curious Katy Perry moment," Ingrid reminds her. "Yeah, that's how I know it's bullshit," retorts Desiree (1.5, "It Gets Better?"). Recognizably ironic to those familiar with Akhavan's steadfast insistence on self-identifying as bisexual, here Desiree projects her self-appraisal onto others while reiterating stereotypes of bisexuality as a self-serving fabrication à la Perry's star-making single "I Kissed a Girl." Ingrid will go on to call Desiree out on indulging precisely this form of "bisexual privilege" in her manipulation of sexual labeling to befit her inbetweener status.

INGRID: When you're with a guy and you want to look hotter you say I'm your girlfriend, and when you're with lesbians you say I'm your partner, and when you talk to your mom on the phone you say I'm your friend because you're afraid to come out to her.

DESIREE: I won't lie; I use different language with different people. I try to mimic them and mirror them to make them more comfortable. (1.8, "Cooperative")

As this exchange indicates, *The Slope* retains an ironic distance that *Appropriate Behavior* breaches in transforming the gay "smack-talking" of the web series into narrative form, where Shirin's closeted code-switching proves unpalatable to Maxine. *Appropriate Behavior*'s seriocomic (rather than wholly ironic) treatment gives more nuanced expression to this particular aspect of bisexuality alterity, which can permit so seamless a cultural positioning as to render the bisexual overly adaptive, from the viewpoint of a queer politics of visibility. Yet its engagement through ironic vignette in *The Slope* makes this bisexually enabled "having it both ways" less defensible than in *Appropriate Behavior*, where viewers are encouraged to identify and empathize with Shirin. Neither are Desiree's Iranian American roots and its significance for her relationship with her family as pronounced in *The Slope*. But perhaps more valuably, this ironic positioning reveals Akhavan's reluctance to invest too wholly in bisexuality or any identity, wary of how such fixed formations elide the changing, contingent nature of desire and subjectivity—even if Desiree's ultimate dismissal of questioning as a cop-out makes hay of her alter ego's hypocrisy.

Though by season two Desiree concedes her own bisexuality and that of women, she falls back on cliché in denying the validity of male bisexuality: "It's a scientific fact, there's no such thing as male bisexuals. But female sexuality is fluid, like the river. I flow in and out of love with the person not the gender" (2.1, "Talking Space"). Calling out the flaky utopianism of "fluidity" as a framework for conceiving desire while invoking science to "disprove" male bisexuality, *The Slope* lampoons the blatantly gendered ways, on gay and straight sides of the aisle, in which bisexuality is alternately valorized (in women) as a liberation from categorization and dismissed (in men) as what *Sex and the City*'s Carrie Bradshaw (Sarah Jessica Parker) once called "a layover on the way to Gaytown."

Desiree elsewhere revels in stereotypes of bisexuality as enticingly elusive and trendy: "This is what it is to be bisexual. I'm here, I'm there, I'm with men then I'm with women. You can't pin me down. I'm an enigma. The only people cooler than bisexuals are transgendered." On this last point, Ingrid vehemently disagrees, "I'm gonna be honest with you. I don't get transmen. I don't know why they just don't identify as butch lesbians. I don't know why they have to change their bodies to be the other sex—the more privileged sex. To me that is the ultimate form of sexism" (1.3, "Queer Programming"). Ingrid echoes normative conflations of gender and sexuality in understanding gender variance as synonymous with same-sex preference, while invoking trans-exclusionary radical feminist, or TERF, rhetoric in deriding "sexist" transmen as aspirants to male privilege.

Exaggeratedly performing her role as old-school dyke, Ingrid satirizes both straight culture and a second-wave lesbian feminist sensibility nostalgic for the "good old days" when femmes were femmes and butches were butches—deemed preferable to what she disparages, in another episode, as the "unnatural" sacrilege of femme-on-femme weddings (1.4, "Bottoms Up?"). When it suits her interest (or threatens her ego), Desiree shares this distaste for the "deviant" pansexuality of queer Millennials, jealously demanding of a dude reading *Middlesex* who ogles Ingrid, "What kind of a sick perverted fuck goes after lesbians who look like 14-year-old boys?" (1.2, "Pretty People"). But more often it's twentysomething Desiree who plays naïf to jaded thirtysomething

Ingrid, who delivers *The Slope*'s most offensive rant after Desiree's friend Markus beats a hasty retreat upon Ingrid's arrival:

> INGRID: Probably going to go blow some guy off of Grindr.... Gay guys are like the worst versions of straight women. They spend money they don't have on clothes that don't fit them. They worship these miniature size versions of real dogs that they buy from breeders and then they shove them in these fancy purses and use them as accessories. It's disgusting. Oh, and have you ever heard of AIDS?
> DESIREE: Ingrid, you're being super-judgmental right now, and nobody gets AIDS anymore.
> INGRID: No, Desiree, lesbians don't get AIDS. Lesbians. (2.4, "Pride and Prejudice")

Moving from slut-shaming gay men to playing on conservative conceptions of AIDS as punishment for gay male promiscuity, this exchange takes its gleeful sacrilege to the limits of acceptable humor. The further irony is that as a lesbian claiming authority to gay-bash, Ingrid's putdowns sound shocking (albeit ironically so), yet they mockingly replicate perspectives from within the gay community. They contain both the sexual moralism of abstinence activists like Larry Kramer and the self-congratulatory belief among some lesbians in their exemption from sexual threat.

In their roles as *The Slope*'s odd couple, Akhavan performs the ironic distancing and arch dismissal that Halberstam associates with the camp archive of antisocial gay cultural production, while Jungermann embodies the "dyke anger" that Halberstam claims is needed "in order to embrace a truly political negativity." Their snarky dismissals of positivity, pride, and most things homonormative—from marriage equality to *The L Word*—provoke a contrarian challenge to homonormativity's attempt to commodify queerness and contain its disruptive potential. As Halberstam describes, "In this work, a queer aesthetic is activated through the function of negation rather than in the mode of positivity; in other words, the works strive to establish queerness as a mode of critique rather than as a new investment in normativity or life or respectability or wholeness or legitimacy."[106]

Unburdened by the need to defuse their sexual representations and politics for mainstream palatability, the comedic web series emerged, at least initially, as an alternative sphere of queer media production and a queer discursive mode that defamiliarizes dominant LGBTQ scripts. Not surprisingly given its "superficial, homophobic" stance, *The Slope* failed to achieve legacy TV adaptation—unlike contemporaneous breakout web series *Broad City*, *High Maintenance* (Katja Blichfeld and Ben Sinclair, 2012–15; HBO, 2016–), and *The Misadventures of Awkward Black Girl* (retitled *Insecure*; Issa Rae, 2011–13; HBO, 2016–). Yet it paved the way for Akhavan's and Jungermann's respective first features alongside a veritable cottage industry of similarly irreverent bad queer women's comedic web series, including Jungermann's sophomore effort, "homoneurotic" *F to 7th* (2013–14).[107]

And so, whereas commercial television maintains its skittishness when it comes to depicting central LGBTQ+ characters as anything short of saintly, *The Slope* and the other series that followed in its wake and that share its sensibility double down with provoc*auteur* alter egos who are not just as bad-behaving, self-absorbed, and entitled as straight female characters such as Hannah Horvath (if not as sociopathic as straight male characters like Tony Soprano, Don Draper, or Walter White). The characters in *The Slope* and other series are also bad queers—both in rejecting the insistence on positivity and pride in gay representational politics and in troubling queer discourse's self-image as politically and ideologically enlightened. These web series' willingness to mock, or at least question, mandates of LGBTQ+ representational politics stems from their marginal industrial status and postmodern ironic sensibility. In addition to naming them bad queer, but rather than relying on the fraught term *post-queer*, I offer *late queer*. The term is inspired by Fredric Jameson's formulation of late capitalism as a cultural sensibility symptomatic of postindustrial, transnational economic structures, particularly regarding the mediatization of culture as enabled by conglomerization.[108] In this framework, late queer signifies the exhaustion of traditional "normalization through representation" approaches that promote affirmative visibility and humanizing/universalizing rhetoric. Unlike the LGBTQ+ cultural products that endorse the capitalistic structures that enable them—*Queer Eye (for the Straight Guy)* (Bravo, 2004–7; Netflix, 2018–), for example—these bad queer web series distance themselves, to various degrees, from homonormativity through their representational politics as well as through their positioning vis-à-vis media conglomerates' financial and ideological control. In critiquing both gay discourse and the queer discourse that has arisen to challenge it, these series function as metacommentaries on LGBTQ+ and queer representation by challenging gay criticism and queer theory's long-held standards of evaluation: for the former, signifiers of visibility and authenticity in depicting sex and intimacy and discursive reinforcement of affirmative, assimilatory identity politics; for the latter, totalizing discourses of queer subjectivity and experience as progressive, antifoundationalist, and political.

With their historical span from New Queer Cinema to "It Gets Better" and beyond, Cholodenko and Akhavan create work that challenges gay and queer formations and discourses that prioritize inclusiveness and radicalism. Their perspective as sexual inbetweeners permits their pivoting across industrial and ideological realms to a degree that is advantageous in our late capitalist and late queer era, in which programming lesbian/bisexual women specifically allows for what Julia Himberg calls "multicasting" as a means for targeting increasingly fragmented audiences.[109] Yet the recent, promising proliferation of bisexual characters notwithstanding, most contemporary queer auteurs still reflect compulsory monosexuality's imperative to shape characters and narratives in a binary logic of desire. Cholodenko and Akhavan instead resist sexual and political pigeonholing, and thus traverse the dividing lines of sexuality and screen media to establish a site of inbetweenness on all counts.

NOTES

1. Dorothy Snarker, "Is This the End of the Model Gay Character?" *Indiewire*, November 17, 2015, https://womenandhollywood.com/is-this-the-end-of-the-model-gay-character-44c077b76073/.

2. Lisa Henderson, "Simple Pleasures: Lesbian Community and *Go Fish*," *Signs* 25, no. 1 (1999): 41.

3. Arlene Stein and Kenneth Plummer, "'I Can't Even Think Straight': Queer Theory and the Missing Sexual Revolution in Sociology," in *Queer Theory/Sociology*, ed. Steven Seidman (Malden, MA: Blackwell, 1996), 134.

4. Harry M. Benshoff, "(Broke)back to the Mainstream: Queer Theory and Queer Cinemas Today," in *Film Theory and Contemporary Hollywood Movies*, ed. Warren Buckland (New York: Routledge, 2009), 193; emphasis in original.

5. Jenna Wortham, "When Everyone Can Be 'Queer,' Is Anyone?" *New York Times Magazine*, July 12, 2016, https://www.nytimes.com/2016/07/17/magazine/when-everyone-can-be-queer-is-anyone.html?_r=0.

6. Bret Easton Ellis, "In the Reign of the Gay Magical Elves," *Out*, May 13, 2013, https://www.out.com/news-opinion/2013/05/13/bret-easton-ellis-gay-men-magical-elves.

7. RuPaul Charles, "RuPaul Charles," interview by Marc Maron, *WTF*, episode 498, May 19, 2014, audio, 1:24:29, https://www.wtfpod.com/podcast/episodes/episode_498_-_rupaul_charles.

8. The positive appraisal of Waters appears in J. D. Borden, "John Waters on Caitlyn Jenner: 'We Can't Make Fun of Her?'" *Indiewire*, August 7, 2015, https://www.indiewire.com/2015/08/john-waters-on-caitlyn-jenner-we-cant-make-fun-of-her-241129/. The negative appraisal of Waters reads in full: "John Waters is the worst kind of transphobic bigot. Thinking he is a true progressive. Maybe in 1970, but today he is shockingly regressive." @allisonpastries, Twitter post, December 29, 2015, 1:40 a.m., https://twitter.com/allisonpastries/status/681726357013839872.

9. Ellis, "In the Reign of the Magical Gay Elves."

10. Barbara Johnson, *A World of Difference* (Baltimore: Johns Hopkins University Press, 1987), 14.

11. David M. Halperin, *Saint Foucault: Towards a Gay Hagiography* (New York: Oxford University Press, 1995), 106.

12. Roxane Gay, *Bad Feminists: Essays* (New York: Harper Perennial, 2014), x–xi.

13. Eve Oishi, "Bad Asians: New Film and Video by Queer Asian American Artists," in *Countervisions: Asian American Film Criticism*, ed. Darrell Y. Hamamoto and Sandra Liu (Philadelphia: Temple University Press, 2000), 221–41.

14. See Kobena Mercer, "Black Art and the Burden of Representation," *Third Text* 4, no. 10 (1990): 61–78.

15. Akhavan uses *Persian* and *Iranian* interchangeably in referring to her family's pre–Iranian Republic national heritage and diasporic identity.

16. David V. Ruffolo, *Post-Queer Politics* (New York: Routledge, 2009), 169.

17. See Kimberlé Williams Crenshaw, "Mapping the Margins: Intersectionality, Identity Politics, and Violence against Women of Color," *Stanford Law Review* 43, no. 6 (July 1991): 1241–99.

18. See Sharmila Sen, *Not Quite Not White: Losing and Finding Race in America* (New York: Penguin, 2018).

19. See Maria San Filippo, "Breaking Upwards: The Creative Uncoupling of Desiree Akhavan and Ingrid Jungermann," *Feminist Media Studies* 19, no. 6 (December 2019): 991-1008. See also Maria San Filippo, "Serial Offender: *The Bisexual* (2018)," *Journal of Bisexuality* 20, no. 3 (September 2020): 233–43.

20. José Esteban Muñoz, *Disidentifications: Queers of Color and the Performance of Politics* (Minneapolis: University of Minnesota Press, 1999), 31.

21. Cholodenko quoted in Christine Spines, "Down to Earth," *Film Comment* (July–August 2010): 42.

22. Teresa de Lauretis, "Queer Texts, Bad Habits, and the Issue of a Future," *GLQ* 17, no. 2–3 (2011): 244.

23. B. Ruby Rich, "A Queer and Present Danger: The Death of New Queer Cinema?" in *New Queer Cinema: The Director's Cut* (Durham, NC: Duke University Press, 2013), 133. See also Rich, "A Queer Sensation," *Village Voice*, March 24, 1992, 41–44.

24. Jack Halberstam, "The Kids Aren't Alright!" *Bully Bloggers*, July 15, 2010, https://bullybloggers.wordpress.com/2010/07/15/the-kids-arent-alright/.

25. Quoted in Spines, "Down to Earth," 43; emphasis in original.

26. Worldwide grosses for *High Art* ($1.9 million), *Laurel Canyon* ($4.4 million), and *The Kids Are All Right* ($34.8 million) all considerably exceeded their production budgets.

27. Quoted in B. Ruby Rich, "A Path of Her Own [Interview with Ally Sheedy]," *Advocate*, no. 761 (June 9, 1998): 46.

28. Lee Wallace, *Lesbianism, Cinema, Space: The Sexual Life of Apartments* (New York: Routledge, 2009), 61.

29. Quoted in Holly Willis, "Lisa Cholodenko (1964–)," in *Independent Female Filmmakers: A Chronicle through Interviews, Profiles, and Manifestos*, ed. Michele Meek (New York: Routledge, 2019), 53.

30. See Maria San Filippo, *The B Word: Bisexuality in Contemporary Film and Television* (Bloomington: Indiana University Press, 2013).

31. Maria Pramaggiore, "High and Low: Bisexual Women and Aesthetics in *Chasing Amy* and *High Art*," *Journal of Bisexuality* 2, no. 2/3 (2002): 263–64.

32. Jodi Brooks, "*The Kids Are All Right*, the Pursuits of Happiness, and the Spaces Between," *Camera Obscura* 29, no. 1 (2014): 113–14.

33. Richard Porton, introduction to "Gay Family Values: An Interview with Lisa Cholodenko," *Cineaste* 35, no. 4 (Fall 2010): 14.

34. Quoted in Saul Austerlitz, "Same Sex—With the Same Family Issues," *Boston Globe*, July 11, 2010, http://archive.boston.com/ae/movies/articles/2010/07/11/lisa_cholodenko_wanted_her_film_the_kids_are_all_right_to_reflect_every_family_and_every_familys_individual_vulnerabilities/.

35. Fiona Cox, "Fab Lesbianism and Family Values: Costuming of Lesbian Identities in *The L Word* and *The Kids Are All Right*," in *Fashion Cultures Revisited: Theories, Explorations, and Analysis*, 2nd ed., ed. Stella Bruzzi and Pamela Church Gibson (New York: Routledge, 2013), 255.

36. Lanre Bakare, "Mark Duplass: 'There's No Excuse Not to Make Films on Weekends with Friends,'" *Guardian*, March 15, 2015, https://www.theguardian.com/film/2015/mar/15/mark-duplass-south-by-southwest-sxsw.

37. Quoted in Spines, "Down to Earth," 43.

38. Suzanna Danuta Walters, "The Kids Are All Right but the Lesbians Aren't: Queer Kinship in US Culture," *Sexualities* 15, no. 8 (2012): 924.

39. Halberstam, "The Kids Aren't Alright."

40. Lisa Duggan, with Kathryn Bond Stockton, "Only the Kids Are All Right," *Bully Bloggers*, July 30, 2010, https://bullybloggers.wordpress.com/2010/07/30/only-the-kids-are-all-right/.

41. Halberstam, "The Kids Aren't Alright."
42. Porton, introduction to "Gay Family Values," 15.
43. Walters, "The Kids Are All Right," 922.
44. Cynthia Lucia and Richard Porton, "Gay Family Values: An Interview with Lisa Cholodenko," *Cineaste* 35, no. 4 (Fall 2010): 18.
45. Jasbir Puar and Karen Tongson, "The Ugly Truth about Why the Kids Are All Right," *VelvetPark*, January 20, 2012, www.velvetparkmedia.com/blogs/ugly-truth-about-why-kids-are-all-right.
46. Halberstam, "The Kids Aren't Alright."
47. Puar and Tongson, "The Ugly Truth."
48. See "'The Kids Are All Right': HBO Still Considering Series," *HuffPost TV*, August 1, 2012, https://www.huffpost.com/entry/the-kids-are-all-right-hbo-series_n_1730584.
49. Delphine Letort, "Age and Gender in the Minseries Adaptation of Elizabeth Strout's *Olive Kitteridge*," *Adaptation* 9, no. 1 (2015): 90.
50. Clara Bradbury-Rance, "Querying Postfeminism in Lisa Cholodenko's *The Kids Are All Right*," in *Postfeminism and Contemporary Hollywood Cinema*, ed. Joel Gwynne and Nadine Muller (Basingstoke, UK: Palgrave Macmillan, 2013), 39–40.
51. Letort, "Age and Gender," 87, 90.
52. See, for example, Stephanie Merry, "Frances McDormand, Now in the Role of the Golden Globes Grumpy Cat," *Washington Post*, January 11, 2015, https://www.washingtonpost.com/news/arts-and-entertainment/wp/2015/01/11/frances-mcdormand-now-in-the-role-of-the-golden-globes-grumpy-cat/?utm_term=.100539d3c120.
53. Frances McDormand, "Like Olive Kitteridge, Actress Frances McDormand Was Tired of Supporting Roles," interview by NPR Staff, *All Things Considered*, NPR, October 31, 2014, audio, 8:10, https://www.npr.org/2014/10/31/360183633/like-olive-kitteridge-actress-frances-mcdormand-was-tired-of-supporting-roles.
54. For a discussion of *The Slap*'s Australian adaptation and its cultural and industrial contexts, see Constantine Verevis, "Whose Side Are You On? *The Slap* (2011/2015)," *Continuum: Journal of Media and Cultural Studies* 29, no. 5 (2015): 769–80.
55. See, for example, John Anderson, "'The Slap' Review: A Show You'll Love to Hate," *Wall Street Journal*, February 5, 2015, https://www.wsj.com/articles/the-slap-review-a-show-youll-love-to-hate-1423180421. Verevis also quotes a sample of IMDb posts for the US version: "'I snickered when I saw the title' (9 February 2015); 'the show looks absurd—like a Park Slope stroller war' (24 January 2015); and 'I thought it was a parody . . . and

then I realised it was a real show [and] I'm like WHAT? A show about a guy who slaps some one [sic] else's child? This is just beyond ridiculous for a concept' (18 January 2015)." Verevis, "Whose Side Are You On?": 778.

56. Cholodenko's recent television work has been as a multi-episodic director on HBO dramatic series *Here and Now* (Alan Ball, 2018), canceled after one season, and on Netflix miniseries *Unbelievable* (2019)—based on a real-life serial rape case—which was respected but viewed as overly ponderous by critics. Her upcoming directorial venture is on Showtime's English-language remake of Danish hit series *Rita*, to star Lena Headey.

57. Bakare, "Mark Duplass."

58. See, for example, Peter Bradshaw, "Jack Nicholson's *Toni Erdmann* Remake: Seven Changes Hollywood Will Make," *Guardian*, February 8, 2017, https://www.theguardian.com/film/filmblog/2017/feb/08/jack-nicholsons-toni-erdmann-remake-seven-changes-hollywood-will-make.

59. Bradbury-Rance, "Querying Postfeminism," 40.

60. Desiree Akhavan, "What Is Appropriate Behavior?" Dr. S. T. Lee Distinguished Lecture in the Humanities, Penn Humanities Forum, University of Pennsylvania, Philadelphia, September 16, 2015.

61. Akhavan quoted in So Mayer, *Political Animals: The New Feminist Cinema* (New York: I. B. Tauris, 2015), 147.

62. Quoted in Boris Kachka, "Desiree Akhavan Wants to Move Beyond the 'Bisexual Persian Lena Dunham' Tag," *Vulture*, January 11, 2015, https://www.vulture.com/2015/01/desiree-akhavan-girls-appropriate-behavior.html. In a tongue-in-cheek reference to Akhavan's own participation in such postfeminist strategies of self-empowerment, Shirin is assured by the steely proprietress of a lingerie store, "Just because your breasts are small doesn't mean they aren't legitimate."

63. Desiree Akhavan, "Desiree Akhavan (Appropriate Behaviour) on High Art," filmed March 12, 2015 at BFI Flare: London LGBTQ Film Festival, London, video, 5:29, https://www.youtube.com/watch?v=fDacKuo1pgU.

64. Jess Alcamo, "Appropriate Behavior—An Interview with Writer/Director Desiree Akhavan," 4:3, June 15, 2014, https://fourthreefilm.com/2014/06/appropriate-behavior-an-interview-with-writerdirector-desiree-akhavan/.

65. Quoted in Nick Levine, "Desiree Akhavan Q&A on Appropriate Behaviour, Sex Scenes and Changing How Marginalised Communities Are Depicted in Film," *NME*, March 5, 2015, https://www.nme.com/blogs/nme-blogs/desiree-akhavan-qa-on-appropriate-behaviour-sex-scenes-and-changing-how-marginalised-communities-are-17916.

66. See Rebecca Beirne, "New Queer Cinema 2.0? Lesbian-Focused Films and the Internet," *Screen* 55, no. 1 (Spring 2014): 129–38.

67. Beirne, "New Queer Cinema 2.0?": 131.

68. Quoted in Alcamo, "Appropriate Behavior." *Girls* was also reported as having high viewership numbers among middle-aged men, though it is thought likely that this finding does not accurately reflect viewership among younger people who were watching without directly paying for an HBO subscription.

69. Quoted in Alcamo, "Appropriate Behavior."

70. Quoted in Nick Dawson, "Desiree Akhavan and Ingrid Jungermann," *Filmmaker*, 25 New Faces of 2012, 2012, https://filmmakermagazine.com/people/desiree-akhavan-and-ingrid-jungermann/#.WXilPIqQxsM.

71. The source for Akhavan's quote at chapter's start is Desiree Akhavan and Emily Danforth, "'Miseducation of Cameron Post' Creators Take Aim at Gay Conversion Therapy," interview by Terry Gross, *Fresh Air*, NPR, July 25, 2018, audio, 43:43, https://www.npr.org/2018/07/25/632242898/miseducation-of-cameron-post-creators-take-aim-at-gay-conversion-therapy.

72. Quoted in Celia Wickham, "Interview with Desire Akhavan," *Berlin Film Journal*, May 2015, berlinfilmjournal.com/2015/05/interview-with-desiree-akhavan/.

73. Jack Halberstam, *The Queer Art of Failure* (Durham, NC: Duke University Press, 2011), 94.

74. Frank Krutnik, "Love Lies: Romantic Fabrication in Contemporary Romantic Comedy," in *Terms of Endearment: Hollywood Romantic Comedy of the 1980s and 1990s*, ed. Peter William Evans and Celestino Deleyto (Edinburgh: Edinburgh University Press, 1998), 24.

75. Akhavan recalled her response to Ahmadinejad's remarks in Desiree Akhavan and Emily Danforth, "'Miseducation of Cameron Post' Creators."

76. Luciano quoted in Elizabeth Freeman, *Time Binds: Queer Temporalities, Queer Histories* (Durham, NC: Duke University Press, 2010), 3.

77. Whitney Monaghan, *Queer Girls, Temporality, and Screen Media: Not "Just a Phase"* (Basingstoke, UK: Palgrave Macmillan, 2016), 156.

78. Claire Perkins, "My Effortless Brilliance: Women's Mumblecore," in *Indie Reframed: Women's Filmmaking and Contemporary American Independent Cinema*, ed. Linda Badley, Claire Perkins, and Michele Schreiber (Edinburgh: Edinburgh University Press, 2016), 148–50.

79. See San Filippo, *The B Word*.

80. For a discussion of bisexual representation in contemporary television, see Caroline Framke, "How Bisexuality on TV Evolved from a Favorite Punchline to a Vital Storyline," *Vox*, May 16, 2018), www.vox.com

/culture/2018/5/16/17339992/bisexual-representation-tv-callie-rosa-darryl. See also Maria San Filippo, "The Politics of Fluidity: Representing Bisexualities in 21st Century Screen Media," in *The Routledge Companion to Media, Sex, and Sexuality*, ed. Feona Attwood, Brian McNair, and Clarissa Smith (New York: Routledge, 2017), 70–80.

81. Quoted in Alex Davidson, "Bisexual Healing: Desiree Akhavan on Appropriate Behavior," British Film Institute, June 24, 2015, https://www.bfi.org.uk/news-opinion/news-bfi/interviews/bisexual-healing-desiree-akhavan-appropriate-behaviour.

82. Desiree Akhavan, "What Is Appropriate Behavior?" While these two remain the most infamous bisexual celebrities, a number of more aspirational figures (including Abbi Jacobson, Janelle Monáe, and Evan Rachel Wood) have emerged in the last few years.

83. Quoted in Davidson, "Bisexual Healing."

84. Quoted in Kachka, "Desiree Akhavan Wants."

85. Quoted in Hadley Freeman, "Desiree Akhavan on *Appropriate Behaviour* and Not Being the 'Iranian Bisexual Lena Dunham,'" *Guardian*, March 5, 2015, https://www.theguardian.com/film/2015/mar/05/desiree-akhavan-appropriate-behaviour-not-being-iranian-bisexual-lena-dunham.

86. Akhavan, "What Is Appropriate Behavior?"

87. Quoted in Kachka, "Desiree Akhavan Wants." For my discussion of *The Bisexual* as it relates to Akhavan's creative praxis and uncoupling with Ingrid Jungermann, see San Filippo, "Breaking Upwards."

88. Akhavan and Danforth, "'Miseducation of Cameron Post' Creators."

89. Electrelane, "To the East," by Emma Gaze, Mia Clarke, Rosamund Jean Murray, Verity Susman, on *No Shouts No Calls*, BMG Music, 2016.

90. Perkins, "My Effortless Brilliance," 148–50.

91. Quoted in Wickham, "Interview with Desiree Akhavan."

92. Quoted in Kate Erbland, "How 'Appropriate Behavior' Filmmaker Desiree Akhavan Avoided the Second-Film Slump by Getting the Hell out of Hollywood," *Indiewire*, October 27, 2017, https://www.indiewire.com/2017/10/appropriate-behavior-desiree-akhavan-second-film-1201891367/.

93. Quoted in Dawson, "Desiree Akhavan and Ingrid Jungermann."

94. Akhavan quoted in Wickham, "Interview with Desiree Akhavan."

95. See Maria San Filippo, "'Just Because I'm a Lesbian Doesn't Mean I'm Evolved': The 'Bad Queer' Politics of Queer Women's Comic Web Series," *Velvet Light Trap* 85 (Spring 2020): 65–77.

96. Ellis, "In the Reign of the Gay Magical Elves." See Eve Ng, "A 'Post-Gay' Era? Media Gaystreaming, Homonormativity, and the Politics of

LGBT Integration," *Communication, Culture and Critique* 6, no. 2 (2013): 258–83.

97. *Dyke TV* was a half-hour cable access, magazine-format television program. See Candace Moore, "The D Word," in *Loving the L Word*, ed. Dana Heller (London: I. B. Tauris, 2013), 191–207. *The F Word* was produced by Smell My Productions at the Milky Way Lounge, www.faithsoloway.com/fword.html.

98. Aymar Jean Christian, "Indie TV: Innovation in Series Development," in *Media Independence: Working with Freedom or Working for Free?* ed. James Bennett and Niki Strange (New York: Routledge, 2014), 161.

99. Margaret Lyons, "Lesbians Are Having the Best Summer Ever on TV," *Vulture*, July 25, 2013, https://www.vulture.com/2013/07/lesbians-are-having-the-best-summer-ever-on-tv.html.

100. Ellis, "In the Reign of the Gay Magical Elves."

101. See, for example, Cynthia Belmont, "Has Queer Culture Lost Its Edge?" *Salon*, August 6, 2017, https://www.salon.com/2017/08/06/has-queer-culture-lost-its-edge/.

102. Halberstam, *The Queer Art of Failure*, 23.

103. Jeffrey Sconce, "Irony, Nihilism, and the New American 'Smart' Film," *Screen* 43, no. 4 (Winter 2002): 369.

104. See San Filippo, *The B Word*.

105. Quoted in Trish Bendix, "Ingrid Jungermann and Desiree Akhavan on 'The Slope' and Writing Funny Lesbian Jokes," *AfterEllen*, March 30, 2012, http://www.afterellen.com/people/99781-ingrid-jungermann-and-desiree-akhavan-on-the-slope-and-writing-funny-lesbian-jokes/3#DOKXGGtj5OK2z3EU.99.

106. Halberstam, *The Queer Art of Failure*, 110–11.

107. See San Filippo, "'Just Because I'm a Lesbian.'"

108. See Fredric Jameson, *Postmodernism, or, the Cultural Logic of Late Capitalism* (Durham, NC: Duke University Press, 1991).

109. See Julia Himberg, "Multicasting: Lesbian Programming and the Changing Landscape of Cable TV," *Television and New Media* 15, no. 4 (2014): 289–304.

Epilogue

Still Taboo? Provocative Acts, Vulnerable Viewing

> The concrete institutional forms of sexuality at any given time and place are products of human activity. They are imbued with conflicts of interest and political maneuver, both deliberate and incidental. In that sense, sex is always political. But there are also historical periods in which sexuality is more sharply contested and more overtly politicized. In such periods, the domain of erotic life is, in effect, renegotiated.
>
> Gayle Rubin, "Thinking Sex"

> It's in our vulnerability... that our strength truly lies (if only because our capacity to feel for everyone else lies there, too).
>
> Pico Iyer, "The Humanity We Can't Relinquish"

AS THIS BOOK HAS DEMONSTRATED, today's screen media rely more than ever on sexual provocation as a path to commercial and creative vitality, and so it has been a difficult book to finish. In contemporary media, nearly every day new provoc*auteurs* and provocations call out for attention, and the bar for what is deemed provocative in any cultural moment is in a process of constant transformation. As I cautioned at the outset, this book does not aim comprehensively to cover the expanse of sexual provocation in 21st century screen media, but rather to present illustrative case studies that employ provocation in constructive, though not prescriptive, ways. The case study approach was necessary not only because of the sprawling scope of sexually provocative content in contemporary screen media, to which no single book could do justice, but more importantly because it is imperative that any given figure or work be assessed individually and, as A. O. Scott was quoted in the prologue urging, reassessed at turbulent cultural moments. At the outset I posited the importance of understanding provocation in terms of degree and purpose to determine whether a given provocauteur or provocation is merely self-interested and sensationalist (motivated primarily by attention-seeking and profit), or ventures further to be transgressive (boundary pushing) or even subversive (boundary dismantling). The question of "to what end?" is critical as well. My contention throughout has been that screening sexual provocation, while certainly about extending the boundaries of what kinds of (and how much) sex are shown, is as much or more about pushing the envelope on the politics of its representation. I follow Gayle Rubin in her call for a radical theory of sexuality that supports a politics embracing sexual variation and freedom of sexual expression. To that end, I have highlighted works that encourage us toward "thinking sex," with the aim of renegotiating, or even radically reimagining, its norms.

But there is another mode of thinking "radically" about sex that looms menacingly over our present cultural landscape. This one is prescriptive and restrictive and derives from political constituencies perceived as conservative and liberal alike. As inspiring and motivating as it is to write about something so urgent and continuously unfolding, it is simultaneously dispiriting to observe the political tide turn—from elements of the right as well as the left—against provocation, sexual and otherwise. In the summer of 2018, it emerged that the American alt-right movement was, with tragic irony, using comedians' jokes against them, feigning moral outrage in an effort to silence dissent against the present administration. The alt-right agitator Mike Chernovich targeted the Twitter feeds of such comedians as Michael Ian Black, Anthony Jeselnik, and Patton Oswalt, alongside *Community* creator Dan Harmon and *Guardians of the Galaxy* franchise director James Gunn, as a means to ignite a smear campaign aimed at discrediting liberal celebrities through allegations of pedophilia.[1] The episode highlights the importance of digital media, for it is precisely the accessibility, plasticity, and permanence (however disguised as ephemerality) of the internet, particularly the easily retrievable and manipulable record of Twitter posts, that enables this strategy. As one target of manufactured outrage from the alt-right, Jeselnik, tweeted in response, "Scrolling through my timeline for offensive tweets is like looking for a needle in a needle store on customer appreciation day."[2] Oswalt pointed out that tweets used to incriminate him were taken from a series of jokes he had crafted precisely to illustrate how remarks taken out of context can be unintentionally damning.[3]

Though Oswalt was the outlier in using humor to instructive ends, a closer look at the context of these jokes deemed to go "too far" would reveal that their creators were guilty of nothing worse than "totally failed and unfortunate efforts to be provocative"—as James Gunn admitted of his own decade-old incriminating tweets, which resulted in his being summarily fired by Disney.[4] Yet it is precisely our careful parsing of these provocations—something that neither Disney (in firing Gunn) nor Twitter (in taking no substantive action against those abusing its service in spreading disinformation) would properly do—that allows us to grasp their relative value for our cultural conversation and "the conflicts of interest and political maneuver" (in Gayle Rubin's terms) behind their being recirculated.[5] Ultimately these jokes might not yield sufficiently worthwhile insights to qualify as the kind of constructive use of provocation I advocate here, but to censor them or condemn their creators would be to subject them to the same weaponizing as the alt-right did in willfully misconstruing and misusing them.

It is troubling as well to witness a corollary push, from groups with whom I feel far more closely aligned, to censor cultural representations conflated, and therefore deemed to be on par, with outright acts of abuse or assault. Such was the sentiment informing a push for the Metropolitan Museum to remove Balthus's painting *Thérèse Dreaming* from its walls.[6] Though the Met took a firm position in refusing to make any concessions around the work's display, the debate that ensued among art critics and cultural commentators (which was conducted largely online) thoughtfully reassessed the artist and his work, both its power and its disturbing elements. In so doing, it effectively produced a virtual wall label to substitute for that which the Met declined to add.

As these two controversial cases attest, both comedy and art, alongside screen media, act as forums for establishing and contesting what is taboo at a given moment, and can even serve directly to influence public policy. Comic George Carlin legendarily satirized the broadcasting restrictions of the FCC in his 1972 "Seven Words You Can't Say on Television" monologue—although in that case, a radio broadcast of Carlin's routine resulted in a Supreme Court decision upholding the FCC's regulation of material it defines as indecent, a ruling that continues to limit broadcasters' freedom of expression.[7] Even if Carlin's satirical protest proved a bridge too far at the time, the *FCC v. Pacifica* decision continues to be contested (as recently as 2012, in a stated objection by Justice Ruth Bader Ginsberg) for the leeway it gives the FCC in determining what qualifies as indecent, and for its curtailing of First Amendment rights.[8] Carlin's routine had further lasting effect: while the "seven dirty words" remain taboo, broadcasters have compensated by creatively incorporating language not included on the FCC's "indecent" list, and swearing emerged alongside sex as a vital mode of brand differentiation for cable programming.

Like freedom of sexual expression, freedom of artistic expression is important precisely because the terms for what is transgressive are always shifting, in large part because, as *FCC v. Pacifica* demonstrates (and as Gayle Rubin also notes), those terms are always political. Free expression is a valuable means by which we address the need continually to renegotiate the politics of desire and representation in order to make the sexual/political sphere more inclusive and more open. These boundaries of the provocative tell us a great deal about the culture we inhabit. Exploring our complex responses to genuinely provocative works and investigating what is troubling about them and why lead to an understanding of current logics of desire and, going back to Rubin, how we might renegotiate "the domain of erotic life." Rather than implement a newfangled production code in which artistic and sexual values are coterminous and no act of "sex perversion" (as classical Hollywood's Production Code Administration formally termed it) goes undisciplined, we should embrace these provocative works for providing the impetus for and the means by which to reassess our moral and ethical frameworks around sex. As the historical and cultural vicissitudes of sexual variation attest, "one person's perversion is another's normality."[9]

What I have striven to do, perhaps provocatively, in these pages is to (re)assess and even commend screen artists and artworks that provoke (and indeed may offend) in order to illustrate the productive potential of provocation to rethink sexualities and suggest liberatory possibilities. Given the cultural relativity and continual redefining of what is still taboo, I offer as one constant of provocation that it involves vulnerability. The very prevalence of provocation suggests a certain commercial vulnerability for artworks, the need for works to stand out in an increasingly overcrowded ecosystem. Yet it is also a vulnerable position that provoc*auteurs* inhabit, not only in deliberately placing themselves in the crosshairs of political controversy but also in forgoing the impulse to ensconce themselves within an armor of aesthetic safety and moral certainty—in choosing, to use the comedian's term, to "work blue."

The self-revelation ventured by Lena Dunham and by those performers and media creators who defy the dictate against exposure of the (de-phallicized) penis constitutes such a show of vulnerability, as does Desiree Akhavan's ironic owning up to being "superficial [and] homophobic." Similarly, the cases explored below describe a comedian and short story writer respectively giving voice to issues of sexual compulsion and consent that have heretofore been culturally silenced. Effectively engaging these kinds of provocative texts calls for a critically informed position and a willingness to embrace ambiguous meanings and ambivalent responses. This kind of careful, reflective approach to personally and culturally divisive works characterizes training in the humanities, central to which is the process of grappling with texts rich in nuance and ambiguity.

Even in the most challenging cases of works that could be said to go too far—provocations so intent on voicing or showing what is taboo that they may seem insensitive, oblivious, or even harmful to those on the receiving end—we might find it valuable, rather than a liability or a danger, to confront such works, provided that confrontation takes place consensually and with appropriate ethical parameters in place (not unlike those that guide BDSM practices). To face these sorts of discomforting works requires a mode of engagement that entails making oneself vulnerable as a spectator, and that heeds the danger of disregarding (literally, looking away from) the sometimes-uncomfortable truths that such work puts forward. My thinking here is informed and inspired by contemporary feminist philosophical theory's exploration of "the experience of vulnerability for what it may provide in terms of ethical and political provocation." Ann V. Murphy formulates this idea as follows: "The claim would be that there is something in the experience of one's own vulnerability that allows for a productive appreciation of the vulnerability of others, particularly when vulnerability is understood to be constitutive of the human condition, despite the disparate ways it might be realized in experience." In extending this thinking about the relevance of an acknowledgment of vulnerability to the realm of spectatorial reception, we can imagine how the escapist and reflective qualities attributed to screen media allow for a safe but productive means of attaining what Murphy describes as the "redemptive and aspirational" potential of this position of vulnerability.[10]

This reading strategy is one that *New York Times* internet culture critic Amanda Hess suggests certain viewers will find familiar. "Women and other marginalized audiences are already accustomed to managing the cognitive dissonance of finding meaning in art that ignores us, or worse. Drawing connections between art and abuse can actually help us see the works more clearly, to understand them in all of their complexity, and to connect them to our real lives and experiences—even if those experiences are negative."[11] Following from Murphy and Hess, and recalling Pico Iyer's quote at the beginning of this chapter about vulnerability's value in fortifying a sense of our shared humanness, I contend that engaging with taboo-breaking works—rather than censoring or turning away from them—can forge empathy and be empowering, and so ultimately be cathartic and connective, personally and culturally.[12]

Vulnerability, then, is not only a driver of provocation and a wager ventured by its practitioners but also a reception position that carries its own risks and rewards. This is not to be glib about artwork's ability to empower or to minimize the very real effects of trauma. Rather, it is an invitation to art to do its job of allowing artists and audiences a relatively safe haven for the exposure and exploration of human flaws and moral contradictions. Art that fully reflects the world we live in will better position us to cope with its complexities and to imagine more fulfilling possibilities than will art that falls back on flawless (and thus not humanlike) role models and unambiguous moral directives—which is not to say that screen narratives should not present aspirational figures or imagine positive transformation. But it is a strong indication of the need to navigate our immensely fraught times that provocation has emerged as a key mode—perhaps the key mode—in realms of contemporary media that are robust and thriving, from film festival programming to cable TV dramedies to women-directed indies to queer web series. Alongside the selections from screen media that I have examined up to this point and will conclude with below, I wish to weave in some brief discussion of the value of vulnerability for provoc*auteurs* and provocations from two final frontiers of 21st century "old media": stand-up comedy and short fiction.

SHOCK COMEDY AND TAKING SEXUAL PROVOCATION #TOOFAR

"It's so hard to shock. Really hard. But to shock is not a goal, it's a medium."[13] This reflection, voiced in an op-ed for *The Guardian* by provoc*auteur* Gaspar Noé upon the release of his 1999 film *Seul Contre Tous (I Stand Alone)*, suggests first the cultural jadedness that had already taken hold at the close of the last century. Two decades later, as sex becomes more and more explicit on more and more screens, raising the bar for what is considered shocking or scandalous, what remains taboo? This "anything goes" permissiveness has been opposed by formidable resistance to works and creators that go "too far"—whether by exceeding ostensibly rightful bounds of appropriate expression or cultural appropriation, or more malignantly by using means or taking positions deemed exploitative or repugnant.

In chapters 1 and 3, I pointed to how provocations judged to go too far by filmmakers Lars von Trier and Catherine Breillat (and, to a less impudent degree, Lena Dunham) have compromised their respective provoc*auteur* brands, perhaps beyond repair. Of course, in all these cases, it has not been the images these creators brought to the screen, but rather their publicly uttered remarks, that proved damning. Where they might succeed in rising above the clutter in the short term, the more sustainable and substantive mode of provocation that the best aspects of their creative output attain is regrettably undermined by these pronouncements, which lack the humility and humanity exhibited in that work.

This simultaneous enticement to and threat of going too far suffuses another realm of contemporary media currently enjoying a golden era: stand-up comedy. Writing in 2015, *New York Times* cultural critic Jason Zinoman weighed the form's perennially boundary-pushing power against today's reactionary redrawing of lines demarcating what's taboo: "Comedians have never been able to joke about provocative subjects without repercussions, and what's often overlooked is how, during the past few decades, the ability of comics to push the line of good taste for a national audience has actually dramatically increased.... The real consequence of the proliferation of joke controversies is that the realm of the taboo has appeared to expand."[14]

In the wake of this expansion, the extreme genre of "shock comedy" has grown increasingly prominent in stand-up and in comedy overall. I observed at this book's outset screen media's preoccupation with showing what typically goes unseen; this shares a kinship with comedy's drive to say what goes unsaid—and hence to shock. Not surprisingly, shock comedy relies as much on sex as do screen provoc*auteurs* and provocations. In thinking about the second sentiment expressed by Gaspar Noé in the quote that begins this section, this parallel push to up the ante of provocation suggests that, in both screen art and stand-up comedy, the medium is the message. It continually strives to test its own limits of what can be shown and spoken.[15] Recently, however, both realms have been met with mounting resistance to what is perceived as their going too far—in the parlance of the social media hashtag and internet meme developed to function as an outrage-fueled media watchdog.

Beyond drawing the boundary of what goes too far in content (i.e., that some topics may still be taboo), the perceived provocation of certain creative works has soared with revelations about their makers and has endowed those works with evidentiary power. In the prologue, I used the case of *Blue Is the Warmest Color* filmmaker Abdellatif Kechiche to encourage a bracketing of considerations of an artist's character in evaluations of that artist's work. I argued that "the aesthetic alibi" (as historian Martin Jay termed the ethical immunity afforded to artists) must not keep our critical estimation of an artwork or cultural text divorced from its terms of production, but neither should we reduce the moral character of a work to that of its maker.[16]

In thinking about how this question of separating art from artist applies to the realm of stand-up comedy, again the medium is paramount for the way it invites us to read comedians as revealing themselves to a far greater extent than in most other types of performance. Two figures whose art has been retrospectively shown to imitate (or at least relate in troubling ways to) life are dismaying precisely because they threaten to collapse the distinction between performer and (real) person. As *New York Times* critics Manohla Dargis and A. O. Scott have suggested, both Louis C.K. and Woody Allen have seemed to be trolling their critics and fans by increasingly dissolving the boundaries between their lives and work.[17]

Reassessing C.K.'s work in light of the revelations about his sexual misconduct, critics have pointed to such loaded material as his *Saturday Night Live* opening monologue from 2015. It was rebuked at the time for going too far as C.K. marveled at the powerful compulsiveness exhibited by child molesters. At the risk of being overly provocative myself, I find it a useful joke to examine for what it reveals about the timbre and temporality of the taboo:

> There is no worse life available to a human than being a caught child molester, and yet they still do it. From which, you can only really surmise, that it must be *really good*. I mean from their point of view, not ours, but from their point of view, it must be *amazing* for them to risk so much.... If somebody said to me "if you eat another Mounds bar you will go to jail and everyone will hate you," I

would stop eating them. Because they do taste delicious, but they don't taste as good as a young boy does—and shouldn't!—to a child molester. (42.17, "Louis C.K./The Chainsmokers")

This monologue's strategy for going too far shares with Lars von Trier's comments at Cannes a recognition of the undeniable humanity of figures—child molesters, Hitler—who have been demonized in nearly every other cultural realm. Though plenty of people recoiled from both utterances, that C.K. got laughs (from some) while von Trier was greeted with appalled silence stems from the audience's understanding the former as provocative in a meaningful way. The audience is allowed (to paraphrase Aristotle) to entertain compassion for such figures without accepting their actions. In other words, C.K. was relying on the critical distancing that irony permits, and (now paraphrasing F. Scott Fitzgerald) with which we can accept two opposing ideas: that child molesters (or Hitler) are both unimaginable and all too human. We can agree that we are extraordinarily fortunate that our compulsion is for Mounds bars rather than molesting children, yet isn't our sense of moral superiority to child molesters at least partly a matter of luck, of our being drawn to candy bars while molesters are drawn to children? von Trier's remarks, however, lacked the necessary distancing to endow them with the reassuring framing of irony, and so they seemed to reinforce rather than challenge prejudice. They were provocative to no apparent purpose, and within an inappropriate context. Whereas C.K. was without question performing a comedy monologue, von Trier's performance, though he claimed at intervals during his rambling to be joking, was not clearly legible as such. Nor was a film festival press conference an appropriate space for such a performance, jokes about Hitler being sufficiently provocative to require a clearly delineated performative space and tone (such as that which permits Mel Brooks's *The Producers* to register as farcical).

Now marked by the revelations about his own failures of empathy and care for others, C.K.'s monologue—plus a good amount of material from his stand-up, FX series *Louie* (2010–15), and film *I Love You, Daddy* (2017)—no longer feel as if they have the necessary distance from his own actions. Their ostensible purpose (an audacious reckoning with the psychology of pedophilia, or sexual compulsion more generally) is overshadowed by what several critics construed as their actual purpose: a smokescreen for C.K.'s own sexual misconduct.[18] In C.K.'s case, then, the adage that comedy is "tragedy plus time" requires the addendum "but not too much time"—as the locus of shock shifted from the brutal honesty of his comedy to the dishonest brutality of his treatment of women colleagues. The "too far" element of the provocation was not the content of the joke itself, which was on but not over the edge, but that C.K. had lost the moral authority to push the edge in this way. What had seemed before to be daring revelation came to look like concealment and hypocrisy. These revelations undermined an important basis of the joke, which itself hinges on vulnerability: the comedian's sensitivity to our shared vulnerability as humans. And so C.K.'s provocation proved vulnerable itself, when it was revealed that he had failed to be sufficiently sensitive to women's vulnerability, particularly to their sense of the difficulty of saying no, to the gendered and professional inequities that made consent a more complicated notion for his female colleagues than it was for him.

Here we can reflect back on the extreme vulnerability that the sexual provocations of *Blue Is the Warmest Color* and *Stranger by the Lake* called for on the part of their performers. The actors' self-exposure infuses those films with an intimacy and pathos that deepens and cuts against what Linda Williams calls their "hard-core eroticism," employing sex scenes and nudity not simply for sensationalism and arousal but, as discussed in the prologue and chapter 2, respectively, to defamiliarizing and de-phallicizing ends.[19] Moreover, both films narratively thematize vulnerability, in exploring the openness to pain that being in love (or lust) entails, the emotional and physical risks that accompany intimacy, and the specific liability constituted by being queer in a straight world. Where the two films diverge most noticeably is in the markedly differing experiences around safety and agency reported by their performers and the gendered inflection of those reports. It was revealed that Kechiche's insufficient care for Exarchopoulos and Seydoux left them vulnerable in a way that recalled C.K.'s victims, and in a manner that, as with C.K.'s oeuvre, significantly compromises the work.

Leaving C.K. aside for the moment, far from the "death of irony" predicted after 9/11, comedy has been intensely irony-rich and shock-inducing in the new millennium, but its time might be up. First, Netflix's newfound domination over stand-up (the company released twenty-six comedy specials in 2016, and since then has upped the output to at least one per week) may have a mainstreaming effect, in which comedy is made palatable for wide release, though it is also possible that it will create further incentive for attention-getting shock. As I argued in chapter 4, drawing on Jeffrey Sconce's view that irony's brutal honesty underwrites its political potential, using ironic delivery to present provocative ideas can both reveal the contours of and challenge accepted beliefs.[20] Using irony in the way that "superficial, homophobic lesbians" Desiree Akhavan and Ingrid Jungermann do in their web series *The Slope* to mock their own community's overinvestment in constricting standards of decorum works to challenge the policing of speech. It does so effectively because it registers an understanding of the pain wrought by stigmatizing language ("tragedy") yet from the relatively safe distance of 2010's Brooklyn ("time"). Even as their "It Gets Better?" mock-PSA suggests that things have not gotten and won't get better, the very fact that they can deploy irony as they do makes the case that things are, in fact, better. Again, context is key, particularly with regard to who is doing the joking. To be "homophobic" in the way that Akhavan and Jungermann are in *The Slope* requires some claim to ownership of the identity "queer," and with it the vulnerability that such an identity position carries in a heteronormative culture. Thus, with its reliance on irony—a grasp of opposing ideas—shock comedy testifies to the importance of close reading, particularly in an era of recombinant media and remix culture, and in the face of far more dangerous decontextualizing of jokes being done by the alt-right.

For some in the audience, of course, it is always already taboo to use certain terms or inherently damaging to joke about homophobia. Others may be similarly persuaded of this perspective by the 2018 viral sensation *Nanette*, distributed by Netflix and described by the *New York Times* as the "most discussed comedy special in ages"—not least because it abandons comedy at its halfway point.[21] In it, lesbian comedian Hannah Gadsby announces her retirement (since rescinded, in the wake of her breakout success) as a result of her recognition that her self-deprecating humor prolonged the trauma that provided her punch lines, and deeming laughter no longer an effective means of engaging empathy or challenging prejudice. She remarks sarcastically, "I told lots of cool jokes about homophobia. Really solved that problem." Though here, too, she is joking (much as she does in mocking the adage that laughter is the best medicine, saying "I reckon penicillin might give it a nudge"), Gadsby is asking comedy to do something that it can't, and doesn't properly try to do: "solve" real-world problems. Comedy may help transform attitudes by holding retrograde ideas up to ridicule and so participate in the process of changing norms, but it can hardly be expected to achieve on its own a massive social transformation. Indeed, the humor of both of those jokes rests on our awareness of how exaggerated an expectation that would be. The provocation at the core of Gadsby's special, which might have had an attitude-transforming (if not world-changing) effect, was sexual in the sense that it was bound up in her identity as a woman and a lesbian. As Gadsby observes, "People really only feel safe when men do the angry comedy. I do it and I'm just an angry lesbian ruining all the fun and banter." The same is true in the case of shock comedy's permissiveness around what comedian Whitney Cummings calls "dirty words coming out of pretty mouths," which allows women comics to spill sexual truths, yet in ways that can be commodified (they are, after all, "pretty") and contained (as "raunchy" but rarely angry).[22]

This moratorium on women's anger in comedy discourse speaks to Lauren Berlant's reminder, in analogizing predators and jokesters, that both are protected by their invulnerability—that is, by their privilege: "by control over time and space and the framing of consequences in domains of capital, labor, institutional belonging, and speech situations where the structurally vulnerable are forced to 'choose their battles' or just act like a good sport."[23] Because comedy, like screen media, remains the province of the privileged—those with greater access to and control over the cultural conversation, who in our moment continue to be white cishet men—our (re)assessments of its provoc*auteurs* and provocations must therefore take note of how power is conferred, and how it might be challenged. Going back to Noé's conception of shock as a medium, comedy and screen media are primed for this challenge precisely because of their ability, some might say compulsion, to say and show that which is taboo.

To consider a final example of sexual provocation in recent shock comedy that shows it is not the province of stand-up alone, I turn back to screen media and chapter 1's discussion of the scandal film as a promotional strategy for rising above the clutter of festival programming and other art cinema circuits. While I concur with Mette Hjort's strictures against what she calls a "shotgun method of provocation" that employs "mockery combined with the refusal to commit to a position," I hesitate to agree that "the refusal to provide answers becomes in effect a refusal to develop a coherent argument" and thus weakens the power of provocation.[24] While Hjort was taking issue with von Trier specifically, her characterization echoes the response to the work of provoc*auteur* Paul Verhoeven, whose 2016 film *Elle* serves as an illustrative final millennial watercooler movie.

Verhoeven claimed, "I could never have made this film in the US, with this level of authenticity" and that "no American actress would ever take on such an amoral movie."[25] So the film was shot in France, and Verhoeven cast Isabelle Huppert as Michèle. After being raped in her home in the film's opening scene, Michèle plays a cat-and-mouse game with her assailant—though whether she is out for revenge or reenactment becomes increasingly unclear. As one of the most talked about films at Cannes (where it premiered) and of the year, the work was provocative not only because of its graphic, male-authored depiction of a woman's experience of sexual violence and its deliberately opaque treatment of Michèle's motives in going after her attacker but also for what seemed, given the subject matter, its inappropriately lighthearted tone. "Screwball sadomasochism" was a term used in one review, which went on to note that, not for the first time in his career, Verhoeven nimbly constructs the film to be read both straight and satirically, as either "a statement of feminist empowerment or masochism."[26] In her offhand remark to friends at dinner, "I suppose I was raped," her rejection of the role of victim, and her disbelief in the authorities' ability and willingness to protect and serve, Michèle shares with Catherine Breillat's women characters a refusal of the cultural script for how rape survivors ought to speak, feel, and act in the wake of their experience. Also like Breillat, Verhoeven's stance toward his protagonist's response to rape is not the amoral stance toward rape that his comment above might suggest; rather, it is nonmoralizing. In provocatively suggesting that nonconsensual sex may not preclude attraction to one's attacker, Verhoeven's ambiguity valuably allows for a nonprescriptive, genuinely provocative exploration of trauma's effects and of perverse desire—but without ever conclusively linking the former to the latter.

Ultimately, however, what Huppert called Verhoeven's "perpetual ambiguity" serves as a crutch, similar to what Hjort calls von Trier's "refusal to commit to a position."[27] The ambiguity permits Verhoeven to deflect what might be the more stringent provocation to come from a committed position (if not a firm conclusion or pat solution) vis-à-vis the subject matter. In this sense, Verhoeven's approach is not unlike that of some shock comedy in its overreliance on irony. To reassess Verhoeven's provocation with a challenge to his privilege, as Berlant urges, suggests that behind its distancing and opacity, he exerts formidable control that, in a film about a woman's response to rape, seems "too far" removed.

Elle's casting proved vital in this regard, with feminist critics hailing Huppert's legendary combination of physical fragility and steely will as providing a necessary counterbalance to Verhoeven's impassivity.[28] Reminiscent of the sort of "resistance through charisma" that Richard Dyer attributes to Rita Hayworth's character in *Gilda* (Charles Vidor, 1946), Huppert's performance bends the material to her will and so contests the privilege and control on Verhoeven's part that might otherwise compromise the film's ability to resonate with (especially women) viewers.[29] What started out as an opportunistic provocation and perverse (male) fantasy on Verhoeven's part about a woman attracted to trauma becomes, through Huppert's indomitable presence, about a woman who takes command of her own vulnerability. Only in this way does *Elle* succeed as a productive provocation, superseding the "mockery" that Verhoeven's light touch might seem to inject, even if the film lacks the committed position and coherent argument that might have made it a more compelling meditation on rape culture and (thinking of its title) the shared experience of all women of misogyny and sexism. The next section explores how another millennial watercooler-worthy provocation concerning a woman's response to a sexual encounter, this one nonviolent but still wounding, again hinges on gendered authorship in its power to provoke.

CONFESSING (BAD) SEX: THE PROVOCATION OF "CAT PERSON"

Having started by asking what is still taboo—that which seems enduringly capable of provoking—it seems evident that provocation is crucially subject not only to tone but to timing, to the cultural sensitivity of a given moment and milieu. That an "old media" work of short fiction published in the august literary publication *The New Yorker* went viral says as much about the #MeToo moment as it does about the work itself. After its publication in the December 11, 2017, issue, Kristen Roupenian's short story "Cat Person" set Twitter aflame with retweets and discussion, and went on to be the magazine's most read online fictional piece that year (and the second most read overall, surpassed only by journalist Ronan Farrow's first investigative piece on Harvey Weinstein).[30] The social media storm around "Cat Person" suggests that while new media (e.g., online magazines, social networking sites) can be competitors with old media (e.g., print and terrestrial radio, but also now film and legacy TV), they can also extend the reach of and breathe new life into those older media forms.

The story of a female college student's short-term, sexually unsatisfactory relationship with a somewhat older man conducted largely by text message was, by *The New Yorker*'s account, slated for publication with an eye to its relevance in the current climate, though probably with only the vaguest hope of creating, as Roupenian did, a millennial watercooler story (in two senses, being that the author is herself a Millennial).[31] "Cat Person" was not unprecedented as a woman-authored literary treatment of a loaded sexual topic being widely disseminated and inspiring an outpouring of interest. In 2013, Patricia Lockwood's poem "Rape Joke," which indirectly commented on controversies in the comedy world by rejecting the idea of building a joke on rape, alighted online after appearing in the literary journal *The Awl*, striking the same resonant chord as "Cat Person" in blending topicality, creativity, and controversy.[32] Though fictional, "Cat Person" no doubt also benefited from its resemblance to a mode du jour known as the personal essay, which might be rebranded as the "too-personal essay" for its compulsively tell-all approach to autobiographical (or autofictional) stories frequently featuring sexual episodes or confessions. Some of the more scandalous examples include Daphne Merkin's spanking memoir "Unlikely Obsession," also published in *The New Yorker*, and former Balanchine ballerina Toni Bentley's memoir about female erotic submission and anal sex, *The Surrender*.

The flourishing of this form in recent years is often attributed to what Brian McNair characterizes as the "striptease culture" of sexual commodification and consumerism, which he traces to a larger cultural leaning toward "self-revelation . . . exposure" and "public intimacy."[33] Related to and fed by the new narcissism of a social media–fueled "selfie culture," the too-personal essay also has its roots in the material realities of digital journalism culture. *New Yorker* staff writer Jia Tolentino, a former scribe of personal essays, has since written them off as being an underpaid (and sometimes unpaid) commodification of women's experiences fueled by online page-view metrics for advertising sales. The genre "creates uncomfortable incentives for writers, editors, and readers alike. Attention flows naturally to the outrageous, the harrowing, the intimate, and the recognizable."[34] In Tolentino's estimation, such narratives are of questionable value (literally and figuratively) to their makers, except perhaps in the rare instances that they prove career making. But in recounting episodes of "bad sex," they avail themselves of the strategy of applying sexual provocation to newfound digital forums used by the "bad queer" web series creators examined in chapter 4.

When the screen that most people regard most frequently in any given day—the smart phone—was given the moniker "portable electronic confessional" by sociologist-philosopher Zygmunt

Bauman, it would seem that displays of sexual provocation stemming from the old media—or "old new media"—on which this book largely focuses will be displaced by self-revelations created using newer platforms and likely by younger producers.[35] Thinking back to Lena Dunham's early adoption of such channels with her YouTube short videos, digital distribution provides opportunities for self-expression for young women specifically, from which we can expect a "level of authenticity" in relating women's experiences of sex (and of sexual violence) to vie with that which Verhoeven claimed for *Elle*. Though Tolentino's warning about the commodification of such stories needs heeding, especially as video-hosting and -sharing sites also become increasingly ad-driven, the too-personal essay—whether penned or filmed—holds significant potential for counteracting the disempowerment created by women's being socialized not to articulate their needs and experiences.

At the same time that a culture of (sexual) oversharing has cultivated the too-personal essay alongside naked selfies, women continue to be discouraged from communicating openly and honestly about (and during) sex. It is noteworthy but not surprising that a key component of the appeal of "Cat Person" was the story's articulation of women's shared experience of feeling unable to speak up in the course of a bad sexual encounter. Many commentators noted the extent to which the Twitter response to the story was split along gender lines. Women tended to identify with the story's account of feeling helpless to put the brakes on a bad sexual encounter—one whose badness is precisely wrapped up in the man's failure to notice that the woman is experiencing the sex as bad. One of the story's fans created an @MenCatPerson Twitter handle because she was "feeling frustrated with the number of men who seemed to completely miss the point of what the author was trying to do."[36]

With its hints at the age-determined power imbalance between the couple, "Cat Person" might conceivably have been written by the woman who publishes an online tell-all of her encounter with a well-known author in season six of *Girls* in the "American Bitch" episode discussed in chapter 3. That Lena Dunham's alter ego Hannah Horvath is herself a published author of too-personal essays permitted *Girls* to self-reflexively address how the gendered and generational "entertainment" of sexual confession is symptomatic of what Feona Attwood diagnoses as "a culture in which sex signifies both the truth of the self and its performance; authenticity and artifice."[37] A critic for *The Guardian* likens "Cat Person" to another moment in *Girls*—the season two episode "On All Fours," also discussed in chapter 3—in which Dunham probes what popular culture regards as the "blurred lines" of consent and the sometimes thorny distinction between bad sex and sexual assault.[38] On this front, "Cat Person's" popularity and cultural resonance were surely boosted by the appearance of its nonfictional corollary in the contemporaneous case of pseudonymous photographer "Grace's" bad date with comedian Aziz Ansari, as reported in the online women's news and lifestyle publication Babe.net. No doubt because it was bound up with celebrity journalism and involved actual people, response to the latter story suffered even more from the misdirected attention and unproductive outrage that characterized the shallowest social media reactions to "Cat Person." In so doing, it undercut the potential, according to an article in *Jezebel*, "for actually talking about the socially ingrained cultural and political disparity that shows itself in dating scenarios."[39]

Where that potential was more effectively realized was in the cultural conversation that resulted from "Cat Person." What is perhaps most striking in all this is that the simple fact of a woman representing how a sexual encounter feels, relating women's experience of unsatisfactory sex, seems unprecedented and somehow scandalous and divisive—in a word, provocative. The furor around the story suggests that any attempt to articulate the experience of marginalized sexualities (which includes that of women) retains tremendous urgency and remains a focal point of social and cultural anxieties. It also suggests the ongoing necessity for, and value of, sexual provocation. It is precisely the role of provocation, as I've explored throughout this book, to give voice to what had been rendered unspeakable, and to sort through the messiness of desire to achieve some form of clarification.

Even accounting for the sort of analog and digital manipulations previously discussed (from *Blue Is the Warmest Color*'s prosthetic vaginas to *American Gods*' CGI penises), that Roupenian's written representation of sex bears less of the indexical relationship to reality than the screened sex examined throughout this book demonstrates that sexual provocation need not rely on audiovisual imagery. What was provocative about "Cat Person" was the explicitness not of its sex but of its confession, which, despite being fictional, was overwhelmingly regarded as speaking truth. As noted in the quote by Carol Siegel towards the start of chapter 1, to encourage radical conceptualizations of sex does not necessitate a work's depicting sex explicitly. As evidenced by "Cat Person," one can make a sex radical work absent sex (or its visualization on-screen) simply by showing women unable to enact sexual "freedoms" due to the gendered inequities of their lived realities. As was seen in its creators' choice to largely mask the screening of gay male sex in HBO's *Looking*, a sexually provocative work can provoke precisely by defying the pressure to screen sex and instead of talking about it with "boring" yet revealing honesty.

All these battlegrounds of screen imagery, stand-up comedy, and short fiction have much in common with another contemporary realm where battles over provocation are being fought: the academy. All are forums founded on showing the unseeable, saying the unsayable, and "talking about difficult stuff," as Laura Kipnis puts it in her celebration of the university "as a refuge for complexity, a setting for the free exchange of ideas."[40] Instead, the "neoliberalization" of the academy and the constraints on open dialogue that have descended on (especially American) college campuses have rendered intellectual freedom vulnerable—of which I, as a not-yet-tenured professor writing a book on sexual provocation, am all too aware.[41] In an era in which, as Kipnis writes, "speaking honestly about sexual realities has become taboo," I maintain my conviction that there is an important place for meaningful and responsible practices of provocation in the broader classroom of the 21st century screen mediascape, and that such media play an irreplaceable role in showing (or telling) the truth about sex.[42] This is not to overlook that truth is plural and discursively bound or to ignore its mediated nature in representation, but rather to acknowledge that despite those qualifications, the concept of sexual truth and the aims of its representation remain meaningful. This is also not to argue that screen media should serve as an untrammeled receptacle for the sexual id, as any engagement with an erotic fantasy scenario must include active informed consent—both among creative collaborators and between media creators and consumers—and conscientious regard for the impact of representations, in keeping with the ethics of provocation I have weighed throughout. The same holds for conversations in actual classrooms, and in this book I hope to have modeled how sexually provocative works can and should be critically engaged among consenting adults in university settings, in respectful but rigorous exchanges that compel our being vulnerable in our openness to challenging material and complex ideas.

What we are in danger of losing with the disintegration of the humanities is, after all, no less than what we stand to lose by turning away from art itself. Perhaps exceptional among the arts if only for its ability to speak so accessibly and to represent reality with such immediacy, screen media act as an acute means of engaging with and thus understanding all of human variation. As Roger Ebert judged, "Movies are the most powerful empathy machine in all the arts."[43] Questions of how representation plays into reality and how art effects change are ones that have long been pondered without clear-cut answers having been achieved, and I will hardly be so hubristic as to offer definitive conclusions about the impact of or social effects produced by the forms of provocation I champion here.

Yet as much potential as I see in these old, new, and still emergent screen media, I am mindful that as our media technologies and practices transform, so do our forms of censorship. As the aforementioned misuse of Twitter by the alt-right illustrates, any medium or platform can be leveraged for power and propaganda, and that need not condemn the medium entirely. But what of any individual performance or work? To return briefly to Louis C.K.—and, in so doing, to offer one final provocation of my own—HBO's decision (in the wake of his admission to sexual misconduct) to remove his comedy specials and *Lucky Louie* from its streaming services is a form of censorship, albeit a relatively mild one, and challenges us to question where to draw the line—both for content distributors and as consumers. (Those questions have already begun: All shows in which he played an authorial role? All his late night show guest appearances? Fan-created videos of his stand-up acts posted to YouTube? His new stand-up special, "Sincerely Louis C.K.," released after he admitted misconduct?) To the argument that one can, in this age of torrenting and the persistent reemergence of previously expunged online content, always find a means of accessing such material seems to pass the buck, and relying on extralegal back channels to ensure the availability of material is not ultimately productive of much except (perhaps) denying its malfeasant creator some monetary reward. Would censoring those films produced by Miramax and the Weinstein Company repair the damage done by their fallen former leader or merely rob us of a great many works that provide alternative perspectives and challenge the toxic masculinity Harvey Weinstein personifies?

These are not merely rhetorical questions in the contemporary climate, and so I encourage—would even go so far as to prescribe—conversation over censorship. As the comedian Cameron Esposito, in her 2018 stand-up special *Rape Jokes*, responds to those shock comics who "cry censorship" when they are critiqued for off-color jokes, it is not censorship but rather feedback that they are receiving. And that is precisely what is needed most at this transformative cultural moment. As I hope to have conveyed with my analyses of provocative works from across the 21st century screen mediascape, feedback is the more productive alternative to censorship, not only in pointing out what is problematic about certain works while still allowing them to be seen and heard but also in, effectively, opening them up to meanings and understandings that their authors may not have intended or imagined. In that spirit, I hope to have contributed productively, if provocatively, to the conversation, and I welcome the feedback to come.

NOTES

1. See Christina Cauterucci, "The Far Right's Pedophilia Smear Campaign Is Working," *Slate*, July 25, 2018, https://slate.com/human-interest/2018/07/james-gunn-dan-harmon-mike-cernovich-the-far-rights-pedophilia-smear-campaign-is-working.html.
2. @anthonyjeselnik, Twitter post, July 21, 2018, 5:30 p.m.
3. See Matthew Olson, "The Account That Cried 'Pedophilia': Conservative Troll Tries to Smear Patton Oswalt with Oswalt's Own Deliberately Misleading Tweets," *Digg*, July 23, 2018, digg.com/2018/patton-oswalt-nambla-tweets-gunn-ban-cernovich.
4. Quoted in Zack Sharf, "James Gunn Issues Statement Reacting to Disney Firing, Offers 'Deepest Apologies' for Offensive Tweets," *Indiewire*, July 20, 2018, https://www.indiewire.com/2018/07/james-gunn-responds-disney-fired-guardians-of-the-galaxy-1201986202/. Disney announced in March 2019 that Gunn had been rehired to helm the third installment in the franchise.
5. Gayle Rubin, "Thinking Sex: Notes for a Radical Theory of the Politics of Sexuality," in *Culture, Society and Sexuality: A Reader*, 2nd ed., ed. Richard Parker and Peter Aggleton (New York: Routledge, 2007), 243.
6. The petition presented to the Met called for either removal of the work or a recontextualization of its presentation (by offering a warning to

visitors or amending its wall description to be more instructive), but the Met declined to do either. See Ginia Bellafante, "We Need to Talk about Balthus," *New York Times*, December 8, 2017, https://www.nytimes.com/2017/12/08/nyregion/we-need-to-talk-about-balthus.html.

7. The decision *FCC v. Pacifica Foundation* (1978) empowered the FCC to prohibit what it deems obscene, indecent, or profane language from terrestrial radio and network television broadcasts in the interest of shielding underage listeners, and to penalize broadcasters accordingly. Follow-up rulings established the "safe harbor" window (when children can be reasonably expected not to be listening).

8. See Scott Bomboy, "Looking Back: George Carlin and the Supreme Court," *Constitution Daily*, July 3, 2018, https://constitutioncenter.org/blog/george-carlin-and-the-supreme-court-36-years-later.

9. Julie Peakman, *The Pleasure's All Mine: A History of Perverse Sex* (London: Reaktion, 2013), 7.

10. Ann V. Murphy, *Violence and the Philosophical Imaginary* (Albany: State University of New York Press, 2012), 67–68. See also Anu Koivunen, Katariina Kyrölä, and Ingrid Ryberg, *The Power of Vulnerability: Mobilising Affect in Feminist, Queer, and Anti-Racist Media Cultures* (Manchester: Manchester University Press, 2019).

11. Amanda Hess, "How the Myth of the Artistic Genius Excuses the Abuse of Women," *New York Times*, November 10, 2017, https://www.nytimes.com/2017/11/10/arts/sexual-harassment-art-hollywood.html.

12. Iyer made this statement in praise of the novels of Graham Greene. Pico Iyer, "The Humanity We Can't Relinquish," *New York Times*, August 11, 2018, https://www.nytimes.com/2018/08/11/opinion/sunday/the-humanity-we-cant-relinquish.html.

13. Gaspar Noé, "I'm Happy Some People Walk Out during My Film. It Makes the Ones Who Stay Feel Strong," *Guardian*, March 12, 1999, https://www.theguardian.com/film/1999/mar/12/features3.

14. Jason Zinoman, "Political Correctness Isn't Ruining Comedy. It's Helping," *New York Times*, October 20, 2015, https://www.nytimes.com/2015/10/21/arts/television/political-correctness-isnt-ruining-comedy-its-helping.html.

15. Noé, "I'm Happy Some People Walk Out."

16. Quoted in Hess, "How the Myth of the Artistic Genius Excuses the Abuse of Women."

17. Manohla Dargis and A. O. Scott, "Hollywood on the Brink," *New York Times*, January 3, 2018, https://www.nytimes.com/2018/01/03/movies/hollywood-on-the-brink.html.

18. See, for example, David Sims, "How Louis C.K. Used Comedy as a Smokescreen," *Atlantic*, November 13, 2017, https://www.theatlantic.com/entertainment/archive/2017/11/how-louis-ck-used-comedy-as-a-smokescreen/545681/.

19. See Linda Williams, "Cinema's Sex Acts," *Film Quarterly* 67, no. 4 (2014): 9–25.

20. See Jeffrey Sconce, "Irony, Nihilism, and the New American 'Smart Film,'" *Screen* 43, no. 4 (Winter 2002): 249–69.

21. Judy Berman, "'Nanette' Is the Most Discussed Comedy Special in Ages. Here's What to Read about It," *New York Times*, July 13, 2018, https://www.nytimes.com/2018/07/13/arts/television/nanette-hannah-gadsby-netflix-roundup.html.

22. Quoted in Maureen Dowd, "Dirty Words from Pretty Mouths," *New York Times*, February 28, 2015, https://www.nytimes.com/2015/03/01/opinion/sunday/maureen-dowd-dirty-words-from-pretty-mouths.html.

23. Lauren Berlant, "The Predator and the Jokester," *New Inquiry*, December 13, 2017, https://thenewinquiry.com/the-predator-and-the-jokester/.

24. Mette Hjort, "The Problem with Provocation: On Lars von Trier, Enfant Terrible of Danish Art Film," *Kinema: A Journal of Film and Audiovisual Media*, 2011, https://doi.org/10.15353/kinema.vi.1236.

25. Verhoeven quoted in interview by Claire Vassé, *Elle* press kit, 2016, https://www.festival-cannes.com/en/films/elle.

26. Rachel Donadio, "'Elle,' Starring Isabelle Huppert as a Rape Victim Who Turns the Tables, Rivets Critics," *New York Times*, June 3, 2016, https://www.nytimes.com/2016/06/04/movies/elle-starring-isabelle-huppert-as-a-rape-victim-who-turns-the-tables-rivets-critics.html.

27. Verhoeven (quoting Huppert) quoted in Vassé, *Elle* press kit; Hjort, "The Problem with Provocation."

28. See Michael Nordine, "'Elle' Review Roundup: Paul Verhoeven's Controversial Return Draws Universal Acclaim for Isabelle Huppert," *Indiewire*, May 22, 2016, https://www.indiewire.com/2016/05/elle-review-roundup-paul-verhoevens-controversial-return-draws-universal-acclaim-for-isabelle-huppert-289025/.

29. See Richard Dyer, "Resistance through Charisma: Rita Hayworth and *Gilda*," in *Women and Film Noir*, new ed., ed. E. Ann Kaplan (London: BFI, 1998), 115–22.

30. See Kristen Roupenian, "Cat Person," *New Yorker*, December 11, 2017, https://www.newyorker.com/magazine/2017/12/11/cat-person.

31. Claire Fallon, "Why a *New Yorker* Short Story about Bad Sex Went Viral," *HuffPost*, December 11, 2017, https://www.huffpost.com/entry/new-yorker-cat-person-short-story_n_5a2f0389e4b01598ac475cfb.

32. Patricia Lockwood, "Rape Joke," *The Awl*, July 25, 2013, https://www.theawl.com/2013/07/patricia-lockwood-rape-joke/.

33. Brian McNair, *Striptease Culture: Sex, Media and the Democratization of Desire* (New York: Routledge, 2002), 81, 98.

34. Jia Tolentino, "The Personal-Essay Boom Is Over," *New Yorker*, May 18, 2017, https://www.newyorker.com/culture/jia-tolentino/the-personal-essay-boom-is-over.

35. Zygmunt Bauman, *Consuming Life* (Cambridge: Polity, 2007), 3.

36. See Estelle Tang, "Enjoy Seeing Men Spectacularly Miss the Point of That Viral 'Cat Person' Story," *Elle*, December 11, 2017, https://www.elle.com/culture/books/a14406222/men-respond-cat-person-kristen-roupenian/.

37. Feona Attwood, "Sexed Up: Theorizing the Sexualization of Culture," *Sexualities* 9, no. 1 (2006): 84.

38. Matilda Dixon-Smith, "*Cat Person* Is Familiar to Women Who Feel Powerless to Stop a Sexual Encounter," *Guardian*, December 11, 2017, https://www.theguardian.com/commentisfree/2017/dec/12/feeling-powerless-to-stop-a-sexual-encounter-cat-person-is-familiar-to-many-women.

39. Julianne Escobedo Shepherd, "Babe, What Are You Doing?" *Jezebel*, January 16, 2018, https://jezebel.com/babe-what-are-you-doing-1822114753. Some found that missed potential recaptured in the release of and response to the 2019 stand-up special *Aziz Ansari: Right Now*, in which Ansari addressed at length the incident and its aftermath.

40. Laura Kipnis, *Unwanted Advances: Sexual Paranoia Comes to Campus* (New York: Harper, 2017), 5, 17.

41. Although I wrote this manuscript beforehand, my tenure was conferred before the book went into production.

42. Kipnis, *Unwanted Advances*, 33–34.

43. Roger Ebert, "Ebert's Walk of Fame Remarks," *RogerEbert.com*, June 24, 2005, https://www.rogerebert.com/rogers-journal/eberts-walk-of-fame-remarks.

BIBLIOGRAPHY

Aftab, Kaleem. "*Blue Is the Warmest Colour* Actresses on Their Lesbian Sex Scenes: 'We Felt Like Prostitutes.'" *Independent* (London), October 4, 2013. https://www.independent.co.uk/arts-entertainment/films/features/blue-is-the-warmest-colour-actresses-on-their-lesbian-sex-scenes-we-felt-like-prostitutes-8856909.html.

Akhavan, Desiree. "Desiree Akhavan (Appropriate Behaviour) on High Art." Filmed March 12, 2015, at BFI Flare: London LGBTQ Film Festival, London. Video, 5:29. https://www.youtube.com/watch?v=fDacKuo1pgU.

———. "What Is Appropriate Behavior?" Dr. S. T. Lee Distinguished Lecture in the Humanities, Penn Humanities Forum, University of Pennsylvania, Philadelphia, September 16, 2015.

Akhavan, Desiree, and Emily Danforth. "'Miseducation of Cameron Post' Creators Take Aim at Gay Conversion Therapy." Interview by Terry Gross. *Fresh Air*, NPR, July 25, 2018. Audio, 43:43. https://www.npr.org/2018/07/25/632242898/miseducation-of-cameron-post-creators-take-aim-at-gay-conversion-therapy.

Alcamo, Jess. "Appropriate Behavior—An Interview with Writer/Director Desiree Akhavan." 4:3, June 15, 2014. https://fourthreefilm.com/2014/06/appropriate-behavior-an-interview-with-writerdirector-desiree-akhavan/.

Anderson, Ariston. "Asia Argento Fires Back After Catherine Breillat Defends Harvey Weinstein." *Hollywood Reporter*, March 31, 2018. https://www.hollywoodreporter.com/news/asia-argento-fires-back-catherine-breillat-defends-harvey-weinstein-1098829.

Anderson, John. "'The Slap' Review: A Show You'll Love to Hate." *Wall Street Journal*, February 5, 2015. https://www.wsj.com/articles/the-slap-review-a-show-youll-love-to-hate-1423180421.

Angelo, Adrienne. "Sexual Cartographies: Mapping Subjectivity in the Cinema of Catherine Breillat." *Journal for Cultural Research* 14, no. 1 (2010): 43–55.

Anton, Saul. "Interview: Catherine Breillat Opens Up about 'Romance,' Sex and Censorship." *Indiewire*, September 23, 1999. https://www.indiewire.com/1999/09/interview-catherine-breillat-opens-up-about-romance-sex-and-censorship-82059/.

Attwood, Feona. "Art School Sluts: Authenticity and the Aesthetics of Alt-porn." In *Hard to Swallow: Hard-Core Pornography on Screen*, edited by Claire Hines and Darren Kerr, 42–56. London: Wallflower, 2012.

———. "Sexed Up: Theorizing the Sexualization of Culture." *Sexualities* 9, no. 1 (2006): 77–94.

Austerlitz, Saul. "Same Sex—With the Same Family Issues." *Boston Globe*, July 11, 2010. http://archive.boston.com/ae/movies/articles/2010/07/11/lisa_cholodenko_wanted_her_film_the_kids_are_all_right_to_reflect_every_family_and_every_familys_individual_vulnerabilities/.

Bakare, Lanre. "Mark Duplass: 'There's No Excuse Not to Make Films on Weekends with Friends.'" *Guardian*, March 15, 2015. https://www.theguardian.com/film/2015/mar/15/mark-duplass-south-by-southwest-sxsw.

Barnes, Brooks. "At Sundance, a Focus on Fetishes and Flatulence." *New York Times*, January 24, 2016. https://www.nytimes.com/2016/01/25/movies/at-sundance-a-focus-on-fetishes-and-flatulence.html?emc=edit_th_20160125&nl=todaysheadlines&nlid=6998640&_r=0.

Bataille, Georges. *Erotism: Death and Sensuality*. Translated by Mary Dalwood. San Francisco: City Lights, 1986.

Bauman, Zygmunt. *Consuming Life*. Cambridge: Polity, 2007.

Beardsworth, Liz. "What to Say about *Stranger by the Lake*." *Empire*, February 21, 2014. https://www.empireonline.com/movies/features/say-strangers-lake/.

Beirne, Rebecca. "New Queer Cinema 2.0? Lesbian-Focused Films and the Internet." *Screen* 55, no. 1 (Spring 2014): 129–38.

Bellafante, Ginia. "We Need to Talk about Balthus." *New York Times*, December 8, 2017. https://www.nytimes.com/2017/12/08/nyregion/we-need-to-talk-about-balthus.html.

Belmont, Cynthia. "Has Queer Culture Lost Its Edge?" *Salon*, August 6, 2017. https://www.salon.com/2017/08/06/has-queer-culture-lost-its-edge/.

Bendix, Trish. "Ingrid Jungermann and Desiree Akhavan on 'The Slope' and Writing Funny Lesbian Jokes." *AfterEllen*, March 30, 2012. https://www.afterellen.com/people/99781-ingrid-jungermann-and-desiree-akhavan-on-the-slope-and-writing-funny-lesbian-jokes/3#DOKXGGtj5OK2z3EU.99.

Benshoff, Harry M. "(Broke)back to the Mainstream: Queer Theory and Queer Cinemas Today." In *Film Theory and Contemporary Hollywood Movies*, edited by Warren Buckland, 192–213. New York: Routledge, 2009.

Berlant, Lauren. "The Predator and the Jokester." *New Inquiry*, December 13, 2017. https://thenewinquiry.com/the-predator-and-the-jokester/.

Berlant, Lauren, and Michael Warner. "Sex in Public." *Critical Inquiry* 24, no. 2 (Winter 1998): 547–66.

Berman, Judy. "'Nanette' Is the Most Discussed Comedy Special in Ages. Here's What to Read about It." *New York Times*, July 13, 2018. https://www.nytimes.com/2018/07/13/arts/television/nanette-hannah-gadsby-netflix-roundup.html.

Bersani, Leo. *Is the Rectum a Grave? And Other Essays*. Chicago: University of Chicago Press, 2010.

Bertolucci, Bernardo. "Bertolucci par Bertolucci." Conversation moderated by Serge Toubiana and Jean-François Rauger. *Leçon de cinéma*, Cinémathèque Française, Paris, September 14, 2013. Video, 1:57:53. https://www.canal-u.tv/video/cinematheque_francaise/lecon_de_cinema_bertolucci_par_bertolucci.13144.

Best, Victoria, and Martin Crowley. *The New Pornographies: Explicit Sex in Recent French Fiction and Film*. Manchester: Manchester University Press, 2008.

Beugnet, Martine. *Cinema and Sensation: French Film and the Art of Transgression*. Edinburgh: Edinburgh University Press, 2007.

Billington, Alex. "First Look: Charlotte Gainsbourg in Lars von Trier's 'Nymphomaniac.'" *First Showing*, February 6, 2013. https://www.firstshowing.net/2013/first-look-charlotte-gainsbourg-in-lars-von-triers-nymphomaniac/.

Bilmes, Alex. "Inside Shame." *Esquire*, January 14, 2012. https://www.esquire.com/uk/culture/film/news/a965/the-long-read-inside-shame/.

Birkin, Jane, and Charlotte Gainsbourg. Conversation moderated by Dennis Lim. Film at Lincoln Center, New York, January 29, 2016. Accessed on *The Close-Up*, no. 69, February 3, 2016. Audio, 45:05. https://www.filmlinc.org/daily/the-close-up-jane-birkin-and-charlotte-gainsbourg/.

Blair, Elaine. "The Loves of Lena Dunham." *New York Review*, June 7, 2012. https://www.nybooks.com/articles/2012/06/07/loves-lena-dunham/.

Blay, Zeba. "The Way Lena Dunham Talks about Black Men Is Peak White Entitlement." *HuffPost*, September 6, 2016. https://www.huffpost.com/entry/the-way-lena-dunham-talks-about-black-men-is-peak-white-entitlement_n_57cecdfde4b0e60d31e00ebc.

Bomboy, Scott. "Looking Back: George Carlin and the Supreme Court." *Constitution Daily*, July 3, 2018. https://constitutioncenter.org/blog/george-carlin-and-the-supreme-court-36-years-later.

Borden, J. D. "John Waters on Caitlyn Jenner: 'We Can't Make Fun of Her?'" *Indiewire*, August 7, 2015. https://www.indiewire.com/2015/08/john-waters-on-caitlyn-jenner-we-cant-make-fun-of-her-241129/.

Bordo, Susan. *The Male Body: A New Look at Men in Public and Private*. New York: Farrar, Straus and Giroux, 1999.

Bordwell, David. "Art Cinema as a Mode of Film Practice." In *Film Theory and Criticism*, 7th ed., edited by Leo Braudy and Marshall Cohen, 649–57. New York: Oxford University Press, 2009.

Bradbury-Rance, Clara. "Querying Postfeminism in Lisa Cholodenko's *The Kids Are All Right*." In *Postfeminism and Contemporary Hollywood Cinema*, edited by Joel Gwynne and Nadine Muller, 27–43. Basingstoke, UK: Palgrave Macmillan, 2013.

Bradshaw, Peter. "Jack Nicholson's *Toni Erdmann* Remake: Seven Changes Hollywood Will Make." *Guardian*, February 8, 2017. https://www.theguardian.com/film/filmblog/2017/feb/08/jack-nicholsons-toni-erdmann-remake-seven-changes-hollywood-will-make.

Breslaw, Anna. "Director of *Girls* Porn Slams Lena Dunham for Being Too Conservative." *Jezebel*, June 1, 2013. https://jezebel.com/director-of-girls-porn-slams-lena-dunham-for-being-too-510837480.

Brooks, Jodi. "*The Kids Are All Right*, the Pursuits of Happiness, and the Spaces Between." *Camera Obscura* 29, no. 1 (2014): 110–35.

Bruni, Frank. "The Bleaker Sex." *New York Times*, April 1, 2012. https://www.nytimes.com/2012/04/01/opinion/sunday/bruni-the-bleaker-sex.html.

Buchanan, Kyle. "How to See Ben Affleck's Penis in *Gone Girl*." *Vulture*, October 1, 2014. https://www.vulture.com/2014/10/how-to-see-ben-affleck-nude-penis-gone-girl.html.

———. "Looking at 'Looking': How the HBO Series Reexamined Itself for Season 2." *New York*, December 29, 2014. https://www.vulture.com/2014/12/how-looking-reexamined-itself-for-season-2.html.

Buckingham, Peter, and Michael Gubbins (Sampo Media). "Insight Report: *Stranger by the Lake*." BFI, February 19, 2015. www.bfi.org.uk/sites/bfi.org.uk/files/downloads/bfi-insight-report-stranger-by-the-lake-2015-02-19.pdf.
Butler, Eleri. "Catherine Breillat: Anatomy of a Hard-Core Agitator." In *Peep Shows: Cult Film and the Cine-Erotic*, edited by Xavier Mendik, 57–69. London: Wallflower, 2012.
Butler, Judith. *Bodies That Matter: On the Discursive Limits of "Sex."* London: Routledge, 1993.
Capino, José B. "Seminal Fantasies: Wakefield Pool, Pornography, Independent Cinema and the Avant-Garde." In *Contemporary American Independent Film*, edited by Chris Holmlund and Justin Wyatt, 155–73. New York: Routledge, 2005.
Cauterucci, Christina. "The Far Right's Pedophilia Smear Campaign Is Working." *Slate*, July 25, 2018. https://slate.com/human-interest/2018/07/james-gunn-dan-harmon-mike-cernovich-the-far-rights-pedophilia-smear-campaign-is-working.html.
Cavitch, Max. "Sex after Death: Francois Ozon's Libidinal Invasions." *Screen* 48, no. 3 (Autumn 2007): 313–26.
Charles, RuPaul. "RuPaul Charles." Interview by Marc Maron. *WTF*, episode 498, May 19, 2014. Audio, 1:24:29. https://www.wtfpod.com/podcast/episodes/episode_498_-_rupaul_charles.
Christian, Aymar Jean. "Indie TV: Innovation in Series Development." In *Media Independence: Working with Freedom or Working for Free?* edited by James Bennett and Niki Strange, 159–81. New York: Routledge, 2014.
Cochrane, Kira. "Carey Mulligan: 'I Haven't Seen Myself in the Mirror for a Decade.'" *Guardian*, January 15, 2012. https://www.theguardian.com/film/2012/jan/15/carey-mulligan-naked-mirror-decade.
Coleman, Lindsay, ed. *Sex and Storytelling in Modern Cinema: Explicit Sex, Performance and Cinematic Technique*. New York: I. B. Tauris, 2016.
Coleman, Lindsay, and Carol Siegel, eds. *Intercourse in Television and Film: The Presentation of Explicit Sex Acts*. Lanham, MD: Lexington Books, 2018.
Constable, Liz. "Unbecoming Sexual Desires for Women Becoming Sexual Subjects: Simone de Beauvoir (1949) and Catherine Breillat (1999)." *MLN* 119, no. 4 (September 2004): 672–95.
Conway, Kelley. "Sexually Explicit French Cinema: Genre, Gender, and Sex." In *A Companion to French Cinema*, edited by Alistair Fox,

Michel Marie, Raphaëlle Moine, and Hilary Radner, 461–80. Malden, MA: Wiley-Blackwell, 2015.

Corliss, Richard. "Films That Are Good in Bed." *Time*, November 18, 2001. http://content.time.com/time/magazine/article/0,9171,184984,00.html.

———. "Sex and *Shame* in Venice: Michael Fassbender Is a Real X-Man." *Time*, September 5, 2011. http://content.time.com/time/arts/article/0,8599,2091805,00.html.

Corrigan, Timothy. *A Cinema without Walls: Movies and Culture after Vietnam*. New Brunswick, NJ: Rutgers University Press, 1991.

———. "The Commerce of Auteurism: Coppola, Kluge, Ruiz." In *A Cinema without Walls: Movies and Culture after Vietnam*, 101–36. New Brunswick, NJ: Rutgers University Press, 1991.

Cox, Fiona. "Fab Lesbianism and Family Values: Costuming of Lesbian Identities in *The L Word* and *The Kids Are All Right*." In *Fashion Cultures Revisited: Theories, Explorations, and Analysis*, 2nd ed., edited by Stella Bruzzi and Pamela Church Gibson, 249–60. New York: Routledge, 2013.

Crenshaw, Kimberlé Williams. "Mapping the Margins: Intersectionality, Identity Politics, and Violence against Women of Color." *Stanford Law Review* 43, no. 6 (July 1991): 1241–99.

Daalmans, Serena. "'I'm Busy Trying to Become Who I Am': Self-Entitlement and the City in HBO's *Girls*." *Feminist Media Studies* 13, no. 2 (2013): 359–62.

D'Acci, Julie. "Defining Women: The Case of *Cagney and Lacey*." In *Private Screenings: Television and the Female Consumer*, edited by Lynn Spigel and Denise Mann, 168–201. Minneapolis: University of Minnesota Press, 1992.

Dargis, Manohla. "Is Lars von Trier Trolling Us?" *New York Times*, May 16, 2018. https://www.nytimes.com/2018/05/16/movies/lars-von-trier-the-house-that-jack-built-cannes-film-festival.html.

———. "Seeing You Seeing Me: The Trouble with 'Blue Is the Warmest Color.'" *New York Times*, October 25, 2013. https://www.nytimes.com/2013/10/27/movies/the-trouble-with-blue-is-the-warmest-color.html.

Dargis, Manohla, and A. O. Scott. "Hollywood on the Brink." *New York Times*, January 3, 2018. https://www.nytimes.com/2018/01/03/movies/hollywood-on-the-brink.html.

Das, Lina. "I Felt Raped by Brando." *Daily Mail* (UK), July 19, 2007. https://www.dailymail.co.uk/tvshowbiz/article-469646/I-felt-raped-Brando.html.

Daum, Meghan. "Lena Dunham Is Not Done Confessing." *New York Times*, September 10, 2014. https://www.nytimes.com/2014/09/14/magazine/lena-dunham.html?_r=0.

Davidson, Alex. "Bisexual Healing: Desiree Akhavan on Appropriate Behavior." British Film Institute, June 24, 2015. https://www.bfi.org.uk/news-opinion/news-bfi/interviews/bisexual-healing-desiree-akhavan-appropriate-behaviour.

Davies, Ben, and Jana Funke, eds. *Sex, Gender, and Time in Fiction and Culture*. Basingstoke, UK: Palgrave Macmillan, 2011.

Dawson, Nick. "Desiree Akhavan and Ingrid Jungermann." *Filmmaker*, 25 New Faces of 2012, 2012. https://filmmakermagazine.com/people/desiree-akhavan-and-ingrid-jungermann/#.WXilPIqQxsM.

Dean, Tim. *Unlimited Intimacy: Reflections on the Subculture of Barebacking*. Chicago: University of Chicago Press, 2009.

Dixon-Smith, Matilda. "*Cat Person* Is Familiar to Women Who Feel Powerless to Stop a Sexual Encounter." *Guardian*, December 11, 2017. https://www.theguardian.com/commentisfree/2017/dec/12/feeling-powerless-to-stop-a-sexual-encounter-cat-person-is-familiar-to-many-women.

Doane, Mary Ann. "Film and the Masquerade: Theorising the Female Spectator." In *The Sexual Subject: A Screen Reader on Sexuality*, 227–43. New York: Routledge, 1992.

Donadio, Rachel. "'Elle,' Starring Isabelle Huppert as a Rape Victim Who Turns the Tables, Rivets Critics." *New York Times*, June 3, 2016. https://www.nytimes.com/2016/06/04/movies/elle-starring-isabelle-huppert-as-a-rape-victim-who-turns-the-tables-rivets-critics.html.

Doty, Alexander. *Flaming Classics: Queering the Film Canon*. New York: Routledge, 2000.

Dowd, Maureen. "Dirty Words from Pretty Mouths." *New York Times*, February 28, 2015. https://www.nytimes.com/2015/03/01/opinion/sunday/maureen-dowd-dirty-words-from-pretty-mouths.html.

Dry, Jude. "Alia Shawkat Made 'Duck Butter' Queer after Male Actors 'Seemed Uncomfortable' with Intimate Sex Scenes." *Indiewire*, April 27, 2018. https://www.indiewire.com/2018/04/duck-butter-alia-shawkat-lesbian-sex-scenes-1201957653/.

Duggan, Lisa. "The New Homonormativity: The Sexual Politics of Neoliberalism." In *Materializing Democracy: Toward a Revitalized Cultural Politics*, edited by Ross Castronovo and Dana D. Nelson, 175–94. Durham, NC: Duke University Press, 2002.

Duggan, Lisa, with Kathryn Bond Stockton. "Only the Kids Are All Right." *Bully Bloggers*, July 30, 2010. https://bullybloggers.wordpress.com/2010/07/30/only-the-kids-are-all-right/.

Dunham, Lena. "Harvey Weinstein and the Silence of Men." *New York Times*, October 9, 2017. https://www.nytimes.com/2017/10/09/opinion/harvey-weinstein-lena-dunham-silence-.html.

———. "Lena Dunham on Sex, Oversharing and Writing about Lost 'Girls.'" Interview with Terry Gross, *Fresh Air*, NPR, September 29, 2014. Audio, 44:59. https://www.npr.org/templates/transcript/transcript.php?storyId=352276798.

———. *Not That Kind of Girl: A Young Woman Tells You What She's "Learned."* New York: Random House, 2014.

———. "One of a Kind," *Lenny*, letter no. 72, February 7, 2017. http://independentonlinenewsreporter.blogspot.com/2017/02/lena-dunhams-sexual-healing.html.

———. "Retouched by an Angel," *Lenny*, letter no. 24, March 8, 2016. https://www.lennyletter.com/story/lena-dunham-doesnt-want-her-photos-retouched.

Durnell, David. "Woman's Body as an Anatomy of Hell: Nihilism, Recursion and Tragedy in Breillat's *Anatomy of Hell*." *OffScreen* 10, no. 7 (July 2016). https://offscreen.com/view/anatomy_of_hell.

Dyer, Richard. *Only Entertainment*, 2nd ed. New York: Routledge, 2002.

———. "Resistance through Charisma: Rita Hayworth and *Gilda*." In *Women and Film Noir*, new ed., edited by E. Ann Kaplan, 115–22. London: BFI, 1998.

Ebert, Roger. "Ebert's Walk of Fame Remarks." *RogerEbert.com*, June 24, 2005. https://www.rogerebert.com/rogers-journal/eberts-walk-of-fame-remarks.

Edelman, Lee. *No Future: Queer Theory and the Death Drive*. Durham, NC: Duke University Press, 2004.

Eggers, Dave. "A Cultural Vacuum in Trump's White House." *New York Times*, June 29, 2018. https://www.nytimes.com/2018/06/29/opinion/dave-eggers-culture-arts-trump.html.

Electrelane, "To the East." By Emma Gaze, Mia Clarke, Rosamund Jean Murray, Verity Susman, on *No Shouts No Calls*. BMG Music, 2016.

Ellis, Bret Easton. "In the Reign of the Gay Magical Elves." *Out*, May 13, 2013. https://www.out.com/news-opinion/2013/05/13/bret-easton-ellis-gay-men-magical-elves.

Erbland, Kate. "How 'Appropriate Behavior' Filmmaker Desiree Akhavan Avoided the Second-Film Slump by Getting the Hell out of

Hollywood." *Indiewire,* October 27, 2017. https://www.indiewire.com/2017/10/appropriate-behavior-desiree-akhavan-second-film-1201891367/.

Exarchopoulous, Adèle, and Léa Seydoux. "The Stars of 'Blue Is the Warmest Color' on the Riveting Lesbian Love Story." Interview by Marlow Stern, *Daily Beast,* September 1, 2013. http://www.thedailybeast.com/the-stars-of-blue-is-the-warmest-color-on-the-riveting-lesbian-love-story.

Fallon, Claire. "Why a *New Yorker* Short Story about Bad Sex Went Viral." *HuffPost,* December 11, 2017. https://www.huffpost.com/entry/new-yorker-cat-person-short-story_n_5a2f0389e4b01598ac475cfb.

Fallon, Kevin. "How *Looking* Helped Jonathan Groff to Like Being Gay." *Daily Beast,* July 20, 2016. http://www.thedailybeast.com/how-looking-helped-jonathan-groff-learn-to-like-being-gay.

Feidelson, Lizzie. "The Sex Scene Evolves for the #MeToo Era." *New York Times,* January 14, 2020. https://www.nytimes.com/2020/01/14/magazine/sex-scene-intimacy-coordinator.html?nl=todaysheadlines&emc=edit_th_200119?campaign_id=2&instance_id=15176&segment_id=20459&user_id=659d4416c49fb088c697ae5b351de3af&regi_id=69986400119.

Feeney, Nolan. "Netflix and On-Demand Aren't Killing 'Water-Cooler TV'—They're Saving It." *Atlantic,* September 30, 2013. https://www.theatlantic.com/entertainment/archive/2013/09/netflix-and-on-demand-arent-killing-water-cooler-tv-theyre-saving-it/280113/.

Fernandez, Maria Elena. "Why Full-Frontal Nudity Was All Over TV in 2015." *Vulture,* December 22, 2015. https://www.vulture.com/2015/12/full-frontal-male-nudity-was-all-over-tv-in-2015.html.

Foucault, Michel. *Discipline and Punish: The Birth of the Prison.* Translated by Alan Sheridan. New York: Pantheon, 1978.

———. *The History of Sexuality.* Vol. 1, *An Introduction.* Translated by Robert Hurley. New York: Random House, 1978.

Fouz-Hernández, Santiago, ed. *Mysterious Skin: Male Bodies in Contemporary Cinema.* London: I. B. Tauris, 2009.

Fox, Alistair. "The New Anglo-American Cinema of Sex Addiction." In *Transgression in Anglo-American Cinema: Gender, Sex and the Deviant Body,* edited by Joel Gwynne, 9–23. New York: Wallflower Press, 2016.

Fox-Kales, Emily. "*A ma soeur!* Erotic Bodies and the Primal Scene Reconfigured." *Journal for Cultural Research* 14, no. 1 (2010): 15–26.

Framke, Caroline. "How Bisexuality on TV Evolved from a Favorite Punchline to a Vital Storyline." *Vox,* May 16, 2018. https://www.vox

.com/culture/2018/5/16/17339992/bisexual-representation-tv-callie-rosa-darryl.

Freeman, Elizabeth. *Time Binds: Queer Temporalities, Queer Histories*. Durham, NC: Duke University Press, 2010.

Freeman, Hadley. "Desiree Akhavan on *Appropriate Behaviour* and Not Being the 'Iranian Bisexual Lena Dunham.'" *Guardian*, March 5, 2015. https://www.theguardian.com/film/2015/mar/05/desiree-akhavan-appropriate-behaviour-not-being-iranian-bisexual-lena-dunham.

Frey, Mattias. *Extreme Cinema: The Transgressive Rhetoric of Today's Art Film Culture*. New Brunswick, NJ: Rutgers University Press, 2016.

Fuchs, Cynthia J. "The Buddy Politic." In *Screening the Male: Exploring Masculinities in the Hollywood Cinema*, edited by Steven Cohan and Ina Rae Hark, 194–210. New York: Routledge, 1993.

Fuller, Sean, and Catherine Driscoll. "HBO's *Girls*: Gender, Generation, and Quality Television." *Continuum: Journal of Media and Cultural Studies* 29, no. 2 (2015): 253–62.

Fung, Richard. "Looking for My Penis: The Eroticized Asian in Gay Video Porn." In *How Do I Look? Queer Film and Video*, edited by Bad Object-Choices, 145–68. Seattle: Bay Press, 1991.

Gay, Roxane. *Bad Feminists: Essays*. New York: Harper Perennial, 2014.

Gettell, Oliver. "Ryan Reynolds on the Man Who Made His 'Penis Look Perfect' in *Deadpool*." *Entertainment Weekly*, February 10, 2016. https://ew.com/article/2016/02/10/ryan-reynolds-deadpool-makeup-penis-look-perfect/.

Glenn, Clinton. "British Social Realism and Queerness in Andrew Haigh's *Looking* (2011)." *Journal of Interdisciplinary Studies in Sexuality* 1 (2013): 75–83.

Goldman, Andrew. "Grumpus Maximus." *New York Times*, June 17, 2011. https://www.nytimes.com/2011/06/19/magazine/inside-the-bald-angry-head-of-louis-ck.html.

Goudet, Stéphane, and Claire Vassé. "One Soul with Two Bodies: An Interview with Catherine Breillat." DVD notes on *Fat Girl*, Criterion Collection. Original interview appeared in *Positif*, no. 481 (March 2001): 26–30.

Greer, Germaine. "The Connection between Art and Exhibitionism." *Guardian*, January 28, 2008. https://www.theguardian.com/artanddesign/artblog/2008/jan/28/theconnectionbetweenartand.

Gwynne, Joel, ed. *Transgression in Anglo-American Cinema: Gender, Sex and the Deviant Body*. New York: Columbia University Press, 2016.

Hagland, David, and Daniel Engber. "Was That the Worst Episode of *Girls* Ever?" *Slate*, February 10, 2013. https://slate.com/culture/2013/02/girls-on-hbo-one-man-s-trash-episode-5-of-season-2-reviewed-by-guys.html.

Hahn, Kathryn. Interview by Jesse Thorn. *Bullseye*, Maximum Fun, December 6, 2019. Audio, 31:14. https://maximumfun.org/episodes/bullseye-with-jesse-thorn/kathryn-hahn/.

Halberstam, Jack. "The Kids Aren't Alright!" *Bully Bloggers*, July 15, 2010. https://bullybloggers.wordpress.com/2010/07/15/the-kids-arent-alright/.

———. *The Queer Art of Failure*. Durham, NC: Duke University Press, 2011.

Hale, Mike. "'Euphoria' Review: HBO Raises the Stakes on Teenage Transgression." *New York Times*, June 14, 2019. https://nyti.ms/2Xbf4AB.

Halperin, David M. *Saint Foucault: Towards a Gay Hagiography*. New York: Oxford University Press, 1995.

Hattenstone, Simon. "Lena Dunham: 'People Called Me Fat and Hideous, and I Lived.'" *Guardian*, January 10, 2014. https://www.theguardian.com/culture/2014/jan/11/lena-dunham-called-fat-hideous-and-i-lived.

Hazlett, Courtney. "Lena Dunham Explains Her Thighs—And the 'No-Pants' Look." *Today*, October 9, 2012. https://www.today.com/entertainment/lena-dunham-explains-her-thighs-no-pants-look-1C6358990?franchiseSlug=todayentertainmentmain.

Henderson, Lisa. "Simple Pleasures: Lesbian Community and *Go Fish*." *Signs* 25, no. 1 (1999): 37–64.

Hess, Amanda. "How the Myth of the Artistic Genius Excuses the Abuse of Women." *New York Times*, November 10, 2017. https://www.nytimes.com/2017/11/10/arts/sexual-harassment-art-hollywood.html.

———. "'I Feel Pretty' and the Rise of Beauty-Standard Denialism." *New York Times*, April 23, 2018. https://www.nytimes.com/2018/04/23/movies/i-feel-pretty-amy-schumer-beauty.html?login=email&auth=login-email.

———. "The Lustful Middle School Girl Rises." *New York Times*, February 22, 2019. https://www.nytimes.com/2019/02/22/movies/pen15-eighth-grade-middle-school-girls.html.

Hester, Helen. "Perverting the Explicit: Catherine Breillat's Visual Vocabulary of Desire." In *Tainted Love: Screening Sexual Perversion*, edited by Darren Kerr and Donna Peberdy, 47–62. London: I. B. Tauris, 2017.

Hiatt, Brian. "Girl on Top." *Rolling Stone*, February 28, 2013. https://www.rollingstone.com/movies/movie-news/lena-dunham-girl-on-top-237146/.

Himberg, Julia. "Multicasting: Lesbian Programming and the Changing Landscape of Cable TV." *Television and New Media* 15, no. 4 (2014): 289–304.

Hirsch, Foster. *Detours and Lost Highways: A Map of Neo-Noir*. New York: Limelight, 1999.

Hjort, Mette. "The Problem with Provocation: On Lars von Trier, Enfant Terrible of Danish Art Film." *Kinema: A Journal of Film and Audiovisual Media*, 2011. https://doi.org/10.15353/kinema.vi.1236.

Horek, Tanya, and Tina Kendall, eds. *The New Extremism in Cinema: From France to Europe*. Edinburgh: Edinburgh University Press, 2013.

Hornaday, Ann. "Sex Is Disappearing from the Big Screen, and It's Making Movies Less Pleasurable." *Washington Post*, June 7, 2009. https://www.washingtonpost.com/lifestyle/style/sex-is-disappearing-from-the-big-screen-and-its-making-movies-less-pleasurable/2019/06/06/37848090-82ed-11e9-933d-7501070ee669_story.html?utm_term=.8d9441e694d5.

Illouz, Eva. *Hard-Core Romance*: Fifty Shades of Grey, *Best-Sellers, and Society*. Chicago: University of Chicago Press, 2014.

Iyer, Pico. "The Humanity We Can't Relinquish." *New York Times*, August 11, 2018. https://www.nytimes.com/2018/08/11/opinion/sunday/the-humanity-we-cant-relinquish.html.

Jagernauth, Kevin. "'Blue Is the Warmest Color' Director Says the Film Shouldn't Be Released and He Thought of Replacing Léa Seydoux." *Indiewire*, September 24, 2013. http://www.indiewire.com/2013/09/blue-is-the-warmest-color-director-says-the-film-shouldnt-be-released-he-thought-of-replacing-lea-seydoux-93327/.

James, Nick. "Looks That Paralyze." *Sight and Sound* 11, no. 12 (2001): 20.

Jameson, Fredric. *Postmodernism, or, the Cultural Logic of Late Capitalism*. Durham, NC: Duke University Press, 1991.

———. *Signatures of the Visible*. New York: Routledge, 1990.

Johnson, Barbara. *A World of Difference*. Baltimore: Johns Hopkins University Press, 1987.

Johnson, Lauren. "This GIF Shows You Just How Photoshopped Justin Bieber's Calvin Klein Ads Were." *Adweek*, January 9, 2015. https://

www.adweek.com/creativity/gif-shows-you-just-how-photoshopped
-justin-biebers-calvin-klein-ads-were-162280/.

Johnson, Liza. "Perverse Angle: Feminist Film, Queer Film, Shame." In "Beyond the Gaze: Recent Approaches to Film Feminisms," edited by Kathleen McHugh and Vivian Sobchack. Special issue, *Signs* 30, no. 1 (Autumn 2004): 1361–84.

Juhasz, Alexandra. "The Phallus UnFetishized: The End of Masculinity as We Know It in Late-1990s 'Feminist' Cinema." In *The End of Cinema as We Know It: American Film in the Nineties*, edited by Jon Lewis, 210–21. New York: New York University Press, 2001.

Jung, E. Alex. "*Westworld's* Simon Quarterman Thinks Every Actor Should Try Full-Frontal Nudity." *Vulture*, April 22, 2018. https://www.vulture.com/2018/04/westworld-season-2-simon-quarterman-interview.html.

Juzwiak, Rich. "*Looking*? Mmmmm, Maybe Another Time." *Gawker*, January 17, 2014. https://gawker.com/looking-mmmmm-maybe-another-time-1502622759.

Kachka, Boris. "Desiree Akhavan Wants to Move Beyond the 'Bisexual Persian Lena Dunham' Tag." *Vulture*, January 11, 2015. https://www.vulture.com/2015/01/desiree-akhavan-girls-appropriate-behavior.html.

Kang, Inkoo. "Catherine Breillat to Make First English-Language Film." *Indiewire*, May 20, 2014. https://womenandhollywood.com/catherine-breillat-to-make-first-english-language-film-3c87fa5fccaa/.

Keesey, Douglas. *Catherine Breillat*. Manchester: Manchester University Press, 2015.

———. "They Kill for Love: Defining the Erotic Thriller as a Film Genre." *CineAction* no. 56 (2001): 44–53.

Kelso, Tony. "And Now No Word from Our Sponsor: How HBO Puts the Risk Back into Television." In *It's Not TV: Watching HBO in the Post-Television Era*, edited by Marc Leverette, Brian L. Ott, and Cara Louise Buckley, 46–64. New York: Routledge, 2008.

Kerner, Aaron Michael, and Jonathan L. Knapp, eds. *Extreme Cinema: Affective Strategies in Transnational Media*. Edinburgh: Edinburgh University Press, 2016.

Kerr, Darren, and Donna Peberdy, eds. *Tainted Love: Screening Sexual Perversion*. New York: I. B. Tauris, 2017.

"'The Kids Are All Right': HBO Still Considering Series." *HuffPost TV*, August 1, 2012. https://www.huffpost.com/entry/the-kids-are-all-right-hbo-series_n_1730584.

Kinser, Jeremy. "Looking's Daniel Franzese on His HIV-Positive Bear Character, Being Completely Naked on Screen and Why He Came Out Publicly." *Queerty*, January 11, 2015. https://www.queerty.com/lookings-dan-franzese-on-his-hiv-positive-bear-character-being-completely-naked-on-screen-and-why-he-came-out-publicly-20150111.

Kipnis, Laura. "Sexual Paranoia Strikes Academe." *Chronicle of Higher Education*, February 27, 2015. https://www.chronicle.com/article/Sexual-Paranoia-Strikes/190351.

———. *Unwanted Advances: Sexual Paranoia Comes to Campus*. New York: Harper, 2017.

Knegt, Peter. "'Looking' in the Mirror: Mourning the Loss of Television's Great Gay Catharsis." *Indiewire*, March 25, 2015. https://www.indiewire.com/2015/03/looking-in-the-mirror-mourning-the-loss-of-televisions-great-gay-catharsis-215569/.

Kohn, Eric. "'Holiday' Review: Devastating Danish Drama Has the Most Unsettling Rape Scene Since 'Irreversible'—Sundance 2018." *Indiewire*, January 26, 2018. https://www.indiewire.com/2018/01/holiday-review-isabella-eklof-rape-sundance-2018-1201921797/.

Koivunen, Anu, Katariina Kyrölä, and Ingrid Ryberg, eds. *The Power of Vulnerability: Mobilising Affect in Feminist, Queer, and Anti-Racist Media Cultures*. Manchester: Manchester University Press, 2019.

Konstantinovsky, Michelle. "Why Lena Dunham's Body Matters (And Why It's Ridiculous That It Does)." *Hello Giggles*, April 26, 2012. https://www.huffpost.com/entry/why-lena-dunhams-body-matters_n_1458765.

Kramer, Larry. *The Tragedy of Today's Gays*. New York: Tarcher, 2005.

Kristeva, Julia. *Powers of Horror: An Essay on Abjection*. Translated by Leon S. Roudiez. New York: Columbia University Press, 1982.

Krutnik, Frank. "Love Lies: Romantic Fabrication in Contemporary Romantic Comedy." In *Terms of Endearment: Hollywood Romantic Comedy of the 1980s and 1990s*, edited by Peter William Evans and Celestino Deleyto, 15–36. Edinburgh: Edinburgh University Press, 1998.

Krzywinska, Tanya. *Sex and the Cinema*. New York: Wallflower, 2006.

Kyrölä, Katariina. "Squirming in the Classroom: *Fat Girl* and the Ethical Value of Extreme Discomfort." In *Unwatchable*, edited by Nicholas Baer, Maggie Hennefeld, and Laura Horak, 317–22. New Brunswick, NJ: Rutgers University Press, 2019.

Lane, Anthony. "New Love." *New Yorker*, October 28, 2013. https://www.newyorker.com/magazine/2013/10/28/new-love.

Lattanzio, Ryan. "From Gaspar Noé to Jeremy Saulnier, Cinema Provocateurs Head to Toronto." *Indiewire*, August 11, 2015. https://www.indiewire.com/2015/08/from-gaspar-noe-to-jeremy-saulnier-cinema-provocateurs-head-to-toronto-185575/.

———. "'Girls' Creator Lena Dunham Poses for Playboy and Answers 20 Questions." *Indiewire*, March 14, 2013. https://www.indiewire.com/2013/03/girls-creator-lena-dunham-poses-for-playboy-and-answers-20-questions-198982/.

de Lauretis, Teresa. "Queer Texts, Bad Habits, and the Issue of a Future." *GLQ* 17, no. 2–3 (2011): 243–63.

Lehman, Peter. "Crying Over the Melodramatic Penis: Melodrama and Male Nudity in Films of the 90s." In *Masculinity: Bodies, Movies, Culture*, edited by Peter Lehman, 25–41. New York: Routledge, 2001.

———. *Running Scared: Masculinity and the Representation of the Male Body*, new ed. Detroit: Wayne State University Press, 2007.

Lehman, Peter, and Susan Hunt. "*Californication*: Trouble in Body Guy Paradise." *Flow*, 2008. www.flowjournal.org/2008/12/californication-trouble-in-body-guy-paradise-peter-lehman-arizona-state-university-susan-hunt-santa-monica-college/.

———. "From Casual to Melodramatic: Changing Representations of the Penis in Films of the 70s and 90s." *Framework* 40 (Spring 1999): 69–84.

———. *Lady Chatterley's Legacy in the Movies: Sex, Brains, and Body Guys*. New Brunswick, NJ: Rutgers University Press, 2010.

"Lena Dunham Apologises for Defending *Girls* Writer Accused of Sexual Assault." *Guardian*, November 19, 2017. https://www.theguardian.com/culture/2017/nov/20/lena-dunham-apologises-for-defending-girls-writer-accused-of-sexual-assault.

Letort, Delphine. "Age and Gender in the Minseries Adaptation of Elizabeth Strout's *Olive Kitteridge*." *Adaptation* 9, no. 1 (2015): 86–97.

Leverette, Marc. "Cocksucker, Motherfucker, Tits." In *It's Not TV: Watching HBO in the Post-Television Era*, edited by Marc Leverette, Brian L. Ott, and Cara Louise Buckley, 123–51. New York: Routledge, 2008.

Leverette, Marc, Brian L. Ott, and Cara Louise Buckley, eds. *It's Not TV: Watching HBO in the Post-Television Era*. New York: Routledge, 2008.

Levine, Nick. "Desiree Akhavan Q&A on Appropriate Behaviour, Sex Scenes and Changing How Marginalised Communities Are Depicted in Film." *NME*, March 5, 2015. https://www.nme.com/blogs/nme-blogs/desiree-akhavan-qa-on-appropriate-behaviour-sex-scenes-and-changing-how-marginalised-communities-are-17916.

Lewis, Jon. *Hollywood v. Hard Core: How the Struggle over Censorship Created the Modern Film Industry.* New York: New York University Press, 2002.

———. "Real Sex: Aesthetics and Economics of Art-House Porn." *Jump Cut,* no. 51, Spring 2009. http://www.ejumpcut.org/archive/jc51.2009/LewisRealsex/index.html.

Lockwood, Patricia. "Rape Joke." *The Awl,* July 25, 2013, https://www.theawl.com/2013/07/patricia-lockwood-rape-joke/.

Loist, Skadi. "Crossover Dreams: Global Circulation of Queer Film on the Film Festival Circuits." *Diogenes,* November 7, 2016: 1–16. https://doi.org/10.1177/0392192115667014.

Lowder, J. Bryan. "Why Is *Looking* So Boring?" *Slate,* January 21, 2014. www.slate.com/blogs/outward/2014/01/21/looking_hbo_s_gay_show_is_boring_and_bad_for_gays_straights.html.

Lucia, Cynthia, and Richard Porton. "Gay Family Values: An Interview with Lisa Cholodenko." *Cineaste* 35, no. 4 (Fall 2010): 14–18.

Lunceford, Brett. *Naked Politics: Nudity, Political Action, and the Rhetoric of the Body.* Lanham, MD: Lexington Books, 2012.

Lyons, Margaret. "Lesbians Are Having the Best Summer Ever on TV." *Vulture,* July 25, 2013. https://www.vulture.com/2013/07/lesbians-are-having-the-best-summer-ever-on-tv.html.

Maciak, Philip. "The *Girls* Finale." *Los Angeles Review of Books,* April 24, 2017. https://lareviewofbooks.org/article/the-girls-finale/#!.

Macnab, Geoffrey. "Sadean Woman." *Sight and Sound* 14, no. 12 (2004): 20–22.

Manjoo, Farhad. "We Have Reached Peak Screen: Now Revolution Is in the Air." *New York Times,* June 27, 2018. https://www.nytimes.com/2018/06/27/technology/peak-screen-revolution.html.

Marcus, Stephanie. "Jon Hamm Asks That You Please Stop Talking about His Penis." *HuffPost,* April 23, 2014. https://www.huffpost.com/entry/jon-hamm-penis_n_5200589.

Margulies, Ivone. *Nothing Happens: Chantal Akerman's Hyperrealist Everyday.* Durham, NC: Duke University Press, 1996.

Marshall, Kelli. "The Anatomical Part Mysteriously Missing from 'Masters of Sex.'" *Alternet,* September 29, 2014.

Martin, Brett. *Difficult Men: Behind the Scenes of a Creative Revolution: From The Sopranos to The Wire to Mad Men and Breaking Bad.* New York: Penguin, 2013.

Martin, Nina K. *Sexy Thrills: Undressing the Erotic Thriller.* Urbana: University of Illinois Press, 2007.

Mason, Charlie. "*The Leftovers*' Boss: 'There's No Excuse Not to Show More Dongs' on Television." *TVLine*, June 4, 2017. https://tvline.com/2017/06/04/the-leftovers-justin-theroux-naked-nudity-full-frontal/.

Mayer, So. "In Praise of Soft Cock." *cléo: A Journal of Film and Feminism* 5, no. 1 (2017). cleojournal.com/2017/04/20/praise-soft-cock/.

———. *Political Animals: The New Feminist Cinema*. London: I. B. Tauris, 2015.

McCabe, Janet, and Kim Akass. "Sex, Swearing and Respectability: Courting Controversy, HBO's Original Programming and Producing Quality TV." In *Quality TV: Contemporary American Television and Beyond*, edited by Janet McCabe and Kim Akass, 62–76. London: I. B. Tauris, 2007.

McCammon, Ross. "Lena Dunham Is Building an Empire." *Esquire*, November 13, 2012. https://www.esquire.com/news-politics/a16688/lena-dunham-interview-1212/.

McClintock, Pamela. "Fassbender on Fire." *Hollywood Reporter*, January 18, 2012. https://www.hollywoodreporter.com/news/thr-cover-michael-fassbender-shame-nudity-dangerous-method-282859.

McDormand, Frances. "Like Olive Kitteridge, Actress Frances McDormand Was Tired of Supporting Roles." Interview by NPR Staff, *All Things Considered*, NPR, October 31, 2014. Audio, 8:10. https://www.npr.org/2014/10/31/360183633/like-olive-kitteridge-actress-frances-mcdormand-was-tired-of-supporting-roles.

McNair, Brian. *Striptease Culture: Sex, Media and the Democratization of Desire*. New York: Routledge, 2002.

McNutt, Myles. "Game of Thrones: 'The Night Lands' and Sexposition." *Cultural Learnings*, April 8, 2012. https://cultural-learnings.com/2012/04/08/game-of-thrones-the-night-lands-and-sexposition/.

Mercer, Kobena. "Black Art and the Burden of Representation." *Third Text* 4, no. 10 (1990): 61–78.

Merry, Stephanie. "Frances McDormand, Now in the Role of the Golden Globes Grumpy Cat." *Washington Post*, January 11, 2015. https://www.washingtonpost.com/news/arts-and-entertainment/wp/2015/01/11/frances-mcdormand-now-in-the-role-of-the-golden-globes-grumpy-cat/?utm_term=.100539d3c120.

Messi, Pamela. "Yahima Torres Talks about Her Role as Sarah Baartman in the Film by Abdellatif Kechiche." *African Women in Cinema*, November 7, 2010. https://africanwomenincinema.blogspot.com/2010/11/yahima-torres-talks-about-her-role-as.html.

Miller, Julie. "Tom Hardy Is Filming a Period Adventure Drama in the Nude." *Vanity Fair*, February 9, 2016. https://www.vanityfair.com/hollywood/2016/02/tom-hardy-nude-taboo.

Monaghan, Whitney. *Queer Girls, Temporality, and Screen Media: Not "Just a Phase."* Basingstoke, UK: Palgrave Macmillan, 2016.

Moore, Candace. "The D Word." In *Loving the L Word*, edited by Dana Heller, 191–207. London: I. B. Tauris, 2013.

———. "Getting Wet: The Heteroflexibility of Showtime's *The L Word*." *Cinema Journal* 46, no. 4 (2007): 3–23.

Moorman, Jennifer. "Women on Top: The Work of Female Pornographers and 'Sexperimental' Filmmakers." PhD diss., University of California, Los Angeles, 2014.

Morris, Wesley. "After Normal: *Looking*, Michael Sam, and the State of Gay Culture." *Grantland*, February 21, 2014. grantland.com/features/after-normal/.

———. "Hump Day: The Utterly OMG 'Magic Mike XXL.'" *Grantland*, July 2, 2015. http://grantland.com/hollywood-prospectus/hump-day-the-utterly-omg-magic-mike-xxl/.

———. "Last Taboo: Why Pop Culture Just Can't Deal with Black Male Sexuality." *New York Times*, October 27, 2016. https://www.nytimes.com/interactive/2016/10/30/magazine/black-male-sexuality-last-taboo.html?_r=0.

Morrissey, Tracie Egan. "What Kind of Guy Does a Girl Like Lena Dunham 'Deserve?'" *Jezebel*, February 11, 2013. https://jezebel.com/what-kind-of-guy-does-a-girl-who-looks-like-lena-dunham-5983437.

Moyer, Justin. "On the Political Necessity of Seeing a Gay Man's Erection on HBO." *Slate*, January 29, 2014. https://slate.com/human-interest/2014/01/why-doesnt-looking-hbos-gay-show-show-real-queer-sex-or-erections.html.

Mueller, Hannah. "'At Least Let Us See Them Before You Cut Them All Off!' The Gendered Representation of Nudity in Contemporary Quality TV." In *Contemporary Quality TV: The Auteur, the Fans, and Constructions of Gender*, edited by Ralph J. Poole and Saskia Fürst Heidelberg: Universitätsverlag Winter, forthcoming.

———. "'Jupiter's Cock!' Male Nudity, Violence and the Disruption of Voyeuristic Pleasure in Starz' *Spartacus*." In *The New Peplum: Essays on Sword and Sandal Films and Television Programs since the 1990s*, edited by Nicholas Diak, 135–54. Jefferson, NC: McFarland, 2017.

Muir, Kate. "Lars von Trier's Cannes Return Proves Festival Is Still in Thrall to Male Privilege." *Guardian*, April 20, 2018. https://www

.theguardian.com/film/2018/apr/20/lars-von-trier-persona-non-grata-cannes-film-festival-times-up.

Mulvey, Laura. "Visual Pleasure and Narrative Cinema." *Screen* 16, no. 3 (October 1975): 6–18.

Muñoz, José Esteban. *Disidentifications: Queers of Color and the Performance of Politics*. Minneapolis: University of Minnesota Press, 1999.

Murphy, Ann V. *Violence and the Philosophical Imaginary*. Albany: State University of New York Press, 2012.

Murphy, Kevin. "Hell's Angels: An Interview with Catherine Breillat on *Anatomy of Hell*." *Senses of Cinema*, no. 34 (February 2015). http://sensesofcinema.com/2005/on-recent-films-34/breillat_interview/.

Nash, Meredith, and Ruby Grant, "Twenty-Something *Girls* v. Thirty-Something *Sex and the City* Women." *Feminist Media Studies* 15, no. 6 (2015): 976–91.

Neale, Steve. "Masculinity as Spectacle." *Screen* 24, no. 6 (1983): 2–16.

Needham, Gary. "Closer Than Ever: Contemporary French Cinema and the Male Body in Close-Up." In *Mysterious Skin: Male Bodies in Contemporary Cinema*, edited by Santiago Fouz-Hernández, 127–42. London: I. B. Tauris, 2009.

"Next Episode of 'Girls' to Feature Lena Dunham Shitting Herself during Gyno Exam While Eating a Burrito." *The Onion*, March 14, 2013. https://www.theonion.com/next-episode-of-girls-to-feature-lena-dunham-shitting-h-1819574677.

Ng, Eve. "A 'Post-Gay' Era? Media Gaystreaming, Homonormativity, and the Politics of LGBT Integration." *Communication, Culture and Critique* 6, no. 2 (2013): 258–83.

Nguyen, Hoang Tan. *A View from the Bottom: Asian American Masculinity and Sexual Representation*. Durham, NC: Duke University Press, 2014.

Noé, Gaspar. "I'm Happy Some People Walk Out during My Film. It Makes the Ones Who Stay Feel Strong." *Guardian*, March 12, 1999. https://www.theguardian.com/film/1999/mar/12/features3.

Nordine, Michael. "Catherine Breillat Says Asia Argento Is a 'Traitor,' Harvey Weinstein Isn't That Bad, and She's Against #MeToo." *Indiewire*, March 29, 2018. https://www.indiewire.com/2018/03/catherine-breillat-asia-argento-harvey-weinstein-jessica-chastain-me-too-1201945040/.

———. "'Elle' Review Roundup: Paul Verhoeven's Controversial Return Draws Universal Acclaim for Isabelle Huppert." *Indiewire*, May 22, 2016. https://www.indiewire.com/2016/05/elle-review-roundup

-paul-verhoevens-controversial-return-draws-universal-acclaim-for-isabelle-huppert-289025/.

Nordyke, Kimberly. "Howard Stern Apologizes to Lena Dunham, Says She's Not 'Just a Talentless Little Fat Chick' (Audio)." *Hollywood Reporter*, January 15, 2013. https://www.hollywoodreporter.com/news/howard-stern-apologizes-lena-dunham-412824.

Norwalk, Brandon. "HBO Should Renew *Looking*, Even Though Nobody Watches." *AV Club*, March 9, 2015. https://tv.avclub.com/hbo-should-renew-looking-even-though-nobody-watches-1798277314.

Nussbaum, Emily. "Hannah Barbaric." *New Yorker*, February 11 and 18, 2013. www.newyorker.com/magazine/2013/02/11/hannah-barbaric.

———. "It's Different for 'Girls.'" *New York*, April 2012. nymag.com/arts/tv/features/girls-lena-dunham-2012-4/index1.html.

Obenson, Tambay. "SAG-AFTRA Issues New Rules for Sex Scenes With 'Intimacy Coordinators.'" *Indiewire*, January 29, 2020. https://www.indiewire.com/2020/01/sag-aftra-intimacy-coordinators-1202206891/.

Oishi, Eve. "Bad Asians: New Film and Video by Queer Asian American Artists." In *Countervisions: Asian American Film Criticism*, edited by Darrell Y. Hamamoto and Sandra Liu, 221–41. Philadelphia: Temple University Press, 2000.

Olson, Matthew. "The Account That Cried 'Pedophilia': Conservative Troll Tries to Smear Patton Oswalt with Oswalt's Own Deliberately Misleading Tweets." *Digg*, July 23, 2018. digg.com/2018/patton-oswalt-nambla-tweets-gunn-ban-cernovich.

Peakman, Julie. *The Pleasure's All Mine: A History of Perverse Sex*. London: Reaktion, 2013.

Perkins, Claire. "My Effortless Brilliance: Women's Mumblecore." In *Indie Reframed: Women's Filmmaking and Contemporary American Independent Cinema*, edited by Linda Badley, Claire Perkins, and Michele Schreiber, 138–53. Edinburgh: Edinburgh University Press, 2016.

Perren, Alisa. "sex, lies and marketing." *Film Quarterly* 55, no. 2 (2001): 30–39.

Phillips, John. "Catherine Breillat's *Romance*: Hard Core and the Female Gaze." *Studies in French Cinema* 1, no. 3 (2001): 133–40.

Piepenburg, Eric. "'Magic Mike' Is Big Draw for Gay Men." *New York Times*, July 4, 2012. https://www.nytimes.com/2012/07/05/movies/magic-mike-with-channing-tatum-draws-gay-men.html.

Poole, Ralph J. "Wasting God's Gift? The Ruined City and the 'Melodramatic Penis.'" *Anglia* 132, no. 2 (2014): 310–35.

Porton, Richard. Introduction to "Gay Family Values: An Interview with Lisa Cholodenko." *Cineaste* 35, no. 4 (Fall 2010): 14–15.
Pramaggiore, Maria. "High and Low: Bisexual Women and Aesthetics in *Chasing Amy* and *High Art*." *Journal of Bisexuality* 2, no. 2/3 (2002): 243–66.
Price, Brian. "Catherine Breillat." *Senses of Cinema*, no. 23 (December 2002). sensesofcinema.com/2002/great-directors/breillat/.
Puar, Jasbir, and Karen Tongson. "The Ugly Truth about Why the Kids Are All Right." *VelvetPark*, January 20, 2012. www.velvetparkmedia.com/blogs/ugly-truth-about-why-kids-are-all-right.
Quandt, James. "Flesh and Blood: Sex and Violence in Recent French Cinema." *Artforum*, February 2004. https://www.artforum.com/print/200402/flesh-blood-sex-and-violence-in-recent-french-cinema-6199.
Radner, Hilary. *The New Woman's Film: Femme-centric Movies for Smart Chicks*. New York: Routledge, 2017.
Rich, B. Ruby. "*Blue Is the Warmest Color*: Feeling *Blue*." Criterion Collection, February 2014. https://www.criterion.com/current/posts/3072-blue-is-the-warmest-color-feeling-blue.
———. "A Path of Her Own [Interview with Ally Sheedy]." *Advocate*, no. 761 (June 9, 1998): 46.
———. "A Queer and Present Danger: The Death of New Queer Cinema?" In *New Queer Cinema: The Director's Cut*, 130–37. Durham, NC: Duke University Press, 2013.
———. "A Queer Sensation." *Village Voice*, March 24, 1992, 41–44.
Riesman, Abraham. "Bryan Fuller Demanded a Reshoot of *American Gods*' Gay Sex Scene Because It Wasn't Gay Enough." *Vulture*, May 14, 2017. https://www.vulture.com/2017/05/american-gods-gay-sex-scene-bryan-fuller.html.
Roberts, Soraya. "Hollywood and the New Female Grotesque." *Longreads*, December 2018. https://longreads.com/2018/12/17/hollywood-and-the-new-female-grotesque/.
———. "Naked If I Want To: Lena Dunham's Body Politic." *Salon*, February 9, 2013. https://www.salon.com/2013/02/09/naked_if_i_want_to_lena_dunhams_body_politic/.
Roiphe, Katie. "Working Women's Fantasies." *Newsweek*, April 4, 2012. https://www.newsweek.com/working-womens-fantasies-63915.
Romney, Jonathan. "Women in Love." *Sight and Sound* (December 2013): 38–42.

Rosenbaum, Jonathan. "Real Sex in Movies." October 5, 2018. https://www.jonathanrosenbaum.net/2018/10/real-sex-in-movies/.

Rosenberg, Alyssa. "5 Productive Ways to Ask Lena Dunham about the Nudity on 'Girls.'" *Think Progress*, January 10, 2014. https://thinkprogress.org/5-productive-ways-to-ask-lena-dunham-about-nudity-on-girls-67253fdcf72a/.

Rosewarne, Lauren. *American Taboo: The Forbidden Words, Unspoken Rules, and Secret Morality of Popular Culture*. Santa Barbara, CA: Praeger, 2013.

Roupenian, Kristen. "Cat Person." *New Yorker*, December 11, 2017. www.newyorker.com/magazine/2017/12/11/cat-person.

Rowe (Karlyn), Kathleen. *The Unruly Woman: Gender and the Genres of Laughter*. Austin: University of Texas Press, 1996.

Rubin, Gayle. "Thinking Sex: Notes for a Radical Theory of the Politics of Sexuality." In *Culture, Society and Sexuality: A Reader*, 2nd ed., edited by Richard Parker and Peter Aggleton, 143–89. New York: Routledge, 2007.

Ruffolo, David V. *Post-Queer Politics*. New York: Routledge, 2009.

Russo, Mary. *The Female Grotesque: Risk, Excess, Modernity*. New York: Routledge, 1994.

Ryzik, Melena. "Transforming a Body—And a Performance." *New York Times*, January 5, 2012. carpetbagger.blogs.nytimes.com/2012/01/05/transforming-a-body-and-a-performance/.

San Filippo, Maria. *The B Word: Bisexuality in Contemporary Film and Television*. Bloomington: Indiana University Press, 2013.

———. "Breaking Upwards: The Creative Uncoupling of Desiree Akhavan and Ingrid Jungermann." *Feminist Media Studies* 19, no. 6 (December 2019): 991–1008.

———. "'Just Because I'm a Lesbian Doesn't Mean I'm Evolved': The 'Bad Queer' Politics of Queer Women's Comic Web Series." *Velvet Light Trap*, no. 85 (Spring 2020): 65–77.

———. "The Politics of Fluidity: Representing Bisexualities in 21st Century Screen Media." In *The Routledge Companion to Media, Sex, and Sexuality*, edited by Feona Attwood, Brian McNair, and Clarissa Smith, 70–80. New York: Routledge, 2017.

———. "Serial Offender: *The Bisexual* (2018)." *Journal of Bisexuality* 20, no. 3 (September 2020): 233–43.

———. "A Tale of Two Suzannes: *À nos amours* (*For Our Loves*, 1983) and *Suzanne* (2013)." *Senses of Cinema*, no. 77 (December 2015). sensesofcinema.com/2015/feature-articles/a-nos-amours-and-suzanne/.

Schoonover, Karl, and Rosalind Galt. *Queer Cinema in the World*. Durham, NC: Duke University Press, 2016.
Sconce, Jeffrey. "Irony, Nihilism, and the New American 'Smart' Film." *Screen* 43, no. 4 (Winter 2002): 249–69.
Scott, A. O. "My Woody Allen Problem." *New York Times*, January 31, 2018. https://www.nytimes.com/2018/01/31/movies/woody-allen.html.
Sebag-Montefiore, Clarissa. "How to Make Sex Scenes Natural and Non-threatening? Cue the 'Intimacy Coordinator.'" *New York Times*, January 22, 2019. https://www.nytimes.com/2019/01/22/arts/movie-sex-scenes-safety-intimacy-coordinator.html.
Secher, Benjamin. "Catherine Breillat: 'All True Artists Are Hated.'" *Telegraph* (London), April 8, 2005. https://www.telegraph.co.uk/culture/film/starsandstories/3672302/Catherine-BreillatAll-true-artists-are-hated.html.
Sedgwick, Eve. *Touching, Feeling: Affect, Pedagogy, Performativity*. Durham, NC: Duke University Press, 2003.
Sen, Sharmila. *Not Quite Not White: Losing and Finding Race in America*. New York: Penguin, 2018.
Setoodeh, Ramin, and Brent Lang. "Sundance 2015: The Festival of Sex on the Slopes." *Variety*, January 29, 2015. https://variety.com/2015/film/markets-festivals/sundance-2015-the-festival-of-sex-in-the-slopes-1201418884/.
Sharf, Zack. "'God's Own Country' Director Criticizes Distributor for Censoring Gay Sex Scenes on Prime Video." *Indiewire*, May 20, 2020. https://www.indiewire.com/2020/05/gods-own-country-director-amazon-prime-censored-movie-1202232433/.
———. "James Gunn Issues Statement Reacting to Disney Firing, Offers 'Deepest Apologies' for Offensive Tweets." *Indiewire*, July 20, 2018. https://www.indiewire.com/2018/07/james-gunn-responds-disney-fired-guardians-of-the-galaxy-1201986202/.
———. "'Mektoub My Love' First Reactions Enraged by 'Blue Is the Warmest Color' Director's 'Masturbatory' Male Gaze." *Indiewire*, September 7, 2017. https://www.indiewire.com/2017/09/mektoub-my-love-reviews-male-gaze-abdellatif-kechiche-1201873810/.
———. "'Normal People' Producer Slams Pornhub for Circulating Sex Scenes: 'Deeply Disrespectful.'" *Indiewire*, May 21, 2020. https://www.indiewire.com/2020/05/normal-people-producer-sex-scenes-pornhub-1202232767/.
Shepherd, Julianne Escobedo. "Babe, What Are You Doing?" *Jezebel*, January 16, 2018. https://jezebel.com/babe-what-are-you-doing-1822114753.

Siegel, Carol. *Sex Radical Cinema*. Bloomington: Indiana University Press, 2015.
Sims, David. "How Louis C.K. Used Comedy as a Smokescreen." *Atlantic*, November 13, 2017. https://www.theatlantic.com/entertainment/archive/2017/11/how-louis-ck-used-comedy-as-a-smokescreen/545681/.
Sklar, Robert. "A Woman's Vision of Shame and Desire: An Interview with Catherine Breillat." *Cineaste* 25, no. 1 (December 1999): 24–26.
Snarker, Dorothy. "Is This the End of the Model Gay Character?" *Indiewire*, November 17, 2015. https://womenandhollywood.com/is-this-the-end-of-the-model-gay-character-44c077b76073/.
Spicer, Andrew. *Film Noir*. London: Longman, 2002.
Spines, Christine. "Down to Earth." *Film Comment* (July–August 2010): 40–43.
Stasi, Linda. "New 'Girl' on Top." *New York Post*, January 24, 2013. https://nypost.com/2013/01/04/new-girl-on-top/.
Stein, Arlene, and Kenneth Plummer. "'I Can't Even Think Straight': Queer Theory and the Missing Sexual Revolution in Sociology." In *Queer Theory/Sociology*, edited by Steven Seidman, 129–44. Malden, MA: Blackwell, 1996.
Stephens, Elizabeth. "The Spectacularized Penis: Contemporary Representations of the Phallic Male Body." *Men and Masculinities* 10, no. 1 (2007): 85–98.
Tang, Estelle. "Enjoy Seeing Men Spectacularly Miss the Point of That Viral 'Cat Person' Story." *Elle*, December 11, 2017. https://www.elle.com/culture/books/a14406222/men-respond-cat-person-kristen-roupenian/.
Taormino, Tristan, Celine Parreñas Shimizu, Constance Penley, and Mireille Miller-Young, eds., *The Feminist Porn Book: The Politics of Producing Pleasure*. New York: The Feminist Press, 2013.
Teeman, Tim. "Yes, *Looking* Is Boring. It's the Drama Gays Deserve." *Daily Beast*, January 24, 2014. http://www.thedailybeast.com/yes-looking-is-boring-its-the-drama-gays-deserve.
Tharrett, Matthew. "How Big Is Your Favorite 'Looking' Man?" *Queerty*, March 7, 2014, https://www.queerty.com/how-big-is-your-favorite-looking-man-20140307.
Thornham, Sue. "'Starting to Feel Like a Chick': Re-visioning Romance in *In the Cut*." *Feminist Media Studies* 7, no. 1 (2007): 33–46.
Tolentino, Jia. "The Personal-Essay Boom Is Over." *New Yorker*, May 18, 2017. https://www.newyorker.com/culture/jia-tolentino/the-personal-essay-boom-is-over.

Tommasini, Anthony. "Looking for a Breakthrough? You'll Have to Wait." *New York Times*, January 14, 2001. https://www.nytimes.com/2001/01/14/arts/television-radio-looking-for-a-breakthrough-you-ll-have-to-wait.html.

Travers, Ben. "'The Leftovers' Longest Running Joke: A Timeline of Every Reference to Justin Theroux's Penis." *Indiewire*, May 29, 2017. https://www.indiewire.com/2017/05/the-leftovers-justin-theroux-penis-every-dick-joke-timeline-1201833541/.

Tripodi, Francesca. "Fifty Shades of Consent?" *Feminist Media Studies* 17, no. 1 (2017): 93–107.

Tsai, Caroline. "'Mektoub, My Love: Intermezzo': Abdellatif Kechiche's Torturous, Four-Hour Sequel Is the Butt of the Joke [Cannes Review]." *The Playlist*, May 24, 2019. https://theplaylist.net/mektoub-my-love-intermezzo-cannes-review-20190524/.

Tsika, Noah A. *Pink 2.0: Encoding Queer Cinema on the Internet*. Bloomington: Indiana University Press, 2016.

Tulloch, John, and Belinda Middleweek. *Real Sex Films: The New Intimacy and Risk in Cinema*. New York: Oxford University Press, 2017.

de Valck, Marijke. "Conversion, Digitization, and the Future of Film Festivals." In *Digital Disruption: Cinema Moves On-Line*, edited by Dina Iordanova and Stuart Cunningham, 117–29. St. Andrews, Scotland: St. Andrews Film Studies, 2012.

———. *Film Festivals: From European Geopolitics to Global Cinephilia*. Amsterdam: Amsterdam University Press, 2011.

VanArendonk, Kathryn. "Hannah Horvath: Why Do We (Still) Hate Thee So?" *Vulture*, April 13, 2016. https://www.vulture.com/2016/04/hannah-horvath-why-do-we-still-hate-thee-so.html.

Vassé, Claire. "Interview with Paul Verhoeven." *Elle* press kit, 2016. Accessed July 26, 2019. https://www.festival-cannes.com/en/films/elle.

Verevis, Constantine. "Whose Side Are You On? The Slap (2011/2015)." *Continuum: Journal of Media and Cultural Studies* 29, no. 5 (2015): 769–80.

Vincendeau, Ginette. "Sisters, Sex, and Sitcoms." DVD notes on *Fat Girl*, Criterion Collection. Original essay appeared in *Sight and Sound*, December 2001: 18–20.

Wallace, Lee. *Lesbianism, Cinema, Space: The Sexual Life of Apartments*. New York: Routledge, 2009.

Walters, Suzanna Danuta. "The Kids Are All Right but the Lesbians Aren't: Queer Kinship in US Culture." *Sexualities* 15, no. 8 (2012): 917–33.

Wells, Gwendolyn. "Accoutrements of Passion: Fashion, Irony, and Feminine P.O.V. in Catherine Breillat's *Romance*." *Sites* 6, no. 1 (2002): 51–66.

Wenger, Daniel. "'Looking,' Marriage, and the New Gay Sadness." *New Yorker*, March 22, 2015. www.newyorker.com/culture/culture-desk/looking-marriage-and-the-new-gay-sadness.

Wickham, Celia. "Interview with Desire Akhavan." *Berlin Film Journal*, May 2015. berlinfilmjournal.com/2015/05/interview-with-desiree-akhavan/.

Williams, James S. "Re-siting the Republic: Abdellatif Kechiche and the Politics of Reappropriation and Renewal." In *Space and Being in Contemporary French Cinema*, 187–232. Manchester: Manchester University Press, 2013.

Williams, Linda. "Cinema's Sex Acts." *Film Quarterly* 67, no. 4 (2014): 9–25.

———. *Hard Core: Power, Pleasure, and the "Frenzy of the Visible."* Expanded ed. Berkeley: University of California Press, 1999.

———. *Screening Sex*. Durham, NC: Duke University Press, 2008.

———. "When the Woman Looks." In *The Dread of Difference: Gender and the Horror Film*, edited by Barry Keith Grant, 15–34. Austin: University of Texas Press, 1996.

Williams, Linda Ruth. *The Erotic Thriller in Contemporary Cinema*. Bloomington: Indiana University Press, 2005.

Willis, Holly. "Lisa Cholodenko (1964–)." In *Independent Female Filmmakers: A Chronicle through Interviews, Profiles, and Manifestos*, edited by Michele Meek, 49–62. New York: Routledge, 2019.

Wilson, Emma. "Deforming Femininity: Catherine Breillat's *Romance*." In *France on Film: Reflections on Popular French Cinema*, edited by Lucy Mazdon, 145–57. London: Wallflower, 2001.

Wolcott, James. "Ms. Dunham Regrets." *Vanity Fair*, February 2018. https://www.vanityfair.com/hollywood/2017/12/can-lena-dunham-recover-from-her-mistakes.

Wolff, Zoã. "Léa and Adèle." *Interview*, November 2013. https://www.interviewmagazine.com/film/lea-seydoux-adele-exarchopoulos.

Wood, Robin. *Hollywood from Vietnam to Reagan . . . and Beyond*. New York: Columbia University Press, 2003.

Woods, Faye. "*Girls* Talk: Authorship and Authenticity in the Reception of Lena Dunham's *Girls*." *Critical Studies in Television* 10, no. 2 (Summer 2015): 37–54.

Wortham, Jenna. "When Everyone Can Be 'Queer,' Is Anyone?" *New York Times Magazine*, July 12, 2016. https://www.nytimes.com/2016/07/17/magazine/when-everyone-can-be-queer-is-anyone.html?_r=0.

Yuan, Jada. "Adam Scott and Jason Schwartzman on Their Sundance Comedy *The Overnight* and Prosthetic Penises." *Vulture*, January 26, 2015.

https://www.vulture.com/2015/01/scott-and-schwartzman-on-the-overnight-penises.html.

Zinoman, Jason. "Political Correctness Isn't Ruining Comedy. It's Helping." *New York Times,* October 20, 2015. https://www.nytimes.com/2015/10/21/arts/television/political-correctness-isnt-ruining-comedy-its-helping.html.

Zuckermann, Esther. "The 'Girls' Parody Porn Stars Just Want Lena Dunham to Understand." *Atlantic,* May 31, 2013. https://www.theatlantic.com/entertainment/archive/2013/05/girls-parody-porn-stars/314687/.

ACKNOWLEDGMENTS

THEY SAY THE SECOND BOOK is the hardest. In this case, the writing proved less challenging than the surrounding circumstances of life. In the years the manuscript has taken to complete, the academy and the world beyond have been transformed, in many ways for the worse. This book is, in part, a response to those changes as well as a coping mechanism, and I trust that meeting the challenges of recent years has fortified me for whatever lies ahead.

That future landscape has grown still more uncertain as of this writing, in the summer of 2020, with the coronavirus pandemic altering the course of life in grave and far-reaching ways. I have already begun reflecting on the ways in which what I explore and advocate for in these pages may be substantially affected, perhaps even undone, by the pandemic's impact on media creation and reception. From writers' rooms to production sets to film festival premieres to movie theaters to viewing parties to college and university classrooms, the forums for creating, celebrating, and contemplating screen art may be irrevocably transformed. At the same time, I expect that the media climate and cultural conditions will evolve to make for even more streamable content and virtual viewing, such that this book's premise—that sexual provocation functions ever more significantly in our 21st screen mediascape—will hold true.

My concern, looking ahead, is that the contexts and conditions for experiencing and engaging with the artworks and ideas that I see as indispensable to realizing the potential in screening sexual provocation that this book proposes are increasingly at risk of being compromised or corrupted, as are the material and intellectual resources and securities I have depended on to write, and publish, this book. Due to encroaching threats and widening inequities not created, but severely exacerbated, by the present crisis, I write this book's final words not entirely (as I had at one time expected) with relief—despite having the immense good fortune to have found a secure home at a supportive academic institution in a profession I cherish—but rather with a heightened sense of trepidation. For all of us within academe, it is a harrowing prospect that our collective endeavors—creating knowledge, teaching students, sharing in transformative dialogue, mentoring and learning from colleagues—are bound to endure their most formidable challenge yet. I pledge to muster my energies and maintain my resolve for the difficult struggles ahead.

Knowing my indebtedness to so many, I wish in closing to give particular thanks to a few. I am fortunate to have received encouragement from colleagues who published early versions of what would become my third and fourth chapters. Thank you to the editors of *The Velvet Light Trap* for including my article on Catherine Breillat and Lena Dunham in the 2016 "Performance and the Body" special issue, and to their anonymous reviewers for their valuable feedback. Thank you as well to Linda Badley, Claire Perkins, and Michele Schreiber for inviting me to write about Lisa Cholodenko for their 2016 edited collection *Indie Reframed: Women's Filmmaking and Contemporary American Independent Cinema*, and to Edinburgh University Press for its publication.

Once again, the talented team at Indiana University Press has made me feel supported and delighted at seeing long hours of mental toil transformed into something I am proud to send out into the world. Janice Frisch was this book's initial acquisitions editor, and while she left before its completion, I am grateful for her early championing of the project and for her transferring me into the equally trustworthy hands of succeeding editor Allison Chaplin. Editorial project manager Darja Malcolm-Clarke's expertise has again made me marvel at seeing my manuscript transformed into an object of beauty, and my appreciation as well to Carol McGillivray for attentively overseeing its copyediting and typesetting.

In these precarious times, having the support of an academic institution is a privilege, and I am thankful to Goucher College for the research leave that granted me the most precious resource: time. My colleagues and students, both there and elsewhere along my circuitous route through academe, have provided much professional sustenance and intellectual stimulation, for which I am greatly appreciative. I feel highly fortunate to be welcoming this book into the world from my new home in the Department of Visual and Media Arts at Emerson College, which I am confident will provide a nurturing environment in the years to come.

Thank you to Janet Bergstrom, Caroline Light, and Timothy Shary for having confidence in me early on and for continuing to advocate on my behalf. My thanks as well to Kyle Stevens, who has generously proffered his camaraderie and commiseration these last few years, and whose trust in my potential made possible my latest professional adventure as editor of *New Review of Film and Television Studies*.

My UCLA classmates and now colleagues continue to offer much inspiration and empathy; though they are usually a phone line or screen away, their understanding of the joys and travails of this profession are invaluable. Thank you especially to Maya Montañez Smukler and Jennifer Moorman for always reminding me of the importance of talking about women filmmakers and sex scenes (in that order).

Those significant others from every realm of my life are all deeply appreciated; my sincere thanks for bearing with me during the rough stretches and for being alongside me on the joyful occasions. A special recognition to Ivey Rucket for her friendship.

Though they may not entirely appreciate my provocations, my family has been steadfastly supportive, for which I am immensely thankful. Their hard work inspires and fuels my own.

Vernon Shetley encouraged this project from its inception, shared in countless generative conversations along the way, and contributed his supremely skilled editing expertise in helping me shepherd this book to completion. I dedicate it to him, with my deepest gratitude.

Maria San Filippo
Cambridge, Massachusetts
June 2020

INDEX

3D, 32, 44, 50, 70
36 fillette (Breillat), 175, 201, 242n27
#5050x2020, 24n3
9 1/2 Weeks (Lyne), 218

A24, 56
ABC Studios, 160n127
abject(ion), 14, 41, 80, 226, 234, 288; embodiment, 171, 193–215; owning one's, 82, 169, 193–215, 238, 240
abortion. *See* reproductive rights
Abramović, Marina, 179
abstinence, 22, 115, 227
Abus de faiblesse (*Abuse of Weakness*, Breillat), 234
academe, 62–63, 249n99, 372–73
Academy Awards, 2, 24n2, 56, 88, 91, 288, 299
Academy of Motion Picture Arts and Sciences (AMPAS), 260
ACT UP, 156n71, 254
Adlon, Pamela, 128
adultery. *See* (in)fidelity
Affleck, Ben, 35, 57, 69, 129
ageism, 120, 239, 286–89
Ah-ga-ssi. See *The Handmaiden* (Park)
AIDS, 38, 107, 115–16, 118, 134, 142, 144, 147, 155n70, 156n71, 340

Ai no korîda. See *In the Realm of the Senses* (Ōshima)
Akerman, Chantal, 11–12, 13, 19, 246n59
Akhavan, Desiree, 9, 40–43, 51, 165–66, 252, 255, 257, 259–63, 267, 294–10, 311–23, 324–26, 327–30, 363; as "bad queer" provoc*auteur*, 40–43, 51, 255, 257, 260–61, 263, 267, 296, 299–300, 333–34, 355; and bisexuality, 260, 262, 299, 301, 312–22, 325, 335, 337–39; and Lena Dunham, 294–96, 299–300; as inbetweener, 42, 255, 260–61, 263, 298, 312–13, 315–17, 330, 342–43; as/and Iranian American (representation), 260, 262, 273, 294, 297, 299–300, 309, 315–17, 321–24, 338, 344n15; and Ingrid Jungermann, 43, 263, 330–41, 363–64
Alexandra, Charlotte, *177*, 201
alienation. *See* distanciation
Allen, Woody, 6, 299–300, 302, 304–*05*, 360
Almodóvar, Pedro, 73–74
alter ego, 17–18, 128, 166, 171, 184, 202, 207, 225, 236, 259–61, 271–74, 291, 295, 297–98, 315, 327, 330, 334–42
altporn, 242n24. *See also* art porn; pornography

alt-right, 352–53, 364, 374
Alvarez, Frankie J., 131–32, 160n128
À ma soeur. See *Fat Girl* (Breillat)
Amazon Prime Video, 122, 145, 154n53, 160n124
AMC (American Movie Classics), 121
American Gigolo (Schrader), 102–03
American Gods (Starz), 150, 372
American Psycho (Ellis), 256
AMPAS. See Academy of Motion Picture Arts and Sciences
anal sex. See sex, anal
Anatomie de l'enfer (*Anatomy of Hell*, Breillat), 170, 177–82, 203, 217, 243n34
Anderson, Paul Thomas (P. T.), 93
anilingus, 102, 141, 147, 190. See also sex acts
Annapurna Pictures, 56
Annie Hall (Allen), 43, 299–305, 306–11, 325
Ansari, Aziz, 371, 378n39
(anti-)aspirational(ism), 106, 168–69, 188, 200, 206, 238, 259
(anti-)assimilation, 253, 257–58, 281, 297, 324, 333–34, 342
(anti-)identitarian(ism), 106, 253, 257, 264. See also identity politics
Antin, Eleanor, 198, 246n59
antisemitism, 262, 308
Apatow, Judd, 53, 69, 78–79
Appropriate Behavior (Akhavan), 42–43, 262–63, 294, 296–310, 311–23, 324–26, 327, 330, 335–36, 338; distribution/exhibition and reception of, 43, 294, 296–300, 311, 313, 320; relation to *Annie Hall*, 43, 300–12, 317, 325
appropriation: cultural, 8, 14, 232, 358; feminist-queer, 40, 106, 139, 175, 182, 193, 200, 306, 324; of language, 301, 334–35; of pornographic conventions, 33, 40, 48, 106–07, 112, 121, 167, 174–75, 182–83, 193, 215

Araki, Gregg, 267
Argento, Asia, 186, 244n41
art cinema. See cinema, art
art film. See cinema, art
art house cinema. See cinema, art house
art porn, 36–37, 41, 55, 170, 174–75, 187, 189, 193, 234. See also pornography
Aselton, Katie, 329
Asian, bad. See bad Asian (Oishi)
Asymmetry (Halliday), 249n100
At Play in the Fields of the Lord (Babenco), 73
Attenberg (Tsangari), 202
auteur(ism), 17, 24n6, 40, 45, 47, 49–50, 95, 176, 242n24, 245n47, 342. See also provoc*auteur* autocritique; pornography, autocritique of
avant-garde film. See cinema, avant-garde

Baartman, Saartjie, 13–14
Bacon, Kevin, 123, 204
bad Asian (Oishi), 259
bad feminist (Gay), 258
Bad Love (Breillat), 249n102
Bad Moms (Lucas and Moore), 53
bad Persian, 260, 298–99, 316–20, 322, 324. See also Desiree Akhavan; inbetweener/ness, racial; Iranian-American
bad queer, 7, 42, 60, 118, 148, 254–62, 264, 266–68, 286, 289, 296, 302, 304, 306–09, 312, 315, 330–33, 335–37, 341. See also Desiree Akhavan; Lisa Cholodenko
Baker, Becky Ann, 126, 211
#BalanceTonPorc, 2, 24n3, 235
Ballad of Sexual Dependency, The (Goldin), 269
Bang Gang (une histoire d'amour moderne) (*Bang Gang (A Modern Love Story)*, Husson), 37
barebacking, 115–17, 119

Baron Cohen, Sacha, 86
Bartlett, Murray, 132, 135
basic cable. *See* cable television, basic
Basic Instinct (Verhoeven), 52, 214, 228
Bataille, Georges, 106, 117, 175
BDSM, 35, 54–55, 60, 104, 130, 217, 219–20, 227, 295, 356, 368
Beaches (Marshall), 316–17
Beautiful Agony, 48
Before Midnight (Linklater), 35
Bell, Kristen, 78–79
Bening, Annette, 146, 265, 280
Berenger, Tom, 73
Berlinale (Berlin International Film Festival), 44, 47
Berry, Halle, 73
Bertolucci, Bernardo, 4–5, 18, 21, 24n9
bestiality, 52
Betti, Laura, 205
Beur cinema, 15, 26n22
Bieber, Justin, 69
Billings, Alexandra, 94
biphobia, 313, 317, 319
Bisexual, The (Channel 4/Hulu), 262, 321
bisexual(ity), 40, 42–43, 92, 117, 252, 260, 274–79, 294, 297–301, 312–22, 337–39, 342
Bitter Tears of Petra von Kant, The (Fassbinder), 270
Black, Jack, 51
Black, Michael Ian, 353
Black Venus (Kechiche), 13–14
Blair Witch Project, The (Myrick and Sanchez), 57, 327
Blockers (Cannon), 152n19
blog(ging), 43, 108, 119, 123, 144, 154n50, 266–67, 282–85, 332
blowjob. *See* sex, oral
Bluebeard (Breillat), 234
Blue Is the Warmest Color (Kechiche), 1–10, 11–15, 16–26, 35, 39, 45, 47, 92, 105–06, 362, 372

Blue Is the Warmest Color (Maroh), 8, 15
Blumberg, Stuart, 266, 293
Bob & Carol & Ted & Alice (Mazursky), 86
bodily fluids, 7, 188, 200–22, 225
body double, 89, 99, 109, 112, 181
body guy (Lehman and Hunt), 80, 102–05
Body Heat (Kasdan), 96
body image, 84, 137, 168, 207, 209, 212, 221. *See also* Lena Dunham; penis size; shame
Bomer, Matt, 58
bondage. *See* BDSM
Bonnaire, Sandrine, 242–43n27
Boogie Nights (Anderson), 92, 125
Borat: Cultural Learnings of America for Make Benefit Glorious Nation of Kazakhstan (Charles), 152n19
Bound (Wachowskis), 9, 110
Boys in the Band (Friedkin), 115
Boys in the Sand (Poole), 115, 144
brand(ing), 53, 59, 111, 135; of film festivals, 45, 49–52, 60; of provo*cauteurs*, 4, 40, 47, 49, 176, 186, 197, 206, 236–37, 267, 286, 295–96, 298–99, 358; of queerness, 255, 331, 336; of television, 121–22, 135–36, 144–45, 187–88, 245n47, 258–59, 331, 336, 354
Brando, Marlon, 4–5, 18, 24n9
Brand, Russell, 80
Breaking Bad (AMC), 61, 260, 341
breakout (film et al.), 7, 105, 176, 297, 330, 341, 364
breasts, 35, 73, 84–85, 199, 210–11, 296, 329. *See also* nudity, female
Brechtian. *See* distanciation
Breillat, Catherine, 3, 7, 36–37, 40–42, 47, 96, 106, 120, 165–86, 314, 356; and abjection, 41, 171, 200–05, 225–26, 240; and corpo*reality*/female embodiment, 7, 41, 120, 171, 180, 182, 193, 200–05, 215, 225, 240, 255; as feminist (*see* feminism/t and/

Breillat, Catherine (*Continued*) as Catherine Breillat); as provo-*cauteur*, 3, 41, 47, 106, 165–66, 169, 172–73, 175–77, 186, 234–35, 237–38, 255, 294–96, 358; relation to pornography, 37, 41, 169–71, 173–86, 188–89, 193, 234; and women's self-degradation/subjugation, 42, 168, 171, 215–19, 227, 356; and women's self-formation, 42, 168–69, 171, 175, 193, 201–02, 204, 215–16, 218–19, 223, 225, 236, 240, 314, 366

Bresson, Robert, 114, 248n87
Brice, Patrick, 51, 77, 81, 130, 327
Bridesmaids (Feig), 53
Bright, Susie, 9
British Board of Film Classifications (BBFC), 177
Broad City (web series; Comedy Central), 238, 341
Brokeback Mountain (A. Lee), 58, 108, 265
bromance, 39, 51, 53, 76–80, 86–88, 152n19
Bromans (ITV2), 70
Bronze, The (Buckley), 11, 51
Brooks, Louise, 17
Brown Bunny, The (Gallo), 50
buddy film, 76–77
Buskfilms, 7
butch, 95, 146, 160n127, 198, 260, 281–82, 314, 336, 339. *See also* dyke; nonbinary
Buying Naked (TLC), 150n1

cable television, 32–34, 52, 132, 160n124, 198, 221; basic, 36, 121–22, 157n89; premium, 36, 76, 121, 145, 157n89, 172, 191, 292. *See also* individual channels
Cagney & Lacey (ABC), 146, 160n127
Call Me by Your Name (Guadagnino), 108
Campbell, Naomi, 249n102
Camping (HBO), 235

Campion, Jane, 39, 95–100, 102–103, 105
cancel culture, 258. *See also* censorship
Cannes Film Festival, 2–3, 7, 14, 20, 23n1, 45–50, 52, 66n33, 105–06, 117, 356. *See also* film festival(s); Palme d'Or
Canterbury, Stuart, 189
Caplan, Lizzy, 123
Carlin, George, 354
carnivalesque, 199, 254
Carrie (De Palma), 203
Carroll, Lewis, 201–02, 225
Casar, Amira, 179, 181
Castillo, Raúl, 141, 160n128
casual sex, 115–16, 147, 284, 293, 302–03. *See also* gay promiscuity
"Cat Person" (Roupenian), 368–72
Cavedweller (Cholodenko), 267
celibacy. *See* abstinence
censorship, 37, 46, 50, 57, 66n40, 71, 108, 174, 177, 304, 353–54, 357, 374–75
Ce vieux rêve qui bouge. *See That Old Dream That Moves*
CGI, 65n29, 150, 372
Chaiken, Ilene, 5, 335
Chance, Alex, 189
Channel 4 (UK), 262, 321
Charles, RuPaul. *See* RuPaul
Chasing Amy (Smith), 313–14
Chastain, Jessica, 4–5, 24n9
Chernovich, Mike, 352–53
Chicago, Judy, 203
childbirth, 120, 182, 233
child molester. *See* pedophilia
Cholodenko, Lisa, 40, 42–43, 51, 146, 252, 255, 257, 259–61, 270–72, 279–94, 296–98, 313–14, 332, 342–43, 347n56; as "bad queer" provo*cauteur*, 43, 51, 255, 257, 260–61, 263–68, 272, 286, 297, 312; as inbetweener, 42, 260–63, 272–75, 277–80, 293–94, 297, 334, 342–43. *See also* Jewishness
chronobiopolitics, 311
chromonormativity, 311, 324–27

cinema: art, 8, 13–14, 19, 35–37, 45, 108, 112–13, 115–16, 120–21, 139, 172, 174–75, 188, 304, 365; art house, 7, 45, 62, 172, 264; crossover, 108, 154n49, 280, 336; exploitation (*see* sexploitation); Hollywood, 9, 33–36; 52–56, 59–60, 70–71, 285 (*see also* sex scene, Hollywood-style); independent (indie) cinema, 34–36, 53–54, 64n19, 80–81, 108, 260, 265–67, 280, 297, 299, 302–03, 327–28, 330, 333–34; Indiewood, 53, 56, 198, 270; multiplex, 7, 35, 52–53, 55, 62; virtual, 34, 38, 60, 62, 407
Cinemark, 23n2
Cinémathèque Française, 4
cinéma vérité, 183
Cinemax, 136
Cinerama, 32
Cineworld, 154n50
C. K., Louis, 127–28, 135, 360–63, 374
class. *See* social class
Clinton, Hillary, 250n105, 250n111
Clooney, George, 91
closet(ed), 144, 294, 310, 316, 319, 322–23, 336. *See also* coming-out (narrative)
Code (Era). *See* Production Code (Administration)
code-switching, 134, 314, 338
coitus. *See* sex
Coleman, Olivia, 239
Colin, Grégoire, 178–79
College Humor, 121, 123
Color of Night (Rush), 73
comedy: animal, 304; cringe, 78; irony/ic, 78, 84, 106, 171, 187–88, 216–17, 297, 303, 308, 316, 318, 325, 334–36, 340–41, 352–53, 355, 361, 363–64, 367; parodic (*see* parody); potential to effect change, 364; raunch, 53, 78, 365; romantic (*see* romantic comedy); sex, 86; shock (*see* shock comedy); stand-up (*see* stand-up comedy); and time, 360, 362–63, 368

coming-out (narrative), 106, 270, 274, 278, 306, 309–10, 318–20, 322, 324, 330
Compliance (Zobel), 51
compulsory monosexuality, 274–75, 320, 342
computer generated imagery. *See* CGI
Concussion (Passon), 9
condom. *See* safe(r) sex
convergence, media, 8, 34, 44, 267
coronavirus. *See* COVID
corp*oreality*, 7, 41, 73–74, 76, 81, 112, 120, 127, 139, 168, 170, 205–06, 212–15, 225, 240, 255. *See also* abject(ion) embodiment; Catherine Breillat and corp*oreality*/female embodiment; defetishization of female embodiment; Lena Dunham and corp*oreality*/embodiment; embodiment; nudity
Costa, Laia, 9
counterpublic (sphere), 38, 62
Courbet, Gustave, 120
COVID, 38, 60, 66n33
Creative Nonfiction (Dunham), 219
Creep (Brice), 81, 327
Creep 2 (Brice), 81, 130, 327–30
Criterion Collection, 2, 7, 194
crowdfunding. *See* Kickstarter
cruising. *See* gay cruising
Cruising (Friedkin), 115, 156n72
Crying Game, The (Jordan), 57, 67n41, 92, 107, 149
Cui, Zi'en, 150
cultural sex hierarchy (Rubin), 118, 143
cum shot. *See* money shot
cunnilingus, 8, 20, 102, 283–84. *See also* sex acts

Da 5 Bloods (S. Lee), 66n33
Daly, Tyne, 146, 160n127
Daniels, Stormy, 70
Dating Naked (VH1), 69
Davidson, Jaye, 149

Deadpool (Miller), 71
death drive. *See* Thanatos
Deep Throat (Damiano), 21
defamiliarization, 10–12, 182, 193, 199, 258, 334, 341, 362. *See also* distanciation
defetishization: of female embodiment, 75, 127, 171, 178, 193, 199, 202, 211, 296; of penis, 40, 74, 108–09, 137; of sex scenes, 181, 183, 192, 202. *See also* corpo*reality*; embodiment; female gaze; penis, (non)phallic; nudity; sex scenes
Deladonchamps, Pierre, 106, *112*
Delpy, Julie, 35
Deneuve, Catherine, 235
dephallicize. *See* phallic(ism); penis, (non-)phallic
Desert Hearts (Deitch), 253
Despentes, Virginie, 240n5
Destroyer (Kusama), 239
Diary of a Teenage Girl (Heller), 51
dick jokes. *See* penis jokes
dick pics, 70, 220
Die Büchse der Pandora. See *Pandora's Box* (Pabst)
digital: culture, 33–34, 60–61, 117, 122, 160n124, 190, 267; 298–99, 327, 353, 368–70; technologies, 33–34, 61, 65n29, 328, 372
dildo, 94–95, 108–09, 179, 320
direct address, 176, 183, 271, 303
discipline, self-. *See* embodiment, regulation of
discipline, sexual. *See* BDSM
disidentification (Muñoz), 263, 275, 282, 285, 293
distanciation, 11–12, 106, 180, 182–84, 188, 303, 357
distribution (film), 8, 21, 34, 45, 260, 298–99. *See also* VOD
docuporn, 180. *See also* art porn; pornography
Dogme 95, 48. *See also* von Trier, Lars

Dogville (von Trier), 49
Dolan, Xavier, 47
domination, sexual. *See* BDSM
Dornan, Jamie, 55
Driver, Adam, 168, 212
drug use, 43, 52, 124, 133, 190, 265, 269, 271, 297, 317
D Train, The (Mogel and Paul), 51, 80
dual address, 313–14. *See also* LGBTQ+ mainstreaming
Ducey, Caroline, 176, *181*, 243n29
Duck Butter (Arteta), 9
Dumont, Bruno, 240n5
Dunham, Carroll, 158n99
Dunham, Lena, 3, 7, 40–41, 43, 126–27, 137, 165–75, 195, 214, 263, 267, 293–94, 356, 358, 370–71; and abjection, 41, 169, 171, 193–200, 208–09, 215, 218, 238, 240; and corpo*reality*/embodiment, 7, 42, 126–27, 168–69, 171–73, 189, 193, 197–99, 205–09, 210–15, 225, 240, 255, 296 (*see also* body image; nudity and Lena Dunham); as feminist (*see* feminism/t and/as Lena Dunham); privilege of, 41, 168, 172, 199, 229, 235–37, 239, 259, 285, 299–300, 341; as provoc*auteur*, 3, 40–42, 126, 138, 165–67, 169–73, 196–97, 226, 228, 235, 237–39, 255, 293, 299–300, 355–56, 358, 370; relation to porn, 170–71, 173–75, 186–91, 193, 240, 296; and self-degradation/subjugation, 42, 168–69, 171, 198–99, 219–25, 227, 233, 315; and women's self-formation, 42, 171, 202, 208–09, 215–16, 218, 225, 236, 371
Dunye, Cheryl, 267
Duong, Anh, 268, 297
Duplass Brothers, 81, 129, 327–29
Duplass, Mark, 129, 280, 292, 327–29
Duras, Marguerite, 243n34
Du soleil pour les gueux. See *Sunshine for the Poor*
D Word, The (Snyder), 331

dyke, 122, 160n127, 242n24, 246n59, 252, 281–82, 301, 306, 334–35, 339–40. See also butch
Dyke TV, 331

Eastern Promises (Cronenberg), 71
Easy (Netflix), 231–32
Eighth Grade (Burnham), 239
ejaculation, 87, 111–12, 119, 137, 170, 177–78, 182, 221. See also money shot
Elle (Verhoeven), 234, 356, 366–37, 370
Ellis, Bret Easton, 256–57, 263, 297, 330, 333
emasculation, 78–83, 90, 99, 103–04, 130, 144, 148
embodiment: abject (see abject(ion) embodiment); female/feminist, 75, 120, 127, 171–72, 197, 182, 211–12, 246n59 (see also Catherine Breillat and corp*oreality*/female embodiment; defetishization of female embodiment; nudity, full-frontal female); nude (see nudity); male, 40, 72, 75 (see also nudity, full-frontal male); regulation of, 200, 206; trans, 87, 149. See also corp*oreality*; Lena Dunham and corp*oreality*/embodiment
Emmanuelle (Jaeckin), 176
Emmy Awards, 145, 168, 209, 238
enema, 143
Eros, 114
erotic/ism: BDSM (see BDSM); hardcore (Williams), 8, 175, 362; intimacy (see intimacy, erotic); memoir (see memoir, erotic); same-sex, 191–92, 212, 269; thriller, 39, 52, 73, 76, 94–96, 100, 102–104, 109–17, 119–20, 155n70
Esposito, Cameron, 375
ethics: of artists, 6, 185–86; of provocation, 4, 49, 373; of relationality, 118; of screening sex, 7, 186; sexual, 113–13, 119

Euphoria (HBO), 122, 124
Exarchopoulos, Adèle, 1–2, 4–5, 7–9, 10, 14, 15, 18–19, 22, 23n1, 363
l'exception culturelle française. See French cultural exception
exhibition (film): online (see streaming); theatrical, 2, 35, 50, 52–53, 298 (see also cinema)
exhibitionism (corporeal), 41, 110, 192, 196, 206, 239, 315
exotic dancing, 59, 71, 82, 97

Facebook Watch, 122
Fagbenle, O-T, 160n128
Fandor, 60
fantasy. See sexual fantasy
Fassbender, Michael, 88, 89–90, 91–93, 130
Fassbinder, Rainer Werner, 106, 264, 270
Fatal Attraction (Lyne), 52
Fat Girl (Breillat), 170, 180, 183–84, 185, 201, 204–05, 209, 217, 243n34, 296, 314
Favourite, The (Lanthimos), 239
FCC (Federal Communication Commission), 76, 121, 157n89, 332; v. Pacifica, 354–5, 376n7
fellatio, 8, 50, 98–99, 105, 141, 201, 227. See also sex, oral
female: adolescence (see girlhood); audience, 53–59, 95, 199, 357, 367; gaze, 98, 103, 173, 178; Gothic, 110, 116, 227; grotesque, 198, 239; masochism, 116, 168, 216, 218, 356, 366 (see also BDSM); voice, 104, 166, 171, 180, 198, 209, 225–26, 228, 232; writing (see writing, women's)
feminine hygiene products. See tampons
feminine masquerade, 196
feminism/t: activism, 3, 177, 198–200, 250n111; antiporn, 169, 177, 189, 191; Catherine Breillat and/as, 41–42,

feminism/t: activism (*Continued*)
167–70, 175, 189, 193, 200, 203, 234, 240, 243n34, 256, 259, 296; criticism/theory, 12, 33, 56, 98, 198, 200, 210, 235, 237, 241n11, 256, 258, 261, 265, 264, 281, 285, 305, 356, 367; discourse/ideology, 73, 122, 169, 194, 197–98, 221, 235, 258–59, 268, 279, 287, 289, 313, 334, 339; Lena Dunham and/as, 41–42, 167–70, 175, 187, 189–90, 193–94, 196–97, 199–200, 205–06, 209, 212, 221, 223–24, 228, 235, 238, 240, 256, 259, 296; empowerment, 169–70, 200, 206, 224, 347n62, 356, 366; filmmaking, 13, 39, 51, 80, 83, 109, 234–35, 242n24, 265, 300, 305; masculinity (*see* butch); (performance) art, 169, 197–98, 203, 246n56; (non)prescriptive, 42, 168, 170, 197–98, 223–24, 259; provocation's potential/use for, 39–40, 76, 95, 105, 135, 165, 175, 193, 197, 259, 296; (self-)formation, 42, 171, 215, 223–26, 236; trans-exclusionary radical, 339. *See also* art porn; bad feminist; female gaze; female voice; postfeminism; writing, women's
femme, 260, 281–82, 314, 317, 339
femme fatale, 110, 116
femmephobia, 147
Ferrell, Will, 86, 293
Feuchtgebiete. See Wetlands (Wnendt), 202
Fifty Shades Darker (Foley), 54
Fifty Shades Freed (Foley), 54
Fifty Shades of Grey (James), 54, 55, 62, 218, 227
Fifty Shades of Grey (Taylor-Johnson), 35, 54, 59–60, 62
film distribution. *See* distribution (film)
film festival(s), 34, 36, 45, 62, 260, 361, 365; economies of, 36; LGBTQ+,

105, 260, 298–99. *See also individual festivals*; red carpet
filmgoing. *See* moviegoing
film noir, 96, 110–11
Fingersmith (Waters), 14
Flanagan, Bob, 74
Fleabag (Amazon), 238
fluid(ity). *See* sexual fluidity
Flynn, Gillian, 57
Focus Features, 53
Forgetting Sarah Marshall (Stoller), 78–79, 80, 82, 84, 88
Foster, Meg, 160n127
Fosters, The (Freeform), 332
Fountain, The (Dunham), 166, 194–95, 196, 207
Fox, The (Rydell), 278
Fox Searchlight, 53
Foxy Brown (Hill), 284
Franco, James, 57
Franzese, Daniel, 137, 138, 139
Fred Ott's Sneeze (Dickson), 194
Freeheld (Sollett), 252–54
Frémaux, Thierry, 66n33
French cultural exception, 47, 172
frenzy of the visible (Williams), 8, 102, 119, 170, 177–79, 204
frottage. *See* sex acts, lesbian
Frugiuele, Cecilia, 321
F to 7th (Jungermann), 341
Full-frontal. *See* nudity, full-frontal
Full Monty, The (Cattaneo), 58, 71
F Word, The, 331
FX Networks, 32, 121, 129, 145

Gadsby, Hannah, 364
Gaiman, Neil, 150
Gainsbourg, Charlotte, 45–46, 48
Gaitskill, Mary, 219
Gallo, Vincent, 50
Game of Thrones (HBO), 32, 139, 207, 260
gay: audience (*see* LGBTQ+ audience); bars, 20, 89, 309; commodification

of, 140, 270–72, 340; cruising, 106, 111, 119, 140; erotics, 110–11; film (history), 144, 253, 265 (see also individual films); film(makers), 43, 74–75 (see also individual filmmakers); (as) identity (term), 105–06, 252–58, 261–63; male intimacy, 76, 108, 116, 119–20, 132, 139, 140, 142, 145, 192–3; marriage (see marriage equality); (role) model, 252, 259, 334; /queer pathology, 107, 110, 115–18; porn (see pornography, gay); p/Pride, 20, 253, 306, 308, 318, 341; promiscuity, 107, 115, 117–18, 139, 325, 340; /queer subculture, 55, 116, 119; representation, 7, 39–40, 42–43, 45, 105–08, 110–12, 115, 121, 131–50, 252–54; sex (see sex, gay/queer)
gaystreaming. See LGBTQ+ mainstreaming
gender nonconformity/variance. See nonbinary
Genet, Jean, 107
genitalia. See nudity
Génovès, André, 176
Gen Z, 237
Gere, Richard, 102–03
Gigolos (Showtime), 150n1
Girlfriends (Weill), 325
girlhood, 51, 106, 175–76, 183–84, 201–02, 208, 217–19, 225–26, 239
Girls (HBO), 40–41, 126–27, 135, 158n99, 166, 168, 170, 206–14, 219, 226–34, 237–93, 259, 285, 294–96, 315, 327, 371; body politics of, 127, 168, 196, 199, 205–15, 238–39, 240n1 (see also nudity and Lena Dunham); female friendship in, 192–93, 212; and HBO, 126, 135, 137, 172, 187–9, 348n68; sex scenes in, 41, 168, 186–91, 219–25, 227
Girls Gone Wild (franchise), 56
Girls Trip (M. Lee), 53, 58

GLAAD, 60, 67n46, 107, 256–57
Glee (Fox), 331
Glover, David, 221
Glow (Netflix), 204
Godrèche, Judith, 81, 84
God's Own Country (F. Lee), 108, 154n53
Go Fish (Troche), 265, 313–14, 320
Golden Girls, The (NBC), 144
Golden Globe Awards, 206, 288
Goldwyn Films, 154n53
Gomez, Selena, 56, 190
Gone Girl (Fincher), 35, 57, 60, 69, 71, 129
Graduate, The (Nichols), 325–26
Grindr, 140, 159n116, 340
Groff, Jonathan, 131, 135, 139–40, 143
Guiraudie, Alain, 7, 36–37, 39, 94–95, 105–07, 109, 111, 113, 115–18, 120, 156n72, 182, 234
Gunn, James, 353, 375n4

Haigh, Andrew, 39–40, 131, 135–36, 139, 145
Hahn, Kathryn, 122, 204
Halliday, Lisa, 249n100
Hamm, Jon, 69–70
Handmaiden, The (Park), 14
Haneke, Michael, 234
Hangover, The (Phillips), 53
Hangover Part II, The (Phillips), 152n19
Hannah Takes the Stairs (Swanberg), 328
Hamilton, David, 244n41
hard-core. See pornography, hard-core
Hardy, Tom, 70
Haring, Keith, 146
Harmon, Dan, 353
Harold and Kumar Escape from Guantanamo Bay (Hurwitz and Schlossberg), 152n19
Harris, Neil Patrick, 146
Haynes, Todd, 267–68

HBO (Home Box Office), 32, 121–31, 134–37, 139, 144–45, 160n124, 172, 187–88, 199, 212, 228, 244n47, 286, 374
Henderson, Rebecca, 300, 310
heteroflexibility, 78, 134, 141–42, 325
heteromasculinity, 39, 75, 78, 86, 89, 94, 105, 135, 149, 200–02, 218
heteronormativity, 59, 67n46, 77, 110, 116–17, 135, 146, 170, 178, 191, 254, 257, 261, 263, 277, 280, 282, 312, 316, 320, 333, 337, 364
heteropatriarchy. See patriarchy
heterophallicism. See phallic(ism)
High Art (Cholodenko), 42–43, 262, 264–72, 273–78, 280, 288, 292, 297–98, 314, 328, 345n26
high concept (Wyatt), 54, 299
High Maintenance (website; HBO), 341
Hitchcock, Alfred, 57, 67n41, 113, 304
HIV-AIDS. See AIDS
Hoffmann, Gaby, 211
Holiday (Elköf), 52
Hollywood cinema. See cinema, Hollywood
Holy Girl, The (Martel), 202
homme fatal, 109–10, 113, 115–16, 119–20
homoeroticism, 39, 76, 78, 80, 110
homonormativity, 42–43, 60, 67n46, 115–16, 132, 145–46, 254, 257, 264–65, 281, 285–86, 297, 312, 320, 325, 333–34, 340, 342
homophobia, 20, 71–72, 78, 92, 107–08, 133–34, 139, 144–45, 154n50, 157n92, 243n34, 263, 301, 10, 330, 334, 341, 363–64
homosociality, 39, 76–78, 80, 136–37
Honoré, Christophe, 106
Hooker on Campus (Dunham), 194
Hottentot Venus. See Saartjie Baartman
House That Jack Built, The (von Trier), 49

Houston, Shine Louise, 242n24
Hudgens, Vanessa, 56
Hughes, Howard, 57
Hulu, 122, 145
Humpday (Shelton), 80, 86
Hung (HBO), 124–25, 127, 135
Huppert, Isabelle, 356–57
Hustler, 189–91
Hutcherson, Josh, 284

identification: authorial, 17–18; spectatorial, 80, 84, 171, 183–85, 199, 212, 312, 338
identitarian(ism). See anti-identitarian(ism); identity politics
identity politics, 105, 253, 262, 334, 342
Idiots, The (von Trier), 177
IFC Center, 23n2
I Love Dick (Soloway), 204, 238
I Love You, Daddy (C. K.), 362
inbetweener/ness: industrial, 42, 260–61, 266, 268, 270–71, 275, 277–78, 280, 293–94, 297, 330, 342; racial, 260, 272–73, 306, 317; sexual, 42, 255, 260–61, 266, 268, 272–75, 279, 294, 297–98, 311, 337, 342
incest, 87, 91
Incredibly True Adventures of Two Girls in Love, The (Maggenti), 265
indecency. See obscenity
independent (indie) cinema. See cinema, independent (indie)
indie TV, 332. See also web series
Indiewood. See cinema, Indiewood
(in)fidelity, 18–19, 87, 318
Insecure (HBO), 341
Instagram, 198, 236
intercourse, sexual. See sex
Interior. Leather Bar. (Franco and Mathews), 156n72
Internal Affairs (Figgis), 110
intersectionality (Crenshaw), 39, 42, 261–62, 272–73, 288, 299

In the Cut (Campion), 39, 96–101, 104–05, 109, 113, 115
In the Realm of the Senses (Ôshima), 21
intimacy: coordinator, 21; emotional, 83, 88, 93, 97, 204, 215–16, 220, 226; erotic, 5, 9, 171, 179, 184, 234; regulation of, 38, 156n83; spectatorial, 12. See also gay male intimacy
Iranian-American, 40, 43, 260, 262, 294, 309, 317, 321–24, 338, 344n13. See also Desiree Akhavan; bad Persian; inbetweener/ness, racial
irony. See comedy, ironic
Irreversible (Noé), 50, 52
It Gets Better (Project), 336–37, 342, 363
It's My Turn (Weill), 292

Jacob, Gilles, 23n1
Jacobs, Gillian, 226
James, E. L., 54, 218
Jaws (Spielberg), 56
Jenner, Caitlyn, 256
Jeselnik, Anthony, 353
Je Tu Il Elle (Akerman), 11–12, 13, 246n59
Jewishness, 260–62, 272–73, 302, 306–08. See also Lisa Cholodenko
Jones, Cleve, 146
Jungermann, Ingrid, 43, 263, 330–41, 349n87, 363–64

Kalin, Tom, 267
Karpovsky, Alex, 191, 214, 219
Keaton, Diane, 301, 305
Kechiche, Abdellatif, 1–2, 4–7, 9–26, 92, 234, 360, 363
Keitel, Harvey, 73, 96
Khanjian, Arsinée, 205
Kickstarter, 302, 331
Kidman, Nicole, 239
Kids (Clark), 56

Kids Are All Right, The (Cholodenko), 42–43, 146, 257, 260, 264–66, 275–83, 284–86, 288, 291–93, 297, 313–14, 332, 345n26
kinetoscope, 33
King of Escape, The (Guiraudie), 106
Kinsey (Condon), 92
Kirke, Jemima, 168, 197, 212
The Kiss (Edison/Heise), 32, 304
Konner, Jenni, 235, 293
Korine, Harmony, 56
Kramer, Larry, 115, 340

LaBruce, Bruce, 106
Lacy, Jake, 190
Lady Chatterley's Lover (Lawrence), 102
Langraf, John, 32
La niña santa. See *The Holy Girl* (Martel)
Lannan, Michael, 39–40, 131, 135–36, 139–40
la petite mort. See orgasm
Last Mistress, The (Breillat), 186, 234
Last Seduction, The (Dahl), 96
Last Tango in Paris (Bertolucci), 4–5, 18, 21
Laurel Canyon (Cholodenko), 265–66, 275–79, 296, 298, 345n26
La vie d'Adèle, La. See *Blue Is the Warmest Color*
La vie de Marianne. See *The Life of Marianne*
Law, Andrew, 160n128
Lawrence, Jennifer, 190
LeBeouf, Shia, 48, 70
Le bleu est une couleur chaude. See *Blue Is the Warmest Color* (Maroh)
Lee, Jiz, 242n24
Lee, Lorelei, 242n24
Lee, Spike, 66n33
Leftovers, The (HBO), 70, 130
legacy television, 331–33, 341, 368. See also network television; cable television

Leigh, Janet, 67n41
Leigh, Jennifer Jason, 97
lesbian: bed death, 276–77, 282–83, *310*; film (canon), 9, 265; filmmaker, 12, 273 (*see also individual filmmakers*); film distribution, 298; /queer (in)authenticity, 7, 282–83, 320, 342, 370; relationships, 277, 279–86; representation, 110, 282–83. *See also* sex acts, lesbian
Le soupirail (*The Opening*, 1974), 176
lesploitation, 7–8, 123, 192, 277, 299. *See also* sexploitation; marketing, exploitation
Less than Zero (Ellis), 256
LGBTQ+: activism, 137, 146, 199, 336–73; audience, 58, 106–07, 132–33, 135, 140–41, 154n49, 282, 313; community/culture, 117, 209, 309, 331–34; discourse/rhetoric, 297, 330–32, 341–42; film festivals (*see* film festivals, LGBTQ+); language usage, 252, 256, 301–02, 334–35; literature, 306; mainstreaming, 60, 108, 132, 144, 146, 192, 253–54, 257, 260, 265, 282, 298, 331, 331; politics, 6, 67n46, 254–57, 262, 279, 282, 309, 334; pride (*see* gay p/Pride); programming, 134, 256, 336, 342; representation, 252–54, 266, 270–71, 297, 331–33 (*see also individual films*); web series, 331–33, 341–42, 358, 369 (see also *The Slope*); youth (*see* queer youth)
L'homme facile (*A Man for the Asking*). See *A Man for the Asking* (Breillat)
Liberté (Serra), 60
Life of Marianne, The (Marivaux), 15
L'inconnu du lac. See *Stranger by the Lake* (Guiraudie)
Lindelhof, Damon, 130
live tweeting. *See* Twitter
Locarno Film Festival, 235
Lockwood, Patricia, 368

LOGO, 331
long take, 11–12, 120, 183
Looking (HBO), 39–40, 120, 131–38, 139–43, 144–48, 160n128, 188, 372
Looking for Mr. Goodbar (Brooks), 216
Looking: The Movie (Haigh), 145
Louie (FX), 129, 362
Love (Noé), 44, 50, 70, 234
Lucky Louie (HBO), 128–29, 374
L Word, The (Showtime), 5, 134, 330–32, 336, 340
Lyne, Adrian, 52, 218
Lynskey, Melanie, 129

Mad Men (AMC), 259–60, 341
Magic Mike (Soderbergh), 58–60
Magic Mike Live, 59, 67n44
Magic Mike XXL (Jacobs), 58–60
Making Love (Hiller), 108, 253
Malady of Death, The (Duras), 243n34
male buddy film. *See* buddy film
male gaze (Mulvey), 8, 13–14, *15*, 18, 20, 40, 76, 123, 215; reversal of, 95–96, 102, 105, 173, 178. *See also* visual pleasure
Mamet, Zosia, 168, 212
Manet, Édouard, *17–18*
Man for the Asking, A (Breillat), 175
Mapplethorpe, Robert, 146, 149
Marivaux, Pierre de, 15
marketing: exploitation, 56; niche (*see* nichification); viral (*see* viral marketing). *See also* lesploitation; sexploitation
Maroh, Julie, 1, 7, 10, 23n1
Maron, Marc, 204, 231–32
marriage equality, 2, 42, 265, 279–80, 340
Marsden, James, 51
masochism. *See* BDSM; female masochism
Masters of Sex (Showtime), 123
masturbation, 81, 85, 100, 118, 129, 137, 179, 183, 190, 196, 213

McCarthy, Mary, 219
McConaughey, Matthew, 58
McDormand, Frances, 276, 286–89
McEnany, Abby, 122
McGregor, Ewan, 73
McQueen, Steve, 87, 91–92
Mean Girls (Waters), 137
meat shot, 181–82. *See also* pornography
meet-cute, 300–03, 308, 317, 324, 334
Mektoub, My Love: Canto Uno (Kechiche), 20
Mektoub, My Love: Intermezzo (Kechiche), 20
Melancholia (von Trier), 47
melodramatic/comic binary. *See* penis, melodramatic/comedy binary
meme, 57, 69–70, 190, 288, 359
memoir, erotic, 175, 226; tell-all, 70, 166, 226–28, 368
ménage à trois. *See* threesome
menstruation, 179, 203–04
merkin, 84
Mesquida, Roxane, 183–84
#MeToo, 2, 22–23, 24n3, 124, 231, 235, 288, 291, 368
Meyers, Nancy, 53
Meyer, Stephenie, 54
Millennial(s), 40, 187, 237, 255, 257, 267, 327, 331, 333, 368
millennial watercooler movie, 7, 34–35, 39, 44, 52, 60–61, 234, 237, 293, 356; story, 368. *See also* watercooler TV
Miramax, 37, 51, 57, 67n41, 92, 108, 374. *See also* Harvey Weinstein
Misadventures of Awkward Black Girl, The (Rae), 341
Miseducation of Cameron Post, The (Akhavan), 260
misogyny, 78, 187, 232, 243n34, 304, 313, 367
Mitchell, Radha, 268, 272
Modern Family (ABC), 108

money shot, 36, 50, 102, 109, 111, 114, 117, 119, 140, 150, 177–78, 222. *See also* ejaculation; pornography
monogamy: 85, 116, 146, 156n72, 222, 277–78, 286
Moonlight (Jenkins), 256
Moore, Julianne, 146, 253, 265, 280, 283
Moore, Mary Tyler, 238
Moore, Susanna, 97
Morley, Simon, 74
Mortensen, Viggo, 71
Moss-Bachrach, Ebon, 158n99
mother(hood), 55, 81, 165, 197, 202, 205, 211, 217, 225, 233, 246n59, 265, 272–73, 279, 285, 287, 297, 309, 320, 322
moviegoing, 34, 37–38, 50, 59–60
movie theater. *See* cinema
Mr. Man, 73
Mrs. Fletcher (HBO), 122
Mr. Skin, 73
Mouchette (Bresson), 248n87
MPAA (Motion Picture Association of America). *See* ratings, MPAA
MPPDA (Motion Picture Producers and Distributors of America), 66n40
Mubi, 60
Mulholland Drive (Lynch), 110
Mulligan, Carey, 88, 90
multiplex. *See* cinema, multiplex
mumblecore, 80, 328
mumblegore, 81, 327
Muybridge, Eadweard, 31–33, 63n1

Naked and Afraid (Discovery), 150n1
Naked Attraction (UK Channel 4), 150n1
Naked Vegas (Syfy), 150n1
Nanette (Gadsby), 364
narrowcasting. *See* nichification
National Endowment for the Arts (NEA), 51, 66n35
NC-17. *See* ratings

neoliberal(ism), 42, 67n46, 259, 261, 311, 372
Netflix, 7, 20, 35, 50, 66n33, 122, 145, 160n124, 292, 363
network television, 76, 290, 292, 330
New French Extremity, 47, 106, 167
New Queer Cinema, 40, 43, 51, 64n19, 66n35, 253, 255, 263, 265, 267, 270, 274, 292, 298, 342
Newton, Thandie, 124
New Yorker, The, 61, 368
New York Film Festival, 175
nichification (of audience), 43, 52, 255, 298–99, 330–32, 342
Nicholson, Jack, 293
Nin, Anaïs, 218, 226
Noé, Gaspar, 44, 47, 50, 70, 234, 240n5, 358–59, 365
(non)belonging, 118, 260, 262–63
nonbinary (gender identity), 94, 198, 260. *See also* butch; trans
nonphallic masculinity. *See* phallic(ism)
Normal People (BBC Three/Hulu), 190, 244n51
Notaro, Tig, 127, 199
Not That Kind of Girl (Dunham), 166, 172
nude scenes. *See* nudity
nudity: casual (*see* naturalistic nudity); celebrity, 69–70, 73, 87–88 (*see also individual celebrities*); clauses, 73, 212; and Lena Dunham, 137, 166, 172, 196–98, 206–07, 210–12, 213–214, 215, 240, 246n59, 296; full-frontal female, 17–18, 72, 75–76, 84, 90–91, 96, 120, 122–23, 180, 211–12, 214, 293; full-frontal male, 7, 39–40, 57, 60, 72–79, 80, 82–83, 87–89, 92, 96, 97–99, 101–09, 111–12, 122, 124, 126, 128–31, 136–38, 139, 148–50, 152n19, 158n99, 329; gay/queer, 39–40, 74, 105, 231; in art, 13–14, 72, 197–99, 211; (non)naturalistic, 72–73, 75, 77, 79,

93–94, 108–09, 112–13, 124, 149–50, 199, 211–12, 240, 296; political use of, 240; public, 196; realness of, 72–73, 91, 112, 129, 171–72; shooting of, 184–85 (*see also* intimacy coordinator; sex scenes); (non)spectacular(ized), 72–74, 97, 198–99; topless (*see* breasts); trans, 67n41, 149. *See also* merkin; selfies
Nymph()maniac (von Trier), 48–49, 57, 65n29
Nyswaner, Ron, 253

Obergefell v. Hodges, 309. *See also* marriage equality
obscenity, 36, 46, 66n35, 175, 217, 376n7
Olive Kitteridge (Cholodenko), 260, 286–89, 292
Olive Kitteridge (Strout), 286–87
Olympia (Manet), 17–18
onanism. *See* masturbation
One Mississippi (Amazon), 127
One More Lesbian, 7
opening weekend, 35, 54–58. *See also* exhibition
open TV (Christian). *See* indie TV
Opie, Catherine, 198, 246n59
oral sex. *See* sex, oral
Orange Is the New Black (Netflix), 84, 332
orgasm, 15, 48, 81, 101–02, 120, 141, 170, 178, 187, 192, 204, 219, 282–83
orgy, 37, 45, 86, 118
Orlan, 198, 246n59
Oscars. *See* Academy Awards
Ôshima, Nagisa, 21
Oswalt, Patton, 353
The Outlaw (Hughes), 57
Overnight, The (Brice), 51, 77, 80–83, 84–87, 99, 109
Oz (HBO), 124
Ozon, François, 47, 106, 111, 234
Ozpetek, Ferzan, 150

Pabst, G. W., 17
Page, Ellen, 253
Palme d'Or, 2, 20, 105. *See also* Cannes Film Festival
pandemic. *See* AIDS; COVID
Pandora's Box (Pabst), 17
pansexual. *See* sexual fluidity
Paou, Christophe, 106, *112*
Parillaud, Anne, 178–79
Paris 05:59: Théo & Hugo (Ducastel and Martineau), 44–45
Park, Chan-wook, 14
parody, 11, 55, 121, 123, 125, 169, 188–91, 196, 209, 253, 336. *See also* comedy
Pathé, 20
patriarchy, 13, 97, 99, 104, 108, 110, 116, 169, 200, 215, 221, 291
Payne, Alexander, 334
PC. *See* political (in)correct(ness)
PCA. *See* Production Code (Administration)
peak TV, 32, 34
Peccadillo Pictures, 105, 299
pedophilia, 175, 353, 360–62. *See also* sex, underage; sexual violence
Peet, Amanda, 130
PEN15 (Erskine and Konkle), 239
penetration, sexual. *See* sexual penetration
penis: anxiety, 69, 81, 90, 102, 107–08, 119; of color, 142, 147–50; comic, 77–80, 83, 86, 88, 126–29; erect, 36, 71, 87, 98, 127, 136–37, 178–79; flaccid, 73–74, 79, 95, 101, 104, 119, 126, 178; gay/queer, 107–08, 136–38, 139; jokes, 78–80, 83–84, 88, 91, 131; Lehman's melodramatic/comic representational binary of, 69, 77, 86, 92, 95, 104, 109, 125–26, 131, 136, 138, 149; melodramatic, 83, 86–90, 92–94, 125, 149; (non)phallic, 39, 60, 72–74, 79, 83, 87, 92, 94–96, 99, 105, 109, 145, 147–150, 179, 356 (*see also* defetishization of penis); prosthetic, 73, 78, 80, 82–83, 84, 88–89, 93, 99, 101, 109, 124, 127, 178–79, 229, 231; regulation of, 72, 75–76, 136; -sighting, 35, 57, 69–70; size, 73–74, 79–85, 89, 91–92, 94, 103, 117, 123, 125, 137, 148; (de-)spectacular(ized) (*see* defetishization of penis; penis, (non)phallic); as taboo, 69, 150; uncircumcised, 142, 148; (un)veiled, 71–72, 76, 86, 89, 92–93, 95, 102, 104, 108–09, 113, 125, 129, 178, 229. *See also* dick pics
period sex, 203–04. *See also* menstruation; tampons
Persian-American. *See* Iranian-American
Personal Best (Towne), 278
personal essay. *See* memoir
phallic(ism): authority, 71, 83–84, 95–96, 108, 179; masculinity, 72–74, 94, 104, 132; mystique, 74, 93, 136; penis as, 71–74, 79–80, 86, 89–90, 93–95, 99, 108–09, 125–28, 149–50, 178; tropes, 277; visual economy, 39–40, 71–74, 123, 138–39, 144. *See also* penis, (non-)phallic
Philadelphia (Demme), 108, 253, 265
Philadelphia Film Festival, 50
philosophy in the bedroom, 180–81, 186–88
Pialat, Maurice, 242n27
Piano, The (Campion), 96
Piano Teacher, The (Haneke), 234
Pike, Rosamund, 57
platforms, streaming. *See* streaming platforms
Playboy, 199, 205, 240n1
pleasure principle. *See* Eros
Plemya. *See The Tribe* (Slaboshpytskyi)
political (in)correctness, 43, 172, 227, 256, 283, 294–95, 297, 300–01, 303, 309, 333, 335
Poole, Wakefield, 115

Pornhub, 8, 190, 244n51
pornification. *See* porn culture
Pornocratie (Breillat), 177
pornography: aesthetic of realness in, 174–75, 181, 183, 187; (auto)critique of, 41, 169–71, 173–74, 182, 189, 296; boundaries of, 21, 36–37, 41, 77, 112–13, 115, 120–21, 170, 173–75, 188, 193, 296; conventional/s, 8–10, 13, 41, 71, 76, 87, 93, 98–99, 101, 106, 111, 149, 170, 173, 180, 183, 187, 193, 221; culture, 35, 43, 186–90, 221, 224, 368; dyke, 8, 242n24; ethics of, 190–91; hard-core, 8, 107, 174, 178, 189, 222; gay, 40, 107–08, 115–16, 119, 148–49, 176, 284, 313; girl-on-girl, 8, 10, 14, 23n1, 191; history of, 31–32, 111; lactation, 82, 84; lesbian (*see* dyke porn); MILF, 122; performers, 70, 92–93, 109; sites, 7–8, 244n51; soft-core, 56, 76, 95, 111, 133, 139, 174, 176, 244n41; studies, 36; theater, 119; of the visual, 31, 114. *See also* altporn; art porn; docuporn
postfeminism, 116, 169–70, 200, 206, 224, 237, 268, 287, 292. *See also* feminism
pregnancy, 37, 204, 211, 233
Pressure (Dunham), 192
Pretty Woman (Marshall), 216
privilege: bisexual, 337; cis(het) (male), 13, 49, 172, 229, 256, 268, 291, 304, 339, 364–65; cultural/social, 135, 172, 199, 261–62, 276, 284, 365; femme, 317; unexamined, 166, 227, 239, 285; white, 148–49, 172, 199, 259–60, 306. *See also* Lena Dunham, privilege of
Production Code (Administration), 57, 66n40, 140, 355
Professor Marston and the Wonder Women (Robinson), 292
prophylactic. *See* safe(r) sex

Prop(osition) 8 (California), 23n2, 279–80. *See also* marriage equality
prosthesis. *See* penis, prosthetic; vagina, prosthetic. *See also* dildo.
prostitution. *See* sex work
provoc*auteurs*, 4, 24n6, 34, 36–37, 40–42, 45–50, 60, 95, 105–06, 111, 126, 165–93, 199, 234, 237, 240, 255, 262–63, 266, 285, 293–94, 312, 327, 329, 342, 355. *See also individual* provoc*auteurs*
Psycho (Hitchcock), 57, 67n41, 111
public(s) sex. *See* sex, public(s)
Puffy Chair, The (Duplass Brothers), 327
Puppetry of the Penis (Morley), 74

quality television, 32, 39, 76, 121–23, 126–28, 131–32, 134–35, 144, 150, 172, 210. *See also* cable television
Quarterman, Simon, 124
queer: activism (*see* LGBTQ+ activism); antifuturity, 110, 119; antisociality, 117, 119, 333, 340; bad (*see* bad queer); community/culture (*see* LGBTQ+ community/culture); crossover (*see* LGBTQ+ mainstreaming); erotics, 105, 110; failure, 304, 324, 333; history, 253; (as) identity (term), 42, 86, 253–56, 261, 333, 364; masculinity, 39, 60, 76, 81, 86, 95, 109, 121, 139; negativity, 117–18, 307, 333, 340; oppositionality, 117, 255, 257–58, 333; praxis, 42, 110, 253, 261; radical, 42, 146, 254–55, 258, 263, 280, 307, 335, 342; regulation of, 42, 86–87, 117–18; studies, 6, 36; temporality, 311–12, 323; theory, 111, 117–118, 200, 257–58, 262–63, 274, 311, 333, 342; youth, 5, 20, 137. *See also* LGBTQ+
Queer as Folk (Showtime), 132–34, 147
Queer Eye (for the Straight Guy) (Bravo/Netflix), 342

INDEX   427

R. *See* ratings, R
racism, 31, 148, 235, 259, 284–85
Rae, Issa, 341
Raging Bull (Scorsese), 93
Rannells, Andrew, 192
rape. *See* sexual violence
"Rape Joke" (Lockwood), 368
ratings: MPAA, 67n40, 98, 160n124; NC-17, 2, 8, 23n2, 35, 88, 98; R, 35, 71, 177; TV-MA, 151n14; X, 176–77. *See also* unrated
Réage, Pauline, 219
reality television, 69–70, 150n1, 256, 335–36. *See also individual series*
Real L Word, The (Showtime), 335–36
real sex. *See* sex scenes, (un)simulated
Real Sex (HBO), 136
Real Young Girl, A (Breillat), 166, 170, 176–77, 178, 180, 201, 204, 225–26, 243n34
Rear Window (Hitchcock), 113
Reboux, Anaïs, 183–84, 209
red-band trailers. *See* trailers, red-band
red carpet, 3, 24n4, 44–45, 49–50, 198. *See also* film festivals
reproductive futurism, 117, 304, 311, 324
reproductive rights, 233, 236
Rester vertical. *See Staying Vertical* (Guiraudie)
reverse cowgirl. *See* sexual positions
Rhys, Matthew, 127, 229
Robinson, Angela, 292
Le roi de l'évasion. *See The King of Escape* (Guiraudie)
romance narrative, 54, 56, 105, 115–16
Romance (X) (Breillat), 166, 170, 180–81, 182, 202–03, 216–18, 243n34, 314
romantic comedy, 42, 58, 77, 97, 265–66, 298, 300–02, 304, 311, 321, 324–25. *See also individual films*
Roth, Philip, 232, 249n100
Roupenian, Kristen, 368, 372
Rozema, Patricia, 83

R-rated. *See* ratings, R
Ruffalo, Mark, 99, *101*, 103, 265, 283
RuPaul, 256–57, 309
RuPaul's Drag Race (LOGO; VH1), 256
Russell, Jane, 57
Ryan, Meg, 97, *101*

Sade, Marquis de, 60, 175
sadism, sexual. *See* BDSM
safe(r) sex, 100, 114, 116, 119, 202–04, 224
safeword, 307
Salahuddin, Bashir, 160n128
Sally4Ever (HBO), 11
Sapphic. *See* lesbian
Sarsgaard, Peter, 92
Sartre, Jean-Paul, 16
Saturday Night Live (NBC), 55, 169, 196–97, 360
scandal film(s), 23, 34, 37–38, 45, 54, 56, 80, 365
Schilling, Taylor, 81, 84
Schneemann, Carolee, 179–80, 246n56
Schneider, Maria, 4–5, 24n9
Schumer, Amy, 55, 222, 250n106
Schwartzman, Jason, 81, 83
scissoring. *See* sex acts, lesbian
Scolari, Peter, 126, 211
scopophilia, 12, 176. *See also* male gaze; voyeurism
Score (Metzger), 86
Scott, Adam, 81–83, 84
Second Sex, The (de Beauvoir), 305
Segel, Jason, 78–79, 80, 82, 84
self-discipline. *See* embodiment, regulation of
selfie/culture, 50, 190–91, 213, 220, 231, 369–70
self-inscription, 40, 171, 225, 255, 262, 264, 267, 293–94, 316
self-reflexivity, 14–19, 42, 109, 112, 115–16, 118, 145, 182–85, 191, 209, 213–15, 225–33, 258, 268–71, 285, 294, 302–03, 371

semen. *See* ejaculate
Serra, Albert, 47, 60
Sevigny, Chloë, 50
sex: addiction, 88–90, 222; anal, 4, 8, 115, 120, 133, 142–43, 147, 176, 183, 188, 368; anti-erotic, 168, 184, 191, 200; club, 44–45; gay/queer, 106, 117, 120, 132–33, 136, 140–43, 192 (*see also* sex acts, lesbian); hierarchy (*see* cultural sex hierarchy); intergenerational, 120; oral, 101, 133, 216–17, 229–30 (*see also* anilingus; cunnilingus; fellatio); period (*see* period sex); -positive, 119, 122, 140, 170, 307; public(s), 38, 59, 118–20, 156n83; radicalism, 31, 34, 38–39; rough, 303 (*see also* BDSM); seropositive, 138, 142; spectacularized, 53, 110; tape, 49; underage, 23n1, 51, 244n41, 307 (*see also* pedophilia); (un)protected, 8 (*see also* barebacking; safe(r) sex); vaginal, 8, 102, 183; work, 5, 125, 194
sex acts: gay, 140, 372; lesbian, 8–12, 283–84, 313. *See also* anilingus; cunnilingus; fellatio; sex, gay/queer
Sex and the City (HBO), 187, 244n47, 339
Sex and the City (King), 53
Sex Is Comedy (Breillat), 109, 170, 178–79, 184, 228
sex, lies, and videotape (Soderbergh), 37, 51
sexploitation, 32–33, 37, 56–57. *See also* lesploitation; marketing, exploitation
sexposition, 32, 35, 139, 188
sex scene(s): aesthetics of, 7, 9–11, 14, 13, 102, 174; authenticity of, 1, 4, 7, 9–10, 21, 284; duration of, 11, 14, 22, 183; gay, 7–8, 109, 120; girl-on-girl (*see* pornography, girl-on-girl); Hollywood-style, 9–10, 22, 102, 171, 175, 181, 187, 193; (non-)choreographed, 1, 4, 8; (non-)consensual, 3–4; explicitness of, 2, 7–8, 14, 37, 41, 44, 76, 108, 112, 120, 122, 133–34, 139, 141, 147, 150, 154n49, 154n53, 171–72, 174, 190, 204, 228; lesbian, 2, 7–10, 75, 192, 283–84; naturalism of, 36, 46, 100–101, 133, 187, 192, 240; realism of, 7, 9, 13, 21, 37, 136, 139; (un-)simulated, 4, 20, 34, 36, 112, 172, 176–77, 181, 183. *See also individual films*; orgy; threesome
sexual: assault (*see* sexual violence); awakening, 6, 102, 201–02, 265; coercion, 51, 139, 185–86, 222, 229; compulsion, 356, 360–62; consent, 42, 100, 122, 186–87, 189–90, 218, 220–24, 229–30, 233, 356, 362, 371, 373 (*see also* sex scene(s), (non-)consensual); domination (*see* BDSM); exploitation, 6, 229; fantasy, 100, 113–14, 116, 183, 202–03, 221, 224–26, 277, 303; fetish(ism), 41, 52; fluidity, 40, 106, 266, 276–79, 338–39; humiliation, 24n9, 78–79, 85, 122, 215, 219, 225; impotence, 89, 93; inbetweener (*see* inbetweener, sexual); intimacy (*see* intimacy, sexual); *jouissance*, 117; misconduct, 362, 374; moralism, 37, 67n40, 107, 113–15, 117–19, 216, 340, 356; norms, 34, 38, 352; pathology, 90, 119, 138; penetration, 8, 85, 183, 216, 243n34; perversity, 35, 44, 73, 86, 88–91, 104, 110, 119, 201, 355–56; positions (*see* sexual positions); publics (*see* sex public(s)); realism, 5, 13, 50, 125, 165, 171, 201; role-play, 125, 186–87, 216–17, 221–24, 307; (self-)degradation, 169, 171, 201, 216–25, 227, 240; (self-)subjugation, 42, 60, 170, 198–9, 206, 219, 233, 296; slave (*see* BDSM); subjectivity, 40, 113, 119, 168, 171, 193, 240, 313, 338; submission (*see* BDSM); surrender, 122, 139,

215–16, 224; taboo, 39, 43, 354–59; transgression (*see* transgress(ive)); trauma, 24n9, 55, 227–28, 233, 357, 364, 366; truth, 5, 40, 170, 173–75, 365, 371–73; vanilla, 141, 303, 307; verisimilitude (*see* sexual realism); violence, 5, 51–52, 144, 179, 206, 216–18, 227, 233, 235, 244n41, 248n87, 314, 356–57, 370–71; virginity, 147, 183–84, 201–02
sexuality, 1, 31, 34, 36; theory of, 352
sexually transmitted disease. *See* STD
sexual positions: missionary, 142; reverse cowgirl, 8
Seydoux, Léa, 2, 4–5, 8, *10*, *15*, *18*, 22, 363
shame, 6, 41, 82, 84, 91, 117, 134, 144, 147, 200–01, 203–09, 211, 216–18, 221, 223–26, 229, 236, 314, 323
Shame (McQueen), 87–88, *89–90*, *91–94*, 130
Shawkat, Alia, 9
She Done Him Wrong (Sherman), 32
Sheedy, Ally, 268–69, 272
Shelton, Lynn, 80, 329
Sherman, Cindy, 198, 246n59
shock comedy, 359, 364–65, 367, 375
Showalter, Michael, 330
Showtime, 121–22, 131, 134, 145, 331
Siffredi, Rocco, 176–*81*, 242n29
Sigur Rós, 70
Simmons, Laurie, 197
sitcom, 128, 201
Slap, The (NBC), 277, 289–92
Sleeping Beauty, The (Breillat), 234
Slope, The (web series), 42–43, 263, 316–18, 327, 330–41, 363
smart film (Sconce), 334
smart phone, 369
social class, 6, 86, 285
social media, 34, 41, 43, 57, 62, 13, 140, 154n50, 232, 236–37, 239, 267, 290, 302, 358, 368, 371
Soderbergh, Steven, 37, 51, 58

soft butch. *See* butch
soft-core. *See* pornography, soft-core
Solondz, Todd, 334
Soloway, Faith, 331
Soloway, Joey, 238
Sopranos, The (HBO), 259, 341
Sorrow and the Pity, The (Ophüls), 308, 310
South by Southwest, 52, 292
spanking. *See* BDSM
Spera, Hillary, 9
Spielberg, Steven, 23n1, 56
Spring Breakers (Korine), 56, 238
Sprinkle, Annie, 198, 246n59
stand-in. *See* body double
stand-up comedy, 43, 222, 303, 358–65
Stanford, Leland, 31, 63n1
Starz (basic cable channel), 121–22, 145
statutory rape. *See* sex, underage; sexual violence. *See also* pedophila
Staying Vertical (Guiraudie), 120, 182
STD (sexually transmitted disease), 37, 224. *See also* AIDS
Stern, Howard, 206
Stewart, Kristen, 50
Stiller, Ben, 78–79
Stoler, Shirley, 225
Stone Butch Blues (Feinberg), 306, 309–10, 311, 322–23
Stonewall (Emmerich), 253–54
Story of O, The (Réage), 218–19
Strand Releasing, 105
Stranger by the Lake (Guiraudie), 7–8, 39, 105–*112*, 113–21, 131, 133, 138–40, 154n49, 154n50, 156n72, 190, 362
strap-on. *See* dildo
streaming: culture, 33–34, 61 (*see also* digital culture); platforms/sites, 60, 122, 154n49, 160n124. *See also* individual platforms/sites
stripping, *see* exotic dancing
Strout, Elizabeth, 286–87
submission, sexual. *See* BDSM

subversion, 33, 38, 42, 82, 118, 125, 194, 199, 215, 255–57, 280, 352. *See also* transgress(ion)
Sundance Film Festival, 44, 46, 51–52, 64n19, 80, 260, 267, 298. *See also* film festival(s)
Sunshine for the Poor (Guiraudie), 155n70
Superbad (Mottola), 203
surrogate character (author's). *See* alter ego
surveillance, 75, 97, 100, 117–18
Swanberg, Joe, 231
sweeps week, 131
Swimming Pool (Ozon), 234
swingers, 51, 81
Swiss Army Man (Kwan and Scheinert), 51–52
Swordfish (Sena), 73

Taboo (BBC One/FX), 70
Talented Mr. Ripley, The (Minghella), 110
Talladega Nights: The Legend of Ricky Bobby (McKay), 86
tampon, 11, 203–04
Taomino, Tristan, 242n24
Tatum, Channing, 58–59, 67n44
Taylor-Johnson, Sam, 54
Taxicab Confessions (HBO), 136
Team America: World Police (Parker), 11
Téchiné, André, 106
Ted (MacFarlane), 53
Tell Me You Love Me (HBO), 83, 135
Telluride Film Festival, 45
TERF (trans-exclusionary radical feminist). *See* feminism, trans-exclusionary radical
Thanatos, 114
That Old Dream That Moves (Guiraudie), 105
theater, movie. *See* cinema
theatrical release. *See* exhibition, theatrical

Thérèse Dreaming (Balthus), 354
There's Something About Mary (Farrellys), 78–80
Theroux, Justin, 70
This Ain't Girls XXX (Canterbury), 189
Three Billboards Outside Ebbing, Missouri (McDonagh), 288
threesome, 192, 277, 296, 307, 313, 318, 325
Tickled (Farrier and Reeve), 52
TikTok, 34
Time's Up (movement), 2, 24n3, 124, 288, 291
Tiny Furniture (Dunham), 166, 170, 194, 197, 207–08, 212
TMZ, 198
Togetherness (HBO), 129
Tom of Finland, 108
Toni Erdmann (Ade), 292
#TooFar, 359
Toronto International Film Festival, 44
Torres, Yahima, 13–14, 25n20
Tovey, Russell, 135
trailers (movie), 57; red-band, 35, 58, 60; teaser, 48, 60
Trainwreck (Apatow), 53
trans, 94–95, 122, 149, 253, 256, 307, 339. *See also* nonbinary
transgress(ive): art, 107, 354–55; ideological/moral, 54, 115, 253, 258; literature, 107; lure of, 37, 46, 55; representation, 7, 40, 77–78, 86, 95, 121–22, 133, 150, 173; potential, 33, 352; programming, 124; regulation of, 56; erotic/sexual, 35, 47, 86, 115, 118. *See also* subversion
Transparent (Amazon), 94, 238, 332
transphobia, 94, 256
Trevverow, Colin, 328
The Tribe (Slaboshpytskyi), 51
Trier, Lars von. *See* Von Trier, Lars
Trinh Thi, Coralie, 240n5

Troche, Rose, 265, 267
Trouble, Courtney, 242n24
Trump, Donald, 62, 70, 239, 250n111
Tsai, Ming-liang, 47, 106, 150
Tumblr, 70, 229–30
TV-MA. *See* ratings, TV-MA
Twentieth Century Fox, 69
Twilight (Meyer), 54, 306
Twitter, 62, 154n53, 189, 210, 236, 244n41, 290, 353, 368, 370, 374

Úbeda, Carina, 203
uncanny, 10, 13, 180–81, 201
Une vieille maîtresse. See *The Last Mistress*
Une vraie jeune fille. See *A Real Young Girl*
Unfinished Business (Scott), 152n19
Universal Pictures, 55–56
Unmarried Woman, An (Mazursky), 325
unrated, 8, 14, 98–99, 172
unruly woman (Rowe Karlyn), 193–94, 209

vagina: 120, 180, 201, 214, 222, 225; prosthetic, 25n14, 372; *See also* sexual penetration; sex, vaginal
Van Sant, Gus, 267–68
Venice Film Film, 20
Vénus Noire. See *Black Venus* (Kechiche)
Verhoeven, Paul, 52, 234, 356, 370
VHS/VCR, 33, 111
video games, 34
viewing, communal, 61; time-shifted, 61. *See also* moviegoing; streaming
Vimeo, 330–31
viral marketing, 34, 48, 54, 57
virginity. *See* sexual virginity
visibility. *See* LGBTQ+ representation
visual pleasure, 13, 73, 97, 103, 106, 171, 180, 183–84, 271

VOD (Video on Demand), 154n49, 299
Von Trier, Lars, 45, 47–49, 358, 361
Vow of Chastity, 48
voyeurism, 12, 14, 33, 91, 96–98, 110, 112–14, 123, 182–83, 271, 277
vulnerability, 44, 119, 144, 213, 351, 355–57, 362–64, 367, 373

Wachowski, Lana, 9
Wachowski, Lilly, 9
Wahlberg, Mark, 92
Walk Hard: The Dewey Cox Story (Kasdan), 152n19
Waller-Bridge, Phoebe, 238
watercooler TV, 60–61, 290
Waters, John, 256–57, 297, 343n8
Waters, Sarah, 14
Wauthion, Claire, 11–12
web series, 36, 43, 327, 330–41
Weedman, Lauren, 160n128
Weekend (Haigh), 136
Weill, Claudia, 292
Weiner, Anthony, 70
Weinstein, Harvey, 37, 232, 235, 244n41, 250n105, 368, 374. *See also* Miramax
West, Mae, 32
Westworld (HBO), 124
Wetlands (Wnendt), 202
What Have I Done to Deserve This? (Almodóvar), 73–74
When She Was Good (Roth), 232
White Girl (Wood), 52
white privilege. *See* privilege, white
Wiig, Kristen, 293
Wild (Krebitz), 52
Wilde, Olivia, 206
Wilke, Hannah, 179
Williams, Allison, 158n99, 168, 190, 212
Willis, Bruce, 73
Wilson, Patrick, 210

woman's film, 54
women's filmmaking, 266, 292, 328. *See also individual filmmakers*
Woodman, Francesca, 246n59
Work in Progress (HBO), 122
writing, women's, 19, 168, 219, 225–26, 233, 368–72

X-Men: First Class (Vaughn), 88
X-rated. *See* ratings, X

YouPorn (video-sharing site), 8
YouTube (video-sharing site), 34, 48, 122, 194–5, 198, 207–08, 327, 330–31, 370, 374

MARIA SAN FILIPPO is Associate Professor in the Department of Visual and Media Arts at Emerson College and editor of *New Review of Film and Television Studies*. She is author of the Lambda Literary Award–winning *The B Word: Bisexuality in Contemporary Film and Television* (2013) and editor of the collection *After "Happily Ever After": Romantic Comedy in the Post-Romantic Age* (2021).

www.ingramcontent.com/pod-product-compliance
Lightning Source LLC
Chambersburg PA
CBHW051241300426
44114CB00011B/839